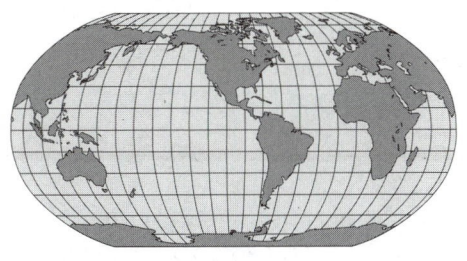

COMPARATIVE FOREIGN POLICY

ADAPTATION STRATEGIES
OF THE GREAT AND EMERGING POWERS

Steven W. Hook, Editor

Kent State University

D0209466

Prentice
Hall

UPPER SADDLE RIVER, NEW JERSEY 07458

Library of Congress Cataloging-in-Publication Data

Comparative foreign policy: adaptation strategies of the great and emerging powers/
Steven W. Hook, editor.
    p. cm.
    Includes bibliographical references and index.
    ISBN 0-13-088789-7
      1. International relations.   2. Comparative government.   I. Hook, Steven W.

JZ1305 .C655 2001
327.1—dc21
                                     2001040942

VP, Editorial director: Laura Pearson
Senior acquisitions editor: Heather Shelstad
Assistant editor: Brian Prybella
Editorial assistant: Jessica Drew
Marketing manager: Claire Rehwinkel
Editorial/production supervision: Kari Callaghan Mazzola
Prepress and manufacturing buyer: Ben Smith
Electronic page makeup: Kari Callaghan Mazzola and John P. Mazzola
Interior design: John P. Mazzola
Cover director: Jayne Conte
Cover design: Jayne Kelly

This book was set in 10/12 New Century Schoolbook by Big Sky Composition
and was printed and bound by Courier Companies, Inc.
The cover was printed by Phoenix Color Corp.

Printed in the United States of America
10   9   8   7   6   5   4   3   2   1

ISBN 0-13-088789-7

Pearson Education LTD., London
Pearson Education Australia PTY, Limited, Sydney
Pearson Education Singapore, Pte. Ltd
Pearson Education North Asia Ltd, Hong Kong
Pearson Education Canada, Ltd., Toronto
Pearson Educación de Mexico, S.A. de C.V.
Pearson Education—Japan, Tokyo
Pearson Education Malaysia, Pte. Ltd
Pearson Education, Upper Saddle River, New Jersey

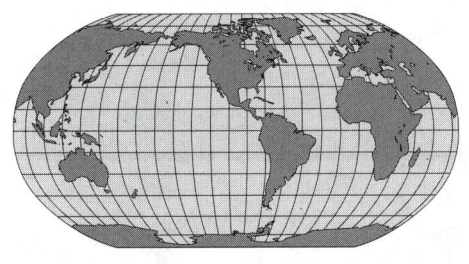

COMPARATIVE FOREIGN POLICY

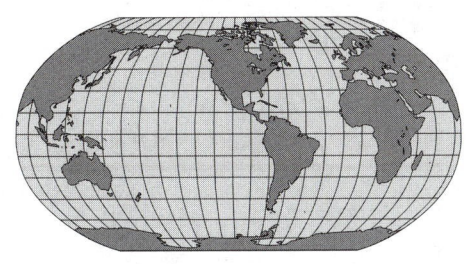

CONTENTS

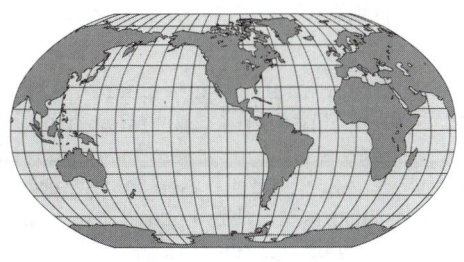

PREFACE

This book is designed to provide students of world politics with a comprehensive yet concise overview of the foreign policies of ten "great and emerging powers" in the early twenty-first century. The chapters, written by leading area specialists, focus on the strategies devised by these powers to adapt to the rapidly changing landscape of the post–Cold War era. As the authors find, the end of the Cold War in 1991 greatly affected the calculations of foreign-policy makers. But their policy responses have, to varying degrees, incorporated many other developments in the international system. These include the widespread adoption by national governments of democratic norms and institutions, accelerating technological and economic integration, the emergence of non-state actors as key players in world politics, and the recognition of transnational problems such as environmental decay and weapons proliferation. All these developments have greatly complicated the task of making foreign policy, a distinctive arena of governance in which internal and external pressures converge and must be reconciled.

The following chapters seek to advance the comparative study of foreign policy by viewing these trends in cross-national perspective and by confronting the central theme of foreign-policy *adaptation* through a common analytic framework. The chosen adaptation strategies are considered in their historical context so that readers may identify recurring patterns from the past and identify their manifestation in current foreign-policy behavior. Further, each author considers the primary governmental and non-state actors involved in the policy-making process, the foreign-policy issues of greatest concern, and the status of key bilateral and multilateral relations.

The authors present their analyses in a clear and straightforward composition style that is most suitable to a readership of advanced undergraduates, graduate students, and professional researchers. Footnoting is therefore limited, with readers being drawn to related studies through extensive parenthetical citations. In this regard, we hope the master bibliography at the end of the book serves as a valuable reference for further study. Finally, to ensure that this book is truly comparative, every opportunity has been taken to cross-reference the chapters and highlight common patterns and findings.

Taken together, the chapters illustrate the divergent ways foreign-policy makers have sought to accommodate the rapid pace of change within the international system during the first post–Cold War decade. As we will find, these strategies achieved their stated goals in some instances, failed in others, and produced ambiguous results in still others. Domestic divisions and crises frequently stymied creative adaptation strategies, forcing attention away from widely recognized international problems and opportunities. For better or worse, the foreign policies of these great and emerging powers have had inescapable consequences—not only for the attainment of their immediate self-interests but also for the resolution of long-term collective problems at the regional and global levels. This snapshot of foreign-policy adaptation, therefore, may well illuminate the prospects for global relations far into the future.

ACKNOWLEDGMENTS

First and foremost, the editor and authors of this book acknowledge the work of the late Roy Macridis, whose eight editions of *Foreign Policy in World Politics* enlightened many generations of students and served as a role model for this book. In this respect, we are pleased that Robert Scalapino, whose analyses of Japanese foreign policy appeared in the Macridis editions, represents a symbolic bridge between the two books. The political science editors at Prentice Hall have enthusiastically supported this continuing effort to present a comprehensive, cross-national review of foreign-policy adaptation. In particular, Beth Gillett Mejia played a decisive role in launching the new project, while Heather Shelstad, Laura Pearson, and Kari Callaghan Mazzola provided invaluable editorial supervision. We also express our gratitude to David Skidmore of Drake University, who provided instructive critiques of individual studies and the book's main themes during the 2001 annual meetings of the International Studies Association. At Kent State University, the research assistance of Jim Bralski, Jeremy Lesh, and Guang Zhang is greatly appreciated. Finally, the project has benefited greatly from the guidance provided by the following reviewers: Sebastian Royo of Suffolk University and Ralph G. Carter of Texas Christian University.

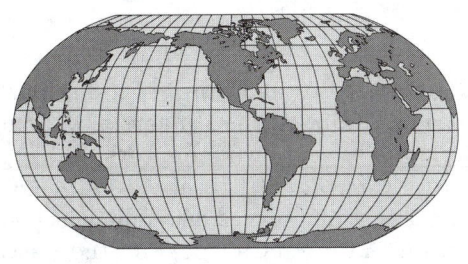

ABOUT THE AUTHORS

WILLIAM A. CLARK is Associate Professor of Political Science at Louisiana State University. A specialist on Soviet and Russian politics, he is the author of *Crime and Punishment in Soviet Officialdom* (1993) and *Soviet Regional Elite Mobility after Khrushchev* (1989). His research on Russia has appeared in such journals as *Electoral Studies, Soviet Studies, Problems of Post-Communism, Presidential Studies Quarterly, The International Journal of Public Administration, Europe–Asia Studies,* and *The Soviet and Post-Soviet Review.* He is currently at work on a book on legislative politics in Russia.

STEVEN W. HOOK is Associate Professor of Political Science at Kent State University. His books include *American Foreign Policy since World War II,* with John Spanier (15th edition, 2000), *National Interest and Foreign Aid* (1995), and the anthology *Foreign Aid toward the Millennium* (1996). His authored and co-authored articles have been published in *World Politics, International Studies Quarterly, Asian Survey, European Security, Democratization,* and other journals. He is currently chair of the Foreign Policy Section of the American Political Science Association.

ANDREW HURRELL is University Lecturer in International Relations and Fellow of Nuffield College, University of Oxford. His major interests include international relations theory, with particular reference to international law and institutions, and the international relations of Latin America, with particular reference to the foreign policy of Brazil and U.S.–Latin American relations. His recent publications include *Hedley Bull on International Society* (2000) and two edited volumes: *Inequality, Globalization, and World Politics,* co-edited with Ngaire Woods (1999), and *Regionalism in World Politics,* co-edited with Louise Fawcett (1995).

MOHSEN M. MILANI is Professor and Chair of the Department of Government and International Affairs at the University of South Florida. In addition to his many articles and book chapters, he is the author of *The Making of Iran's Islamic Revolution: From the Islamic Republic to Monarchy* (2nd edition, 1994). He has served as a fellow at Harvard University, Oxford University's St. Antony's College, and the Fascari University of Venice, Italy. He is currently writing a book on the rule of Iranian President Mohammad Khatami.

ROBERT A. SCALAPINO is Robson Research Professor of Government Emeritus at the University of California at Berkeley. He has published more than 500 articles and 38 books or monographs on Asian politics and U.S.–Asian relations. His books include *The Last Leninists: The Uncertain Future of Asia's Communist States* (1992), *Major Power Relations in Northeast Asia* (1987), *Communism in Korea*, with Chong-Sik Lee (1972), and *Parties and Politics in Contemporary Japan* (1962). He served as editor of *Asian Survey* from 1962 to 1996.

PETER J. SCHRAEDER is Associate Professor in the Department of Political Science at Loyola University–Chicago, where he specializes in comparative foreign policy and international relations theory, especially as both apply to Africa. He is the author of *African Politics and Society: A Mosaic in Transformation* (2000) and *United States Foreign Policy toward Africa: Incrementalism, Crisis, and Change* (1994). His articles have appeared in *The Journal of Modern African Studies*, *African Affairs*, *Politique Africaine*, *World Politics*, *The Journal of Politics*, and *Political Science Quarterly*.

JAMES SPERLING is Professor of Political Science at the University of Akron. A specialist in European politics and integration, he is editor of *Two Tiers or Two Speeds? The European Security Order and the Enlargement of the European Union and NATO* (1999) and co-author of *Recasting the European Order: Security Architectures and Economic Cooperation* (1997). He has authored or co-authored articles in the *British Journal of Political Science*, *Review of International Studies*, *Journal of European Public Policy*, *Contemporary Security Studies*, *West European Studies*, and *German Politics*.

RAJU G. C. THOMAS is Allis Chalmers Professor of International Affairs at Marquette University. He was formerly a visiting scholar or senior fellow at Harvard, MIT, UCLA, the International Institute for Strategic Studies–London, and the University of Wisconsin–Madison. His several books include *Democracy, Security, and Development in India* (1996) and *Indian Security Policy* (1986), along with the anthology *India's Nuclear Security*, co-edited with Amit Gupta (2000). He has published more than sixty journal articles and book chapters on India and South Asia.

DONALD E. WEATHERBEE is Donald S. Russell Distinguished Professor Emeritus at the University of South Carolina and Fellow of the University's Walker Institute of International Studies. He is the author of *Ideology in Indonesia: Sukarno's Indonesian Revolution* (1966), among other publications, and editor of *Southeast Asia Divided: The ASEAN–Indochina Crisis* (1985). His most recent book chapters on Southeast Asian politics include "ASEAN and Indochina: The 'ASEANization' of Vietnam," in Sheldon Simon, editor, *East Asian Security in the Post–Cold War Era* (1993).

HOWARD J. WIARDA is Professor of Political Science and the Leonard J. Horwitz Professor of Iberian and Latin American Studies at the University of Massachusetts–Amherst, Fellow of the Woodrow Wilson International Center for Scholars, and Senior Associate at the Center for Strategic and International Studies. In addition to his many books on Latin America and comparative politics, his work on U.S. foreign policy includes *Cracks in the Consensus: Debating the Democracy Agenda in U.S. Foreign Policy* (1997) and *U.S. Foreign Policy: Actors and Processes* (1996).

LANA L. WYLIE is a Ph.D. candidate in Political Science at the University of Massachusetts–Amherst and currently serves as managing editor of *Political Science Quarterly*. Her current research compares Canadian and U.S. foreign policies toward Cuba. She has published several articles and book chapters on international development and foreign policy and has presented papers at numerous conferences in the United States and Canada.

QUANSHENG ZHAO is Professor and Division Director of Comparative and Regional Studies at the School of International Service of American University in Washington, D.C. He is also Associate-in-Research at the Fairbank Center for East Asian Research of Harvard University. His books include *Interpreting Chinese Foreign Policy* (1996) and *Japanese Policymaking: Informal Mechanisms and the Making of China Policy* (1993). His recent book chapters include "China in East Asia: Changing Relations with Japan and Korea," in Christopher Hudson, editor, *The China Handbook* (2000).

INTRODUCTION: A READER'S GUIDE
TO FOREIGN-POLICY ADAPTATION

Steven W. Hook

Kent State University

W orld politics remains in a profound state of flux more than a decade after the Cold War. A coherent balance of power among nation-states has yet to emerge, prompting some analysts to question the very definition, sources, and utilities of state power. Militarized disputes between countries have been rare in recent years, but internal conflicts produced more than a million casualties in the 1990s. Improved living standards in much of the world, meanwhile, have coincided with a widening gap between the world's richest and poorest inhabitants. Global integration has brought technological advances to much of the world but has also provoked mass protests and terrorist attacks against the perceived agents of globalization.

The widening range of influential actors in global relations further complicates this picture. Democratic transitions in many countries have produced vibrant civil societies that, in turn, have empowered domestic interest groups, news organizations, and public opinion. Not only do intergovernmental bodies such as the World Trade Organization exert greater influence, thousands of nongovernmental organizations (NGOs) have forged links across political boundaries and have demanded collective government action in such areas as human rights, disarmament, poverty, public health, and environmental protection. Terrorist groups have most dramatically changed the face of world politics. In particular, the September 2001 attacks on New York City and Washington, D.C., transformed the foreign-policy priorities and strategies of the United States.

Such complexity makes the task of understanding world politics all the more challenging. The task is especially crucial, however, as more citizens than ever are empowered; as the lines between global, national, and even local problems becomes increasingly blurred; and as the need for collaborative responses to transnational problems becomes more essential.

It is in this spirit that the present volume was conceived. In the chapters that follow, leading area specialists highlight the strategies employed by ten "great and emerging powers" to accommodate the rapid changes taking place around them. Five of these—the United States, Russia, China, Japan, and the European Union (EU)—may be considered "great powers" given their possession of a formidable array of political, economic, social, and military resources.[1] While each of these great powers maintains these assets to widely varying degrees, and while each has experienced acute domestic problems in recent years, all have played a preponderant role in shaping the course of the post–Cold War era. In addition, five "emerging powers" reviewed in this volume—Brazil, India, Indonesia, Iran, and South Africa—draw our attention to important trends within the developing regions of the world. Each of these countries has played a key role in the evolution of regional relations and has exerted significant influence at the global level. In all ten cases, major developments during and after the Cold War—including domestic upheavals and economic crises—have had consequences that extend far beyond their borders.

Our interest in this volume extends beyond the day-to-day activities of these foreign-policy actors. In addition to their outward behavior, we are also concerned with the internal dynamics of each case—the historical, cultural, governmental, and individual forces that have compelled and shaped their various responses to change. Foreign policy rests at a delicate junction between domestic and international politics, and the actions of government leaders in the world arena inevitably reflect these intersecting pressures. Of particular interest, the trend toward democratic governance has produced in many countries more open and decentralized foreign-policy institutions, with clear implications for the daily conduct of foreign affairs.

This central reality becomes all the more evident when we explore the key developments that have provoked foreign-policy adaptation. As we will find, the end of the Cold War was but one of many sources of change. In the case of the People's Republic of China, for example, the most salient turning point was the decision by Deng Xiaoping in the late 1970s to open the country's communist economy to market reforms. Iran's Islamic revolution of 1979 produced fundamental changes in its worldview and foreign policies. In the 1980s, Brazil's struggling economy required new government structures and policies that led to the country's more active engagement in intergovernmental institutions and its adoption of many international norms that it had earlier resisted. And in South Africa, the

---

[1]Although the EU is not a sovereign nation-state, it has adopted many attributes of statehood, including a common currency, and increasingly speaks with one voice on international trade, human rights, sustainable development, and other global concerns.

end of apartheid in 1994 marked a watershed in that country's social, political, and economic history and opened new doors to the outside world.

The foreign policy of the United States, which throughout the Cold War was based on the "containment" of communism, was most directly altered by the Soviet Union's collapse in 1991. Due in part to its prolonged fixation with East–West relations, the U.S. government's response to the new strategic landscape has been uncertain, erratic, and often contradictory. Washington's ambivalent response has been compounded by a low level of public interest in foreign affairs and a protracted struggle between the executive and legislative branches of government over the ends and means of U.S. foreign policy. A central question for the future concerns the capacity of President George W. Bush to overcome these domestic obstacles in advancing a foreign-policy agenda that is markedly different from that of the Clinton administration. Russia's foreign policy, meanwhile, has been greatly restrained by its crushing economic problems, a fact that explains the relative continuity in its recent behavior as compared to that of the Soviet Union under its last leader, Mikhail Gorbachev.

While the focus of this book is on government policies, the authors hardly adopt a state-centric view. As noted earlier, a recurring theme of the chapters concerns the role of increasingly potent nonstate actors, including domestic and transnational interest groups, multinational corporations, and intergovernmental organizations. On their own and in combination with other nonstate actors, these organizations have played a vital role in shaping a more pluralistic policy-making environment within many states. Linkages among these groups provide a source of external leverage that cannot be ignored by political leaders, particularly "those that aspire to belong to a normative community of nations" (Keck and Sikkink 1998, 29). Accommodating this more diffused arena of foreign policy, one which has elevated the importance of state–society relations, thus emerges as a central element of creative foreign-policy adaptation.

A related theme that runs across these chapters involves the widening foreign-policy agendas adopted by political leaders. In the EU, for example, we learn that Germany has adopted an expansive security agenda that combines traditional geopolitical concerns with those relating to drug trafficking, environmental threats, and global epidemics. These same issues have become of greater interest to the Brazilian government, largely in response to demands from a mobilized civil society. Japanese leaders, meanwhile, have made the promotion of global economic development and environmental protection a priority as a result of sustained pressure from foreign governments and international organizations. Meanwhile, South Africa's heightened concern for global democracy and human rights represents an extension of its own democratic transition. And in the United States, "intermestic" issues such as immigration, illegal narcotics, job security, and energy prices have preoccupied foreign-policy makers since the Cold War.

THE STUDY OF FOREIGN-POLICY ADAPTATION

The focus of this volume is on the changes in the formulation and conduct of foreign policy that have been prompted by the many developments noted earlier. Surprisingly, such a focus on foreign-policy change is relatively new in the comparative study of foreign policy. During much of the Cold War, scholarly studies tended to emphasize "continuous patterns of foreign policy, as opposed to restructuring in foreign policy over time" (Rosati, Hagan, and Sampson 1994, 5). This preoccupation with static analysis, Robert Gilpin noted in his pathbreaking study, *War and Change in World Politics* (1981), reflected the immaturity of international relations as a social science. Simply put, coming to grips with state behavior fixed in time and place was a difficult enough enterprise; a more ambitious exploration of *dynamic* behavior would have to come later. Furthermore, Gilpin argued, the neglect of change resulted from the relative continuity of the bipolar Cold War balance of power as well as from an underlying "conservative bias" in Western scholarship. As Gilpin (1981, 6) observed, "The idea of radical changes that threaten accepted values and interests is not an appealing one."

This is not to say that researchers have universally shunned the subject of foreign-policy change and adaptation. Indeed, these were central concerns to James N. Rosenau, whose early study of foreign policy as "adaptive behavior" stimulated a modest, but promising, body of research. Rosenau takes the following viewpoint:

> Any foreign policy behavior undertaken by the government of any national society is conceived to be adaptive when it copes with or stimulates changes in the external environment that contribute to keeping the essential structures of the society within acceptable limits. By *essential structures* we mean those interrelated patterns that constitute the basic political, economic, and social life of a national society. By *acceptable limits* we mean those variations in the essential structures that do not prevent the society from maintaining its basic forms of life or from altering these forms through its own choices and procedures. (1970, 367)

To Rosenau (1970, 368), political leaders are perpetually confronted with shifting conditions at home and overseas that demand responsive adaptation strategies: "Under static conditions—that is, when little or no change is taking place at home and abroad—societies seek to maintain control over the environments through the routine procedures of commerce and the standard practices of diplomacy. Modern life is seldom static, however. Change within and among societies is virtually constant, so that the myriad routinized activities through which each of them controls its ties to the international system are not sufficient to keep its essential structures within acceptable limits."

Rosenau's work was followed by several studies that responded to his call for greater understanding of foreign-policy change. K. J. Holsti's 1982 edited volume, *Why Nations Realign: Foreign Policy Restructuring in the Postwar World*, sought to "confirm that foreign policy change is a subject worthy of systematic analysis." Among his other contributions, Holsti drew an important distinction between "normal" foreign-policy change and the more fundamental process of "restructuring" that entails far-reaching alterations in states' domestic structures, global orientations, and foreign-policy behavior. This distinction is a useful one as it relates to the current volume. Foreign-policy change in Japan, India, and the United States, for example, has been relatively gradual and incremental, whereas the profound changes in the global postures of Russia, Iran, and South Africa have resulted from the transformation of domestic political institutions and state–society relations.

As is also described in the following chapters, a countervailing set of forces commonly *inhibits* creative adaptation in foreign policy. These include the many constraints imposed by the international system, cultural norms, bureaucratic routines and standard operating procedures, and even cognitive processes that discourage policymakers from perceiving altered circumstances and meeting the demand to modify foreign policies accordingly. In this respect, Kjell Goldmann (1988) introduced a useful "checklist" of international, political, administrative, and cognitive "stabilizers" that collectively favor the status quo over even incremental change, let alone fundamental restructuring. The effects of these stabilizers are on display throughout this volume—in the U.S. government's inability to overcome Cold War spending habits and organizational routines; in the Japanese government's resistance to external demands that it adopt reciprocal trade practices; and in the reluctance of the Brazilian, Chinese, Indian, Iranian, and Russian governments to transcend deeply embedded suspicions of outside powers. It must be said, however, that the more prevalent pattern revealed by the authors is one of change rather than continuity in foreign-policy orientations, relationships, and practices.

Students of foreign policy may wish to consider these adaptation strategies in the context of four sources of change advanced by Charles Hermann (1990). These include *external shocks*, such as the end of the Cold War in 1991 or the East Asian economic crisis of 1997–1998, and *domestic restructuring*, such as that undergone by the Iranian and South African governments in 1979 and 1994, respectively. *Bureaucratic advocacy* is a third source of foreign-policy change that can be seen in the Chinese government's emphasis on economic reforms rather than the projection of military power, and in the dominant (and often controversial) foreign-policy role played by Japan's Ministry of International Trade and Industry (MITI). Finally, *leader-driven* change is clearly apparent in the chapter on Russian foreign policy, which emphasizes the personal impact of Mikhail Gorbachev in the country's adoption of a more modest world role. These categories, of course, are not mutually exclusive. Change in foreign policy most often results from concurrent and reinforcing pressures at many levels, foreign and domestic.

Our understanding of the chapters that follow is further enhanced by scholarship that explores the process of foreign-policy *learning*. Breslauer and Tetlock (1991), for example, made sense of Cold War diplomacy by drawing attention to the learning process that unfolded in U.S.–Soviet relations. Among other contributors to the volume, Ernst Haas probed the differences between the processes of policy adaptation and learning, the latter of which he considered more fundamental. In the process of policy adaptation, Haas (1991, 72) found that the "ultimate purpose of the organization is not questioned." Policy learning, by contrast, entails "behavioral changes as actors question original implicit theories underlying programs and examine their original values." Through this learning process, Breslauer (1991, 835) observed how U.S. and Soviet leaders departed from "the worst-case version of the Cold War paradigm through the addition of a collaborative track to the relationship."[2]

While much attention has been paid to the adaptation of individual foreign-policy strategies after the Cold War, comparative or cross-national studies have been rare. In a prominent and early exception to this rule, Keohane, Nye, and Hoffmann (1993) compiled a group of studies that identified the myriad ways European governments and international institutions managed the demise of Cold War competition in Europe. A more recent anthology, edited by Kapstein and Mastanduno (1999), examined the post–Cold War foreign policies of several industrialized countries through the lens of realist theory. Single-country studies of policy adaptation, although more limited in scope, have nonetheless been instructive. Thomas Carothers (1999), for example, discerned a "learning curve" in recent U.S. democratization policy in which the government's previous emphasis on top-down reform yielded to a more elastic approach based upon the support of civil societies. This lesson, as noted by Carothers, has been applied by other aid donors in recent years. Other examples of foreign-policy learning, which often takes place through a difficult process of trial and error, are featured throughout this volume.

Finally, the study of foreign-policy adaptation has been enriched in recent years as scholars have creatively applied the concept of "two-level games." To Robert Putnam (1988, 427), a "puzzling tangle" results as diplomatic negotiations coincide with domestic bargaining over the terms of international agreements. A series of studies edited by Evans, Jacobson, and Putnam (1993) described the evolution and outcomes of this process in such

---

[2]See Simmons (1994) for a subsequent study of "adjustment" to the depression of the 1930s that emphasizes the impact of domestic politics on the foreign economic policies of several industrialized states.

diverse issue-areas as the Arab–Israeli peace process, European weapons development, and U.S. human-rights policy toward Guatemala and Argentina. More recently, Peter F. Trumbore (1998) applied the concept to Anglo–Irish negotiations over the future status of Northern Ireland and found that public opinion played a key role in constraining the options available to both sides. Collectively, these studies remind us to consider the dynamic relationship between domestic and interstate bargaining processes, a point clearly reinforced throughout the current volume.

THE CHAPTERS IN BRIEF

Each of the following chapters tells a distinct story of foreign-policy adaptation. Collectively, they tell much of the story of world politics in this volatile era. Readers should be careful to note and contrast the *sources* of policy change, the varying *objectives* identified by policymakers in the course of change, the divergent *means* by which they implemented new policies, and the wide range of *outcomes* that resulted from their adopted strategies. At the same time, readers should be mindful of the concurrent *impediments* to change in these cases.

The United States is considered first in this volume given its widely acknowledged status as the world's "lone superpower" in the first years of the new millennium. Only the United States has the military and economic resources necessary to project its power on a global scale, and it has done so vigorously since the Cold War. Yet, as Howard J. Wiarda and Lana L. Wylie describe in Chapter 2, the United States emerged from this struggle as an uncertain power. The functions and tactical roles of its unrivaled military forces have been questioned, particularly in cases of international conflict that have not related directly to perceived national interests. Meanwhile, a host of new foreign-policy issues has been placed on the agenda since the Cold War, public opinion has sent mixed signals regarding the country's world role, and a protracted impasse between the Clinton administration and the Republican-led U.S. Congress further prevented the United States from adopting a coherent post–Cold War grand strategy. The contested election of President George W. Bush in November 2000 reflected this lack of unity. Bush raised expectations that a more coherent grand strategy, based more narrowly on U.S. self-interests rather than global concerns, would be adopted. The terrorist attacks in September 2001, however, drastically altered Bush's foreign-policy goals while starkly revealing the reliance of the United States on multilateral cooperation in the face of widely shared threats.

At one level, the case of Russia suggests a process of foreign-policy *restructuring* as described by K. J. Holsti. This is so given that Russia, as a sovereign nation-state, was reborn in 1991 amid the disintegration of the Soviet Union. To William A. Clark, however, Russian foreign policy in the past decade largely resembles that of the late Soviet Union under Mikhail Gorbachev, who recognized the country's deepening economic strains in the mid-1980s and greatly diminished the country's international profile as a result. "Contemporary Russian foreign policy," Clark argues in Chapter 3, "shares more in common with Gorbachev's 'new thinking' than the latter did with the long tradition of Russo–Soviet foreign policy." Continuing internal struggles, both political and economic, have further restricted the capacity of presidents Boris Yeltsin and Vladimir Putin to project Russian power beyond its borders. Gorbachev, Clark observes, represents the pivotal figure in transforming the nature of Russo–Soviet foreign policy, which had demonstrated a remarkable degree of continuity before and after the 1917 revolution that ended the tsarist era.

The People's Republic of China (PRC), by contrast, is a less ambiguous great power today, with the world's largest population, one of its most rapidly expanding economies, and a strong and growing military force that includes nuclear weapons. In Chapter 4, Quansheng Zhao examines the PRC's shift from the revolutionary era of Mao Zedong to a more pragmatic modernization drive launched by his successors. In both eras, Zhao finds, Chinese leaders have consistently placed national autonomy above other goals: "For the PRC, state survival in the international arena is no more important than regime survival domestically." Given this priority, China has adopted a restrained foreign-policy posture, based largely on expanding economic ties overseas, while its government remains preoccupied with maintaining order and political control at home. This does not mean, however, that China does not possess the necessary resources to assume a more assertive role in the future.

In Chapter 5, Robert Scalapino considers the great-power status of Japan today, a status it retains almost exclusively for economic reasons given that Japan maintains Asia's largest economy and the second-largest economy in the world. The Japanese government, however, has endured a prolonged recession that has fueled public demands not only for economic recovery, but also for fundamental social and political reforms. Political leaders in Tokyo have struggled to meet these demands, which have also been voiced by foreign governments and international financial institutions that have viewed Japan as the locomotive of East Asia's political economy. This process of recovery and reform will likely preoccupy Japanese leaders in the foreseeable future. "Along the way," Scalapino concludes, "Japan must shed the excessive reclusiveness and introversion of the past, a step that would enable its leaders to make an even greater contribution to global peace and prosperity."

The European Union, as noted by James Sperling in Chapter 6, is a "curious actor" in world politics given its hybrid, semisovereign status. Sperling makes a distinction between the EU as a foreign-policy "objective," based upon the aspirations of its leaders, and a foreign-policy "actor" that is engaged effectively in the day-to-day functions of foreign policy. To Sperling, the EU's record thus far is mixed. Its conduct of foreign policy remains highly constrained by the preferences of its most influential member states, France, Germany, and Great Britain. Further, the EU has proven incapable of adopting a cohesive position toward regional conflicts, most notably the Balkan wars of the 1990s that ended only after the intervention of the U.S.-led North Atlantic Treaty Organization. Yet the EU has assumed an instrumental role in several issue-areas, particularly in global economic relations, and considerable progress has been made recently toward the adoption of a "common foreign and security policy." At the very least, Sperling concludes, the fatalism of "Euro-pessimists" has not been realized as the EU continues to accumulate an ever-greater degree of autonomy and political influence beyond Europe.

Part II of this volume features the five studies of emerging powers, each of which has experienced fundamental foreign-policy change in separate regions of the developing world. Andrew Hurrell begins in Chapter 7 by exploring the evolution of Brazilian foreign policy since World War II. Hurrell emphasizes a common theme found elsewhere in the book, that of domestic economic and political reform and its spillover effect on foreign relations. He recalls how Brazilian leaders changed course in the 1980s and 1990s and embraced a market-driven economic model designed to make their country more competitive in the rapidly integrating global economy. This policy shift, and the heightened degree of interdependence it entails, has compelled Brazilian leaders to embrace international norms in other areas, including arms control, human rights, and sustainable development.

Similarly, India's government has adapted to the rapidly integrating world economy by implementing market reforms and seeking foreign trade and investment. In Chapter 8, Raju G. C. Thomas underscores this aspect of Indian foreign policy, which, he argues, has been driven by the urgent need to improve the living standards of the country's large population, which now numbers more than one billion. Indian leaders have also sought greater recognition as a major world power; their testing of five nuclear devices in May 1998 was clearly designed to make this point. India's entry into the "nuclear club," however, was soon followed by an even larger number of nuclear tests by neighboring Pakistan, which magnified the highly volatile and unresolved differences between the two South Asian rivals. The perilous regional climate, Thomas notes, has much to do with the Cold War's end and the withdrawal of the superpower antagonists from an active role in South Asia.

Meanwhile, in Southeast Asia, Indonesia has frequently been cited as an emerging power. This is due to the archipelago's massive reach (more than 3,000 miles), its large population of more than 200 million people (including the world's largest Islamic population), and, until the late 1990s, its dynamic and expanding economy. Donald E. Weatherbee considers all these factors in Chapter 9 and finds that Indonesia today, despite its many advantages, has yet to achieve its widely acclaimed potential. Years of repression under presidents Sukarno and Suharto prevented the emergence of a vibrant civil society while the East Asian economic crisis laid waste to the country's advances as a newly industrialized country and has since threatened its democratic reforms. Domestic tensions remain acute in Indonesia, which complied with international demands for the secession of East Timor in 1999 only after a violent crackdown on its population. For better or worse, Weatherbee concludes, Indonesia will remain a vital actor in the region. Either its ultimate emergence as a formidable regional power or its internal dissolution will have profound effects beyond its borders.

In Chapter 10, Mohsen M. Milani identifies the turning point in Iranian foreign policy as the Islamic revolution of 1979. This revolution, he argues, stemmed not simply from religious fervor, but also from Iran's long history of domination by foreign powers—Russia and Great Britain during the imperial era, and the United States during the twentieth century. As Milani describes, the new Islamic government has led Iran through four distinct postrevolutionary phases, each of which relates to the central government's dual concerns for internal security and protection from outside influence. This latter concern, he concludes, has preserved Iran's territorial integrity, a central goal of the 1979 revolution. But the combination of internal repression and international isolation has hindered Iran's capacity to exploit its many assets as a regional power.

Finally, Peter J. Schraeder in Chapter 11 paints a vivid picture of fundamental foreign-policy restructuring in South Africa. This restructuring followed the abolition in 1994 of the apartheid system that systematically excluded the country's majority black population from a meaningful role in political and economic affairs. Newfound democracy in South Africa, Schraeder finds, has produced a more democratic foreign policy: "The process of democratization has favored the emergence and strengthening of a wide variety of state and nonstate actors, all of which are capable of shaping foreign policies." This process is visible in other newly democratic African states that "embody open political systems that, by their nature, permit wider involvement in the foreign policy-making process." In transforming itself from an international pariah to a leader of the "African renaissance" in democratic governance, Schraeder concludes, South Africa has emerged as a vital regional power with growing credibility and influence in global affairs.

The process of foreign-policy adaptation, of course, is a perpetual one, and it remains to be seen what the collective effects of these evolving adaptation strategies will be on regional and global relations. Most broadly, the foreign policies of these great and emerging powers will largely define the extent to which world politics in the second post–Cold War decade will be marked by greater cooperation or competition. Recent experience in this regard has not been encouraging. The convulsions of the 1990s greatly lowered expectations that a peaceful and prosperous "new world order" would replace the turbulence of the Cold War era. Transitions to democracy, furthermore, have proven to be highly fragile, and the creation of a "globalized" economy has not prevented fiscal shocks and trade frictions. For all of these reasons, foreign-policy adaptation will remain a central element of statecraft and a subject deserving close scrutiny by students of world politics.

PART I

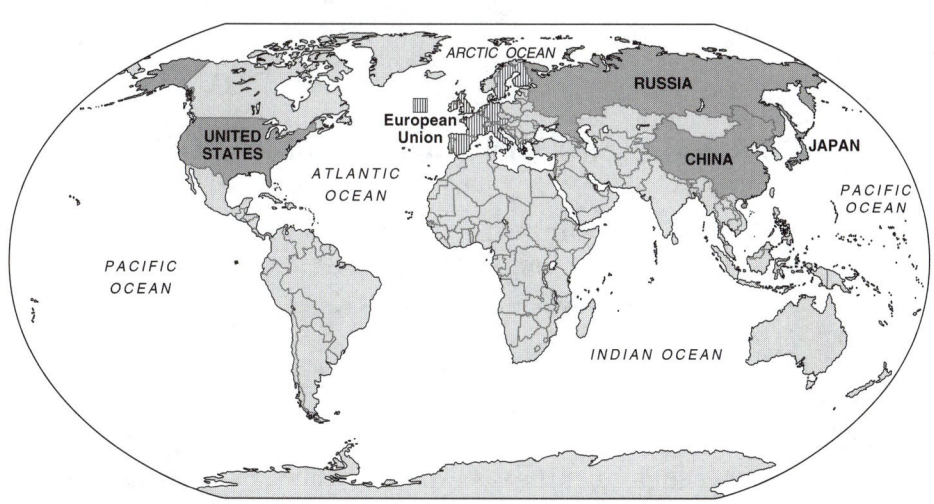

ADAPTATION STRATEGIES OF THE GREAT POWERS

New Challenges in U.S. Foreign Policy

Howard J. Wiarda
Lana L. Wylie

University of Massachusetts

More than a decade after the Cold War, the United States remains the "lone superpower" in world politics. The country's military forces are unrivaled, its economy is still far larger than any of its competitors, and its political system—for all of its well-publicized faults—remains a model that many countries have sought to emulate. Yet the United States is still searching for a new set of foreign-policy principles that reflects the changed conditions in the world, the altered post–Cold War U.S. global position, and the public's desire for greater attention to domestic issues. This search for a clear world role became a fixture of the presidency of Bill Clinton and continues today under President George W. Bush, who came into power in January 2001 after a narrow and controversial electoral victory over Vice President Albert Gore.

Adapting to the post–Cold War era has proven to be an elusive task for U.S. policymakers. The collapse of the Soviet Union, the primary adversary of the United States between 1945 and 1992, forced U.S. leaders to rethink their basic assumptions and strategies. The U.S. government itself, which had been geared to the Cold War struggle for nearly half a century, also required restructuring in order to meet the demands of the new era. The size, structures, and missions of the Defense Department, the State Department, and other agencies of foreign policy all were forced to adapt in their own ways to the new global landscape.[1]

---

[1]For an elaboration on the policy-making environment, see two useful anthologies edited by Scott (1998) and Ripley and Lindsay (1997), respectively.

The country's regional priorities also had to be rethought. During the Cold War, the Soviet Union and the Warsaw Pact were the main focus of U.S. strategic thinking. Since it was widely thought that the plains of Eastern Europe would be the main avenue of Soviet expansion, the political, economic, and military recovery and defense of Western Europe was the central objective of U.S. foreign policy. The Middle East area was also important, both for support of Israel (created in 1948) and because of fears of Soviet penetration of the oil-rich Persian Gulf. As the Cold War set in, East Asia was deemed crucial as a check on Soviet ambitions in this region. Africa, South Asia, and Latin America, by contrast, were thought of as "derivative" regions, important only when the Cold War extended to their shores, but largely ignored the rest of the time.

Since the Cold War, questions have been raised as to whether Russia should be as much a foreign-policy preoccupation as was the Soviet Union. In this regard, the role of the North Atlantic Treaty Organization (NATO) has become ambiguous, along with U.S. relations with the major Western European states and the European Union (EU). Japan, China, and the rest of East Asia have remained priorities, but mainly for economic reasons rather than strategic ones. Meanwhile, turmoil in South Asia—particularly the emergence of India and Pakistan as rival nuclear powers—has demanded attention from Washington. Given that the perceived Soviet threat to the Middle East is gone, U.S. leaders have focused on economic rationales to justify activism in the region, along with ongoing concern for the security of Israel. The U.S. government has looked toward Latin America with greater interest given its growing economies and emerging democracies as well as its complex interdependence with the United States itself. Beyond economic relations, emerging priorities such as drug trafficking, immigration control, and environmental concerns resonate strongly in U.S.–Latin American relations. As for Africa, the United States has shifted its focus toward humanitarian concerns, largely in response to widening regional conflicts across the continent. Given its lack of strategic importance to Washington, however, Africa is likely to receive less overall attention by the Bush administration.

The experience of the post–Cold War period demonstrates that the United States, as the world's most powerful nation-state, continues to have global commitments, interests, and obligations that cannot be abandoned just because the Cold War is over. President Clinton came to recognize this central fact, as did his successor. But the U.S. government's approach toward all these areas has yet to fully reflect the transformed environment. A more coherent adaptation strategy thus remains vital, as does a clear articulation of U.S. interests and priorities.

In the midst of these uncertainties, U.S. leaders have been engaged in a sometimes vigorous, sometimes torpid discussion of what the shape and direction of its foreign policy should be. President George H. W. Bush (father of the current president) welcomed the arrival of a "new world order" in 1992, but he lacked the strategic and conceptual vision that was needed to translate this cliché into a concrete strategy for U.S. foreign policy. His successor, Bill Clinton, first settled upon the concept of "assertive multilateralism," then shifted to "engagement and enlargement" when the earlier formulation was criticized as a result of perceived failures in such places as Somalia and Haiti (see Hyland 1999). The enlargement theme begged the question "enlargement of and for *what*?" and also seemed awkward as a rallying cry.

Upon taking office in 2001, George W. Bush and his advisers also struggled to outline a grand strategy, citing only a need for the United States to remain strong and focus on its national interests. Bush's pledges to redirect U.S. foreign policy were reflected in his early appointments to key foreign-policy positions: General Colin Powell as secretary of state, Condoleezza Rice as national security adviser, and Donald Rumsfeld as secretary of defense. Vice President Richard Cheney, who had served as defense secretary in the "first" Bush administration, quickly became the primary power broker in the White House. The president and his advisors signaled a rejection of the humanitarian interventionism of the Clinton administration and a shift toward more narrow concerns related to U.S. national security. They also called for greater defense spending, including the deployment of a nuclear missile-defense system, and promised a harder line toward Moscow and Beijing. However, given the slim margin of victory that brought the Bush administration to power in the November 2000 elections, and given the divided control of Congress between the Republican and Democratic parties beginning in June 2001, a clear and cohesive statement of U.S. foreign-policy goals and strategies remained out of reach.

The articulation of a coherent foreign policy was further hindered by the absence of a clear enemy to replace the Soviet Union or, more broadly, international communism. The United States identified several "rogue states"—including Iran, Iraq, Libya, and North Korea—but none of these could be considered a strategic threat to the United States in the same way the Soviet Union had been. Certain issues—illegal drugs, ethnic strife, terrorism, nuclear proliferation, environmental decay, and illegal immigration—were also elevated in importance in the wake of the Cold War. But these problems did not threaten to destroy the United States, as Soviet nuclear weapons could, and proved fickle as leading foreign-policy issues.

Until the September 2001 terrorist attacks on New York City and Washington, D.C., none of the rogue states, nor any of the issues noted earlier, sufficiently stirred the public imagination, secured the necessary Congressional budget support, or demonstrated the staying power sufficient to replace "containment" as the focal point of U.S. foreign policy. The deadly assaults on the World Trade Center and the Pentagon focused the energies of the Bush administration toward an inescapable foreign threat, although its scope and the means required to counter the terrorist challenge were difficult to ascertain.

A more general debate has been revived in the absence of anticommunism as a basis of U.S. foreign policy. Clinton, who sought an expansive U.S. world role, criticized the "new isolationists" in Congress, which was controlled by the Republican party for the final six years of his presidency. For their part, Congressional leaders rejected the president's "romantic interventionism" in the absence of clear U.S. national interests. This struggle between Clinton and Congress remained unresolved as the United States pursued an inconsistent, and often incoherent foreign policy. It remains to be seen whether the new administration of George W. Bush will be able to reverse this trend and achieve a consensus with Congress regarding the ends and means of U.S. foreign policy.

In this chapter, we assess the foreign policy of the United States as it continues to adapt to the complex environment of the post–Cold War era. In our historical review, we first consider how the scope of U.S. foreign policy steadily broadened as the nation expanded from a regional to a global power. Specifically, we describe how a grand strategy based on detachment from the European powers ultimately gave way to a foreign policy of global activism that identified U.S. interests in virtually every corner of the world. Even as the United States adopted such global ambitions, however, many Americans resisted the government's growing involvement in "foreign entanglements" and favored a return to the "splendid isolation" of the nineteenth century. We then turn our attention to the many emerging issues confronting U.S. foreign-policy makers after the Cold War. Finally, we consider the shifting sources of U.S. foreign policy at the global, societal, and governmental levels. We focus on the growing number of players in the foreign-policy game, in particular, economic interest groups, government agencies, ethnic groups, and international organizations.

As we will argue, the more pluralistic policy-making environment of the post–Cold War era has pushed the United States in different directions—toward a more active world role in some cases, toward retrenchment in others—depending upon the foreign-policy issue at hand. In this sense, the fragmented nature of U.S. foreign policy has greatly hindered the task of adapting to the post–Cold War era with a distinctive and coherent grand strategy. The United States is not the only country with an increasingly democratic foreign policy; such a trend has become commonplace as more countries have adopted representative institutions and practices. The United States is, however, the world's most powerful nation, and the only remaining superpower with global responsibilities. Consequently, the outcome of these complex and overlapping struggles over U.S. foreign policy have profound implications not only for its own peace and prosperity, but also for the stability of the world and the international system.

U.S. Foreign Policy in Historical Perspective

The foreign policy of the United States has evolved in many ways since the country's independence. The shifting balance between isolationism and internationalism has been among the most interesting of the changes in U.S. foreign policy. Throughout this history there have been periods when isolationist ideas dominated, and other times—primarily in the post–World War II period—when the United States pursued a distinctly internationalist agenda.

The isolationist impulse sprang from the foundations of the U.S. experience (see Varg 1963). The first settlers journeyed across the Atlantic Ocean in order to escape British rule, and their descendants fought to sever themselves completely from Great Britain. The presence of vast oceans that separated the United States and Europe served to further instill the sense that the United States was, and should be, separated from European affairs. As President George Washington observed (quoted in Rappaport 1966, 29) in his farewell address, "Europe has a set of primary interests, which to us have none or a very remote relation. Hence she must be engaged in frequent controversies, the causes of which are essentially foreign to our concerns."

Throughout the nineteenth century, Americans generally kept their backs to Europe, concentrating on expanding their own borders westward. The United States acquired the vast Louisiana territory from France in 1803, then forcibly wrested control of Florida from Spain and the southwestern states from Mexico. In a major foreign-policy pronouncement, President James Monroe declared in 1823 that the entire Western Hemisphere should be free of European interference. The Monroe Doctrine not only warned Europeans to stay out of the Western Hemisphere, but also shaped the U.S. relationship with its southern neighbors. Latin America and the Caribbean thus occupied a distinctive space within U.S. foreign policy. Although formally independent, they were considered to be within the "sphere of influence" of the United States.

This preponderant hemispheric role was further exemplified by the Spanish-American War of 1898, when President William McKinley felt justified in intervening in Cuba's war with Spain, acquiring Puerto Rico, and establishing a protectorate over Cuba. The war heralded a new phase in U.S. foreign relations, which soon assumed a global reach. The United States was quickly becoming a significant world power, with the economic and military might needed to back up such status. The United States, having also gained control of the Philippines from Spain, colonized the islands rather than grant them independence. Through its "open-door policy," U.S. leaders discouraged the European powers from dividing China into economic spheres of influence. As McKinley declared, isolationism had become "no longer possible or desirable."

In 1904, President Theodore Roosevelt added a new dimension to the Monroe Doctrine. In what has become known as the Roosevelt Corollary to the doctrine, Roosevelt asserted the right of the United States "to the exercise of an international police power" within the hemisphere. Wielding its "big stick," the United States intervened militarily in Colombia, the Dominican Republic, Haiti, Mexico, Nicaragua, Panama, and Cuba during the first decades of the twentieth century. Political leaders in Washington often justified these interventions on the normative grounds of promoting democratic order, but economic self-interests often lurked barely beneath the surface.[2] Despite these interventions, isolationist sentiment remained strong. The United States entered World War I in 1917 three years after the conflict had begun in Europe and only after the German navy began to sink U.S. merchant ships. Once the war was over, the United States quickly demobilized. Despite President Woodrow Wilson's involvement in the design and creation of the League of Nations, the United States remained outside of this new international organization. The onset of the Great Depression during the 1930s furthered the revival of isolationism.

In the years leading up to World War II, the United States was determined to remain uninvolved in the developing conflict. The U.S. Congress enacted numerous neutrality acts in the mid-1930s that attempted to prevent future American engagement in Europe. Despite these efforts, the United States could not remain aloof from the conflict indefinitely. President Franklin Roosevelt recognized that the allies needed U.S. support and slowly chipped away at the isolationist wall built around the United States. The wall was toppled completely when the Japanese attack on Pearl Harbor on December 7, 1941, forced the United States to enter the war. This time, the United States intervened not just as another great power, but as a superpower intimately tied into the international system. The United States thus played a decisive role in both theaters of combat, the Western Pacific and Europe.

After the war, it was no longer possible for the United States to turn inward, to return to isolationist "normalcy." The European powers and Japan were devastated. The war effort, on the other hand, had rescued the U.S. economy from the depression while greatly strengthening U.S. military forces. As the Cold War set in, the United States remained the only power that could counter the aggressive behavior of the Soviet Union. Thus the U.S. war machine was not completely demobilized after World War II as it had been in 1918. To the contrary, by 1947–1948 the United States was committed to a major expansion of its military forces in order

---

[2]This question spawned a lively *revisionist* literature on U.S. diplomatic history in the late twentieth century. For the classic example, see Williams (1959).

to "contain" Soviet power.[3] As a result, the United States became a major power on a permanent basis (see Hook and Spanier 2000).

The U.S. government embraced its role as the leader of the anticommunist alliance. "I believe it must be the policy of the United States to support free peoples who are resisting attempted subjugation by armed minorities or by outside pressures," President Harry Truman asserted in 1947 (quoted in Rappaport 1966, 329–330). "The free peoples of the world look to us for support in maintaining their freedoms.... Great responsibilities have been placed upon us by the swift movement of events." The military aid programs approved under the Truman Doctrine were accompanied by a large-scale economic aid program to Western Europe, known as the Marshall Plan, and a major reshaping of U.S. military and intelligence institutions.

Polls taken at that time demonstrated that a majority of Americans supported their government's new international posture (Wiarda 1996, 38). The victory of communist forces in China's civil war, which resulted in the creation of Mao Zedong's People's Republic of China in 1949, further solidified the anticommunist consensus. In 1950, the United States led the United Nations–sponsored effort to repel North Korea's invasion of South Korea. Later in the 1950s, President Dwight Eisenhower ordered a buildup of U.S. nuclear forces, the creation of a global web of military alliances, and numerous covert interventions in such countries as Iran and Guatemala. The globalization of the Cold War reached its most dangerous point in 1962, when it was discovered that the new communist regime in Cuba was installing nuclear missiles that had been shipped secretly from the Soviet Union. President John F. Kennedy's refusal to permit such missile deployments prompted a head-on collision with Moscow, which withdrew the missiles after nearly two weeks of tense negotiations.

Public support for the containment policy reached a turning point in the 1960s, when the United States intervened on a massive scale in Southeast Asia. Despite its military superiority, the United States was unable to prevent North Vietnam from taking control of South Vietnam and unifying the country under communist rule. American actions in Vietnam deeply divided the public. Despite the government's claim that the fall of Vietnam would profoundly alter the global balance of power, many doubted the "domino theory" and questioned why the United States was involved in this conflict, located thousands of miles away, in a region that was previously unknown to most Americans. Large-scale U.S. casualties—in addition to the even greater destruction imposed by U.S. forces on the Vietnamese people—prompted antiwar demonstrations and demands for

---

[3]The containment policy was designed by George Kennan, a Russo-Soviet specialist in the U.S. State Department who became head of its policy-planning staff.

withdrawal. Many Americans, who had previously viewed the United States as an "exceptional" world power, no longer saw it as a role model for others to follow (see Kattenburg 1980).

As the U.S. involvement in Vietnam was winding down, President Richard Nixon sought to stabilize superpower tensions. In the view of his national security adviser, Henry Kissinger, the nation needed a new approach that would prevent future crises and proxy wars. The *détente* policy, designed to promote "a vested interest in cooperation and restraint," led to a series of summit meetings between U.S. and Soviet leaders and the beginning of negotiations to limit, then reduce, the size of the nuclear arsenals maintained by each superpower. The Strategic Arms Limitation Talks (SALT) represented a cornerstone of *détente* and provided a basis for deep cuts in nuclear stockpiles in the 1980s.[4] The Nixon administration also established diplomatic relations with China as part of the *détente* policy, a move that exploited the break between Moscow and Beijing that had become apparent since the early 1960s.

Under President Jimmy Carter, the United States further shifted its foreign policy away from Cold War competition. Carter proclaimed that human rights would become a primary consideration in U.S. foreign policy and he sought to improve relations between the United States and the dozens of developing countries that had been trapped in the Cold War cross-fire. His efforts were frustrated, however, after the Soviet Union invaded Afghanistan in 1979 and after a neo-Marxist regime took control of Nicaragua in Central America. Most crippling to Carter's presidency, anti-American activists in Iran seized control of the U.S. embassy in November 1979 and held dozens of Americans hostage for more than a year.

The experiment with *détente* and the emphasis on human rights in the developing world ceased entirely with the election of Ronald Reagan in 1980. Reagan's rhetoric—the Soviet Union had once again become the "evil empire"—was followed by on-again, off-again conflict and confrontation between the superpowers. Under the so-called Reagan Doctrine, the U.S. government pledged to support groups fighting Soviet-backed regimes worldwide. The United States launched a major military build-up during Reagan's first term, doubling the size of its defense budget, and vowed to escalate the arms race further through the development of a space-based, missile-defense shield, dubbed "Star Wars." Reagan sought to put maximum pressure on the Soviet regime in order to accelerate its demise.

By the mid-1980s, changes within the Soviet Union foreshadowed the end of the Cold War. The Soviet Union had been suffering from an internal economic crisis that was, in part, brought about by the escalating arms

---

[4]The SALT process paved the way for the Strategic Arms Reduction Treaties (START), which called for even deeper cuts in nuclear arsenals.

race. Soviet leader Mikhail Gorbachev realized that Moscow could no longer afford to match the United States in military spending. Through the *glasnost* and *perestroika* initiatives, Gorbachev sought to introduce political freedoms in the Soviet Union and to make its command economy more efficient. But by then the Soviet Union was showing increasing signs of crisis in multiple areas: economic, social, political, generational, ideological, and moral. By the end of the decade, the Soviet Union had withdrawn from Afghanistan, relaxed its internal political and economic controls, and allowed the rise of noncommunist governments in Eastern Europe.

Gorbachev's reforms led directly to the collapse of the Soviet Union. In 1989, the Berlin Wall, the long-standing symbol of the Cold War, came down amid cheers across Central Europe. With Germany reunited in 1990 and the Eastern European governments in the midst of democratic transitions, the territories of the Soviet Union demanded their own independence from Moscow. The secession of the largest territory, Russia, along with Ukraine and several Islamic republics, capped the Soviet Union's free fall. The Cold War had finally ended—peacefully, and on terms that exceeded the most optimistic expectations of U.S. leaders and their allies.

KEY CONCERNS AFTER THE COLD WAR

The end of the Cold War brought understandable relief to governments and mass publics throughout the world. The "doomsday clock" was set back. International security was no longer overshadowed by fear of a cataclysmic nuclear war. In the United States, long-neglected domestic problems could finally receive the government's attention. President George Bush welcomed the arrival of a "new world order" which, he presumed, would feature greater democracy, peace, and prosperity throughout the world. Yet in many ways, the demise of the Soviet Union presented its own problems for U.S. foreign policy. As Soviet official Georgy Arbotov (quoted in Kegley and Wittkopf 1996, 68) warned his U.S. counterparts in 1991, "We are going to do a terrible thing to you. We are going to deprive you of an enemy." The Soviet Union then followed through with this "threat" by disappearing from the map.

Not only had the Soviet Union vanished, but so had many Cold War–related issues. Suddenly, a new grand strategy would be required. Bilateral and multilateral alliances would seek new missions, and the differences between allies and adversaries of the United States would become more ambiguous. Confusion resulted as the long-standing focus of U.S. foreign policy vanished. During the Cold War, when the enemy and threat were clear, policymakers were encouraged to put away their political and bureaucratic differences and to respond with single-minded purpose. Now that the threat was less clear, the domestic rivalries and political squabbles surrounding foreign policy returned to the surface.

All of this led foreign-policy makers to seek out a creative adaptation strategy that suited the new international context (see Posen and Ross 1996–1997). As noted previously, a central line of debate concerned the *extent* of U.S. involvement overseas and provoked familiar arguments between isolationists and internationalists. A second and related issue concerned the *nature* of U.S. involvement. This debate reflected long-standing differences between two contending schools of thought, idealism and realism.

The *idealist* position included conservative as well as liberal proponents. Among conservatives such as Joshua Muravchik (1991) of the American Enterprise Institute for Public Policy Research, the promotion of democracy emerged as a central priority in U.S. foreign policy. In his view, the United States should eschew other and sometimes contrary diplomatic, political, strategic, and economic interests (as in Kuwait, Saudi Arabia, and China, for example) in its effort to "export democracy." The liberal position, represented by such scholars as Larry Diamond (1992) and the journal *Democracy*, viewed the promotion of democracy less as an instrument of U.S. national interests and more as a moral imperative.

The *realist* position, represented most visibly by former Secretary of State Henry Kissinger, had long been known for a hard-headed defense of the national interest, devoid of moralistic or idealistic concerns. To realists, a foreign regime's internal affairs (including human rights violations) should not interfere with the U.S. assessment of its power capability or usefulness to the United States in international politics. Importantly, however, even Kissinger (1994) came to recognize that the United States—perhaps uniquely among nations—could not operate on the basis of "power politics" alone, and that it needed moral purpose and a sense of doing right and good in the world to have a successful foreign policy.

Yet another dimension of the post–Cold War, foreign-policy debate pitted unilateralists against multilateralists. The unilateralists, otherwise known as "aggressive nationalists," believed that, with the collapse of the Soviet Union and the United States being the only remaining superpower, the United States must exercise its power aggressively to end world conflicts and impose a democratic stamp on other nations. This position was strongly argued by neoconservative columnist Charles Krauthammer, who termed the immediate post–Cold War period as the "unipolar moment." Krauthammer stated the following:

> We are in for abnormal times. Our best hope for safety in such times, as in difficult times past, is in American strength and will to lead a unipolar world, unashamedly laying down the rules of world order and being prepared to enforce them. (1990–1991, 24)

This argument reflected the fact that, militarily and strategically, the United States was the only superpower in the Cold War's aftermath. But it ignored the fact that the Congress and public opinion would not support an open-ended global policeman role, that the U.S. economy and its taxpayers could not afford such an ambitious international agenda, that the interests of such *economic* superpowers as Japan and Germany must also be taken into account, and that the more integrated international system of the 1990s placed far more restraints on U.S. power than the unilateralists were willing to acknowledge.

In response to budgetary as well as political restraints, the Clinton administration first proposed a foreign policy more heavily based on multilateralism. The strategy of "assertive multilateralism" called for strengthening the United Nations and other international organizations and for employing their forces and good offices in various local and regional conflicts rather than committing U.S. forces. But multilateralism also faced many problems, particularly in the late 1990s. Allies of the United States and other multilateral partners were often slow to act or had different interests, the United Nations and other international agencies were woefully ill-equipped in carrying out peacekeeping operations in far-flung areas, and many U.S. leaders opposed putting the nation's troops under UN commanders. As time went on, the public and the Republican-led Congress withdrew their support of the policy, and in the face of this opposition, the administration gradually withdrew from its earlier faith in multilateralism.

Amid all of these intellectual debates, the primary agents of U.S. foreign policy struggled to find their way. The Defense Department, after concluding that no major power posed a serious threat to the United States, turned its attention to several "rogue states" (later dubbed "states of concern") that combined strong anti-American sentiments and a stated desire to acquire chemical, biological, or nuclear weapons (see Klare 1995). Iraq provided the Pentagon with an excellent example of the potential dangers presented by such states. Yet even after Saddam Hussein's forces were expelled from Kuwait during George H. W. Bush's presidency, the Clinton administration remained wary of Saddam's military capabilities and intentions. Despite harsh economic sanctions against Iraq that were sponsored by the UN and a protracted effort to block Iraq's effort to build weapons of mass destruction, Hussein remained firmly in power.

THE UNCERTAIN USE OF MILITARY FORCE

The Persian Gulf War demonstrated that the "new world order" anticipated by U.S. leaders would be anything but orderly. The war also revealed that the United States might be tempted to confront other regional conflicts and consider resolving them through military force. Aside from

Iraq's invasion of Kuwait, which clearly threatened U.S. economic interests, the United States became engaged in a variety of humanitarian interventions after the Cold War. American troops were deployed to Somalia in 1992 in order to provide food and other supplies to victims of a prolonged famine, which was made worse by the collapse of the Somali government and civil war. But the intervention failed after U.S. and UN peacekeepers launched an ill-fated effort to apprehend rival warlords and rebuild the Somali state. After U.S. troops were ambushed and the body of one soldier was unceremoniously dragged through the streets, public opinion that was fanned by television coverage demanded that the United States withdraw (see Strobel 1997). Two years later, the United States intervened in Haiti, where a democratically elected government had been forcibly removed by military leaders. But again the intervention succumbed to challenges from indigenous forces.

In each case the United States seemed hesitant to intervene and only did so after much debate within and outside of Congress and the White House. Efforts by the United States in some cases actually hindered the resolution of these problems, which ultimately required the cooperation and reconciliation of the foreign governments and their peoples. By the mid-1990s, when the central African nations of Rwanda and Burundi descended into a genocidal conflict between the Tutsi and Hutu ethnic groups that claimed 800,000 lives, the United States remained passive and unwilling to stop the carnage.

Another casualty of the Cold War's end was Yugoslavia, which was deeply divided along religious and ethnic lines. Without a strong leader at the top, which Marshall Josip Tito provided for many years, and without the threat of Soviet military intervention, Yugoslavia disintegrated into civil war. At first, the United States saw few of its interests affected by these conflicts.[5] But later, affected by gruesome television coverage of Yugoslav President Slobodan Milosevic's campaign of "ethnic cleansing" against Muslims, the United States and its NATO allies intervened. In Bosnia-Herzegovina, they sent peacekeepers to separate the contending factions in 1995 and began building a fragile new government. Four years later in the Yugoslav province of Kosovo, the NATO allies responded to Milosevic's latest atrocities by bombing his troops in Kosovo along with key targets in the heart of Yugoslavia, including the capital, Belgrade. The two sides eventually established a tenuous peace, which only the continued presence of NATO forces seemed capable of maintaining. These interventions were variously praised or criticized, but they did little to resolve the underlying questions regarding a U.S. grand strategy after the Cold War.

---

[5]As Secretary of State James Baker put it, "We don't have a dog in this fight."

Foreign-policy makers sought to maintain a sense of purpose by re-designing Cold War structures. The NATO alliance, formed to prevent Soviet expansion after World War II, lost its main purpose after the fall of the Soviet Union. Many politicians and academics predicted the dissolution of the alliance after its enemy had been vanquished. Not only did NATO survive, however, it grew larger. This was done by redefining NATO as less of a collective military alliance and more as a political club of democracies with shared security concerns. In this spirit, Poland, the Czech Republic, and Hungary were admitted to the "club." To other countries in central and eastern Europe, membership in NATO was dangled as a reward for good behavior, as a stepping-stone into the prosperous EU, and as a protective mantle against Russia's reemergence as a major power. The alliance survived as a new kind of organization, but Russia continued to view NATO as a potential military threat (see Chapter 3 for an elaboration).

A NEW EMPHASIS ON "GEOECONOMICS"

Throughout history, political leaders have routinely utilized economic instruments to shape international relations in their favor. This practice of "economic statecraft" (Baldwin 1985)—involving the terms of trade, global financial flows, and the promotion of domestic firms—joined military defense as a central element of U.S. foreign policy after the Cold War.

All countries today are greatly influenced by economic decisions made outside their borders. Those states that are heavily dependent on export markets or on foreign investment are more vulnerable than others, but all are affected by international economic factors that, to an increasing degree, are beyond their control. Economic globalization—or the coming together of a single world market in addition to national and regional markets—is only the latest expression of international interdependence (see Friedman 2000). The benefits of globalization could be immense for rich and poor countries alike. The integration of the world economy provides individuals with greater choice about where to shop, where to work, and where to invest. It has the potential to allow for specialization, improve efficiency, and spur economic development.

The United States, which possesses the largest economy in the world, is increasingly sensitive to these machinations of international economic and financial pressures. According to the *Central Intelligence Agency's World Factbook* (1998, 8), the United States exported $663 billion in goods and services in 1998 while importing $912 billion in foreign products. The lessons from these statistics are clear. First, the United States is a major player on global trade markets and has a voracious appetite for foreign goods. Second, millions of U.S. jobs can be created or lost by foreign sales or competition.

Americans do not have the resources or inclination to produce everything they require, including many vital resources. In particular, U.S. dependence on oil has at times threatened to paralyze its economy. Twice during the 1970s the price of oil increased dramatically—in 1973–1974, after the Yom Kippur War and the creation of the Organization of Petroleum Exporting Countries (OPEC), and again in 1979, after the Iranian revolution. The impact of these two oil shocks on the United States, the world's largest consumer of energy, was dramatic. As a result, the vast amount of U.S. dollars spent abroad greatly enlarged the national debt and created a serious inflationary crisis. Long lines for gas were not uncommon and U.S. citizens everywhere felt the impact of these events occurring on the other side of the globe. President Carter alleged that the oil cartels were conducting "the moral equivalent of war" against U.S. consumers. As the twenty-first century began, fuel prices soared again and power outages in California reminded Americans once more of their vulnerability to foreign energy sources.

Not only does this vulnerability affect Americans at home. but it also affects U.S. foreign policy. For example, policymakers must balance their concern for human rights abuses in the oil-rich states of Saudi Arabia and Kuwait with the knowledge that these states control U.S. access to this vital resource in the Persian Gulf. The decision of the Bush administration to commit U.S. forces to defend Kuwait against Iraq during the Persian Gulf War was at least partially motivated by the need to secure continued access to Kuwaiti oil. The October 2000 terrorist attack against the *USS Cole*, which was refueling in a Yemenese port, later tested the country's resolve to keep the Persian Gulf open for business.

In terms of routine economic activity, the surge of Web-based business and "e-commerce" makes international purchasing more accessible to the average consumer, bringing exporting and importing to a new level and greatly increasing global economic connectedness. Consequently, U.S. prosperity is becoming even more reliant on international business. In addition, the United States has assumed a leading role in global financial markets. Through foreign direct investments (FDIs), which involve long-term development of companies overseas, and portfolio investments, which include U.S.-based investments in foreign stock, bond, and currency markets, the United States floods the world with capital on a daily basis. These largely private capital flows are accompanied by public funds originating from the World Bank and International Monetary Fund (IMF), to which the United States is the primary contributor.

Economic interdependence, in all its forms, has clear consequences for U.S. foreign policy. It has the potential to offer incredible rewards as well as possible problems. Many skeptics firmly believe that globalization represents a threat to global equality, the environment, and the cultural heritage of parts of the world that may be "swallowed up" by Western corporations and commercial media. The skeptics made this point clear repeatedly in 1999 and 2000 by disrupting the annual meetings of the World Bank, IMF, and World Trade Organization (WTO). If poorly managed, they argued, international economic interdependence has the potential to be damaging not only to the United States, but also (and even more so) to less-secure economies in the developing regions.

Responding to globalization, the Clinton administration elevated foreign economic policy to a central position in its relations with other states. For Clinton, whose agenda as president was primarily focused on spurring economic growth at home, greater competitiveness in world markets emerged as a primary element of his "geoeconomic" strategy. Thus Clinton was a strong supporter of the North American Free Trade Agreement (NAFTA), which more closely connected the U.S., Canadian, and Mexican trade and financial markets. The United States also helped create the grouping known as Asia-Pacific Economic Cooperation (APEC) to promote commerce among the North American and East Asian economies. Clinton also favored closer trade ties between the United States and China. His "engagement" policy was based on the assumption that Beijing's respect for human rights would improve as China developed economically and became more dependent on global trade to sustain its high rate of growth. Although the Chinese government continued to repress political opponents, workers, and religious movements, Clinton endorsed China's entry into the WTO. In September 2000, the U.S. Congress approved "permanent normal trading relations" with China. In the age of globalization, this marked a major foreign-policy accomplishment for the Clinton administration as well as a great leap forward for the Chinese government (see Chapter 4).[6]

A BROADER FOREIGN-POLICY AGENDA

In addition to the key concerns of military intervention and global economic relations, the U.S. government broadened its post–Cold War, foreign-policy agenda to accommodate a variety of newer issues and problems. Narcotics trafficking, immigration pressures, terrorism, environmental decay, and energy "security" all preoccupied the first post–Cold War administration. These issues, described briefly in the following sections, further complicated the formulation and conduct of U.S. foreign policy.

---

[6]Despite growing strains in Sino–American relations after Bush became president in 2001—over U.S. plans for a nuclear missile-defense system, U.S. aerial surveillance of China and Taiwan, and other security-related issues—normalized trade continued between the two countries.

INTERNATIONAL TERRORISM

A critical problem facing the United States today involves international terrorism. For many years, attacks by terrorist groups have posed a direct threat to U.S. interests both at home and overseas. By far the most devastating attack occurred on September 11, 2001, when hijacked U.S. airliners were turned into guided missiles that struck the World Trade Center and the Pentagon. The attacks killed thousands of civilians and traumatized the nation. These and other terrorist strikes have starkly demonstrated the extent of anti-American feelings overseas, primarily among militant Islamic populations.

Fighting terrorism has proven to be a difficult task. By their nature, terrorists are highly secretive and operate outside the traditional boundaries of international diplomacy. Their identities and whereabouts are often unknown, as is their direct involvement in specific terrorist incidents.[7] The U.S. government identified one likely sponsor of international terrorism—the Saudi dissident Osama bin Laden. He was believed responsible for several terrorist attacks, including the cataclysmic 2001 strikes in New York and Washington, D.C., and the bombings of U.S. embassies in Kenya and Tanzania in 1998 that killed 224 people, 12 of them Americans. Bin Laden had long thwarted Western efforts to bring him to justice, hiding his militant followers in the remote, mountainous areas of Afghanistan and Pakistan.

The terrorist attack against the *USS Cole* in October 2000, leaving more than a dozen U.S. sailors dead, posed a similar challenge to the U.S. government. The assault on the destroyer, which was bombed in a Yemenese port during a routine refueling stop, occurred on the same day that tensions between Israelis and Palestinians spilled over into widespread violence by both sides. The U.S. government thus confronted simultaneous military crises in both key subregions of the Middle East: the Arab–Israeli theater close to the Mediterranean Sea, and the Persian Gulf area. But the September 2001 attacks on New York and Washington were the most devastating to the United States, leaving thousands of casualties, forcing the suspension of routine activities across the country for many days, and producing widespread fear and uncertainty.

Cyber-terrorism has emerged as an additional problem for U.S. foreign-policy makers. Questions of security now involve the protection of government and private computer systems. The U.S. government recently formed

---

[7]In most cases, many terrorist groups take credit for a single attack, and U.S. investigators are rarely granted the authority to locate and interrogate suspected terrorists in foreign countries that are hostile toward the United States.

a new department modeled after the Center for Disease Control. The National Infrastructure Protection Center (NIPC), located at the FBI headquarters, is an "information and warfare detection and response center" whose mission is to identify and respond to serious cyber-warfare threats, such as penetration of the banking sector or other critical industries.

It is not hard to imagine how this form of computer-based economic terrorism would be used as a weapon in a future war. According to General Kenneth Minihan, director of the National Security Agency in the late 1990s, there was evidence that recent Chinese government military exercises included the use of computer warfare. Computer hackers clearly demonstrated that this type of terrorism is possible. Internationally based hackers were able to halt business in a number of Internet-based companies in early 2000, demonstrating their ability to disrupt this new form of business and potentially inflict billions of dollars in losses. Keeping government and business sites secure will continue to be a priority as more of the world gets online.

AMERICA'S "WAR ON DRUGS"

The international narcotics trade presented U.S. foreign-policy makers with a new and difficult challenge. It has been estimated that the economic toll from drug abuse and related accidents reached $60 billion a year by the end of the twentieth century, not to mention the loss of life and personal tragedy that affected addicts and those who cared for them (see Smith 1998). As well as addressing the demand side of the problem, U.S. officials focused on the supply of drugs, treating this problem as an international relations issue.

Illegal narcotics mainly enter into the United States through Latin America. Bolivia, Peru, Ecuador, Colombia, Mexico and the islands of the Caribbean are the major producers or trans-shipment points of illegal drugs that find their way into the United States through illegal smuggling. As a result, U.S. diplomatic relations with many of these countries have been dominated by this problem since the last stages of the Cold War. The official labeling of this effort as a "war on drugs" revealed the importance and international emphasis given to this issue in U.S. foreign policy. Accordingly, in December 1989, President Bush sent U.S. forces into the Central American country of Panama to capture its leader, General Manuel Noriega, in part because of his ties to Colombian drug cartels. President Clinton appointed General Barry McCaffrey to lead his administration's drug policy and threatened to cut off aid to enlist cooperation from Latin American countries. Further, under NAFTA, the Mexican government agreed to strengthen its own domestic narcotics enforcement and expand efforts to prevent drug smuggling across the vast U.S. border.

The primary target of the "war on drugs" however, was the South American country of Colombia, which served as a primary source of cocaine production and worldwide distribution. As U.S. foreign-aid programs to most other developing countries fell sharply in the late-1990s, the U.S. government steadily increased its assistance to Colombia. Its leaders were engaged in a virtual civil war against regional drug cartels, which were able to draw on their vast wealth in fending off the cash-starved Colombian government led by President Andres Pastrana. The Clinton administration hoped to make more than $1.3 billion available to Pastrana between 2000 and 2002 that would be used to provide for military training, sixty U.S.-made helicopters, and funds for justice, agricultural, and human-rights initiatives. Even with these funds, however, Colombian leaders would have a difficult time stopping the cultivation and export of *coca*, whose potential value in world markets exceeded that of Colombia's most lucrative legal cash crop, coffee. Thus the civil war dragged on and limited the impact of U.S. financial aid.

IMMIGRATION PRESSURES

Another problem facing the United States today concerns immigration, both legal and illegal. Immigration levels in recent years reached a record pace of 1.1 million annually in the late 1990s, which exceeded the previous peak of about 700,000 annually between 1900 and 1920. The most recent surge went against the findings of the U.S. Commission on Immigration Reform, which called in 1995 for a one-third reduction in legal immigration and stronger efforts by U.S. firms to curb illegal immigration.

The mass movement of populations is certainly not a new issue in the United States, whose origin and rise as a world power were primarily driven by foreign immigration. However, with rising population pressures worldwide and within the United States, this issue has taken on greater significance in the past few decades. During the twentieth century, the source of immigrants gradually shifted from Europe to developing countries—mainly those in Latin America and the Caribbean, but also in East Asia.

The economic disparity between the United States and these regions intensified the immigration pressure on the United States to the point that many Americans felt threatened by the increased numbers of immigrants. The argument was that immigrants would take away the jobs of Americans. Since a significant number of these immigrants did not enter the United States legally, this perception of threat was increased. Further, high levels of immigration strained the political and economic resources—for schools, social agencies, courts, and law enforcement—available in many U.S. cities, particularly those close to the Mexican border in Texas and California. Thus the problems faced primarily by local and state governments made illegal immigration a strong national concern. According to a poll conducted in 1994 by the Chicago Council on Foreign Relations (1995), 72 percent of the respondents stated that "controlling and reducing illegal immigration" should be a "very important" goal of the United States.

During the Cold War, U.S. interventions in Central America and the Caribbean were justified in part on immigration grounds. President Reagan's first secretary of state, Alexander Haig, argued in 1982 that U.S. interventions to prevent the rise of totalitarian or communist states were necessary to avert mass migrations of individuals who would attempt to flee if such regimes were allowed to rule (Teitelbaum 1990, 322). As the threat of Marxist revolutions receded in the late 1980s, and as elected governments gained power across Latin America, U.S. leaders hoped improved conditions in the region would slow the tide of illegal immigration. Regional economic integration through NAFTA was also designed to improve living standards in Mexico sufficiently to encourage its workers to remain in their home country.

Many problems have remained, however. Among other examples, the mass exodus of Cubans into Florida in 1994 created serious problems for state and federal officials. These wide-scale movements of Cubans across the Florida straits were directly responsible for changes in U.S. policy toward Cuba. After the 1994 immigration wave, the Cuban government agreed to step up its restrictions against illegal emigration to the United States, and U.S. officials agreed to accept 20,000 legal Cuban migrants each year. The Clinton administration also tightened other aspects of its Cuba policy (see Pérez 1997, 269).

The United States was also forced to take military action to stop another wave of illegal immigration from Haiti, the poorest country in Latin America, which fell into political and economic chaos in the early 1990s. President Bush ordered the U.S. Coast Guard to forcefully return the hundreds of Haitian "boat people" who had constructed makeshift rafts to bring them to the United States. As a presidential candidate, Bill Clinton opposed Bush's policy, but he reversed his position after taking power in January 1993. The United States then used military force to restore the democratically elected government of Reverend Jean Bertrand Aristide. But in the years that followed, Haiti again succumbed to internal unrest and economic despair. Given the lack of another exodus of refugees, however, the U.S. government did not feel compelled to intervene again. Once again, the linkage between immigration pressures and U.S. foreign policy was clearly demonstrated.

GLOBAL ENVIRONMENTAL DECAY

Environmental problems have major implications for international relations and foreign policy. They do not respect man-made political borders, making them a shared problem requiring coordinated solutions. While some environmental disasters can be contained, most work their way through waterways and into the atmosphere to create health hazards in other regions. For example, in February 2000, poisonous chemicals from a Romanian mine reservoir leaked into the Vaser River and eventually into the Tisza and Danube rivers, affecting Hungary and Ukraine. This crisis followed only weeks after a cyanide spill contaminated the same international waterway. These spills prompted urgent discussions among the governments involved, whose ecosystems had previously been degraded under more than four decades of communist control.

The United States has increasingly been engaged with its neighbors on environmental problems that cross national borders. In particular, environmental issues have often taken center stage in U.S.–Canadian relations since the 1970s. Air pollution originating in the United States causes acid rain that produces extensive damage to the Canadian environment. As a result, Canadian leaders and activists have insisted that a solution to the acid rain problem be incorporated in bilateral treaties and regional pacts such as NAFTA.

Since many environmental issues are global in scope, U.S. officials are also party to much larger multilateral discussions. Global conferences such as the 1992 Earth Summit have drawn much-needed attention to pollution problems and have been attended by thousands of national leaders, representatives of international governmental organizations, nongovernmental organizations (NGOs), and academic specialists. These meetings and the agreements they produce have not only influenced U.S. domestic environmental regulations, but also shaped U.S. foreign policy in other areas. For example, protecting the environment became one of the key post–Cold war missions of the U.S. Agency for International Development (USAID). The agency adopted many of the calls for "sustainable development" outlined in *Agenda 21*, the Earth Summit's concluding document, and pledged more than $600 million annually toward global environmental protection efforts in the late 1990s. The strategy of sustainable development, also adopted by other industrialized states, was designed to encourage economic efforts in less-developed countries that would not impose permanent damage on their ecosystems.

As the world's foremost source of toxic emissions, and as the world's leading consumer of nonrenewable resources, the United States bears a major responsibility for regulating the global environment. But in Washington, political leaders have been deeply divided over exactly how much of this burden should be carried by the United States. Despite strong evidence that growing emissions of fossil fuels have led to global warming, the U.S. Senate refused to ratify the Kyoto Treaty of 1997 that was approved by the Clinton administration and signed by the leaders of thirty-seven other industrialized countries. Under the treaty, these leaders agreed to reduce emission levels to 5 percent below their 1990 levels by 2012.

Many state governors and members of Congress representing industrial states have argued that the strict environmental controls would jeopardize key U.S. industries and slow the nation's economic growth (see Vig and Kraft 1997).

Such views were quickly accepted by the incoming Bush administration, which openly declared the Kyoto Treaty unfit for further consideration by the United States. Bush further enraged environmentalists by declaring that carbon dioxide was not a primary cause of global warming and should thus not be strictly regulated, a reversal of his position as a presidential candidate. By this time, however, the United States was faced with a revived energy crisis, due largely to higher natural gas prices and record levels of demand for gasoline that exceeded the nation's refining capacity. Bush's proposed energy policy—to accelerate oil drilling and the opening of new coal- and nuclear-powered plants rather than encouraging energy *conservation*—clearly placed long-term environmental concerns behind immediate economic needs. Bush's critics also charged that the energy policy, drafted by Vice President Cheney, was designed to favor the oil industry in which both the president and vice president had worked before assuming power.

Beyond these changes, it was clear that U.S. "energy security" had become a central concern that crossed domestic- and foreign-policy domains. Meeting the nation's heavy demand for energy would no doubt require a favorable world market for petroleum and natural gas. Further, the balance to be struck between energy conservation and consumption would have real consequences for the global environment. The question of energy, therefore, became another "intermestic" issue that further complicated the task of foreign-policy adaptation in the United States.

SHIFTING SOURCES OF U.S. FOREIGN POLICY

In many ways, the international environment today is as menacing to U.S. security as were the communist threats of the Cold War. There is not one overriding challenge today, but instead a number of potentially dangerous threats and issues that require effective foreign policies. More so than before, these issues often include a major domestic component. Economic globalization, illegal drug trafficking, immigration pressures, terrorism, and environmental concerns have drawn attention far beyond the U.S. government. They have engaged a wide variety of individuals and groups in other areas as well, including state and local governments, international government organizations, and nongovernmental organizations (NGOs) based in the United States and overseas.

The setting of U.S. foreign policy, therefore, has shifted from one in which policy was made by a relatively small group of elites to one that is the product of an enormous variety of domestic political, bureaucratic, and societal forces. Indeed, the most distinguishing feature of current U.S. foreign policy is the extent of public pressures and the degree to which policy has become democratized. In most other countries, the formulation and conduct of foreign policy remain relatively insulated from these domestic political machinations. The foreign policy of the United States is unique in the degree to which its conduct in world affairs is shaped by domestic political considerations rather than by calculations of the national interest.

In this section we review the shifting sources of U.S. foreign policy. We begin by considering the effects of the transformed post–Cold War balance of power, an important *systemic* source of foreign policy. We then turn our attention to the altered *domestic* environment, which includes the traditional core elites within the U.S. government as well as nonstate actors such as the news media and NGOs. As we argue, the more pluralistic nature of U.S. foreign policy today is one of its defining characteristics, and one that helps explain the erratic performance of the United States in world affairs since the end of the Cold War.

THE BALANCE OF POWER IN FLUX

Even the most powerful country in the world is not immune to the actions of states and other entities beyond its borders. In this respect, prominent realists of the Cold War period argued that a state's actions in the international system could be traced almost exclusively to external forces. To Hans Morgenthau (1948), the struggle for power among nation-states represented the core of international politics; every state's primary goal was to increase its power, both on an absolute basis and relative to other states. Similarly, Kenneth Waltz (1959, 1979) claimed that the anarchic nature of the international system had the greatest influence over a state's actions within that system. In other words, the balance of power among states determined the actions of each.

Many U.S. leaders—from Alexander Hamilton to Theodore Roosevelt, George Kennan, Henry Kissinger, and now President George W. Bush and his key advisers—have viewed international politics through such a realist lens. Even though the United States was fairly secure from European attack for most of its history, the actions of other states played a significant role in U.S. foreign policy during its first century. Widespread concerns about the collapse of the Spanish empire, for example, contributed to growing U.S. involvement in Latin America and the Caribbean in the early 1800s. Fears that the European powers would attempt to fill the resulting power vacuum led directly to the Monroe Doctrine. From the realist perspective, U.S. entry in both world wars was necessary given that Germany was close to gaining control over Europe, a development which would have destroyed the balance of power within and beyond the region.

Of central concern to realists has been the number of "poles," or power centers, in the interstate system. As the two superpowers in the bipolar Cold War, the United States and the Soviet Union were destined to become enemies in this view. Realists of the Cold War era asserted that the Marshall Plan, the Truman Doctrine, and the presence of thousands of U.S. troops in Western Europe long after World War II stemmed not from idealism but from Washington's concerns about the balance of power in Europe. The United States, they argued, was compelled by the logic of bipolarity to prop up its European allies and prevent the expansion of Soviet power. To Waltz (1979, 171), "A war or threat of war anywhere is a concern to both of the superpowers if it may lead to significant gains or losses for either of them. In a two-power competition a loss for one appears as a gain for the other."

Both sides, therefore, attempted to gain as many allies as possible in order to increase their share of the balance. The U.S. government invested enormous amounts of resources worldwide and sought to persuade minor powers to join the Western alliance against communism.[8] American leaders adopted the "domino theory," which presumed that if one ally fell or changed loyalties, other states would inevitably follow. The potential fall of South Vietnam, deemed an important and delicately placed "domino," was therefore unacceptable. The seemingly illogical and disproportionate U.S. effort to salvage South Vietnam arose from this fear.

Since the end of the Cold War, realist thinkers have debated the polarity of the system that emerged from the ruins of the old bipolar structure. Many, like Charles Krauthammer (1991), argued that the United States remained the sole superpower in a *unipolar* world and challenged U.S. leaders to assume greater global responsibility. To other analysts, U.S. preeminence was challenged by other power centers such as the European Union, Japan, China, and, to a lesser extent, emerging powers such as India and Brazil. These scholars (e.g., Layne 1993) foresaw a *multipolar* world and predicted the rise of many regional disputes within this system.

While power in the traditional *realpolitik* sense is understood to be rooted in military strength, the nature of power in the world arena has changed. Military might is no longer the sole predictor of international influence. Of course, political, diplomatic, and economic leverage have long been important. But today these and other ways for international actors to wield influence—by demanding democracy and human rights abroad, for

---

[8]Many states were able to play the Soviets and U.S. governments off against each other, obtaining arms and materials from both sides. For example, at the outset of the Somalia–Ethiopian conflict in 1976, the Soviets supported Somalia. But within a year, Moscow was aiding the Ethiopian side, which had previously received U.S. military aid. Somalia then turned to the Americans for support. Both sides thus used a combination of U.S. and Soviet war materials in fueling their deadly conflict.

example—have become more relevant. Robert O. Keohane and Joseph S. Nye (2001) recognized this development when they popularized the term "complex interdependence" in the 1970s. Its effects have profoundly shaped the agenda of U.S. foreign policy since the Cold War as nonmilitary issues such as economic globalization, environmental concerns, illegal drugs, and immigration have demanded sustained attention from policymakers and a greater degree of coordination with other governments. In this respect, not only is the balance of power widely considered to be in flux today, so are the *sources* of power in the post–Cold War international system.

POLITICAL CULTURE AND PUBLIC OPINION

Increasingly, the external pressures noted earlier cannot be separated from domestic political or societal factors that shape U.S. foreign policy. In fact, most foreign-policy decisions are heavily influenced by domestic factors, and some are ultimately determined by them. For example, while immigration pressures originate in foreign countries, how the U.S. government decides to deal with these pressures relates directly to public opinion, the condition of the U.S. economy, the existing concentration of immigrants in politically sensitive areas, and many other domestic issues. President Clinton's policy toward Cuba was not just affected by the arrival of Cuban refugees, but also by public opinion and electoral politics in southern Florida. Most, if not all, foreign policies are heavily influenced by these kinds of domestic considerations.

In this regard, U.S. political culture—the political values, norms, beliefs, and ideals held by Americans—has an important influence on foreign policy. Political culture is an elusive concept, but most scholars agree that U.S. political culture reflects the liberal tradition that emphasizes popular sovereignty, political equality, and freedom of expression. American "exceptionalism" is closely related to this tradition. Many U.S. citizens believe the nation's values and institutions should be adopted by other countries. Tellingly, the Clinton administration identified the promotion of democracy as a central foreign-policy goal in the 1990s (see Carothers 1999).

The ideas and values of political culture are often expressed through public opinion, which becomes translated into policy through interest groups, the news media, Congress, and political parties. Though generally more concerned about domestic issues, U.S. public opinion has a significant influence over foreign-policy decisions. Democratic theory is based on the premise that a polity has a well-informed citizenry that cares about public affairs and is able to influence its leaders to make the correct policy decisions. However, in reality, most Americans care little about U.S. foreign policy and are woefully ill-informed. Two-thirds to three-quarters of U.S. citizens remain uninterested in developments beyond their borders

(Wiarda 1996, 59). According to a 1994 Chicago Council on Foreign Relations poll (1995), only 33 percent of the respondents were "very interested" in news about other countries; most were interested only in those issues that affected their economic situations. Subsequent surveys have offered similar evidence of scant public knowledge of, and interest in, important foreign-policy issues.

Although most U.S. citizens do not have an extensive knowledge of, or even a strong personal opinion about, most foreign-policy decisions made by their government, public opinion does have an impact. Voting-behavior studies demonstrate that citizens do punish and reward candidates on the basis of their foreign policies. President George H. W. Bush was heavily criticized in the early 1990s for focusing too much on foreign policy at the expense of domestic concerns. This perception contributed to the election of Bill Clinton, whose campaign emphasized domestic (largely economic) issues. Thus, politicians who want to be reelected must respond to public opinion.[9]

INTEREST GROUPS AND THE NEWS MEDIA

Interest groups have been an important part of the U.S. political system throughout its history. The role and impact of such groups in shaping U.S. foreign policy, while rather limited until recently (Zegart 1999, 22–27), will likely become stronger as the policy agenda widens. Yet increasingly, the role of interest groups in the policy-making process has come under attack. The sheer number of interest groups is considered problematic. Today there are over 23,000 interest groups attempting to sway the U.S. government on nearly every foreign-policy issue (Wiarda 1996, 95). The existence of so many groups, which frequently clash with each other over policy goals and choices, has often led to paralysis as decision makers fear offending groups that, collectively, represent a sizable segment of the voting public.

A vivid example of this problem was the outbreak of violence that occurred late in 1999 during the World Trade Organization's (WTO) annual meetings in Seattle. Business groups advocating free trade were challenged by labor, environmental, and human-rights groups that opposed the WTO's growing role. The showdown revealed deep divisions within Congress over U.S. foreign economic policy. In supporting the WTO, a coalition of Congressional Republicans and conservative Democrats backed the Clinton administration, but they faced considerable opposition from a majority of Democrats with strong ties to organized labor. The threat that

---

[9]See Mayhew (1974) for an early, though still relevant, examination of the connection between public opinion, voting behavior, and congressional action.

labor would retaliate in elections had many members scrambling for some midway position that neither fully supported nor opposed the trade body (see Schmitt 2000, A8).

Powerful interest groups are also blamed for promoting narrow-minded policies that place their own self-interests above the national interest. The largest and most powerful groups are charged with wielding virtual control over policy and drowning out dissenting opinion. In particular, business interests have become more active than ever in shaping foreign economic policy by contributing to election campaigns, lobbying Congress for favorable legislation, and acting as advisers to government agencies. Given that a growing share of the U.S. economy derives from international commerce, policymakers are inclined to do more than just listen to these business groups. To critics, the Department of Commerce has become a *de facto* advocate of U.S. business interests, which have used their massive resources to overwhelm less-affluent groups concerned with environmental degradation, human-rights violations, and labor issues. Clinton's support for Chinese entry into the WTO, and Congress's subsequent agreement to normalize Sino–American trade relations, followed an intense lobbying effort that was dominated by business interests (see Hook and Lesh 2002).

Agricultural interest groups have similar foreign-policy goals. Since agricultural products account for approximately 15 percent of U.S. exports, these groups have wielded enormous influence in recent years. Indeed, the Agriculture Department has become to farmers what the Commerce Department is to business: an agency that often lobbies for large agribusiness concerns and not necessarily for public interests (Wiarda 1996, 106). Among other issues, agricultural lobbies have taken on the controversial embargo against Cuba, hoping to lessen the restrictions on the sale of food to Cuba. Agribusiness advocates estimated that U.S. sales of food to the island could total $1 billion (Radelat 1999, 2). Their pressure on the Clinton administration was widely credited with the easing of export restrictions to Cuba in the summer of 2000.

Despite its waning numbers, organized labor remains a powerful interest group representing U.S. workers from every state. Today, organized labor is primarily concerned with the impact of foreign competition on jobs in the United States. When Clinton asked Congress to establish permanent normal trade ties with China in 2000, the labor unions intensified their lobbying, pressured the presidential candidates, and joined with environmental and student groups to protest further globalization. Vice President Albert Gore, the Democratic nominee for president in 2000, relied heavily on support from labor and felt the pressure. Gore, traditionally supportive of free trade, declared that he would, if elected, renegotiate parts of the deal to address labor's concerns (Greenhouse and Stevenson 2000, A8). Thus, even though the heyday of labor's power appears to be over, this interest group continues to wield significant power over U.S. trade policy.

Aside from the economic interests described earlier, there has been an enormous growth in the number of single-issue lobby groups, many of which exist mainly to shape U.S. foreign policy. Among the most well known of these groups are ethnic interest organizations, such as the American Israel Public Action Committee and the Cuban-American National Foundation, which have contributed heavily to election campaigns and maintained aggressive lobbying efforts on Capitol Hill. Also, human rights groups such as Amnesty International, environmental groups such as the Sierra Club and Greenpeace, and religious organizations such as the National Council of Churches have all become visible in foreign policy. Increasingly, NGOs from all over the world have coordinated their efforts through public-information campaigns on the Internet and direct lobbying of political leaders. Although their direct impact on policy outcomes is difficult to measure, these NGOs have played a key role in shaping the foreign-policy agenda and informing government officials and mass publics.

Finally, the U.S. news media also plays an important role in foreign policy. The Cable News Network (CNN) has become a truly global medium, and major newspapers and wire services provide a crucial link in informing U.S. citizens about developments overseas. This link has tangible consequences for foreign policy, including the deployment of multinational peacekeeping forces to end regional conflicts and civil wars. Increasingly, however, news programs have bowed to ratings concerns, emphasizing the most shocking events rather than long-term problems. Furthermore, the major networks report less world news than during the Cold War and have closed many foreign news bureaus, which has made accurate and thorough reporting from overseas more difficult. As a result, foreign-policy issues that U.S. citizens need to understand are often ill-reported, underreported, or not reported at all. Americans are thus becoming even less informed about international-affairs issues, which impairs their ability to make thoughtful assessments of foreign policy. This is a paradoxical trend given that public opinion has more influence on U.S. foreign policy than ever before.

STRUGGLES WITHIN THE U.S. GOVERNMENT

The framers of the U.S. Constitution built a system of overlapping checks and balances. In so doing, they issued an "invitation to struggle" (Crabb and Holt 1992) to Congress and the White House over U.S. foreign policy. For example, the Constitution designates the president as the commander in chief of the armed forces, but only Congress can declare war. Similarly, the president negotiates treaties, but they must be approved by Congress before they become law. Since Congress has the sole power over the appropriation of money, the president needs Congressional support for his foreign-policy initiatives or they will not become reality. This leads to much confusion within the government and also complicates relationships with foreign governments that do not always understand that the U.S. president cannot guarantee that his own government will honor a treaty he has just signed.

The balance of power between the president and Congress over foreign policy has waxed and waned over time. During the Cold War, and during all wars in U.S. history, presidential control over foreign policy has been understood as necessary to prevent the appearance of disunity within the government and to facilitate quick decisions. Yet Congress has often imposed a very significant, perhaps even coequal, influence over foreign policy. After years of Congressional acquiescence early in the Cold War, Congressional involvement in foreign policy increased during and after the Vietnam War. The War Powers Act passed by Congress in 1973 required the president to obtain congressional consent for any long-term commitment of U.S. forces abroad. Over the next twenty years, as the Cold War slowly drew to an end, Congress continued to assert more power over the conduct of U.S. foreign relations.

Greater Congressional power over foreign-policy decisions also increases the impact of political parties on these issues. Congress is the most partisan branch of the U.S. government, in which votes are often cast along party lines. Traditionally, before World War II, the Republican party leaned toward isolationism and the Democratic party was more internationalist. But in the 1950s, the Republican party became more assertive globally. These distinctions broke down in the last stages of the Cold War, and since its demise both parties appear to be mainly internationalist, but with isolationist factions (Wiarda 1996, 125). Despite these similarities, the parties still manage to disagree over foreign-policy decisions. When Congress is controlled by one of the parties and the White House by the other, the chances for stalemate are high. This situation, the product of divided government, is very common and increases the impact of partisanship on foreign policy.

President Clinton took office with a Democratic Congress in 1992, but in November 1994 the Republicans gained control of both houses of Congress. Not only were the two branches in different political hands but each tried to embarrass the other or gain political advantage from their positions. Thus the Senate held up Clinton's nominees to foreign-policy positions, refused to grant Clinton "fast-track" authority in trade negotiations, and rejected the Comprehensive Test Ban Treaty that was previously signed by the president. In turn, Clinton sought to gain political advantage by criticizing Congress for its cutbacks in foreign affairs, foreign aid, and United Nations budgets. Domestic politics regularly took priority over a rational calculation of the national interest.

For a brief time after Bush's arrival in the White House, both the executive and legislative branches were controlled by the Republican party.

This situation changed, however, when Senator James M. Jeffords of Vermont abruptly left the Republican party in the spring of 2001 and declared himself an independent. His move, largely in frustration over the Bush administration's early foreign and domestic policies, shifted control of the Senate to the Democrats by a slim margin of fifty to forty-nine members (Jeffords would be the lone member of the Senate with no formal party affiliation). As a result, Democrats took over the leadership of the Foreign Relations Committee, the Armed Services Committee, and other Senate committees that were actively engaged in U.S. foreign policy. More broadly, Democrats were able to shape the Senate's foreign-policy agenda, which contrasted starkly with that of the Bush administration on such issues as missile defense and environmental cooperation. Since Congress plays such an important role in the foreign-policy process, the defection by Jeffords virtually guaranteed that Bush would not be able to achieve his stated goals in foreign affairs. Only the September terrorist attacks on New York and Washington, D.C., forced the two branches of government to cooperate, demonstrating the crucial role of international crises in shaping the domestic politics of U.S. foreign policy.

Also of note is the impact of bureaucratic politics. This dimension of U.S. foreign policy was first brought to the fore by Graham Allison's (1971) study of the Cuban missile crisis, which demonstrated how the recommendations of different advisers in the Kennedy administration reflected their bureaucratic roles within the government. Most foreign-policy issues are of intense interest to many government agencies. The State Department, the Defense Department, the CIA, and the National Security Council each hold distinctive views toward U.S. foreign relations, as do the increasingly important economic agencies. Their views often reflect bureaucratic self-interests as much as, if not more than, objective assessments of the national interest (Zegart 1999).

The State Department, traditionally the main agent for carrying out U.S. foreign policy, has been losing power relative to the other agencies. Since the Cold War, as foreign economic policy achieved the status of "high politics," a growing number of federal agencies became key players in the formulation and conduct of U.S. foreign policy. Those formerly concerned primarily with domestic matters—such as the Treasury, Justice, and Commerce departments—assumed a vital foreign-policy role in the Clinton administration. Reflecting this change, the president created a National Economic Council to counterbalance the dominant National Security Council.

The effort to restrict the flow of drugs into the United States is a clear example of the complications involved when many agencies have an interest in a particular policy. No fewer than forty-three federal agencies were involved in this effort during the late 1990s. The main responsibility in this area had been granted to the Drug Enforcement Agency (DEA), a division of the Justice Department. The DEA was primarily concerned with prosecuting drug traffickers, but this goal often conflicted with the mandates of the other agencies involved. Since the State Department first and foremost sought productive relationships with other countries, its officials opposed many tactics used by the DEA that threatened these relationships. Both the State Department and the DEA, by carrying out their legitimate roles, thus created interagency tensions that result in a sometimes confusing and incoherent policy (Wiarda 1996, 203).

Another problem is the lack of continuity in U.S. foreign policy. Each administration, for political reasons, seeks to discredit the policy of its predecessor and to strike out in a new direction. During the 2000 election campaign, for example, George W. Bush sought to emphasize the experience and realism that could be expected from his foreign policy in contrast to the perceived naiveté and idealism of the Clinton years. Still, Bush was unable to articulate a clear rationale of U.S. interests, objectives, and priorities any more than his immediate predecessors. Nor did he describe how his cabinet officials would overcome the entrenched bureaucratic rivalries that had proven so disabling in the past. The deep divisions that existed within Congress as Bush took office in January 2001, combined with the persistent malaise and ambivalence among the general public toward foreign policy, prevented the "second" Bush administration from forging a widely accepted foreign policy until the terrorist attacks in September thrust the nation into a new sense of common purpose.

Conclusion

As we have seen, U.S. foreign policy has changed in profound ways throughout its history. The emergence of the United States as a world power early in the twentieth century, its successful interventions in both world wars, and the pressing demands of the Cold War forced the United States to abandon its isolationist tradition and to assert itself globally on a sustained basis. The end of the Cold War precipitated another shift, the direction and outcome of which remain unclear. While each of these periods was initiated by external events, they were also affected by parallel changes in the domestic environment. The greater impact of domestic influences is both a cause and a result of this shift in the foreign-policy decision-making process. Increasingly, U.S. foreign policy reflects the incredible pluralism inherent in U.S. society. Today's foreign policy exemplifies the constantly evolving amalgamation of political alliances, interest groups, and government institutions that make up U.S. society. The power of each entity or interest shifts constantly, depending on the issue under review. All of this greatly complicates the task of adapting the nation's foreign policies to the new systemic context.

Moreover, in the absence of the Soviet threat, U.S. leaders have been able to play politics with foreign policy to a greater degree than was possible when the United States was immersed in the Cold War. In this environment, policy paralysis or confusion characterized much of post–Cold War U.S. foreign policy. Remarkably, it is a testament to the strength and resilience of the U.S. political system that, despite these problems, the United States has managed in many areas to carry out an effective and often successful foreign policy.

The need for a clear and coherent U.S. foreign policy was made painfully clear in the aftermath of the September 2001 terrorist attacks on the World Trade Center and the Pentagon. Although the source and intention of the attacks were not immediately known, the resulting sense of national anxiety and vulnerability was inescapable. Of immediate concern to the Bush administration, which viewed the assault as a declaration of war, was the need to create a worldwide coalition of states and international organizations. Such a coalition, Secretary of State Powell observed, would be essential to counter the escalating challenge not only to the United States, but also to "civilization."

No development since the Cold War so clearly revealed the intimate link between international security and U.S. foreign policy. Furthermore, the terrorist attacks highlighted the interdependent nature of the policy-making environment. Each U.S. bilateral relationship was tested, in some cases strained, by the crisis, and the need for multilateral cooperation through the UN and military pacts was on full display. Finally, the assaults battered the U.S. economy and disrupted economic activity around the world, reinforcing the sense of collective vulnerability.

In these trying circumstances, a new consensus on the direction or goals of U.S. foreign policy might yet be reached that would serve to unify the often contradictory forces of isolationism and internationalism, realism and idealism, and unilateralism and multilateralism. It is hoped that, in the years to come, U.S. leaders will ultimately adapt in creative ways to this new and fluid environment and learn how to incorporate the diversity of goals and opinions that emerge in the decision-making process. An effective and democratic foreign policy is not necessarily a contradiction in terms and should certainly be within reach of the world's "lone superpower."

CHAPTER 3

Russia's Times of Trouble

William A. Clark

Louisiana State University

More than any other country considered in this volume, the Russian Federation has been faced in the past decade with demands of strategic adaptation on a grand scale. Indeed, many of the geopolitical adjustments that have confronted foreign-policy makers in other countries since the Cold War have been prompted by the Soviet Union's demise.

As was the case with the Soviet Union of the late Cold War, Russian foreign policy today is driven primarily by the distressing economic conditions that continue to prevail across the country. Economic decline has been the filter through which Russian foreign-policy ambitions have passed. It has been a very stingy filter, permitting only the most modest of policy aims to proceed and greatly restricting what the Russian government can accomplish in world politics. Rarely have students of international relations witnessed such a decline in stature as that experienced by Russia in the aftermath of the Soviet Union's collapse late in 1991.

Yet Russia remains a great power in many respects. It is the world's largest country, covering nearly seven million square miles, or nearly the combined territory of the United States and the People's Republic of China. Even without the appendages of the former Soviet Union, Russia still maintains borders with Finland and the Baltic states, Eastern Europe, an array of Islamic states, China, Mongolia, and Japan. The country possesses the world's second-largest stockpile of nuclear weapons and a formidable standing army. It remains blessed with enormous deposits of natural and strategic resources, many of which have been hardly tapped.

On the other hand, Russia has struggled to convert these power resources into real influence overseas. It has instead endured the status of a beggar nation, has seen its economic output cut roughly in half, has survived an armed confrontation within the centers of national power, and has embarked upon a series of policy reforms aimed at relieving the burdens of its onerous military commitments.[1] In contrast to the past, Russia's stated foreign-policy positions have recently not carried much weight in the cabinet rooms of the major Western powers.

Whether Russia permanently assumes a diminished role in world affairs or whether it regains its prominence cannot be known. What is clear is that Russia's role in the world is the subject of intense debate within domestic political circles. Its foreign policy has reflected all sides of this debate and has been unpredictable and inconsistent as a result. What is also clear is the likelihood that Russia's times of trouble will not last forever. As stability eventually returns to the country, its foreign-policy goals and possibilities are likely to become untangled from the economic constraints that presently enfeeble them. Only then will debates about Russia's proper place in world affairs be resolved in a more tranquil and reflective environment.

Russia's foreign policy has been in flux ever since its rebirth as an independent, sovereign state on January 1, 1992. President Boris Yeltsin and his aides were forced to create a foreign policy amid profound political and economic changes at home and major structural changes in the international environment. These changes, of course, were closely intertwined. All at once, Russia was forced to refashion its political and economic systems, adjust to a reduced stature in world affairs, and reorient its future role in the international arena. Such a multilayered agenda made it virtually impossible for Russian leaders to perform any one of these tasks satisfactorily (see Reddaway and Glinski 2001).

While contemporary Russia is the primary successor state of the Union of Soviet Socialist Republics (USSR), it is important to establish the many important differences between Russia and the USSR as they affect the current foreign-policy posture and prospects of Russia. Such a comparison will highlight the central reality that Russia today is currently unable to play as significant a role in world affairs as did the USSR during its seventy-four-year existence. Americans during the Cold War were inclined to equate "Russia" and the "Soviet Union" despite the fact that, by the late 1980s, ethnic Russians constituted only 51 percent of the overall Soviet population, the Russian republic covered just 76 percent of Soviet territory, and Russia contributed only about 60 percent of the Soviet Union's economic output. Since the Soviet Union broke up, Russia's population and economy have shrunk further. Its economic output by the late

---

[1]Since 1991, Russia has received more than $66 billion in aid from the United States, the European Union, and leading multilateral lending agencies such as the International Monetary Fund (IMF) and the World Bank (Kahn 2000).

1990s was less than 15 percent of U.S. gross national product (GNP); only in 2000 was there unambiguous GNP growth in Russia.

As a result of this economic plunge, Russia's leaders have been less inclined and less able to play a role in global affairs that could match that of the USSR, which represented one of the two "poles" in the bipolar distribution of global power that existed during much of the Cold War. They have been less *inclined* to do so because the messianic, anti-Western stance of the Soviet period has been abandoned. They have been less *able* to play a key role because of the impact on the military of the drastic decline in the Russian economy during the past decade (see Odom 1998). Indeed, as Alexei G. Arbatov (1998, 83), the deputy chairman of the Russian Parliament's Committee on Defense, argued, "Not since 1941 has the Russian military stood so perilously close to ruin as it does now." Russo-Soviet defense expenditures have declined by about 90 percent since the mid-1980s. As a result, postcommunist Russia has simply not been able to conduct the foreign policy of a superpower. Russia must for the foreseeable future pursue a modest agenda despite its many resources and potential advantages. Whether Russia can reemerge as a global superpower is still an open question, but by no means an impossibility. In any event, its actions will have a significant impact on the course of world politics in the twenty-first century, for better or worse.

This chapter examines the many questions relating to foreign-policy adaptation in Russia as its leaders search for a new identity and role in global affairs. As we will find, the adaptation strategies of Russian leaders have been conditioned by a number of historical factors. These will be identified early in the next section of this chapter, after which a series of ongoing foreign-policy problems is explored. The chapter concludes by returning to the domestic challenges that continue to plague the Russian Federation today. Only with the rehabilitation of the domestic economy and the further institutionalization of a stable, functional domestic polity will Russia be able to contemplate a revived role in world affairs.

FROM TSARS TO COMMISSARS

While the development of post–Cold War Russia represents an abject rejection of many defining aspects of the Soviet Union, one cannot make sense of current trends in Russian foreign policy without first understanding the impact of the Soviet experience on Russian society and government. Scholars of the postcommunist transitions across the former Soviet bloc often describe developments in these areas as "path dependent," meaning that the political, economic, military, and cultural inheritances of these states profoundly frame the options open to their leaders. Such a view certainly applies to Russia's foreign policy as well.

CONTINUITIES BEFORE AND AFTER THE REVOLUTION

Diplomatic historians and political scientists have commonly identified territorial expansionism as one of the major continuities between the foreign policy of tsarist Russia and that of the Soviet Union (see, for example, Zwick 1990; Rubinstein 1985; and Ulam 1974). In the 450 years preceding the Bolshevik Revolution of 1917, the Russian empire expanded from 15,000 square miles in the middle of the sixteenth century to 8.5 million square miles in 1917, an average expansion rate of 50 square miles a day over that period (Zwick 1990, 8). Soviet behavior after the revolution was seen, primarily in the United States and Western Europe, through the prism of this seemingly inexorable will to expand. Indeed, from this perspective, it was only after its victory in World War II that the Soviet Union could claim to have reabsorbed all the lands that were ruled by the last tsar and that "temporarily" regained sovereignty between the world wars.

The Soviet Union came into being after the collapse of the ruling Romanov dynasty during World War I. The old regime had been destabilized by the war, and Tsar Nicholas II himself was weakened by his own feeble attempts to take charge of military matters. It was not surprising in this context that the Bolsheviks, upon seizing power from Aleksandr Kerensky's provisional government in the winter of 1917, would seek for ideological and practical reasons to withdraw Russia from the war. They did so formally on March 3, 1918, with the Brest-Litovsk Treaty that reversed centuries of Russian expansion and cast the Bolsheviks in the role of traitors in the eyes of many Russians. By virtue of Brest-Litovsk, Moscow ceded 1.3 million square miles and approximately 62 million people. These figures represented a loss of some 32 percent of the Russian empire's arable land, 26 percent of its railroads, 33 percent of its factories, and 75 percent of its coal and iron mines. All the Baltic states, Finland, and other territories were abandoned (Zwick 1990, 15–16; Dmytryshyn 1978, 83).[2] Russia's separate peace with Germany caused some consternation among the Western allies, but the Bolsheviks were bracing for a bitter civil war over the control of the post-Russian state. They could not hope to weather such challenges while continuing to prosecute the war against Germany.

By 1922 the Bolsheviks had successfully defeated their opponents in the civil war and began their consolidation of domestic power. In the area of foreign policy, Soviet leaders embarked on a thinly veiled strategy of encouraging revolutionary activity in capitalist states through "independent" organizations, most prominently the Moscow-dominated Communist

---

[2]Two important factors should be considered when evaluating the treaty. First, the Bolshevik government actually did not control the lands it ceded to German control. Second, and related to the first point, Soviet Russia would regain much of this territory later in 1918 after Germany lost the war. Still, the Bolshevik government was roundly vilified at home for agreeing to these terms.

International (Comintern).[3] Meanwhile, Soviet leaders sought relatively normal interstate relations through the People's Commissariat of Foreign Affairs. Very few foreign governments were fooled by this ruse, and relations were badly strained with the established powers of Europe and the United States. Indeed, it was not until 1933 that the United States formally recognized the Soviet government and established diplomatic relations with Moscow.

If the USSR was to be treated as a pariah state in Europe, then it would take steps to organize cooperation with other disaffected states in the region. Primary among such states was Germany, which was harshly punished in the aftermath of World War I. In April of 1922, while attending the Genoa Conference on European Economic Problems, Bolshevik representatives met with German government officials in the nearby town of Rapallo. The two "outlaw states" agreed to the mutual renunciation of war claims as well as the initiation of commercial and diplomatic relations. In a secret protocol of the treaty, Germany was granted the opportunity to train its troops secretly on Russian territory in violation of the Versailles Treaty that ended World War I. In exchange for this right, Germany agreed to equip and train Soviet military forces and assist in the development of the Soviet military industry. The irony of this situation was lost on no one when the Germans later invaded the Soviet Union in 1941 and used information about Soviet terrain and military capabilities that it obtained as a result of the Rapallo Treaty.

World War II cost the Soviet Union dearly as it faced the brunt of the German army. At no time after the German invasion of June 1941 did the Soviet Union face less than 80 percent of the German war effort. Such an onslaught certainly took its toll. Twenty-five million Soviet lives were lost in the war, a fact that is indelibly marked in the minds of all Soviet children who were raised in its aftermath.

Soviet foreign-policy behavior in Eastern and Central Europe in the late 1940s was likewise seen in the West as expansionist and brought Moscow into direct confrontation with the United States and other Western European states. As the formal borders of the USSR expanded after the end of World War II (at the expense of Poland, the Baltic States, Germany, Czechoslovakia, Finland, Romania, and Japan), the extension of a Soviet sphere of influence extending to Germany lay at the root of the emerging Cold War (Rubinstein 1985, 40). Promises made by Stalin at the Yalta summit of February 1945 concerning free and fair elections in liberated

---

[3]The Comintern was created by Vladimir Lenin in 1919 and was composed of nonruling communist parties in many countries. A year later, Lenin imposed twenty-one conditions for membership that ensured Moscow's control over the international communist movement. Lenin's successor, Joseph Stalin, dissolved the Comintern in 1943 as a gesture of goodwill to his wartime allies.

Poland went unfulfilled, and subsequent disagreements over postwar political issues in Europe solidified the Cold War division of Europe into two hostile camps. It was in this context that former British Prime Minister Winston Churchill (quoted in Zwick 1990, 24) warned in March 1946, "From Stettin on the Baltic to Trieste on the Adriatic an iron curtain has descended across the Continent."

Another aspect of Soviet postwar foreign policy was closely related to the imperial tendency noted earlier. The Soviet state throughout its history was militaristic in the sense that military preparedness was given the highest priority in state policy. Just as under the tsars, when Russia was considered the "gendarme of Europe," so the Soviet state was determined to build and maintain a war-fighting capacity unrivaled by its neighbors. While interpretations vary as to the motivation for this aspect of Soviet rule, with some arguing that its military buildup was defensive in nature and others perceiving a more sinister offensive intent, the fact is that the Soviet Union far outspent its neighbors to maintain the largest army in Europe. Three years after World War II, when most of the major combatants had largely demobilized despite the onset of the Cold War, the Soviet military dwarfed those of its ostensible rivals. The Soviet Union had roughly four million soldiers under arms, compared to 645,000 for the United States, 530,000 for Great Britain, and 430,000 for France. Soviet forces, meanwhile, maintained one hundred battle-ready divisions compared to twelve for the United States, ten for Britain, and seven for France. The Soviet Union's 15,000 tanks also exceeded the combined totals of the Western states.

To maintain such a military posture required massive expenditures on the part of the state. "Guns" certainly won out over "butter" as the Soviet Union spent approximately 25 percent of the country's GNP on defense during much of the Cold War, compared to approximately 7 percent by the United States and even less by the Western European powers. The entire economy of the Soviet state was geared toward the maintenance of this military machine, much to the detriment of its civilian economy. It is for this reason that the Soviet Union in the 1960s was derisively referred to as a "Third World country with a First World military."

A third aspect of historical continuity between Russian imperial and Soviet foreign policy was a marked sense of messianism. Just as Russia under the tsars saw itself as the "Third Rome," the Soviet leadership, armed with a radical "scientific" theory of social evolution, set out to spread the influence of Marxism-Leninism from its center in Moscow. Many saw Marxism-Leninism as an ersatz religion, complete with sacred texts, saints and heretics, infidels, inquisitions, and a utopian teleology. Soviet foreign policy was in this sense driven by Moscow's need to be at the center of a worldwide revolutionary movement. Not all scholars of Soviet foreign policy agreed on the level of influence of Marxist-Leninist ideology in the formation of Soviet foreign policy, but successive Soviet leadership groups went to great lengths to justify in ideological terms their foreign-policy behavior and worldview. For many years, widespread optimism about the future of the Soviet system and its "inevitable" triumph resulted from these precepts of state ideology.

Soviet foreign-policy makers, like their tsarist predecessors, also displayed a tendency to overplay their hand. Russia's traditional view of the West was a mixture of love and hate, and many observers noted an inferiority complex *vis-à-vis* the major Western powers. The Soviet pattern was to overcompensate for this ambivalent feeling, to overcommit itself internationally, to make overly ambitious claims, and to gamble with few potential payoffs. The Berlin blockade of 1949 and the subsequent confrontation over the Berlin Wall in 1961, as well as the perilous deployment of nuclear missiles to Cuba in 1962, were the most obvious examples of a Soviet foreign policy that risked much for meager gains.[4]

The repeated crises in Soviet–American relations were accompanied by an unending buildup of nuclear weapons on the part of both superpowers. As the nuclear arms race continued unabated, the United States became mired in the Vietnam War and subsequently fell victim to its most serious economic recession since World War II. In this context, President Richard Nixon sought to restrain the Cold War rivalry by establishing *détente*, or a thawing in bilateral relations with Moscow. This formula proved acceptable to Soviet leader Leonid Brezhnev, who negotiated two Strategic Arms Limitation Treaties (SALT) with the United States. Once again, however, tensions escalated late in 1979 after the Soviet Union invaded Afghanistan and installed a puppet regime in Kabul. President Ronald Reagan, who took office in 1981, denounced the "evil empire" in Moscow as the Cold War reached a new crescendo.

Dimitri K. Simes (1986), a noted Russian émigré scholar, identified four instrumental convictions that served for decades as unassailable articles of faith in Soviet foreign policy: (1) The USSR is engaged in a history-shaping rivalry with industrialized democracies whose very existence threatens its security; (2) the Soviet "periphery" must be made as secure as possible to protect the "core" in Moscow; (3) the USSR's superpower status must be maintained at all costs; and (4) diplomacy is the unreliable instrument of the weak and must always be subordinate to military strength. As in the case of the longer-term historical tendencies noted earlier, which applied equally to the tsarist era as well as the early Soviet period, each of these four instrumental convictions were abandoned in the mid-1980s as the

---

[4]This latent hostility toward the West, if not the recklessness of the previous period, continues today in postcommunist Russia. While the Russian government throughout much of the 1990s enacted what can only be viewed as a pro-Western (or "Atlanticist") policy, many domestic political forces in Russia railed against the "Westernizers" and called for a refocusing of Russian vital interests away from the West.

underlying strains in the Soviet system became apparent. The abandonment of these foreign-policy pillars can be traced to the leadership of Mikhail Gorbachev, who came into office in 1985 representing a younger generation of Communist Party leaders. His short, tumultuous period in power won him the Nobel Peace Prize, but also left him the discredited leader of a deceased country.

GORBACHEV'S "NEW THINKING"

The fundamental sea change in Moscow's foreign policy occurred not at the end of the Cold War, but under the rule of Gorbachev. The changes in Soviet foreign policy between 1985 and 1991 were more dramatic and consequential than those adopted by Yeltsin's Russia, which in many respects were extensions of the Gorbachev model. Indeed, as one observer (Sakwa 1990, 315) noted, under Gorbachev the USSR pursued "one of the most sustained and far-reaching reforms in the principles and conduct of foreign policy in its entire history." Because of these reforms, contemporary Russian foreign policy shares more in common with Gorbachev's "new thinking" than the latter did with the long tradition of Russo–Soviet foreign policy.

One explanation for this may be that Gorbachev, as leader of the USSR, faced many of the same economic constraints on foreign policy that confronted the Russian leadership of Yeltsin and current President Vladimir Putin. At bottom, Gorbachev's "new thinking" and postcommunist Russian foreign policy have both reflected the objective need on the part of the country's leadership to reign in their global ambitions and obligations in the face of severe economic problems. As a driving force in Soviet and Russian foreign policy, this factor cannot be overstated.

Gorbachev always insisted that the changes in Soviet foreign policy he introduced were essential elements of his overhaul of the USSR's domestic structures and systems. In that context, the reforms of the Gorbachev era took the form of three major policy initiatives. In the economic realm, *perestroika* (restructuring) sought to introduce market elements into the Soviet Union's centrally planned command economy. Gorbachev's tinkering in this area, however, was too timid and retained the most statist and self-defeating components of Marxism-Leninism. Real market-based economic reforms, such as those described in Chapter 4 that were launched by China's Deng Xiaoping, were never attempted until Gorbachev's exit from power and the collapse of the USSR. In the social and political realm, by contrast, Gorbachev's policy of *glasnost* (openness or, alternatively, publicity) largely succeeded in opening up public debate and ushering in a new period of candor about the failures of the Soviet system. Before long, however, the criticisms were aimed at Gorbachev himself as he occupied a small political center in the rapidly polarizing debates of the day. Gorbachev was attacked by conservatives for being too democratic, and by democrats for being too conservative. The political center held by the Soviet leader ultimately was not viable and Gorbachev became increasingly isolated and weak.

Gorbachev's third major initiative was his so-called "new thinking" in foreign policy. It is difficult, in light of the fact that he presided over the dissolution of his country, to portray any of Gorbachev's policies as successful. His approach to foreign policy was, however, a progressive one with considerable merit. New thinking entailed several departures from previous Soviet foreign policy: an engagement with the West, a diminution of Cold War tensions, a reduction or suspension of Soviet military and economic aid to erstwhile allies throughout the world, a toleration—if not outright encouragement—of political change in Eastern and Central Europe, and a commitment to serious nuclear arms reductions. Each of these foreign-policy positions was maintained by the post-Soviet governments under presidents Yeltsin and Putin, arguably for the same reasons.

Most tangible in the USSR's new foreign policy were the changes in the armed services, which had traditionally consumed the lion's share of the Soviet state budget to the detriment of other sectors of the economy. Cutting these costs was key to rescuing the economy, but these cuts could only safely take place in an international environment marked by a significant easing of East–West tensions. Starting with his December 1988 speech at the United Nations, Gorbachev initiated a series of significant arms and troop reductions, many of which were unilateral—that is, without the promise of a corresponding cut in Western military expenditures or deployments. In his speech, Gorbachev promised sizeable cuts in conventional military forces in the Soviet Union's Eastern European satellite countries. To be withdrawn were some six divisions, or 500,000 troops: from East Germany (three divisions), Czechoslovakia (two divisions), and Hungary (one division). In June 1989, Soviet Prime Minister Nikolai Ryzhkov outlined plans to cut defense spending by half over the next six years.

To make such cuts without jeopardizing Soviet security, Gorbachev pursued a series of initiatives to reduce tensions with the United States. A series of East–West summits occurred in Geneva (November 1985), Reykjavik (October 1986), Washington (December 1987), Moscow (May 1988), and Malta (December 1989) with the Reagan administration and that of its successor, President George Bush. Moscow also ended its fruitless occupation of Afghanistan, with the final withdrawal of troops occurring in February 1989, and exerted pressure on its Vietnamese ally to withdraw from Cambodia. The Soviet naval base in Cam Rahn Bay, Vietnam, was abandoned in 1990. Finally, in an effort to reduce tensions with China, whose 1950 "treaty of friendship" with the Soviet Union had long since expired, Gorbachev withdrew some 200,000 Soviet troops from Mongolia and Central Asia. The Soviet Union was aggressively engaged in a policy of unilateral retreat from its global ambitions, focusing its energies internally rather than globally.

Unfortunately for Gorbachev, the political opening provided by *glasnost* outpaced the institutional reforms of *perestroika*, and the unraveling of the Soviet bloc was quickly out of control. This process began in Eastern Europe, whose leaders and mass publics gladly accepted Gorbachev's invitation to choose their own destinies. The Soviet client states chose liberation from Soviet hegemony and opted for democratic rights, market-driven economies, and integration with the military, political, and economic systems of the West. The Berlin Wall fell in November 1989, after which the contagion of democratic reform spread to the heart of the Soviet Union itself. In a final act of desperation, communist hard-liners attempted to seize control of the faltering state in August 1991, but their failure to do so merely drove the final nail in the Soviet Union's coffin.

KEY ISSUES FACING RUSSIA TODAY

Boris Yeltsin led the fledgling Russian Federation from its creation until the end of 1999, when he declared himself physically unfit to remain in power and turned the government over to Prime Minister Putin. Throughout this period, the retrenchment of Moscow's foreign policy continued even as Russian leaders sought, largely through rhetorical appeals, to influence the course of the post–Cold War era. The advanced decay of the country's economy and civil society, however, was glaringly apparent, and prevented Russia from commanding real attention from the other great powers. Indeed, Yeltsin's last major diplomatic achievement—withdrawing support for Yugoslav President Slobodan Milosevic's war against Albanian Kosovars in the spring of 1999—was due largely to the threat of suspended aid from Western banks and governments.

This was not the only development in the post–Cold War that revealed the depths of Russia's plight. In this section, several concerns are briefly reviewed, including the eastward expansion of the North Atlantic Treaty Organization (NATO), the deterioration of the Russian armed forces, and the management of Russia's key military asset, its nuclear arsenal. The equally troubling question of Russia's regional relations are examined in the next section.

NATO'S EASTWARD EXPANSION

The question of NATO expansion into the former Soviet bloc has been one the most divisive issues in Russia's post–Cold War relations with the West (Kubicek 1999). Not only did the alliance not dissolve, as most alliances do when their declared adversary is defeated, but NATO actually grew larger. In July 1998, NATO leaders voted to expand the alliance from sixteen to nineteen members by admitting three former members of the Soviet bloc: Poland, Hungary, and the Czech Republic.[5] Thus NATO, created in 1949 primarily to deter a Soviet invasion of Western Europe, was extended to the former borders of the Soviet Union itself.

When one considers that the three states of the Baltic region (Estonia, Latvia, and Lithuania), each a constituent part of the USSR after World War II, were themselves eager to join NATO in its next wave of expansion, and that Ukraine was imagined by some in the West as the key to containing a resurgent Russia (Lieven 1997), it is easy to appreciate the real worries that NATO expansion has provoked in Moscow (Rojansky 1999). Indeed, Russian Prime Minister Evgenii Primakov called the July 1998 vote to expand NATO the "biggest mistake in Europe since the end of World War II."[6] As Michael McFaul (1997–1998, 26) observed, "no political actor of importance in Russia today, including even unabashed pro-Western liberals ... has supported NATO expansion."

The Russian government's prior attitude toward NATO expansion was less clear. As early as August 1993, Yeltsin, while on a state visit to Warsaw, stated publicly that Russia had no objection to Poland's quest to join NATO. Upon Yeltsin's return to Moscow, however, the official Russian position concerning NATO changed. Yeltsin came out in strong opposition to any moves by NATO to incorporate the Central and Eastern European states. Hoping to derail any notions of NATO expansion, Russian officials began a preemptive diplomatic strategy to support an expanded role for the Council for Security and Cooperation in Europe (CSCE) in a pan-European security arrangement. The CSCE alternative to NATO would have effectively excluded the United States from European security matters, something the Russian government found attractive. In November 1993 Foreign Minister Andrei Kozyrev, attending a CSCE meeting in Rome, advocated this enhanced role for the organization. He repeated his call in July 1994, when Russia formally proposed a comprehensive system of collective security in Europe based on the CSCE.[7]

Russia was simultaneously engaged in NATO's newly created Partnership for Peace (PfP), a program that represented the alliance's outreach to the former communist states. The PfP was intended to be a temporary

---

[5]In November 1992, Czechoslovakia, which came into existence at the end of World War I, officially split into two sovereign states: the Czech Republic, with its capital in Prague, and Slovakia, with its capital in Bratislava.

[6]Primakov, the head of the Russia Foreign Intelligence Service from 1991 to 1996, and then Yeltsin's minister of foreign affairs, was elevated to the post of prime minister in September 1998. He held that post until August 9, 1999, when he was sacked in favor of Putin.

[7]The authority of the CSCE, renamed the Organization for Security and Cooperation in Europe (OSCE) in 1995, was strengthened during this period, although it has not assumed the role envisioned by Russia.

halfway house for these states to join NATO. Cognizant of Russian sensitivities about NATO's role in the region, as well as the practical concerns surrounding the integration of former Warsaw Pact military organizations into NATO's command structure, the organization understood that an overly hasty expansion of the alliance into Eastern Europe would be problematic on several fronts. The Partnership for Peace, therefore, was useful in easing the integration of potential new members.

Russia's dual policy of resisting NATO enlargement while advocating an enhanced role for OSCE did not prevent its participation in the PfP, whose framework document was signed by Russian leaders in June 1994. Kozyrev announced at the time that Russia "had no fundamental objections" to NATO expansion, a reversal that came some eight months after President Yeltsin's public statement expressing his opposition to NATO expansion and just a few weeks prior to Russia's call to substitute the OSCE for NATO in European security matters. The inconsistency in Russia's attitude toward these issues was highlighted again in Brussels in November 1994, when Kozyrev refused to sign the PfP documents he had previously approved.

The Russian government, meanwhile, advocated a change in the nature of NATO itself. Arguing that the original role of NATO was no longer relevant given the end of the Cold War and the collapse of the USSR, Russia advocated a transformation of NATO away from a decidedly military alliance and into a more politically centered organization (see Kubicek, 1999). France's traditional role in NATO (formal membership in the alliance but without NATO troops or weapons on its soil, along with an independent command of nuclear forces) served as a model for Russia's preferred NATO profile. Russia's wishes on this front have hardly been satisfied.

In the end, Russia's strategy failed and the reality of NATO expansion forced a reappraisal of the government's official position. Finally, in May 1997, Yeltsin and the leaders of the sixteen NATO states signed the NATO–Russian Founding Act that confirmed for Russia a "consultative" role in NATO deliberations. The agreement created a joint council that meets twice a year to consider questions of mutual security and to facilitate cooperation between NATO and Russia. To say that Russia has a significant role in NATO activities, however, would be an exaggeration. Originally hoping for significant power and perhaps even a veto over NATO decisions concerning the former Soviet bloc, Russian influence over NATO decisions has been negligible.

Yeltsin's erratic stance toward NATO was partially due to the domestic political scene in Russia. As nationalists, communists, and other opponents of Yeltsin's pro-Western policy gained political strength in the 1993 and 1995 parliamentary elections, the Russian government was forced to assume a more confrontational stance on NATO expansion.

Kremlin reformers predicted that NATO expansion would increase the likelihood that domestic politics in Russia would assume an anti-Western bias. (This claim had many defenders in the United States as well.) Russian nationalists, meanwhile, demanded that Yeltsin back Serbia, a longtime Russian ally, in its campaign of "ethnic cleansing" against Muslims in the Yugoslav province of Bosnia-Herzegovina. Military intervention by NATO against Serbia, and the central role played by U.S. negotiators in pushing for acceptance of the 1995 Dayton Accords further enraged Russian nationalists.

The continuing prospect of further NATO expansion has also generated opposition in Moscow. Russian defense analysts argue that bringing the Baltics into NATO would needlessly antagonize the Russian government, give additional credence to hard-liners in Russian politics, push Russia toward increased reliance on its nuclear forces, and encourage Russia to deepen joint military arrangements with such authoritarian states as Belarus.[8] Yet the U.S. government continues to support NATO expansion into the Baltic region. While Russia would certainly not go to war to keep NATO out of the region, NATO's insistence on such a move would further inflame Russian enmity toward the West.

DOWNSIZING RUSSIA'S MILITARY FORCES

This chapter began with a claim of the critical and constraining importance of economic considerations in the making of Russian foreign policy. Nowhere is this factor in greater evidence than in Russia's reform of its military forces, that component of the Soviet state that enjoyed the highest level of popular legitimacy and respect. Thus the stark diminution of Russian military power since the early 1990s (see Odom 1998; Meyer 1995) goes to the core of Russia's current troubled status in the world. It also has left a great many Russian policymakers unsure as to what Russia's proper international role can or should be under present circumstances.

When the Soviet Union dissolved at the end of 1991, Russia inherited from the Soviet military some 2.7 million armed forces, 600,000 of whom were deployed beyond Russia's borders. Over the next decade the size of Russia's military force was reduced significantly to 2.1 million in 1994 and to 1.7 million by 1997. By the end of the decade, Russia's military could claim 1.2 million soldiers in uniform. In 2000, Putin was seeking the further reduction in the Russian military to a "manageable" force of 800,000 (Starobin 2000). Such a force level would represent less than one-fifth of the force levels of the Soviet military in the mid-1980s. Rarely

---

[8]For the first time since 1994, Russia in 2000 landed bombers and nuclear missile carriers in Belarus on a training mission. Belarus President Aleksandr Lukashenko asked Putin to deploy a joint force of 300,000 troops near the border of the new NATO member, Poland.

will a student of politics witness such a determined and rapid *unilateral* reduction in the armed forces of a major power.[9]

The deep cuts in Russia's military budget clearly revealed the inability of the state to sustain a strategic posture beyond the minimal demands of national defense. As a result, state investment in military procurement has also been cut significantly. In 1988, three years after Gorbachev became general secretary of the Communist Party, the Soviet Union was producing annually more than 3,500 tanks, 700 combat aircraft, 20 submarines, and 15 combat ships. By 1997, Russia's comparable figures were reduced to a small fraction of these totals (Arbatov 1998, 108; Meyer 1995, 2). Investment in equipment has become almost negligible, as has research and development of new military technologies. Economic limitations, therefore, continue to exert decisive pressure on Russia's military posture and further prevent the Russian government from embracing a foreign-policy role similar to that of its predecessor. In a word, Russia now faces a classic "guns-or-butter" dilemma that, once resolved, will go a long way in determining its future capacity in foreign affairs.

The consequences of Russia's military decline have been most evident in Chechnya, a separatist territory whose Islamic rebels have been fighting a war of independence since 1994 despite aggressive efforts by Yeltsin and Putin to restore order. Their repeated crackdowns in Chechnya drained the federation's already depleted military budgets, leaving thousands of soldiers unpaid and without adequate weapons or ammunition to continue the counteroffensive against Chechen rebels. Russian leaders could not give up the fight, however, given the ominous message this would send to other potential breakaway republics. But neither could Moscow prevail in the struggle, based as it was on ancient ethnic hatreds and rival territorial claims. It is thus likely that Chechnya will remain a festering wound inside Russia and will continue to distract Moscow's attention away from matters beyond its borders.

NUCLEAR WEAPONS AND STRATEGY

Aside from their conventional forces, Russian foreign-policy makers must also confront serious questions about the country's nuclear arsenal, which, aside from Russia's immense geopolitical reach and natural resources, most ensures it a place among the great powers of the early twenty-first century. As of 1998, Russia possessed about 6,200 nuclear warheads, 1,200 "delivery vehicles," 750 intercontinental ballistic missiles (ICBMs), 380 submarine-launched ballistic missiles (SLBMs), and 70 long-range bombers

---

[9]This point was further punctuated in the summer of 2000 by the sinking of the Russian nuclear submarine *Kursk*, which left its entire crew dead and the Russian navy greatly weakened.

(*Bulletin of the Atomic Scientists* 1998). Other than the United States, no other country comes close to matching Russia's nuclear firepower.

But still, Soviet and Russian leaders, along with their U.S. counterparts, have long recognized the high costs and potential perils of maintaining such large nuclear stockpiles. Thus in 1991, U.S. and Soviet leaders met in Moscow to finalize the first Strategic Arms Reduction Treaty (START), which called for a 30-percent reduction in the nuclear warheads and delivery vehicles possessed by each side.[10] Of course, within six months the Soviet Union ceased to exist and START had to be approved by all the nuclear states of the former USSR. Four of the fifteen Soviet republics— Russia, Ukraine, Belorussia (now Belarus), and Kazakhstan—had strategic nuclear systems on their territory. The politics of the USSR's breakup thus slowed down the ratification process, but START was ratified by Kazakhstan (July 1992), the United States (October 1992), Russia (November 1992), Belarus (February 1993), and Ukraine (November 1993), and the instruments of ratification were formally exchanged on December 5, 1994. By this point, Russia and the United States had begun negotiating a second round of deep cuts (START II) in nuclear warheads.

The START II treaty, signed by presidents Bush and Yeltsin in Moscow in January 1993, reduced the upper limits of strategic nuclear warheads to between 3,000 and 3,500 for each side by 2007. (To place this in perspective, the second SALT treaty, signed in 1988, permitted a combined 26,331 nuclear warheads for the two countries.) In addition, START II eliminated an entire class of land-based, multiple-warhead missiles, which had been at the core of Russia's nuclear deterrent. As a result, there was significant opposition to this treaty in the Russian legislature (the *Duma*). Furthermore, the elimination of nuclear weapons entailed the expensive process of dismantling and destroying these missiles. It was not surprising, then, that Russian domestic opposition to the treaty was strong. Indeed, neither party to the treaty could guide it through the ratification process for some time. Only on January 26, 1996, did the U.S. Senate ratify START II. It would be another four years before the *Duma* ratified the treaty, and only after Putin marshaled the combined efforts of his defense and foreign ministries to lobby reluctant legislators to approve the treaty.

The START process took place within a broader context of nuclear arms negotiations, a fact that helps clarify the ongoing strategies of each country in this area. Among other issues, missile defense is a chronic thorn in the side of arms control negotiators. While START II was being delayed

---

[10]The SALT agreements of the 1970s were misnamed. These treaties did not *limit* the number of nuclear warheads, which actually *increased* in number without violating the treaties, but focused instead on limiting the number of vehicles that delivered those warheads. Once the ability of both sides to place multiple warheads on each missile was perfected, the SALT limitations became virtually toothless. The START negotiations of the 1980s and 1990s, therefore, focused more directly on limiting the number of warheads.

in the ratification process, the Clinton administration embarked on the controversial policy of attempting to amend the 1972 antiballistic missile (ABM) treaty. That treaty limited the USSR and the United States to two approved sites each for the deployment of ABM systems on the premise that too much missile defense was a bad thing for nuclear deterrence. In this view, the nuclear "balance of terror" during the Cold War was preserved by the maintenance of mutual vulnerability on both sides.

During the 1980s the Reagan administration had approved research for a space-based antimissile system. The Strategic Defense Initiative, referred to in the popular media as "Star Wars," quickly emerged as a major issue in the revived Cold War. If the space-based missile interceptors could be made to work—and there was (and remains) serious doubt on this point—it would potentially render a significant portion of the Soviet Union's nuclear arsenal obsolete. Soviet–American summitry in the 1980s revolved around this contentious issue. Soviet leaders continued to demand U.S. abandonment of the plan, which spoiled the first two Reagan–Gorbachev summits in Geneva (November 1985) and Reykjavik (October 1986).

In consistently opposing missile defense, Russian officials "have insisted that Washington's real purpose in reopening ballistic missile defense–related issues is nothing short of negating the only area in which Russia can still lay a legitimate claim to being a great power, the possession of sizeable nuclear forces" (Dobriansky 2000, 142). In this regard, one can expect the Russian government to continue to defend the 1972 ABM treaty and to portray any efforts on the part of Washington to develop a missile-defense system as a violation of the treaty. In this regard, Putin has steadfastly rejected U.S. claims that its slimmed-down ABM system would be designed to thwart missile attacks by "rogue states" (or, in more recent State Department parlance, "states of concern"). Russia's ratification of START II and the Comprehensive Test Ban Treaty in April 2000, after the U.S. Senate rejected the latter treaty in October 1999, sought to remove any perceived rationale for the United States to pursue missile defense.

This rift over missile defense intensified with the coming to power of U.S. President George W. Bush, who made the deployment of missile defenses one of his first orders of business upon taking office in January 2001. Putin responded by endorsing a plan to almost double Russia's defense budget by 2010 if the Bush administration proceeded with the plan. By the time the two leaders met for the first time in June 2001, their dispute over missile defense overshadowed other—more cooperative—aspects of U.S.–Russian relations (see Shanker 2001). No doubt this issue will remain on center stage in future arms-control negotiations, and in overall diplomatic relations, between the two nuclear superpowers.[11]

---

[11]The planned deployment of U.S. missile defenses dismayed not only Russian leaders but also those in China and many European Union governments (see Chapter 2).

CONFRONTING THE "NEAR ABROAD"

Two issues related to Russian policy within the former Soviet Union also merit attention in this chapter. The first concerns Moscow's attempts to protect the interests of ethnic Russians outside the borders of the Russian state. The second issue revolves around Russia's attempts to articulate and defend what might be called a Monroe Doctrine for the "Near Abroad," the Russian term that refers to the other territories of the former Soviet Union. This second concern relates to Russia's role in the Commonwealth of Independent States (CIS), the loosely knit, post-Soviet regional organization that came into being with the abrupt breakup of the Soviet Union.

Each of the constituent parts of the former USSR is now an independent, sovereign state. Russian politicians, however, often cite the historical, military, and economic links that make relations within this "community" a special concern for Moscow. While many Russian politicians and movements were instrumental in the dissolution of the Soviet Union, and while many Russians (Stankevich 1994, 29) make the claim that Russia itself was discriminated against while in the union, most non-Russian citizens of the former Soviet Union and outside analysts viewed Russians in the Soviet Union as the hegemonic ethnic group. Studies of the USSR's political power structure certainly support such a view. It is not surprising, then, that Russia has been viewed with deep suspicion by many of its former partners. Russia is by far the largest and most powerful of the CIS states, and many of its neighbors fear future attempts by Moscow to reestablish a sphere of influence in the former Soviet space.

It must be recalled in this context that the Soviet Union splintered into fifteen separate states without the benefit of extended planning. What were once centrally owned and administered assets now suddenly were located in separate countries. What were once the internal migration patterns of ethnic peoples became salient *immigration* issues among sovereign states. Economic investment and development had been planned for decades on the assumption of a single, unified economic entity. The USSR's electrical grid, oil pipelines, highways, and railroads were designed as one unit, not fifteen. The mere declaration of sovereignty, while emotionally satisfying, achieved nothing toward the resolution of these issues. Many complex and compelling questions remained open: Who owned what? How would compensation be arranged? How would citizenship in the new states be determined? These questions faced each of the governments that emerged from the breakup of the USSR and are still being confronted today.

The final census of the USSR taken in 1989 identified the key problem that brought Russia into adversarial relations with its neighbors: the 25.3 million ethnic Russians who found themselves living outside the borders of Russia when the Soviet Union collapsed. This diaspora constituted nearly

20 percent of all the ethnic Russians living in the Soviet Union at the time of the final Soviet census. Complicating matters further, in several CIS states the ethnic Russian minority was quite sizeable, potentially a powerful political force in domestic affairs.[12] The Russian government predictably found itself defending the interests of these Russians as the new states frequently passed laws that Moscow found discriminatory. As the Russian government used its influence in bilateral affairs with its former Soviet partners on such matters as scheduled troop withdrawals, these smaller and weaker states often complained of Russian heavy-handedness (Teague 1994). The Russian *Duma* in the first few years of independence was markedly more nationalist than was the executive branch under Yeltsin and frequently assumed a strident pose in defending ethnic Russians in the newly independent states.[13]

Most fears concerning Russian interference in the domestic affairs of its former Soviet partners have been allayed. The Russian government was within its rights to be concerned about the treatment of ethnic Russians outside of Russia and pursued this matter with some degree of restraint, the hyperbole of certain Russian politicians and resolutions from the Russian *Duma* notwithstanding. Given Russia's economic trouble through the 1990s, it could ill afford a flood of Russian refugees returning from the Near Abroad, although this migration back to Russia has actually been quite modest. The Russian government has balanced several legitimate considerations in defending ethnic Russians in the new states, and most of the complaints about Moscow's interference on this front have since eased.

Security within the Near Abroad, however, remains a volatile question. Within months of the Soviet Union's collapse, several prominent Russian politicians supported the adoption of a regional policy that was likened to the U.S. 1823 Monroe Doctrine, which effectively closed off the Western Hemisphere to colonial settlements by the major European powers.

Six elements of this Russian doctrine can be identified and combine to designate the former Soviet space as the proper sphere of influence of Russia (Aron 1994). First, Russia claimed that the entire territory of the former USSR constituted a vital region in which Russia's interests were acute. Second, given Russia's historical ties to the region, Moscow asserted its right and duty to be the guarantor of peace and security in the region.

---

[12]Specifically, ethnic Russians comprised more than 10 percent of the local population in eight of the other fourteen republics: Kazakhstan (37 percent), Latvia (34 percent), Estonia (30 percent), Ukraine (22 percent), Kyrgyzstan (22 percent), Belarus (13 percent), Moldova (13 percent), and Turkmenistan (10 percent).

[13]The *Duma*, for example, passed a resolution in May 1992 annulling the 1954 transfer of the Crimea to the Ukraine. In 1993, the *Duma* again crossed Yeltsin by declaring that Sevastopol, the headquarters of the Black Sea fleet located on the Crimean peninsula, was actually part of Russia. While President Yeltsin opposed such acts, they received sizeable popular support in Russia (Kubicek 1999, 556).

Third, Russia warned outside states that it would actively oppose any efforts to increase tensions among the former Soviet republics. Likewise, the fourth element of this doctrine held that Russia would resist any plans to increase the military presence in the states bordering the former Soviet Union. Fifth, Russia reserved for itself the right to serve as the principal peacekeeper of the region.[14] Finally, Russia asserted its nuclear exclusivity on the territory of the former USSR.

The commonwealth, which was created in December 1991 before the final collapse of the Soviet Union, was initially viewed suspiciously by the former republics of the USSR as well as by Western observers. Many anticipated that the CIS would become another Soviet Union, dominated by Moscow. This concern kept a number of the former republics, most notably the three Baltic states and Georgia, out of the CIS. Membership fluctuated as these concerns ebbed and the parties realized that the CIS would never become a potent organization like the European Union, which, as described in Chapter 6, has attained many *supranational* functions in recent years. Instead, the CIS was primarily interested in solving the myriad problems presented by the sudden dissolution of the Soviet Union. Any notion of a unified CIS military structure evaporated as the newly independent states, most notably Ukraine, established their own national armies (Kubicek 1999, 556–560). Likewise, many of the CIS's economic and political arrangements have been dismissed by its members. In a word, the integrationist aspects of the CIS have largely failed to materialize and its role in the policy and process of Russian foreign policy remains marginal at best. Nevertheless, Russian relations with its neighbors in the Near Abroad remain a critical aspect of its foreign policy.

RUSSIA'S PLACE AMONG THE GREAT POWERS

The foreign-policy orientation of Russia since 1991 has reflected the pull and tug of competing visions of Russia's role among the great powers, particularly the United States. For the majority of the postcommunist period, Russian foreign policy has reflected what many call an "Atlanticist" concept, best embodied by Andrei Kozyrev, Russian foreign minister until January 5, 1996. Kozyrev, for years assailed for pursuing a foreign policy too subservient to Western interests, was replaced by Evgenii Primakov, the head of Russia's Foreign Intelligence Service. Russia's foreign policy immediately assumed a more assertive and at times anti-Western

---

[14]While Russia has abandoned those regions of Central and Eastern Europe that were the locus of Cold War antagonisms, it has maintained a troop presence within the Near Abroad. Since the early 1990s Russia has been involved in a variety of nonaggressive military missions in Belarus, Moldova, Tajikistan, Turkmenistan, and in Ukrainian ports of the Black Sea Fleet.

posture. This change in the direction of Soviet attitudes toward the West reflected the conclusions drawn after a failed half-decade of commitment to the Western vision of Russia, as well as an honest appraisal of public opinion and the domestic political scene.

To be sure, the simplified story of the Kozyrev–Primakov transfer of power in the foreign ministry glosses over the fact that the debate about Russia's proper national interest in the post–Cold War era has been raging for years (see Sestanovich 1994). There was hardly a universal appreciation in Russian society of the appropriateness of the Western model, based upon widespread political freedoms and a market-based economy. While Yeltsin and his allies fought hard to emulate this model, a sizeable and powerful lobby advocated a "Eurasianist" orientation, which sought to place Russia as a regional power that acknowledged the unique aspects of Russia's location at the juncture of Europe and Asia. Indeed, most of Russia lies east of the Ural mountains, long considered the dividing line between Europe and Asia. Thus the debate in Russia was seen by many as presenting a dichotomous choice to the nation: Embrace Western notions of Russia's national interests (i.e., democratic politics and market economics), on the one hand, or reject them entirely in favor of a more guarded liberalization and a stronger state with less obligations to the West. This stark dichotomy, as it turned out, was false.

Many Russian observers, such as Nikolai Travkin (1994) and Sergei Stankevich (1994), argued that Russia's true national interest was to balance these dual identities and to construct a foreign policy that reflected this duality. In their view, Russia's national interests were structurally determined by such forces as geography, history, culture, ethnic composition, and political tradition, each of which worked against Russia's wholesale commitment to the West. Russia should, in their view, adopt policies that acknowledge its special role as the primary Eurasian power without falling prey to the imperial temptations of the past.

It is not surprising to learn that these and other Russian "patriots" were the main architects of the Russian Monroe Doctrine described earlier. They did not reject a general rapprochement with the West, but argued convincingly that Russia's interests were not identical to those of the West. In a sense, the rise of "Primakovism" reflected the coming into power of this school of thought (Garnett 1999, 329–330). Neither "Atlanticist" nor imperialist, Primakov and his supporters describe themselves as pragmatists and practitioners of *realpolitik*. For them, Russia's national interests are not subsumed under a Western model. They are distinct and should be pursued separately from those of the West.

Much of recent Russian realism in foreign policy has developed as a result of the conclusion that the hegemonic position of the United States and NATO seriously discounts Russian interests in the region and the world. Following logically from this conclusion is the Russian determination to create a multipolar distribution of power. While Russia is certainly in no position either to advocate or implement a policy seeking to recreate the *bipolar* world of the Cold War era, current policy envisions Russia as a great power that can serve as one of the poles in a *multipolar* world. With this in mind, Russia under Primakov (both as foreign minister and prime minister) sought improved relations in the Middle East (with Iran and Iraq), South Asia (with India), and East Asia (with China). These policies have been maintained since Primakov's exit from government. In fact, if Russia's foreign policies in the Balkans and the CIS have generally failed, its initiatives in the Middle East and Asia have been relatively successful.[15]

Russia's improved relationship with China deserves particular mention. Both states have expressed the conviction that the U.S.-led NATO is intent on keeping Russia and China weak internationally. The same pertains to the missile-defense system being planned by the U.S. government, as noted earlier. Russia, with an eye toward Chechnya, accepts Beijing's positions concerning Tibet and Taiwan, and both states are committed to controlling the spread of Islamic fundamentalism in the region. These bases for cooperation have produced increased Russian arms sales to China, and overall economic trade has increased as well (see Chapter 4). Further, in the late 1990s Russia, China, and the three former Soviet Central Asian republics that border China (Kyrgyzstan, Kazakhstan, and Tajikstan) agreed to reduce and equalize their military forces along their borders. The accidental bombing of China's embassy by NATO aircraft in Belgrade during the 1999 Kosovo conflict solidified the Russo–Chinese commitment to resist NATO's growing influence in world affairs. Such were the improvements in relations between Moscow and Beijing that in November 2000 Chinese Prime Minister Zhu Rongji declared that China's relations with Russia were better than ever. This increasingly close relationship has not gone unnoticed in Washington.

Russia's relations with the West have clearly declined over the past few years as a general sobering of expectations has occurred. The Russian economic reforms pushed by Washington and the IMF have been widely condemned in Russia, and significant resentment has developed. Russia has openly criticized U.S. intervention in the former Yugoslavia and Iraq and has opposed what it has increasingly come to see as a conscious policy of NATO "encirclement" (Garnett 1999, 332). In like fashion, the United States has opposed Russian arms sales to Iran and China and has condemned Russia's harsh assaults on the Chechen rebels. Finally, Russia's conventional military cutbacks have made it more reliant on its nuclear force, something that causes concern in Washington. Notions of a "strategic partnership,"

---

[15]Citing one example, Primakov's intervention in the 1997 Iraqi crisis helped prevent, however temporarily, a new round of U.S.-led air strikes.

once seriously contemplated in the early 1990s, have given way to the reluctant realism of strained, though unbroken relations. In November 1998 Strobe Talbott, the U.S. deputy secretary of state with responsibility for Russian policy, captured the mood in Russo–American relations when he referred to the need for "strategic patience" between the two countries.

This patience may indeed be tested as Putin, upon his election in March 2000, immediately embarked upon a reappraisal of Russia's policy toward the West. Some hints about this reappraisal can be culled from the new National Security Concept signed by Putin in January 2000. Concept 2000, as it is frequently called, reflects the sober realism of the Primakov school of Russian foreign policy. While this document stresses that the greatest threats to Russian security are internal (e.g., ethnic separatism as in Chechnya, the related issue of domestic terrorism, and continuing economic problems), it sees the outside world in a much dimmer light than previous manifestos (Sokov 2000, 85–86). The "hegemonic" tendencies of NATO are frequently assailed, while the notion of a multipolar, integrated, and mutually supporting international system is endorsed. Russia resents the dominance of NATO and its recent propensity to act unilaterally, as a substitute for the UN Security Council, and against the wishes of major states such as Russia and China.

Consistent with Putin's emphasis on strengthening the Russian state domestically, the concept represents a clarion call to those who might be called "Russia Firsters." To Sokov (2000, 87), the doctrine expresses the view that "Russia now has to take care of itself, without listening to advice and guidance that has turned out to be less friendly than it seemed." As the principal purveyor of that advice, the United States can expect a more determined, realistic, and skeptical Russian foreign policy in the future. The Russian government, meanwhile, can expect the same from Washington. Upon his election, President George W. Bush promised a reappraisal of U.S. policy toward Russia that would include a critical assessment of past economic aid programs, the pace of political reforms, and the alleged transfer of Russian military technology to other countries. Thus the perceptions that Russia and the United States have of each other are more skeptical now than they have been since the end of the Cold War.

CONCLUSION

As noted throughout this chapter, Russia's severe economic troubles have been the defining factor in its adaptation to a new world role after the Cold War. This claim is not overly controversial. A more debatable question, by contrast, is when such economic determinism came to dominate the making of Russian foreign policy. It is certainly the case that Gorbachev's attempts to moderate the military competition between the United States and the Soviet Union, an effort that won him the Nobel Peace Prize, were substantially driven by the severe economic constraints facing the Soviet leader. But economic considerations alone do not capture the entire picture.

To a broader extent, born-again Russia has yet to establish its moorings as a great power. That is, the federation has not adapted to a role in global affairs that is both plausible and attractive to a sizeable portion of its leaders and citizens. Outsiders identify any number of different foreign-policy "schools" or "orientations" competing over control of the policy agenda. This chapter has identified "Atlanticists," "Eurasianists," and those who would seek to reconcile the two. Such labels are, of course, artificial, at times fanciful, and more often than not misleading. Many more such labels ("hawks," "doves," "liberals," "centrists," "Westernizers," and "Slavophiles") have been put forward to describe Russian foreign-policy groups and orientations. While in some sense the fabrications of outside analysts, the sheer number of such categories or groups competing in Russian foreign-policy circles provides evidence of the lack of a cohesive Russian national vision in the wake of the Cold War.

That Russia might be unable to articulate a coherent vision of its place in the international arena should not be surprising given the chaotic developments of the past two decades. In fact, the overall thrust of Russian foreign policy has been less severe and threatening than might have been expected. "It remains striking how little interstate war has resulted from Russia's revolution," McFaul (1997/1998, 33) observed. "Russia has displayed little of the belligerent activity that we expect to see from states undergoing radical political and economic transformations." In this context, it may also be viewed as a minor miracle that Russia has been able to preserve even the most basic elements of its democratic and market reforms under such circumstances.

The long-term direction of Russia's foreign policy must await the eventual, and perhaps inevitable, reestablishment of a strong Russian state. As then-Prime Minister Putin (quoted in Sokov 2000, 84) stated in December 1999, "Russia will not soon become, if ever, a carbon copy of, say, the United States or England, where liberal values have deep historical traditions. Among us, the state, its institutions and structures, have always played an exceptionally important role in the life of the country and the people." Beyond this central truth, however, it remains unclear just how Russia will behave in global affairs once its own house is put back in order.

C H A P T E R 4

MODERNIZATION, NATIONALISM, AND REGIONALISM IN CHINA[1]

Quansheng Zhao
American University

Since its inception in 1949, the People's Republic of China (PRC) has experienced enormous internal and external change. After the communist government shifted its domestic focus from revolution to modernization due to the change in leadership—from revolution-minded Mao Zedong to pragmatic Deng Xiaoping—the PRC's foreign policy adapted to the demise of Cold War bipolarity and the emergence of a more complex balance of power. Facing these dynamic changes, the PRC has been forced to adapt not only to maintain its strength and reputation in the international community, but to assure its basic survival.

This chapter provides a broad overview of Chinese foreign policy during and after the Cold War. After first considering the historical legacies of the precommunist period, the chapter reviews the evolution of Chinese leadership from Mao to the present. Of particular concern here is the shift from "vertical" to "horizontal" authoritarianism within the PRC. An array of specific policy areas is then considered, after which the chapter analyzes the key strategies and tactics currently employed by Chinese foreign-policy makers. Finally, the chapter assesses three aspects of Chinese foreign policy—modernization, nationalism, and regionalism—in the context of China's key bilateral relationships.

Let us begin with the widely accepted fact that China has acquired the status of a great power in the international system rather than an outsider that challenges existing norms. The country's population of more

---

[1]The author would like to thank Elizabeth Dahl for research assistance.

than 1.2 billion is the largest in the world, its economic output has topped the $1-trillion level, and its military capabilities are on the rise. The PRC's ability to affect peace and stability has been an important concern of China's neighbors and other nations in the global community. Long after the Soviet Union's collapse in 1991 altered the strategic landscape, this recognition of China's importance has grown stronger. This perception is especially valid given China's growing economic clout, but other vital issue areas—such as the global environment, weapons proliferation, and human rights—are directly affected by China.

An examination of Chinese conduct in foreign policy reveals a mixture of rigidity and flexibility. The government is rigid in terms of sticking to basic principles but is flexible in practical and technical matters. The non-negotiable principles (*yuanze-xing*) are those that involve vital national interests such as regime legitimacy and internal power politics. The negotiable principles (*linghuo-xing*) are those regarded as lesser priorities. The status of an issue may change depending on timing, domestic conditions, and the international environment. Similarly, Chinese leaders make a distinction between "essential" and "rhetorical" principles. Essential principles express China's vital and enduring national interests, including its defense and assertion of sovereignty. Beijing's adherence to these principles will be consistently firm. Rhetorical principles, by contrast, often serve secondary goals that lie outside the immediate scope of policy objectives and are thus open to negotiation.

FROM REVOLUTION TO MODERNIZATION

To understand Chinese foreign policy today, one must pay close attention to the historical legacies that the PRC faced when it was established in 1949. Those legacies stemmed first from the "hundred-year humiliation" that China experienced prior to the PRC's creation, then from the internal chaos that attended the final years of civil war (1946–1949). After the establishment of the PRC, Chinese foreign policy can be divided into three eras that correspond to the regimes of Mao Zedong (1949–1976), Deng Xiaoping (1978–1997), and Jiang Zemin (1997–present). As this section of the chapter makes clear, the central change during the PRC's first half-century involved the shift of national priorities from "revolution," a key concept for Mao, to "modernization," the focus of his successors.

THE HUNDRED-YEAR HUMILIATION

The period known as the hundred-year humiliation spanned roughly from the Opium War of 1839 to the rise of the Chinese communists in the final years of civil war (1946–1949). During this period, China experienced repeated invasions from Western imperial countries such as Great Britain, Germany, France, and Portugal; and from neighboring powers such as Japan and Russia. Britain's victories over China led to enormous Chinese concessions and the loss of Hong Kong. China was effectively carved up during this period by several foreign powers. France occupied the southwest region, Britain the Yangtze River area, Germany the Shandong province, and Japan and Russia the Manchuria area and the far west.

Among the most important of these latter encounters was Japan's victory in the Sino–Japanese war of 1894–1895. China was forced to sign the Treaty of Shimonoseki in which it had to acknowledge the independence of Korea and cede Taiwan to Japan. Animosity toward Japan intensified in the late 1930s and early 1940s as Japan invaded and occupied most of China's territory. Millions of Chinese citizens were killed, injured, and tortured during this struggle, the most notorious incident of which was the Nanjing Massacre of 1937.

Another foreign intervention that left a troublesome legacy in China was the U.S. government's support of Chiang Kai-shek's Nationalist regime during the final stages of China's civil war. American support of Chiang's corrupt and unpopular regime, which persisted despite several attempts at mediation, left traces of distrust toward Washington that remain evident today. This tension is especially apparent in relation to the island of Taiwan, where Chiang's forces relocated after their defeat and created a government in exile that was long recognized by Washington and its allies as the official government representing the entirety of China.

MAO'S REVOLUTIONARY ERA

After the civil war, the victorious communist regime of Mao Zedong assumed control of a country that was decimated by these conflicts. China's weakness was apparent in all dimensions—political, economic, and military. After the communist victory in 1949, the PRC was left severely weakened and vulnerable. The combination of anti-imperialist struggles and internal fighting created tremendous chaos and political uncertainty that left most of the Chinese people in poverty. Mao stuck to his belief that China must undertake "continuous revolution." He recognized that the establishment of a socialist society did not automatically lead to a genuine embrace of the new ideology by the masses. While seizure of political power and ownership from the exploiting classes could be completed within a relatively short period of time, it would take many generations to eradicate remnants of their old ideas and habits. From this, Mao concluded that the struggle and the revolution must continue.

In terms of the PRC's global environment, the Cold War balance of power was dominated by two opposite blocs—capitalist and communist. Virtually every country during that period was forced to make a choice between aligning with the U.S. or Soviet blocs. China was no exception. This bipolar structure profoundly affected Chinese foreign policy under Mao, who signed a Friendship Treaty with Soviet leader Joseph Stalin in 1950. China's alliance with the Soviet Union was consolidated further after the Korean War began in the summer of 1950. Together with the unsettled issue of Taiwan, the lasting effect of the Korean War was that China remained in a confrontational relationship with the United States for the next two decades.

The new Chinese leadership was confronted with the immediate need to establish its legitimacy, an urgent task that was complicated by the rival regime in Taiwan. Domestically, the hostility between Taiwan and the mainland was regarded as a continuation of the civil war. Internationally, it involved the issues of representation in the United Nations and regime recognition in the international community. Both Beijing and Taipei (Taiwan's capitol) claimed that they were the sole legitimate representative of China. The issue of Taiwan, therefore, became critical to the PRC's initial foreign-policy calculations.

Central to Mao's new government was the importance assigned to communist ideology. Although during part of the mid-1940s Mao hoped to develop a cooperative relationship with the United States, the PRC chose a policy of aligning with the Soviet Union.[2] Beijing's decision to side with Moscow against Washington was a predictable result of the U.S.–Soviet Cold War, which had divided the world into two hostile camps. Mao's idea that China must support a world revolution prevailed among the top leadership in Beijing. He pushed his revolutionary ideas to fight against "imperialism" (such as shown by the United States), "revisionism" (a charge made in the 1950s and 1960s against the post-Stalinist Soviet Union), and "reactionism" (a label for India's behavior, as it had engaged with China in a border clash in 1962). All three were viewed as components of a conspiracy to encircle China. These political–strategic considerations during the era of Mao overshadowed other aspects of Chinese foreign policy. In East Asia, China supported North Korea and North Vietnam in their wars against the United States. Those countries that stood with the United States, such as Japan, South Korea, and South Vietnam, were labeled "running dogs of American imperialism."

As Sino–Soviet relations worsened, leading to a military clash along the border in 1969, Mao condemned Moscow's behavior and started to improve the PRC's relations with the United States. At the same time, President Richard Nixon significantly softened U.S. policy toward Beijing, hoping that the PRC would help with a smooth U.S. withdrawal from

---

[2]Mao in 1944 had even raised the possibility of receiving aid from the United States. See Reardon-Anderson (1980, 44–45) for an elaboration.

Vietnam and create a vital wedge in Washington's struggle against Moscow. Thus, starting in 1971, China and the United States began the long process of rapprochement, leading to Nixon's historic visit to China in 1972 and the establishment of diplomatic relations in 1979. Even after Sino–American relations improved, however, Mao continued to advocate struggle against the two Cold War superpowers.

Chinese foreign policy also was affected by domestic factors during this period, especially the Cultural Revolution of 1966–1976. Internally, the Cultural Revolution was launched to purge "capitalist roaders" from the leadership of the Chinese Communist Party. Externally, Mao continued to push his idea of "world revolution." During the peak of the Cultural Revolution, China isolated itself from the outside world as much as possible, making its population one of the least informed about events elsewhere in the world. The PRC paid a heavy price for this dogmatic and isolationist foreign policy, lagging far behind most other countries economically. Strategically, China was encircled by the two superpowers and hostile neighbors, creating a threatening environment. Although in the 1970s Mao made efforts to break the isolation by seeking rapprochement with the United States, Japan, and most of the Western powers, his revolutionary rhetoric and dogmatic principles remained fundamentally unchanged.

DENG'S PUSH FOR MODERNIZATION

The death of Mao in 1976 brought the ten-year Cultural Revolution to an end. After a two-year transitional period under the leadership of Mao's hand-picked successor, Hua Guofeng, Deng Xiaoping achieved the status of China's permanent leader in 1978. This change of leadership marked the beginning of a new period in contemporary Chinese history. The Mao era was a radical revolutionary period highlighted by the Cultural Revolution. The Deng era, by contrast, was a period of pragmatism that led to "a new situation in all fields of socialist modernization." In this respect, the Deng era was a postrevolutionary era, clearly different from the period under Mao's rule in its national priorities and behavior toward the international system.

Under Mao, the regime emphasized revolutionary objectives: dramatic and sweeping social and political reform in the domestic arena and survival as a communist nation in the international environment. This period was characterized by an emphasis on revolutionary ideology, a general disregard for prevailing international norms, and extreme sensitivity to outside threats. In the era of modernization, China moved beyond a single-minded preoccupation with world revolution. As nation-states became increasingly interdependent, particularly in terms of economic integration, the PRC gradually recognized that the concept of regime survival had broader meanings. Deng warned that China faced the danger of losing its *qiuji* (global citizenship) if its economy failed to catch up with that of the other major powers.

In the beginning of 1980, Deng identified several tasks for China to pursue in the decade ahead: to preserve a stable international order, to work on China's "reunification" with Taiwan, and, most importantly, to step up the drive for China's economic modernization. The country quickly underwent a series of domestic reforms, primarily in the economic realm, that pushed the PRC's foreign policy to become more open to the international community.

Four reasons explain Deng's dramatic change in policy. First, as domestic tensions were eased in the postrevolutionary era, Deng acquired greater self-confidence. This confidence was boosted by an emerging national consensus that China must concentrate on economic growth rather than the all-consuming ideological campaigns that prevailed during the Cultural Revolution. Importantly, economic modernization hastened China's integration in the global economy because it required greater contacts with capitalist nations that were in a position to help China achieve its economic goals.

A second rationale underlying Deng's shift in foreign policy was that China's international profile had grown rapidly in the years preceding his rise to power. In 1971, the United Nations voted to admit Beijing as the sole representative of China. As a result, the PRC gained not only UN membership, but also the permanent seat on its Security Council that was previously held by the Taiwan regime. China's arrival as a legitimate actor on the world stage was further punctuated by the visit by President Nixon in 1972 and by the subsequent establishment of diplomatic relations with Japan and the Western European countries. All of this prompted Deng to pursue a less antagonistic foreign policy, particularly toward the Western industrialized nations. His approach was well received overseas as many countries switched their official state recognition from Taiwan to the PRC, a trend that further enhanced China's international stature.

During most of the Mao era, China's actions reflected a strong dissatisfaction with the existing international order. Beijing vigorously criticized existing international organizations, particularly the UN. Even after the PRC joined the UN and gained a permanent seat on the Security Council, its suspicion of the UN and other international organizations still persisted. This outsider position, however, was destined to become a thing of the past when China instituted its reforms under Deng. The PRC began to participate actively in international governmental organizations, including the World Bank, the International Monetary Fund (IMF), and the Asian Development Bank. Generally, China now plays a constructive rather than a disruptive role in these institutions.

Third, even before Deng took power, the influence of communist ideology was increasingly yielding to pragmatism. China's conflicts with the

United States in the 1950s and 1960s, and with the "revisionist" Soviet Union in the 1960s, stemmed from considerations not only of national interest but also of ideology. Beginning in the 1980s, ideological considerations gave way to economic concerns, which in turn compelled Beijing to engage the industrialized states that were formerly declared its enemies. No longer did China regard itself as the center of world revolution. Instead, its leaders often called for world peace and avoidance of intervention in other countries' internal affairs.

In this respect, Deng adopted an "independent" foreign policy that sought both a friendly relationship with the United States and improved ties with the former Soviet Union. In practice, however, Deng moved closer to the West, which was better able to meet the demands of China's modernization drive than was the Soviet bloc or today's Russia. In terms of national security, China's policy also became more flexible, as was seen in China's proposal to set aside territorial disputes in the South China Sea and other areas. Deng also moved Chinese foreign policy from one of "liberation of Taiwan by force" to a notion of *one country–two systems*. In 1978, he told a group of visiting U.S. legislators that Beijing had adopted a policy of "peaceful unification."

Finally, Deng was keenly aware of the rapid economic development taking place elsewhere in East Asia, particularly in countries surrounding China. These included Japan and the newly industrialized economies (NIEs) of South Korea, Taiwan, Hong Kong, and Singapore. Of the "little dragons," all but South Korea were societies composed entirely or chiefly of ethnic Chinese citizens. Recognition of the intensifying economic competition in East Asia stimulated fundamental changes in Beijing's interpretation of national survival and reinforced the notion that economic competition was no less vital to China than political and military confrontation. Deng realized that China was not only far behind the industrialized countries, such as the United States and Japan, but also lagged behind its small neighbors. This status was particularly clear in the high-technology industrial sectors in which the NIEs excelled.

In a revealing departure from previous practice, Beijing became willing to accept all kinds of foreign aid, from World Bank loans to disaster relief funds and Official Development Assistance (ODA) from Japan and other industrialized countries. Numerous forms of economic cooperation were established between China and the West, including massive volumes of foreign direct investment and a growing number of joint ventures with foreign corporations. All of these measures, of course, reflected China's shift from the "command economics" of communism to a market-driven model that allowed for private enterprise and embraced closer ties with the capitalist powers.

The new orientation of Chinese foreign policy was confirmed by what was called Deng's "28-character strategy." This strategy was proclaimed by

Deng in the wake of the Tiananmen Square crackdown of June 1989, when a student-led Chinese prodemocracy movement was crushed by military forces, provoking severe economic sanctions from the West. This situation was further complicated by the collapse of communism in Eastern Europe in 1989 and the disintegration of the Soviet Union during the next two years. The central elements of this strategy were that China should avoid confrontations with the United States (the only superpower), that it should not assume "leadership" of the post-Soviet socialist world, and that China should not intervene in the internal affairs of other countries. In Deng's words, China should "go beyond ideological considerations," "detach (itself) from concrete events," and "try to avoid controversy." If such a strategy were followed, he predicted, China would become a modernized country by the middle of the twenty-first century.

FOREIGN POLICY UNDER JIANG ZEMIN

Jiang Zemin was named in 1989 to the leading position, general secretary of the Chinese Communist Party (CCP), and later became president of the country and chairman of the Central Military Commission. His position was consolidated with determined support from Deng, who died in 1997. While Jiang's policies basically followed Deng's, three new challenges emerged under his rule. The first was the increasing challenge of globalization that propelled China's attempt to integrate further into the world economic system. China's drive to gain membership in the World Trade Organization (WTO) was a prominent by-product of this trend. The second challenge related to the emergence of a distinctive post–Cold War environment in world politics that further eroded the strength of ideological considerations in Chinese foreign policy while increasing the PRC's focus on economic development. The third challenge to Jiang was Taiwan's increasing call for independence, particularly after a historic round of presidential elections in March 2000.

The Jiang regime has sought to develop new policies to cope with all these challenges and to enhance China's position further in the international community. Jiang Zemin and his associates—the so-called "third generation" of leadership—have already begun preparing a fourth generation of leadership as part of their long-term planning. This transition is slated to take place in 2002, when the party leadership is scheduled to change in the National Congress. In 2003, the state leadership, including the presidency and premiership, is also due to be reshuffled.

Despite the many fundamental transformations since the end of the Mao era, China's foreign policy has remained consistent in several key respects. China has resisted temptations to establish regional hegemony in the Asia-Pacific area. It has maintained its support for developing countries and still considers itself part of the "South" in North–South negotiations and disputes. The PRC also remains sensitive to external threats, especially those that are perceived as a challenge to its essential principles of national sovereignty and regime survival. Finally, the formation of foreign policy in China remains highly centralized. The decision-making process in many other fields, such as economic planning and cultural policy, has tended toward decentralization in recent years. Despite broader participation in the policy-making process, however, foreign policy continues to be controlled by a small group of top leaders.

In this respect, the domestic context of current Chinese foreign policy deserves scrutiny. For the PRC, state survival in the international arena is no more important than regime survival domestically, as evidenced by the repression of prodemocracy forces in Tiananmen Square in June 1989. In every country, of course, foreign-policy behavior is affected by the domestic environment. But in the case of China, the close connection between internal conditions—social, political, economic, and institutional—and external actions is worthy of special attention, for it often holds the key to understanding Beijing's behavior overseas. Indeed, for the leadership of the PRC, as former Foreign Minister Qian Qichen noted, "Diplomacy is the extension of internal affairs."

A SHIFT TOWARD COLLECTIVE AUTHORITARIANISM

In the wake of the political and economic reforms following the Cultural Revolution, the Chinese political system and decision-making process has remained fundamentally authoritarian in nature. This characteristic is particularly noticeable in the formulation of foreign policy, which continues to be highly centralized and personalized. That is to say, foreign policy is directed by and highly reflective of a small group of individuals' perceptions, tendencies, and preferences.

Nevertheless, a number of changes occurred under Deng that affected the subsequent process of foreign-policy making. Beijing has moved away from the Mao era, when a single leader dominated foreign-policy making, into a more collective decision-making structure. This "halfway change," which stops short of replacing the authoritarian nature of Chinese politics with a democratic model, still has had an enormous impact on the formulation and conduct of Chinese foreign policy. In this respect, the Chinese policy-making apparatus has shifted from "vertical authoritarianism" to "horizontal authoritarianism."[3] The former term refers to a

---

[3]The terms used here refer primarily to the policy-making process rather than to the nature of the regime itself, although the two have a close connection. "Vertical" and "horizontal" refer only to the scope, character, and nature of participation in the foreign policy-making process, not to the structure of command systems. Indeed, the *conduct* of foreign policy in virtually every country, authoritarian or democratic, takes place within a vertical command system.

policy-making process in which a single leader dominates through a top-down command system. Such a process has often been seen in communist countries, including China. Under Mao, Premier Zhou Enlai, in consultation with members of the Politburo and a small group of foreign affairs specialists, was in charge of foreign affairs. Government institutions and bureaucracies engaged only passively in the formulation of policy; the Ministry of Foreign Affairs (MFA) was involved only in its implementation. International audiences were permitted to hear only one voice on foreign-policy issues.

Horizontal authoritarianism refers to a policy-making process that is still highly centralized, but in which several power centers at the top level represent and coordinate various interests and opinions. Multiple command channels exist within this framework. More players participate in the process and conflicting voices may occasionally represent different interests and policies. In a comparison of the two, horizontal authoritarianism is less personalized and more institutionalized than vertical authoritarianism and therefore *may* lead to a more pluralistic policy-making system. The change that China has undergone has been driven by the lessons of recent history, particularly the Cultural Revolution, the upheavals of which created an unprecedented challenge to regime legitimacy. This legitimacy crisis made the Chinese leaders realize the serious problem of "internal security," prompting a consensus among the post-Mao leadership that, in order to ensure the survival of the communist regime, profound changes in the management of government policy must occur.

BROADENING POLICY AGENDAS

Participation in the policy-making process seems certain to expose new concerns as the foreign-policy agenda expands, especially in cases where these issues do not involve essential principles or vital strategic interests. As China has become more open to the outside world, therefore, its agenda in foreign policy has steadily become more complex and wide-ranging.[4]

In the era of modernization, economic development is a top priority, and as a result, China has become increasingly involved in global markets. The rate of economic growth accelerated drastically since the beginning of Deng's reforms in 1978 and has averaged about 10 percent annually since then. Previously, Mao's emphasis on self-reliance effectively isolated China from the international community, particularly the capitalist economies. When Deng came to power, one of his first changes was to start the process of linking the PRC to the global and regional economies. The integration

---

[4]Such a trend toward widening foreign-policy agendas has been seen in other states undergoing economic and/or political reforms, including Brazil and South Africa (as described in Chapters 7 and 11 of this volume, respectively).

process posed new and often heavy demands on the PRC's foreign policy. External market forces reflect constantly changing consumer demands, levels of supply, and political developments within the major trading powers. Further, Chinese leaders have been forced to reconcile these market forces with the socialist system that remains intact within large segments of the domestic economy.

Defense policy also remains a key concern. Military modernization has been regarded as a main factor in ensuring China's sovereignty. The Persian Gulf War of 1991, with its dazzling display of U.S. weaponry, stunned the People's Liberation Army (PLA). As a consequence, the modernization of military equipment has become a top priority for the Chinese leadership. Consequently, the level of Chinese military expenditures has drawn broad attention and expressions of concern from the other major powers and China's Asian neighbors.

Observers of China have also paid close attention to the PRC's arms sales policy. During the Cold War, China often provided military supplies free of charge to its Asian allies, mostly to North Korea, North Vietnam, and Pakistan. This policy was changed in 1979, when China adopted an "open door" policy in arms sales under Deng. At that point the PLA quickly became a notable arms supplier to the world and established a vast, military-backed network of arms manufacturers that was valued for its ability to generate foreign exchange for the country's modernization drive. Important in this regard, Chinese leaders have made promises to the United States that they would not sell chemical or nuclear weapons material or missile parts to so-called "rogue states" such as Iraq and Iran. The question remains, however, as to the extent to which the Chinese government and PLA continue to promote arms proliferation to such countries despite Western calls for restraint (see Hiebert and Chanda 2000, 16–17).

The issue of human rights in China has also dominated its foreign-policy agenda. Although there was progress in Beijing's respect for human rights under Deng and subsequently under Jiang, China is still widely regarded as lagging significantly behind developed countries. Beijing has insisted that the concept of human rights relates not only to political rights, but also to economic and social rights, which are related to China's economic development and to its cultural and historical background. The Chinese government's views on this point are echoed by its Asian neighbors and by most governments of developing countries (see Fairclough 1993, 22).

After Tiananmen Square, there was a downturn in Sino–American bilateral relations, largely prompted by Washington's concern for China's human rights record and its treatment of political dissidents and their supporters. The Chinese government has sought to overcome foreign sanctions by improving its relations with the United States and other major powers. Nevertheless, pressures from outside may help to bring gradual improvement in human rights conditions within China, particularly through business-affected reforms. As China becomes further integrated into the world economy and international affairs in general, its internal behavior—including its treatment of its citizens—will inevitably be affected by external influences. Indeed, this was the underlying logic of the Clinton administration's "engagement" policy toward China (see Chapter 2).

Also of note, cultural and educational exchanges with foreign countries have increased tremendously since Deng's ascension to power. China began to send students to the United States in the late 1970s, shortly after relations between the two countries were normalized. This flow continued and grew to the point that, by 1990, mainland Chinese students became the largest contingent of foreign students in the United States. In 1993, for example, there were more than 45,000 students from China and 37,000 from Taiwan studying in the United States. They represented the largest and third-largest numbers of foreign students in the country, respectively (Meyer 1994, 56–58). There has also been an influx of foreign students and scholars to China since the late 1970s. Although the total number still remains small when compared with the number of Chinese students abroad, the number has grown rapidly, from 1,800 students in 1982 to more than 25,000 by the late 1990s.

Today, China continues to send a large number of students and scholars to study abroad, primarily in industrialized countries. In addition, Beijing has sent thousands more Chinese officials to these countries on short-term visits to learn about Western societies and institutions. In the case of the United States, for example, scientific and technological exchange programs have linked virtually every U.S. cabinet department with its Chinese counterpart. Moreover, several U.S.-based corporations have conducted educational programs for Chinese officials and managers as a way of developing business opportunities in China. The impact of sending students to the West has been mixed. For example, some students and professional researchers have opted to stay abroad. But since the end of the 1990s there has been a reversal in this trend as an increasing number of overseas scholars and students have returned to China in search of better opportunities. In general, therefore, China has greatly benefitted from the cultural and educational exchanges.

GREATER REPRESENTATION OF LOCAL INTERESTS

Under horizontal authoritarianism, the relationship between the central government and local elites has become much closer. Local interests have started to play a role in foreign policy, particularly in foreign economic relations. This new development stands in contrast to the previous system of vertical authoritarianism, in which the central government controlled virtually all aspects of policy making.

Throughout the period of reform, a gradual loosening of the constraints on local authority has occurred. Local governments—in particular those in the coastal cities or provinces, such as Guangdong, Jiangsu, and Shanghai, as well as in the five "special economic zones" of Hainan, Shenzhen, Zhuhai, Xiamen, and Shantou—have a high degree of authority in terms of economic activities and external economic relations. The central government permits these local governments to retain a portion of the foreign exchange they earn to encourage exports and local economic development.

In a study of China's economic development strategy and its implication for Chinese foreign policy, Naughton (1994, 63) suggested that different regional developments may bring different foreign-policy preferences. He described a "tripartite China" composed of three regions: (1) the economically advanced southern coast, which is relatively affluent, technologically advanced, and highly integrated with foreign economies; (2) the "communist core" in the north and northeast; and (3) the "deep interior" that has been "left out of the growth process to date." Importantly, it is in the prosperous southern provinces where Beijing has granted the greatest freedom of action. With more than 1.2 billion Chinese citizens to feed, clothe, and house, the Chinese government has become dependent upon the revenue derived from the "special economic zones" in the south and more tolerant of their political and social freedoms. Meanwhile, Beijing launched a major campaign in the late 1990s to develop its western frontier.

NATIONALISM AS A FOREIGN-POLICY TOOL

In this rapidly integrating economic context, nationalism has emerged as a leading ideological current behind China's drive toward modernization and one of the primary driving forces behind Chinese foreign policy. In the post–Cold War era, nationalistic feelings appear particularly strong among Chinese intellectuals and government officials. This emphasis on ethnic identity has, of course, been evident in other parts of the world in the wake of the Cold War and its focus on ideological concerns and divisions.

An indication of Chinese nationalism may be seen in the textbook controversy that began with Japan in the 1980s. In 1982, Japan's Ministry of Education was sharply criticized by other Asian governments (including China, Thailand, Hong Kong, and North and South Korea) for revising the description of Japan's wartime behavior in school textbooks. Rather than stating that Japan had "invaded" China and other parts of Asia, the wording was changed to "entered," provoking protests throughout East Asia. Beijing launched a full-scale campaign attacking Japan's revised language. The campaign continued until Tokyo promised to review the disputed terminology prior to Prime Minister Zenko Suzuki's visit to Beijing to mark the tenth anniversary of normalized relations.

The textbook controversy resurfaced in 1985 and 1986, when new editions of textbooks describing Japan's actions in World War II were published. The problem was further exacerbated by Prime Minister Yasuhiro Nakasone's official visit to the Yasukuni Shrine to honor those killed in World War II. The shrine contains the remains not only of Japanese soldiers but also of a number of Japanese war criminals, including General Hideki Tojo, the commander in chief of the Japanese army in China during the war. Following Nakasone's visit, China's news media launched a new wave of criticism against Japanese militarism, triggering student demonstrations in Beijing, Shanghai, and other major Chinese cities, and giving expression to popular nationalistic sentiments.

For the Chinese government, the affair offered an opportunity both to promote nationalism at home and to pressure Japan to make political and economic concessions. An indirect link was established, for example, between the perceived revival of Japanese militarism and the Sino–Japanese trade imbalance, expressed by Chinese student demonstrators in such slogans as "down with the Japanese economic invasion." These and other controversies challenged the widespread assumption that nationalist sentiments would inevitably diminish in the midst of economic globalization. Recent trends in China suggest that nationalism remains a potent social force even in modernizing societies, and a powerful instrument of foreign policy.

THE PRIMACY OF REGIONAL RELATIONS

Another aspect of Chinese foreign policy today is regionalism. This concept emphasizes that China has remained a regional power, concentrating its political, economical, and military activities primarily in the Asia-Pacific region. The concept also refers to China's effort to participate actively in regional institutions such as the Asian-Pacific Economic Cooperation and the Asian Development Bank. China's closer ties with members of the Association of Southeast Asian Nations (ASEAN) countries is demonstrated further by its active participation in the grouping known as ASEAN Plus Three (the primary ASEAN countries plus China, Japan, and South Korea). Despite its global aspirations, Beijing has confined its international activities primarily to the Asia-Pacific area. From Beijing's perspective, the combined area of East Asia and Southeast Asia is critical for Chinese foreign policy, not only in terms of military and political relations, but also in the economic dimension, which has direct implications for China's modernization drive. Given the many cultural, ethnic, and linguistic similarities across the region, as well as geographic proximity, the Asia-Pacific is the most advantageous region within which China can do business.

A revealing way to examine Chinese foreign policy is to look at the country's major trading partners. China's trade with Asian countries is more than with all non-Asian states combined. East Asia and Southeast Asia constitute the bulk of the trading activities, and trade within "Greater China" has also ranked prominently.[5] In 1994, China's trade within East Asia and Southeast Asia constituted slightly more than half of its total trade, compared to about 20 percent with Europe and North America. The importance of this intraregional trade was on full display in 1997 and 1998, when the Asian financial crisis that originated in Thailand quickly spread across the region. This "contagion" effect not only ruptured the region's economic boom, it posed a stark challenge to economic growth throughout the world.

In addition to economic and trade relations, security issues within the Asia-Pacific region are another factor of paramount concern to Beijing. Since the end of the Cold War, the balance of power that prevailed in the region has given way to an uncertain security environment in which friends and allies are more difficult to discern. In addition, domestic conflicts in such countries as Indonesia have produced power vacuums and possible spillover effects elsewhere. Also of concern are China's territorial disputes over the Xisha (Paracel) and Nansha (Spratly) islands with Vietnam and several members of ASEAN. Finally, a potential arms race in East Asia may affect stability in the region.

Taken together, all of these issues have continued to focus Beijing's attention on its Asian neighbors. We now turn our attention to the many bilateral relations that are of central concern to Beijing. As we will find, the Chinese government must simultaneously pursue favorable relations with a diverse array of regional and global powers, many of which were adversaries during much of the twentieth century. In the midst of modernization, however, China has sought to reconcile its differences with these countries.

JAPAN: CHINA'S MOST IMPORTANT ASIAN PARTNER

It is widely recognized that the most important bilateral relationship in East Asian regional affairs is that between China and Japan. Chinese foreign policy toward Japan has been greatly influenced by Beijing's changing perception and interpretation of Japan. From the victory of the communists in 1949 through the early 1970s, Chinese policy toward Japan was strongly influenced by the Cold War. In Beijing, Japan was openly

---

[5]There are different definitions of "Greater China." In a broad sense, it refers to the growing interaction among ethnic Chinese societies around the world. In a narrower sense, "Greater China" focuses exclusively on Hong Kong, Taiwan, and mainland China.

condemned as an agent of U.S. imperialism. Since China normalized its relations with Japan in 1972, this view has changed substantially and much progress has been made in developing diplomatic relations. Today, China uses quite different phrases to describe Japan—such as "good neighbor" and "good friend"—despite the lingering problems between the two countries noted earlier.

This new perception of Japan is primarily reflected in economic relations. Since the normalization of relations in 1972, bilateral trade has flourished. Japan has consistently been a major source of capital, technology, and manufactured imports to China. For example, by the late 1990s Japan was China's top trading partner, accounting for nearly 20 percent of its total international trade.

The issue of "Japanese militarism" is an important subject that reflects Beijing's changing interpretation of Tokyo's intentions toward China. Due to the bitter memory of the Japanese invasion and occupation during World War II, China's well-founded fears of Japanese militarism endure. Beijing has shown itself prepared either to play down or to exploit those fears, depending on China's changing policy agenda. Also of note, a serious territorial dispute persists between China and Japan over the islands the Chinese call "Diaoyu" and the Japanese know as the "Senkakus." The islands are currently under Japanese control. Diaoyu, a cluster of unpopulated rocky islands located between Taiwan and the Ryukyu Islands, has long been a point of dispute between Beijing and Tokyo. Both claim ownership of the islands, which are reported to be in an area possessing significant oil deposits. Nevertheless, neither government has allowed the dispute to undermine the broader bilateral relationship.

Beijing's keen concern over regime legitimacy in the international community can be found in the disputes around the issue of Taiwan in Sino–Japanese relations. Even though Japan issued a number of official statements in 1972 declaring Taiwan to be Chinese territory, Taiwan has continued to remain a potentially volatile issue between China and Japan. Because Japan ruled Taiwan as a colony for so long (1895–1945), some Japanese have pursued a special relationship with Taiwan and would prefer the status quo of separation in the Taiwan Straits. Such opinions irritate the Chinese government, which views any suggestion of "two Chinas" or "one China, one Taiwan" as an unacceptable assault on China's territorial integrity. Despite its pursuit of closer relations with Japan, China is firm on the Taiwan issue.

Beyond such contentious issues as Japanese militarism and the issue of Taiwan, Japan is China's foremost trading partner and China's markets will become increasingly important to Japan. Also of importance, Japan has for many years been the largest donor of bilateral development aid to China.[6] At the same time, China has been one of the largest recipients of foreign direct investment from Tokyo. Through these exchanges, Japan has not only ensured itself a critical and reliable source of raw materials, energy in particular, but has deeply strengthened its position within the Chinese domestic market. The large-scale aid programs have also enhanced Japan's international reputation as one of the world's top aid donors and a "good citizen" in global development efforts (see Chapter 5).

The mutual benefits of this growing economic relationship have been extensive. Beyond the bilateral relationship, growing economic interdependence between Japan and China has far-reaching political and strategic implications. It is believed that Sino–Japanese relations will assume even greater importance across East Asia as Russian ambitions in the region fade more than a decade after the Cold War, and as U.S. policy toward the region has faced its own adjustments. All of this will ensure that Sino–Japanese relations remain close in the years to come.

STRIKING A BALANCE ON THE KOREAN PENINSULA

Modernization, nationalism, and regionalism have all figured into the shift of China's policy toward the divided Korean peninsula. When the Korean War broke out in the summer of 1950, the PRC provided substantial military support to North Korea in its war with South Korea. Strategic, political, and ideological calculations dominated the PRC's Korea policy in this hotspot of the Cold War. Beijing, however, learned some painful lessons from the Korean War. In terms of Chinese casualties, Sino–American relations, and China's ties to its other East Asian neighbors, the war proved costly for China.

There have been sporadic quarrels between Beijing and Pyongyang (North Korea's capital) during the past several decades. Its low point was in 1969, the peak of China's Cultural Revolution, when Chinese and North Korean forces clashed along their border. With Beijing strengthening its ties to Seoul in the mid-1990s, the Beijing–Pyongyang relationship appeared to be cooling. Beijing, Washington, Tokyo, and Moscow had already reached a consensus on prohibiting the development of nuclear weapons in North Korea. The PRC has nevertheless maintained a workable relationship with North Korea, one of the few countries that openly supported Deng's crackdown against student demonstrations at Tiananmen Square.

Given the changing international and domestic environment, Beijing made substantial adjustments in its Korea policy. Despite its openly stated

---

[6]Japan reduced its aid transfers to China in the late 1990s due to its prolonged recession and increasing fears within Japan of China's growing power. The levels of Japanese aid, however, remained high compared to other donors.

alignment with Pyongyang, China long ago ceased to support a North Korean military attack on the South. Since the opening of the Deng era, Beijing has consistently expressed interest in avoiding another major military conflict and, therefore, has a particular interest in the creation and maintenance of a stable situation on the peninsula and the possible unification of North Korea and South Korea.[7]

As the international situation changed, especially after the Eastern European countries and Russia established diplomatic relations with South Korea, the PRC gained sufficient confidence in 1992 to establish diplomatic relations with South Korea. In fact, in the post–Cold War era, Beijing has had strong incentives to develop relations with Seoul because a closer relationship might increase China's leverage in dealing with the Korean problem and with East Asian stability as a whole. South Korea, with one of the most dynamic economies in East Asia, has also become increasingly important as a trading partner for China. As a newly industrialized country and a close neighbor, South Korea can provide China with valuable experience and lessons in terms of economic development, especially in export-led industrialization. South Korean investors have aggressively pursued the Chinese market, primarily in the coastal Shandong Province.

There will inevitably be problems between the PRC and South Korea, whose differing political systems and levels of economic development are sure to contribute to friction. The potential for cooperation will, however, be much greater than that for conflict. Each side, for example, may profitably regard the other as a counterweight to the increasing economic and military strength of Japan. This possibility was confirmed by the fact that Japan's past experience of militarism was jointly condemned by China's President Jiang Zemin and South Korea's President Kim Young Sam during Jiang's state visit to Seoul in November 1995. Overall, however, the prospect of mutually profitable economic ties, as well as the development of conciliatory relations between the two Koreas, are likely to encourage cordial relations between Seoul and Beijing.

CHANGING PERCEPTIONS OF SOUTHEAST ASIA

Beijing's drive for modernization and its desire for regional stability has significantly affected the transformation of China's relations with the nations of Southeast Asia through ASEAN. This rapprochement exemplified China's shift from an ideologically rigid, isolationist policy under Mao to

---

[7]Some scholars believe that, from a security perspective, China would not want to see a united Korea. Chalmers Johnson (1995, 67), for example, argued that Beijing "prefers a structurally divided Korea that is unable to play its full role as a buffer between China, Russia and Japan, thereby giving China a determining influence on the peninsula."

a less doctrinaire, more pragmatic, and cooperative approach favored by Deng and Jiang. Indeed, whereas for Mao China was forced to rely upon itself, for subsequent leaders the very threat of international isolation has been sufficient to inspire a rapid improvement in China's relations with its Southeast Asian neighbors.

In the 1950s and 1960s, China dismissed the members of ASEAN as proxies for the U.S.-led capitalist bloc. Although in the 1970s Beijing changed its view of the nature of ASEAN, its relations with the Southeast Asian countries did not improve immediately. Indonesia, which severed relations with Beijing in 1964 after a failed coup attempt by the Indonesian Communist Party, remained suspicious of Beijing until 1990, when it finally normalized its relations with China (see Chapter 9). China's relations with the countries of Indochina have likewise been far from smooth. Until the early 1970s, the PRC enjoyed a "comrade-plus-brother" type of relationship with Vietnam, fighting first against France in the early 1950s, then against the United States in the 1960s and early 1970s. After the Vietnamese communists achieved national unification, however, Sino–Vietnamese relations worsened rapidly, primarily due to Vietnam's occupation of Cambodia and the territorial disputes along the border and in the South China Sea. To break Vietnam's ambition of dominating Indochina, China launched a punitive war against Vietnam in 1979. The war lasted for less than a month and ended with the voluntary withdrawal of the Chinese troops.

As mentioned previously, one major problem between China and some Southeast Asian countries in the mid-1990s was that a number of disputes remained unresolved, notably territorial claims over some of the South China Sea islands that are rich in oil. As a result, China has conducted military actions to protect its claims in the area. The South China Sea also is important to international shipping, with about one-fourth of the world's shipping traffic, including most of Japan's transport of imported oil. Thus the potential exists for a serious regional crisis to be sparked by a dispute over resource claims and navigation rights.

In general, however, China has viewed Southeast Asia as a critical component of its Asia-oriented foreign policy of the post–Cold War era. Beijing has taken several concrete steps in this direction in the wake of the Tiananmen Square uprising and crackdown. As already noted, Beijing established diplomatic relations with Indonesia and Singapore in 1990. China then normalized relations with Hanoi in 1991 and since 1992 has been actively involved in the UN peacekeeping effort in Cambodia. The normalization of Sino–Vietnamese relations has presented an opportunity for Beijing to exercise its influence in the region. As elsewhere, China's chief concern for Southeast Asia is stability, although the economic opportunities posed by greater regional cooperation have also played a key role in its calculations.

RUSSIA'S STRUGGLES AND CHINA'S RESPONSE

The collapse of the Soviet Union, and the subsequent struggle within Russia to implement economic and political reforms, profoundly influenced China's domestic and foreign policies. China's policy toward Russia has been closely linked with its changing perception of Moscow's declining power. Historic concerns about Russian expansionism have given way to fears regarding political instability within all the post-Soviet republics and the possible impact of its spread to the PRC's western provinces, especially such areas with large minority populations as Xinjiang.

In September 1994, Jiang Zemin paid a key visit to Moscow. With a more comfortable and stabilized bilateral relationship than in previous years, Jiang and Russian President Boris Yeltsin signed a declaration confirming that China and Russia agreed not to aim nuclear missiles at each other, never to use force against each other, and to limit sharply the number of troops stationed along their border. An equally important result of the visit was an economic agreement signed by the two leaders. Yeltsin told Jiang, "We pay much attention to studying the experience of economic reforms in China," referring to China's successful policies and remarkable economic growth during the previous decade. Indeed, bilateral economic relations between the two countries increased rapidly after the Cold War. In 1997, Russia was China's eighth largest trading partner, constituting 2 percent of the PRC's total trade.

One should not, however, ignore potential problems between these two great powers, whose relations have repeatedly shifted between amity and discord. Beijing and Moscow are still in the process of adjusting their policies toward each other. Although Russia has been in a downturn ever since the collapse of the Soviet Union in 1991 (see Chapter 3), its regional influence remains strong. Thus Beijing has worked hard to strengthen ties with Moscow. At the same time, Russia is also eager to secure China's support and shares several grievances with Beijing, including the eastern expansion of the North Atlantic Treaty Organization (NATO), the NATO bombing of Serbia, and foreign (largely U.S.) criticism of Russia's civil war in Chechnya. This conflict has struck a particular chord within the Chinese government, which continues to defend its suppression of separatists in Tibet on similar grounds as those cited by Russian leaders.

With the two powers moving toward closer ties, as demonstrated by public meetings in 2000 between presidents Jiang Zemin and Vladimir Putin, Russia has shown a willingness to help China modernize its military forces. In October 1999, for example, the two countries agreed to conduct joint training and share information on the formulation of military doctrine. As many as 2,000 Russian technicians were employed by Chinese military research institutes working on advanced defense systems, including laser technology, cruise missiles, nuclear submarines, and space-based weaponry. In early 2000, China purchased two Russian-built destroyers worth $800 million each. The first destroyer was deployed and sailed through the Taiwan Straits in February 2000 en route to a Chinese naval base.

Also of note, Chinese and Russian leaders united in July 2000 to criticize U.S. plans to develop a "limited" missile-defense system. They dismissed pledges by the Clinton administration that the system would be designed to repel missiles only from "rogue states" (later called "states of concern" to Washington), not the declared nuclear superpowers. The concerns of the two governments intensified further with the election in November 2000 of U.S. President George W. Bush, who promised an even more aggressive effort to deploy a missile-defense system than that proposed by the Clinton administration. All these developments have sparked reciprocal fears in Washington and elsewhere about Sino–Russian collusion in the military sphere.

A ZIG-ZAG PATTERN IN SINO–AMERICAN RELATIONS

The U.S. interest in China has its roots in the two countries' ambivalent historical relationship. Over time, the character of the U.S.–China relationship has shifted starkly from missionary activities in the nineteenth century to the search for business opportunities today. It has also involved a transition from being wartime allies in World War II to Cold War rivals in the 1950s to 1980s, and then to a "strategic partnership," as confirmed during President Clinton's 1998 visit to China. China's attractions to Washington are its enormous population and rapidly modernized economy, which became virtually the last major untapped market for U.S. firms. Regardless of whether the dreams of profits are fulfilled or not, the fact that China has moved up quickly to become a top trading partner and a leading destination for private investment is a major factor in U.S. foreign policy toward Beijing (see Chapter 2).

For their part, Chinese leaders have attached great importance to their relations with the United States. With the Cold War over, Deng identified several principles to guide Sino–American relations. These principles included *zengjia xinren* ("increase mutual trust"), *jianshao mafan* ("reduce trouble"), *zengjia hezou* ("enhance cooperation"), and *bugao duikang* ("avoid confrontation"). With this guidance, Beijing has attempted, with considerable success, to maintain friendly relations with Washington. Chinese leaders have regarded the United States, along with Japan and the European Union, as major sources of advanced technology, capital, and markets. Although he criticized the PRC on such issues as human rights and unfair trading practices, Clinton made a critical decision in 1994 to de-link the human rights issue from the renewal of China's Most-Favored Nation (MFN) status, thereby removing a major obstacle to bilateral relations. This shift was part of the U.S. "engagement" policy, which used closer economic ties as an incentive for Chinese leaders to respect human rights and support U.S. positions in other areas such as environmental protection and weapons nonproliferation.

On the other hand, as long as the future of Taiwan remains unsettled, the potential for a Sino–American conflict will continue. In the mid-1990s, these relations were threatened after the Republican party's victory in U.S. Congressional elections produced a more pro-Taiwan stance in Washington. Representative Newt Gingrich, Speaker of the House of Representatives, called in July 1995 for the United States to reestablish diplomatic ties with Taiwan. The most visible challenge to Beijing was Clinton's decision to allow then-Taiwanese President Lee Tung-hui to pay a private visit to the United States in June 1995. In making this decision, Clinton was under enormous pressure from Congress, which earlier passed a resolution in favor of granting Lee a visa to the United States. The resolution passed by a vote of 97–1 in the U.S. Senate and unanimously in the House of Representatives. Beijing was particularly angry since it had taken seriously the vow of U.S. Secretary of State Warren Christopher that Washington would not permit Lee's visit.

Showing its anger over Lee's tendency toward independence, as demonstrated by his visit to the United States, the PRC conducted a series of military exercises and missile tests around Taiwan in the summer of 1995 and the spring of 1996. Washington reacted strongly by sending two aircraft carrier groups to the waters near Taiwan. The Chinese felt compelled to react to what they perceived as "hegemonism" and interference in their internal affairs. Clearly, danger remains of a military clash and escalation around the issue of Taiwan between China and the United States.

Economic issues, however, continue to be most influential in Sino–American relations. A key issue in recent years was the negotiation of China's long-term trade relations with the United States. These relations, as noted earlier, were subject to annual reviews by the U.S. Congress. President Clinton sought to end this annual review, which tended to focus on China's human rights situation, and to grant China permanent normal trade relations (PNTR). He received support from Congress, which approved this new status in 2000. This agreement greatly boosted Beijing's effort to become a member of the WTO, seen by Chinese leaders as a vital step toward global economic integration.

The powerful voices of the business community in providing Beijing PNTR status and entrance to the WTO offer a vivid expression of U.S. economic interests in China. Many people believe that China's economic modernization will help to create an enlarged and empowered middle class that will promote civil society and greater democracy. Indeed, this mixed political–economic consideration served as a foundation for the Clinton administration's engagement policy. Yet festering security concerns in the

United States, along with complaints from labor unions that many U.S. jobs would be "exported" to China, created significant, although not decisive, opposition to Sino–American engagement (see Hook and Lesh 2002).

Such stresses and strains are likely to continue. In general, however, the two countries' national interests are not fundamentally in conflict. The strategic foundation that brought them together in 1972 is still largely in place. Whereas President George W. Bush said during his campaign in 2000 that the PRC should be viewed as a "strategic competitor" rather than a "strategic partner," his statement reflected political rhetoric more than a significant policy shift. Washington has consistently recognized the importance of Beijing's cooperation on East Asian and Southeast Asian regional affairs. Above all, global competition for China's emerging domestic market is recognized in Washington. With this vast market in mind, many other Western countries have put economics ahead of politics when dealing with China. Thus the United States has not been alone in "engaging" the PRC; its leaders are unlikely to stray from this course despite their harsh rhetoric.

A clear measure of the level of interdependence between two great powers is how they withstand periodic diplomatic crises that may threaten their bilateral relations. In this respect it was revealing that a major crisis in April 2001 had only limited impact on Sino–American relations. On April 1, a U.S. plane engaged in routine surveillance of China collided with a Chinese military jet and was forced to land in Chinese territory. For several days Chinese leaders refused to allow the Americans to return home, and even then they prohibited the U.S. government from retrieving the damaged spy plane. The two governments exchanged bitter statements throughout the standoff, but in its aftermath U.S. and Chinese leaders were determined not to allow the incident to jeopardize the closer economic relations established under the Clinton administration.

THE TAIWAN DILEMMA

The volatile and seemingly intractable Taiwan issue has remained a high priority in Beijing's foreign policy, reflecting deeply rooted nationalism among China's political leaders as well as its people. For Beijing, unresolved concerns about Taiwan are tied inextricably to China's national sovereignty and regime legitimacy, two essential principles noted in the introduction to this chapter. The PRC's policy on Taiwan, which has remained firm, is also related directly to its interpretation of the domestic and international situation.

For most of the Mao era, the PRC's sense of vulnerability produced a determined assertion of its claim to Taiwan. During the 1950s and 1960s, the PRC was isolated by the West as Taiwan, regarded as representing the entirety of China, was granted China's membership in major international organizations, most notably the UN. With the U.S. Seventh Fleet stationed in the Taiwan Straits, Beijing understandably viewed the United States as a major threat. Japan, which had occupied Taiwan for fifty years prior to 1945 and was firmly allied with the United States in the Cold War, was also considered a potential aggressor. These concerns provided the foundation for Beijing's uncompromising policy toward Taiwan, a policy that left no room for concessions where the issues of sovereignty and regime legitimacy were involved.

Prior to 1979, Beijing attached great importance to the restoration of Taiwan as a province of China and insisted on the "liberation" of Taiwan. Freed from the Maoist ideological straitjacket, however, Deng recognized that it was virtually impossible to incorporate Taiwan into the framework of socialism. Differences in political, economic, and social life had become so great that neither the ruling elites nor the Taiwanese masses would accept a socialist system for the purpose of unification. According to Deng's proposal, after unification Taiwan would be allowed to maintain its foreign economic and cultural ties with other countries, as well as its own political, economic, and social system. Furthermore, it could maintain its own army and independent judicial power. Taiwanese political parties would participate in the leading bodies of the central government, such as the State Council, the Standing Committee of the National People's Congress, and the People's Supreme Court. This proposal, however, was not entirely acceptable to the Taiwanese, for their desires still remained split between independence and eventual unification with the mainland.

With the shift in emphasis from revolution to modernization, and with Beijing's establishment of official relations with the United States in 1979, the PRC has been able to gain important leverage in its relations with Taiwan. All of the major capitals of the world now recognize Beijing as the legitimate ruler of China and officially consider Taiwan to be part of China. More than 180 countries have established relations with the PRC; fewer than thirty countries maintain official relations with Taiwan. This significant change in the diplomatic environment has only strengthened Beijing's resolve not to make any concessions to Taiwanese independence. Furthermore, Beijing has demanded that Taipei not be allowed to become a member of any international governmental organizations such as the UN.

The PRC's Taiwan policy has been complicated further by the dynamics of Chinese domestic politics. No Chinese leader can afford to be cast as *lishi zuiren* (a person condemned by history) for taking action that would permanently split the nation. Such a label would be a lethal blow to any leader engaged in Beijing's continuing power struggles. Given such fears, Beijing has consistently refused to pledge not to use force against Taiwan. Jiang stated in December 1992 that the PRC would adopt "resolute measures" if Taiwan declared independence, a position he then maintained consistently.

Beijing believes that the longer the separation between the mainland and Taiwan continues, the stronger will grow Taiwan's tendency toward independence. It appears necessary, therefore, for Beijing to reassess the Taiwan issue and to understand the political reality of a unified China. Today's Taiwan is different from the Taiwan that was ruled by Chiang Kai-shek. Taiwanese society is fundamentally pluralistic. The democratic structure in Taiwanese politics, represented by party politics and presidential elections, was confirmed with Lee Tung-hui's victory in 1996 and reinforced by Chen Shui-bian's election in March 2000. It is likely, therefore, that cross-strait relations will remain a top priority in both Beijing's and Taipei's calculations and a considerable source of regional tension and potential conflict.

CONCLUSION

In conclusion, modernization, nationalism, and regionalism are general trends in Chinese foreign policy that seem likely to continue well into the twenty-first century and beyond. Obviously, the rapid technological advances of the past two decades cannot be reversed. China will, therefore, remain a key player in the world economy. At the same time, the nationalist impulse has proven to be compatible with economic modernization and remains a potent tool by which Chinese foreign-policy makers pursue their objectives, both at home and abroad. Furthermore, China's importance as a regional power will persist, or even become stronger, if the region becomes more economically integrated—and if Russia and the United States both assume lower profiles in East Asia.

Beijing's interpretation of its internal and external environment will continue to play an important role in the adaptation of Chinese foreign policy. In this respect, perceived threats to the country's national security will continue to override economic opportunities. If Washington is perceived as a threat to China instead of a good partner, or if Taiwan's attempt to gain independence jeopardizes the legitimacy of Beijing's rule, Chinese leaders will likely suspend their relations with Washington or consider military action against Taipei, even at the risk of economic loss and possible direct military confrontation with the United States. Such are the stakes at hand when China's essential principles are perceived to be in jeopardy.

Future consideration of East Asian politics must always take into account the perspective of the major players in the region. For example, China's approach to Japan is still infused with resentment and distrust despite the intimate, and highly profitable, economic ties that have been forged between the two economic superpowers. It is in Beijing's interests to recognize the extremely important role Japan can play in creating a healthy and conducive international environment for China. While focusing on economic exchanges between the two countries, therefore, Beijing would benefit by conducting regular consultations with Tokyo on regional strategic and security issues. In this respect China may recognize that it is legitimate for Japan to attach great importance to strategically important areas such as the South China Sea and to pay attention to sensitive issues such as human rights. As long as Beijing's legitimacy and sovereignty concerns are not threatened, Chinese leaders will be well advised to work closely with Tokyo on a wide range of regional issues, such as stability on the Korean peninsula and continued recovery from the 1997–1998 regional economic crisis.

From the perspective of Washington, it is clearly in the interest of the United States to play a balanced role in order to maintain stability in the Asia-Pacific region. Thus the United States will continue to benefit by maintaining its alliances with regional partners. The U.S.–Japan relationship is deeply rooted and will continue for decades to come. It will not be threatened by closer relations between China and Japan, given the troubled history and intense emotions surrounding this relationship. While the United States itself continues to engage Beijing politically, strategically, and economically, Washington should also encourage Japan to enhance its relationship with China, particularly in the political and security realms. Such cooperation would only enhance stability in the Asia-Pacific region, an outcome that is unarguably in the interest of the United States.

There are understandably different lines of argument regarding how to deal with the "rise of China." Some in Washington continue to promote a Cold War–style containment policy, similar to that used against the Soviet Union. Yet, while recognizing lingering differences, all parties will gain from cooperation rather than confrontation. Stability and prosperity throughout East Asia and along the Pacific Rim will be impossible unless these important relationships are properly handled. As in the past, China will play a crucial role in this process and will exert significant influence not just in East Asia, but on a global scale.

CHAPTER 5

JAPAN'S ECONOMIC ROUTE TO POWER

Robert Scalapino

University of California at Berkeley

Few countries have adapted to major changes in power and influence to the extent Japan has during the past century. In this chapter, I review Tokyo's rise to the status of a world power and its more recent efforts to maintain this status amid constant changes at home and overseas. As I will argue, East Asian security and prosperity in the future continue to depend in large part upon the Japanese government's response to its own capabilities and limitations.

Despite a deep recession that lasted through much of the 1990s, Japan maintains Asia's largest economy and the second-largest economy in the world.[1] The prospects for the future, however, are uncertain. At home, the Japanese economy faces severe constraints stemming from resource dependency and a rapidly aging population. The government, meanwhile, has recently been in the hands of fragile coalitions whose leaders have attracted limited public support. On the international front, Japan's relationship with China is a critical, if usually unspoken concern, as is the country's continuing reliance on Washington for military security. Adaptation to rapidly changing developments at the domestic, regional, and global levels represents a difficult, yet crucial task.

---

[1] Japan's gross national product (GNP) of $4.4 trillion in 1999 was second only to that of the United States, with $8.7 trillion in economic output. For more recent economic indicators, see the World Bank's informative Web site (www.worldbank.org).

THE HISTORICAL BACKGROUND

To understand the nature of Japanese foreign policy today, an appreciation of the country's modern history is essential. For more than two hundred years prior to U.S. Commodore Matthew Perry's arrival in 1853,
Japanese leaders pursued a rigorous policy of isolation from the outside
world. As in the case of modern North Korea, Japan used isolation as a
means of preserving internal stability (see Beasley 1995). Even before
Perry's arrival, however, a small group of Japanese intellectuals had
begun to question the isolationist posture. Some raised the prospect of
leading a commercial revolution rather than fighting against economic
modernization and integration. Others suggested using foreign trade to
acquire military power. How else could the enticing slogan "A rich country, a powerful soldiery" be made a reality? How else could Japan defend
itself against Western imperialism?

JAPAN'S EMERGENCE AS A REGIONAL POWER

Japan's commitment to more assertive foreign policies awaited the Meiji
era, which began in 1867. Political power in the new era gravitated into the
hands of a small group of officials and young leaders from the military
class. Their first major objective in foreign policy was removing the blem-
ish of unequal treaties and attaining "complete independence" from, and
equality with, the Western powers. To accomplish this task required nearly three decades, during which the Western powers demanded a number
of legal and commercial reforms (see Norman 1940). Throughout these
years, modernization progressed by emulating German, French, British,
and American models of industrial development. One of the great strengths
of Japan was its willingness to borrow from others, then modifying the
import to conform with Japanese culture.

By 1900, Japan had become the first Asian country to attain nearly
complete parity with the West in legal terms. It did so in part by assuring
the major powers that it was prepared to abide by the rules of diplomatic
behavior created in the West. In the long struggle to achieve recognition
as an equal, however, latent elements of nationalism often came to the
surface in various forms. Japanese leaders ran grave risks if they were
deemed obsequious to foreign powers, too "pro-Western" in their personal
style, or disrespectful toward Japanese culture. The history of these years
is filled with assassination plots against moderate elements within Japan's
government and society. This was one price to be paid for cultivating nationalism while scarcely daring to admit its excesses.

In a broader sense, Japanese society reacted in a pendulum-like fashion to the West. Periods of intensive borrowing and adaptation were followed by noticeable retreats. Japan wanted to catch up with the West and be accepted as a "civilized" nation, and for certain things Western a genuine fondness existed among many Japanese. On the other hand, when foreign conflicts erupted, the cries of "defend our culture" and "resist the foreigner" grew in volume. If some aspects of Western culture appealed to most Japanese, there was no widespread desire to abandon the mainstream of Japanese culture or custom. This vital fact must be given careful attention in analyzing contemporary Japan.

While there were strong elements of defensiveness in Japanese policy in the Meiji era, the climate was also ripe for Japan to wield its newly found strength abroad. Northeast Asia was largely a vacuum of power, tended haphazardly by China, "the sick man of Asia," and by the stronger but unstable and overly committed forces of tsarist Russia. The Japanese mission seemed even clearer when it could be posed against Western encroachments throughout Asia. The theme "Asia for the Asians" was first applied by Japanese, often by sincere individuals who had a vision of liberating other Asians from backwardness and Western domination. Private societies like the *Genyosha* (Black Current Society) and the *Kokuryukai* (Amur River Society) had such objectives in mind and offered assistance to nationalist movements in China and the Philippines.

Yet as the Sino–Japanese conflict of 1894–1895 graphically demonstrated, Japanese foreign policy had imperialist aspects that could easily overshadow defensive ones. For Japan, the implications of its victory over China were fourfold. The victory marked the beginning of the Japanese empire and served as a further stimulus to industrial growth and general economic development. In addition, the victory caused Japan's global prestige to rise while further promoting the nationalist tides at home together with the prestige of the military class.

Japanese foreign policy now took a new step of major import. To strengthen its position in Asia, Japan concluded an alliance in 1902 with the world's foremost power of this era, Great Britain. Thus fortified, Tokyo dared to challenge Russia two years later, and another victory advanced the Japanese empire, which gained *de facto* control over much of Northeast Asia. Sakhalin and the Kuril islands were brought under Japanese rule. Its control over Korea could no longer be challenged, although outright annexation did not come until 1910. The Manchuria-Mongolia region also fell under the shadow of expanding Japanese power.

Ahead lay an era of unprecedented influence for Japan throughout Asia that derived from much more than military prowess. There is no doubt that most of the Asian world experienced a thrill at the Japanese victory over Russia, which raised hopes throughout the region that the West could be beaten at its own game. But in a broader sense, Japan had become the symbol of modernization by a process of synthesizing new ideas with its indigenous culture. Western science and technology received an enthusiastic reception in Japan, and from this experience the rest of Asia had much to learn (see Lockwood 1968). Japan embarked upon an extensive career as model, tutor, and leader to eager Asians everywhere. Thousands of students flocked to Tokyo and other Japanese centers of learning. The majority came from China, but every section of Asia was represented to some degree. Likewise, Asian nationalist movements found in Japan a haven and source of support.

Already, however, the central problem of Japanese foreign policy in the decades ahead was emerging—that of preserving the thin line between acceptable leadership in Asia and unwelcome domination. World War I was the third conflict within a generation to pay handsome and immediate dividends to the cause of Japanese prestige. Japan captured without difficulty the German holdings on the Chinese Shantung peninsula and in other parts of the Pacific. With this mission accomplished, the nation directed its energies to supplying the Asian markets that were cut off from their normal European contacts, while providing its Western allies with the materials of war. These tasks required further industrial expansion. Indeed, during this period industrial productivity overtook agrarian output as Japan moved into the ranks of industrial societies.

At the close of World War I, there could be no question that Japan had become a world power, the one major country besides the United States to emerge from the war in a stronger position. Its preeminence in East Asia could not be doubted despite the uncertain new force of Bolshevism in Russia. Japan's economic strength had enabled rapid military expansion. Its navy had become the third largest in the world while its army—in size, equipment, and training—dwarfed other forces in its region. Politics was also a wellspring of power, presenting a picture of remarkable stability.

There were indications during the interwar period of the 1920s that Japanese politics might be significantly affected by the democratic tides. The influence of Western liberalism, crowned by the global idealism of Woodrow Wilson, was strongly felt in Japanese intellectual circles. Party government, moreover, assumed new importance. The office of premier was held for the first time by a commoner, and the movement for universal suffrage was receiving widespread support. Japan's first liberal era was opening, bringing with it serious efforts to establish parliamentary and civilian supremacy in Japanese politics. Hence, moderation in foreign policy was possible during this period.

The liberal era was short-lived, however. The major causes for its decline were familiar: economic crisis and depression, political confusion and corruption, and the consequent rise of opponents from the far right and left (see Scalapino 1962). By the early 1930s, the Japanese government faced a series of direct military challenges to civilian control. As a result of a contrived incident, conflict erupted between Japan and China in Manchuria in September 1931. The weaker Chinese forces were quickly defeated, and Tokyo's incursion remained to the Chinese an unacceptable symbol of Japanese aggression.

With Manchuria under complete Japanese control, the militarists could not resist spreading outward toward northern China. The second China incident erupted in 1937 and led eventually to total war and China's defeat (see Iriye 1981). Japan could always find some Chinese allies, whether as a result of the internal rivalries for power in China, sheer opportunism, or some genuine hope that this route might lead to a new and better Asia, freed from Western imperialism. But in the end, Japanese aggression achieved what was most feared: a union of the nationalist and communist forces and many Chinese independents into a nationalist popular front that was bitterly anti-Japanese. Although the salvation of Asia from communism was a central goal of Japanese leaders, their conduct ultimately contributed more than any other external factor to the success in 1949 of communist revolutionaries in China (see Chapter 4).

To concentrate solely on China in this period, however, would be to examine only the most fragile link in Japan's Asia policy, which for all of its militant and aggressive qualities had strong regional appeal. By the 1930s, Japan had developed the concept of a "Greater East Asia Co-Prosperity Sphere," whose basis lay in the rapid strides made by Japanese trade and investment throughout the region. By means of general deflation, changes in currency valuation, industrial rationalization, and extensive state support, Japanese trade came to enjoy highly favorable competitive conditions in East Asia. Western Europeans complained vigorously about the practice of "dumping" in the colonial markets. Japan retorted with charges of economic discrimination and attempted monopoly. Europe's penetration of the Asian market provoked later proposals for an economic bloc led by Japan and divorced from Western control. However, the center of the Japanese appeal to other Asians during this period remained in the sphere of political nationalism. As Japan drifted toward the fascist bloc, Western imperialism in Asia could be attacked with less inhibition than in the past.

These shifts in Japan's behavior were abetted by changes in the strategic scene in Asia. Earlier, Japan had reluctantly given up the Anglo–Japanese alliance, its shield and support for twenty years. In its place were substituted more general agreements among the major powers. The concept of collective agreement was especially attuned to the United States, whose leaders wanted an end to exclusive alliances and who wished to apply moral suasion for restraint. The great symbol of this hope and this era was the famous Kellogg-Briand Pact of 1928 that "outlawed" war as an instrument of foreign policy. A second effort was the move toward disarmament among the great powers, particularly in naval forces.

THE MARCH TOWARD CONFLICT

Tragically, however, hopes for a prolonged period of global harmony after World War I proved to be unfounded, particularly in East Asia. The one international organization intended to underwrite global peace—the League of Nations—quickly proved powerless to displace Japan from Manchuria, an outcome that was foreshadowed by the fact that the United States was not even a member of the League. Consequently, in the name of defending its national interests, Japan could successfully defy the great powers.

The Marco Polo Bridge Incident, which opened Japan's full-fledged conflict with China on July 7, 1937, was in many respects the beginning of another world war for Tokyo. Japanese ground forces, which had gained control of northern China, began their thrust into China's heartland. By August 1937, Tientsin and Beijing had been taken, and in December, the nationalist capital of Nanking was also overwhelmed by Japanese forces. After war in Europe erupted in 1939, new impetus was provided for Japan to extend its hegemonic ambitions in Asia.

Given its vastness, however, China was no easy conquest. A fragile alliance was established between the nationalists and communists, who were joined by many Chinese independents in a nationalist popular front against Japanese forces. Tokyo had fashioned its own Chinese government, installing Wang Ching-wei as head of state, but his regime had very limited support. The costs for Japan steadily mounted in economic and human terms. Military expenditures reached more than one-third of the government budget by 1938, and Japan's heavy industries were hard pressed to meet military demands.

In this setting, Japan looked for new alignments both in Europe and Asia. On September 27, 1940, a Tripartite Pact was signed with Germany and Italy. Japan had now joined forces formally with the fascists, although the alignment was one of mutual utility rather than of comradeship. Increasingly, Japan was being pushed toward confrontation with the Western democracies because of its expansion both in China and in Southeast Asia. One critical issue, moreover, was that of resources, especially oil. When Japan occupied southern Indochina in 1941, the United States froze Japanese assets in the United States and imposed a complete embargo on oil exports. The Netherlands, still in control of the East Indies, did likewise. Japan could not conduct its operations at home or abroad without oil and other critical resources.

The long-standing controversy over whether the confrontation should be with the Soviet Union or with the West was heavily influenced by this issue, but other factors were also involved. In April 1941, when a neutrality agreement was reached with Moscow, Japanese authorities were privately confident that German forces would overrun the Soviet Union, thereby ending the conflict in Europe. Thus, Japan's task lay in "liberating"

East Asia. After negotiations between Tokyo and Washington broke down, Japan struck the United States at Pearl Harbor and other Asia-Pacific installations. As of December 7, 1941, the scope of the ongoing war assumed global proportions (see Iriye 1981).

Even before Pearl Harbor, Japan had begun to stake out an ambitious program for East Asia. In mid-1940, Yosuke Matsuoka had first spoken publicly about the creation of a Greater East Asia Co-Prosperity Sphere. As Japanese power moved southward, efforts were made to signal support for nationalist movements in the region. After Pearl Harbor, and as the war progressed, additional steps were taken. In 1943, "independent" governments were set up in Burma and the Philippines, and pledges were made to the East Indies (Indonesia). Many nationalist forces in Southeast Asia were trained in Taiwan and elsewhere. Even in the final days of the conflict, Japan encouraged various nationalist forces—such as those represented by Sukarno in Indonesia—to take power.

The war, however, was being lost, and by 1944 the handwriting was on the wall. Militant leaders were forced to resign as moderate elements sought to salvage the situation. But the Japanese went to the wrong source (the Soviet Union) in a search for an "honorable peace." The allies, now confident of victory, insisted upon unconditional surrender. The United States sealed its demands with two atomic bombs, which were dropped on the cities of Hiroshima and Nagasaki in August 1945. For Japan, the war proved to be an enormously costly failure that would not soon be forgotten. In its wake, Western and Japanese imperialism in the Pacific had gone down together.

THE U.S. OCCUPATION AND THE COLD WAR

When Japan surrendered on August 15, 1945, its people were forced to reconcile themselves to being a vanquished nation. Under the terms of the Yalta and Potsdam agreements, the Japanese empire was to be dissolved and Japan reduced in size to the approximate boundaries of the pre-1894 era. The homeland was to be occupied for an indefinite period by U.S. forces. For the first time in recorded history, Japanese sovereignty was to be superseded by foreign rule. The objectives of U.S. occupation were clearly stipulated: Action was to be taken to ensure that Japan would never again become a world menace. Total disarmament was to be carried out, and those responsible for past aggression were to be punished. Even the fate of the Emperor was initially unclear, although Japanese leaders gained some assurances on this point during the surrender negotiations.

Along with these essentially negative tasks, the occupation had more constructive goals. Led by General Douglas MacArthur, U.S. occupation forces encouraged democratic movements and built a representative government with the aim of helping Japan eventually regain its independence as a pacific, democratic state. Thus, in September 1945, a radically new era was inaugurated for Japan, one that might be labeled "the era of the American Revolution."

What was to be considered of strategic importance to Japanese foreign policy at this critical juncture? The Western European states, both victors and defeated, had been weakened and faced a lengthy struggle to regain economic strength. Further, their colonial empires were disintegrating, with numerous new countries being born in South Asia and Southeast Asia, as well as elsewhere. The Soviet Union, while horribly damaged by the war, still had a formidable military force and had expanded its reach, with an Eastern European buffer zone under its control. Soviet interventions in East Germany, Czechoslovakia, and Poland alerted the United States to possible trouble as the Cold War emerged. "Containing" communism would become the basis of Western grand strategy, and Japan would play a key role in applying the strategy in the Far East.

The process of creating new nation-states in southern Asia was complex, with both ideological and ethnic–regional divisions creating complications. After initial efforts to implement democratic reforms based upon Western models, many states shifted to military-dominated, authoritarian systems in an effort to achieve stability. Whatever the system, however, domestic concerns fully occupied the Asian governments, which had little or no capacity to project power beyond their boundaries (Scalapino 1989).

While U.S. commitments remained primarily with Europe, the war had raised the Asia-Pacific region to a heightened level of importance in U.S. foreign policy. In addition to the occupation of Japan and South Korea, Washington had extensive new Pacific island territories, responsibilities toward its former colony, the Philippines, and concerns about the future of China, which remained immersed in civil war. Having emerged from the war as the preponderant global power, the United States now had to make crucial decisions as to the nature and extent of its commitments in Asia, a region certain to rise in strategic importance.

It is in this context that the first phase of the U.S. occupation of Japan, and its impact on subsequent Japanese foreign policy, should be viewed. In this brief phase, the emphasis was upon punishment and reform. A new social, economic, political, and military order had to be created, but the old order had to be eradicated first. Japanese military forces were totally disbanded in a remarkably short time. Before the end of 1947, some six million Japanese troops and civilians had been returned from overseas and demobilized. The ministries of war and navy were also abolished. Moreover, a number of individuals were indicted and tried before an international tribunal as war criminals.

In an effort to seal these actions with the stamp of permanency, the famous Article 9 was written into the new Japanese Constitution. "Aspiring sincerely to an international peace based on justice and order, the Japanese people forever renounce war as a sovereign right of the nation and the threat or use of force as a means of settling international disputes," Article 9 stated. "In order to accomplish the aim of the preceding paragraph, land, sea, and air forces, as well as other war potential, will never be maintained. The right of belligerency of the state will not be recognized."

The U.S. vision was for Japan to become "the Switzerland of the Far East." In this case, however, pacifism was added to neutralization. It was a vision that had considerable appeal to the Japanese, who lived amidst rubble, without adequate food or warmth, and with memories of lost relatives, fire raids, and the final cataclysm of the atomic bomb. Criticism of past leaders and institutions was widespread, and a war-weary people turned hopefully to popular rule without being precisely sure of its content.

The reform efforts extended to Japan's commercial relations and industrial development. A central goal in this respect was to restructure the *zaibatsu* system by which Japanese firms were closely intertwined both with each other and with the central government. This effort, however, proved largely futile in the absence of fundamental changes in the traditional structure. "Crony capitalism" survived the storm and was soon to become even stronger than in earlier times—a source of ongoing frustration within the U.S. government during and after the Cold War. In sum, while the U.S. occupation had significant and enduring effects, Japanese culture proved a formidable force and resisted change at many points.

Greatly complicating matters, wartime cooperation between the United States and the Soviet Union was clearly over and the global scale of the Cold War was becoming manifest. Of great concern was the triumph of communist forces in the Chinese civil war, which led in 1949 to the creation of the People's Republic of China (PRC), led by Mao Zedong. The threat of communism spreading both within and beyond Eurasia had become a reality, and areas all along the PRC's periphery emerged as ideological Cold War battlegrounds, as noted in the previous chapter. By this time, U.S. leaders realized that its occupation of Japan was reaching a point of diminishing returns, but also that continuing economic, political, and security ties between the two countries were a mutual necessity. These views were widely shared in Japan. Moreover, the outbreak of the Korean War in June 1950 revealed the ominous security situation in Northeast Asia.

All of this greatly advanced the desirability of a U.S.–Japanese alliance in both Washington and Tokyo. Thus, the negotiations that led to the San Francisco Peace Treaty of 1951 produced a series of decisions that shaped the new Japanese foreign policy. The critical issue pertained to the question of Japanese defense. Two broad alternatives existed. One was to continue down the path of pacifism, which involved seeking universal agreements guaranteeing the sanctity of Japanese territory and backing these with pledges of protection by the United Nations and the United States. The alternative was to acknowledge the Japanese need for and right to military defense, and to underwrite Japanese rearmament with U.S. power. The choice between these two courses would shape many other aspects of Japanese foreign policy.

The Japanese government did not hesitate to support the second alternative, that of a bilateral alliance with the United States as the only course compatible with international conditions and Japanese needs. To adopt a policy of neutralism, it was argued, would make Japan dependent upon the actions of the communist world. Both the economic and political interests of Japan were best served by alignment with the United States, and the 1947 Constitution, properly interpreted, did not prevent military forces for purely defensive purposes.

Independence came officially on April 28, 1952, the day on which the San Francisco Treaty came into effect. Accompanying this treaty was a bilateral Mutual Security Treaty with the United States, which agreed to maintain military bases in Japan until adequate defenses were prepared by the Japanese government. Toward this end limited rearmament was first started in the summer of 1950, shortly after the outbreak of the Korean War. The National Police Reserve was activated in August of that year with an authorized strength of 75,000 men. With the coming of Japanese independence, this number was increased to 110,000, and a small Maritime Safety Force was established in May 1952. In August, these were brought together under the National Safety Agency. Two years later, on July 1, 1954, the name was changed to the Defense Agency, and the armed forces were placed directly under the office of the prime minister, who was authorized to add a small Air Self-Defense Force.

As the gulf between the United States and the two communist powers grew deeper during and after the Korean War, a series of problems was created for Japan. What would its role be should a major conflict erupt? Would U.S. bases in Japan force its direct involvement? In 1959, the Japanese Supreme Court had ruled that the self-defense forces did not violate the Constitution, since all nations had an inherent right to defend themselves. The following year, the U.S.–Japan Security Treaty was revised and strengthened, which further established Japan as a crucial agent of the U.S.-led containment strategy (see Chapter 2).

Events in the ensuing decades reduced the support for a neutralist-pacifist policy both among the Japanese public and political leaders. The PRC's "Cultural Revolution" raised serious questions about trends in that society, as did the later Chinese war with Vietnam in 1979. Nevertheless, when Sino–American relations suddenly improved in 1972, Japan hastened to establish diplomatic relations with Beijing and sought expanded economic relations, with fruitful results largely awaiting the advent of the Deng Xiaoping era.

The Sino–Japanese relationship remained delicate throughout this era despite growing economic ties. The legacy of history hung heavily over the scene, with Chinese leaders continuously warning against the restoration of Japanese militarism. Indeed, some soft support for the U.S.–Japan Security Treaty existed in Beijing during these years due to a desire to avoid an independent Japanese military program and recognizing the need to meet the Soviet threat. Taiwan was also an issue since Japanese ties to this region continued to be extensive. Meanwhile, Japan's relations with the Soviet Union remained frozen despite advances in trade. The unwillingness of Moscow to give up the Northern Territories (the South Kurils) prevented a peace treaty between the two countries from being signed, and extensive Soviet military forces in the Soviet Far East heightened Japanese apprehensions.

Thus, support for the security treaty with the United States remained considerable during most of the Cold War. However, in the aftermath of the Nixon Doctrine of 1969, suggesting limited U.S. commitments in the future and demanding reciprocity by the Asian states, the question of U.S. reliability was raised in certain quarters in Japan. In an effort to satisfy Washington that Japan was prepared to do its share within constitutional limitations, Prime Minister Zenko Suzuki in 1981 pledged that Japan would conduct air surveillance for several hundred miles and sea patrols up to 1,000 miles to the south and east. Japan's defense expenditures were kept to the mandated limit of 1 percent of the government budget, but rapidly increasing economic output caused the military budget to steadily grow. By the early 1980s, the Self-Defense Force numbered some 240,000 well-equipped and well-trained troops.

JAPAN'S ECONOMIC ADVANCES

On the domestic front, these were years of increasing political stability as well as rapid economic expansion, based largely upon export-led industrialization. Since World War II, Japan had plunged into global trade markets and became a world leader in several economic sectors, particularly consumer electronics and automobiles. Japan was less affected than others by the global recession in the 1970s and early 1980s. Its spectacular growth not only moved Japan into the category of a global economic power, but encouraged the use of this wealth in advancing Japan's role in Southeast Asia. Various foreign-aid programs, which first took the form of reparations, were provided directly to recipients in East Asia as well as through international economic agencies.[2]

---

[2]By 1989 Japan was annually providing the largest amounts of Official Development Assistance of any industrialized country. These aid flows were directed primarily toward Japan's neighbors in East Asia, including the PRC, which had also established major trade and foreign-investment ties to Tokyo. See Rix (1996), Hook (1995), and Orr (1990) for an elaboration.

As noted earlier, the Japanese economic system was based upon close interaction between the government and large-scale business, with a cluster of government-supported enterprises holding an extensive market share, especially in financial services and public works. In effect, the Ministry of International Trade and Industry (MITI) and the Ministry of Finance were a part of the economic planning and production process, with resources and income distribution heavily government controlled (see Johnson 1982). The *keiretsu* system, closely managed by the government, permanently tied subcontractors to primary producers. The deep cross-penetration of corporate funding and lifetime employment further solidified the system, which effectively precluded genuine market-based competition or any significant entry of foreign investment. Not surprisingly, Japan recorded large trade surpluses every year. Combined with a high savings rate and low interest charges, capital was extensively available.

The Japanese strategy was widely heralded as a model for other developing Asian societies (see Samuels 1987). Viewed from the United States, Japan stood ten feet tall, its economy and stabilized political system serving as an effective bulwark against communist expansion in East Asia. To many in Washington, however, the revitalized Japan represented a threat—very different from that previously posed by the Soviet Union, but aimed at the vital center of the U.S. economy. As a result, trade frictions between the two countries soon troubled their relationship and continued well past the Cold War.

The Structural Impediment Initiative talks conducted between the United States and Japan during the Bush administration enabled both sides to present their views. Americans demanded broad market-opening measures via the removal of both tariff and nontariff barriers by Japan. For their part, the Japanese urged that the U.S. savings rate be improved, its massive budget deficits curbed, and that U.S. industry concentrate on becoming more competitive. Intensive bilateral negotiations followed with the Clinton administration.

During this period, the appropriate relationship between the economic and security aspects of the U.S.–Japan relationship was widely discussed and debated on both sides of the Pacific Ocean. Some argued that these two elements could and should be separated, because they spoke to different aspects of national interests. The economic issues, moreover, were primarily bilateral in character, whereas the security issues were regional and even global in their implications. Others insisted that sooner or later, unresolved economic issues would inevitably affect the degree of trust and bonding necessary for a meaningful security relationship.

As this debate continued in the early 1990s, the economic picture changed. Japan entered a prolonged recession, with growth rates dropping sharply, unemployment rising, and a serious banking crisis developing because of the mountainous bad loans they had extended, primarily based on overinflated property values. Japan became testimony to the fact that no economic strategy is appropriate for all times. As a result, internal pressure grew for fundamental reforms of the Japanese economy. Key on the reformers' agenda was the deregulation of Japanese firms, the restructuring of the financial system, greater openness to foreign goods, and greater flexibility in all other aspects of the industrial structure. The business community, the news media, and even elements within the government such as MITI spoke of an urgent need for reform if Japan were to remain competitive.

The U.S.–Japan security tie remained strong amid these tensions, and Japanese confidence in the U.S. commitment gradually returned. Quite clearly, the common security interests of the two Pacific powers could be separated from the chronic trade tensions between them. Thus, as the post–Cold War international system took shape, Japanese leaders could feel reasonably confident about their role in Asia and their relations with Washington.

MAKING FOREIGN POLICY IN JAPAN

We now turn to Japanese foreign policy today. Prior to exploring the key issues and relationships in Japanese foreign policy at present, a brief analysis of the Japanese political system is essential as it relates to the formulation of foreign policy. The broad trend has been toward greater political pluralism. Yet despite various reforms and social changes, the essence of policy making continues to lie in collective decisions reached in private, based on consensus involving intricate negotiations and compromises. While Japan has had forceful leaders on occasion such as Shigeru Yoshida and Yasuhiro Nakasone, leadership by a single individual remains foreign to Japanese culture.

In recent times, efforts have been made to increase the role of the legislature, or *Diet*, in policy making. Policy debates have also acquired greater substance. Nonetheless, despite attempts to reduce its power, the bureaucracy continues to be the key actor in the foreign-policy arena. Japan has benefitted from the fact that some of its most talented youth have elected to make governmental service their careers, and corruption, the scourge of many Asian bureaucracies, has been modest, although not absent. With young entrepreneurs in the business world offered new opportunities, whether talent will continue to flow into government remains to be seen. In any case, the current scene continues to display a fusion of conservative forces, with ex-bureaucrats—including those from the foreign ministry—frequently becoming affiliated with big business, or in some cases, entering politics as members of the dominant Liberal Democratic Party (LDP) or other parties (see Masumi 1995).

At the same time, the emphasis on policy-making coordination can be exaggerated. Turf battles are frequent, abetted by intense loyalty to one's inner group. The Ministry of Foreign Affairs has frequently exercised less power in connection with critical foreign policy issues than the Ministry of Finance or MITI (Hook and Zhang 1998). In this respect, Japan's bureaucrats hardly speak with one voice in foreign policy.

Meanwhile, Japanese interest groups, public opinion as revealed in nationwide polls, and a frequently critical news media have added to the current complexities. Among interest groups, the most influential is that of the business community, represented through such groups as *Keidanren* (the Federation of Economic Organizations). From this group comes the chief financial support for the LDP, and within its membership are included the most intimate confidants of conservative politicians. Yet business also is fragmented on many policy issues.

Another powerful lobby is that of agriculture and Japan's rural community, which is greatly overrepresented in the *Diet*. While farmers have progressively become a smaller fraction of the Japanese electorate, and at present frequently draw income from additional sources, Japan's rural areas remain a stronghold of conservative support. The reluctance with which successive administrations have tackled the issue of agricultural protectionism in its many forms and the extensive expenditures on rural public works speak to the continued strength of the farm lobby, both in the key parties and in the bureaucracy (see Woodhall 1996).

Organized labor has made less of a mark on government policies, especially in recent years with the decline of the Japan Socialist Party. The familial structure of Japanese industry, together with the progressive trend toward internationalization, have served to weaken the power of the trade unions. Only when their position coincides with that of other interest groups is their input significant. Other single-issue interest groups, including environmentalists and human rights advocates, have only recently come into view in Japan and thus far have generally had limited political influence on the national scene (see Broadbent 1998). However, spectacular events such as an accident at a nuclear power plant have had an impact, reviving unresolved doubts about Japan's energy security and placing the government on the defensive. In Okinawa, moreover, public opposition to U.S. bases and the misconduct of U.S. personnel became a major source of controversy in the late 1990s and 2000.

Public opinion has had an increasing impact on Japanese foreign policy in recent years. National polls are generally taken seriously by politicians. According to these polls, most Japanese favor close relations with the United States. But increasingly, the public wants Japan to have an equal status with Washington and to pursue independent policies on certain matters. The Russian Federation continues to garner very limited support, with the PRC faring much better. Japanese prejudice against Koreans is still reflected in national surveys but has declined in recent years. Most Japanese consider themselves a part of the advanced industrial world, and the younger generation is strongly attracted to various aspects of Western culture.

In the aftermath of a deep economic recession in the 1990s, the Japanese public remains uncertain about the country's economic prospects. Many have voiced complaints about their quality of life. Housing, education, and the general strains of life in urban areas are of particular concern. On the international front, the public is well aware of Japan's economic friction with other nations, especially the United States. They see trade as a vital matter for Japan, however, and tend to place the blame for such problems on competitors overseas. Regional economic relations have again become a high priority. As concerns about the future of Japan's economic ties with the United States have grown, and as Japan continues to struggle in its trade relations with the European Union (see Chapter 6), there has been increasing support for closer economic interaction with other parts of East Asia.

For all of the changes noted previously, the remarkable aspect of Japanese foreign policy since World War II has been its continuity, or perhaps more accurately, its slow pace of change. One factor has been the continuous conservative control of the political center. The complete LDP dominance of earlier times has ended, however. Japan has recently been governed by relatively fragile coalitions, with frequent changes of top leadership. Thus, it has been difficult to define any innovative strategy for Japan's foreign relations (see Funabashi 1994). For this reason, speculating about the future is a risky enterprise.

KEY CONCERNS FOR JAPAN TODAY

In this section, I briefly discuss the two areas of primary concern for Japanese foreign-policy makers today. The first concern relates to economic matters, which in Japan have become an integral component of its foreign policy. As made clear by the recent East Asian economic crisis, which struck Japan prior to battering the economies of Thailand, Indonesia, and other regional economies in the late 1990s, the success or failure of the Japanese economy has profound implications far beyond its shores. Secondly, Japanese leaders must still grapple with security concerns in the post–Cold War era. These concerns remain acute given the power vacuum created by Russia's ongoing problems, the PRC's economic growth, and other developments in the Asia-Pacific region.

PRESSING ECONOMIC CONCERNS

Economic considerations continue to dominate Japanese foreign policy despite the growing influence of other factors. On economic matters, domestic and international concerns are closely intertwined. Once hailed as Asia's economic "miracle," Japan suffered from the serious downturn of the 1990s, with national output declining, unemployment reaching 5 percent, and massive debts threatening the capacity of the economy to sustain itself. Even Japan's high-profile foreign-aid program, emphasized by Tokyo as a symbol of its arrival as a good citizen in world affairs, had to be reigned in. Some Japanese labeled the 1990s the "lost decade."

As the twenty-first century opened, signs of economic recovery could be discerned. Japanese exports began growing again as neighboring markets in East Asia reopened their doors. Foreign investment was accelerating, but still represented a very small portion of GNP compared to other advanced nations. Perhaps most importantly, Japanese firms were engaged in restructuring programs, reducing production costs, releasing surplus workers, and becoming more competitive in the critical information-technology sector. Yet concerns about the global economy, and particularly that of the United States, contributed to a complex and uncertain picture.

Despite its many problems, however, some of which relate directly to the cozy relationship between business and government that fueled Japan's economic boom in the 1960s and 1970s, the country's residual strengths should never be minimized. The central fact remains that Japan, with a GNP of nearly $5 trillion, still possesses the second-largest economy in the world. This level of output dwarfs even the most dynamic economies elsewhere in East Asia.

Yet fragility continues to mark the scene. Private financial institutions, which seek to recover past loans, are lending new funds very cautiously. The government had advanced stimulus packages totaling 120 trillion yen by mid-2000, which raised the total debts of central and local governments to 645 trillion yen, or 130 percent of the nation's GNP. Given the fact that Japan has the world's largest foreign currency reserves, estimated at $306 billion, this may not pose an acute problem. Yet domestic consumption has remained weak despite aggressive stimulus measures. Moreover, it is clear that pursuing renewed vitality by removing the three past excesses—surplus labor, surplus production facilities, and surplus debt—will be a lengthy, painful process. Nevertheless, it is imperative that economic structural reforms be advanced and that the government concentrate on fiscal reform.

While foreign investment in Japan has been rising, some other Asian countries offer the foreign entrepreneur greater advantages. Singapore, for example, has replaced Japan as the leading Asian destination for U.S. high-technology investments, with $7.5 billion in cumulative manufacturing assets compared to $5.6 billion in Japan. Elsewhere in East Asia, economic reforms following the deep recessions of the late 1990s are likely to produce revived prosperity and greater competitive advantages. In this climate, foreigners operating in Japan want a more entrepreneurial future, with regulatory barriers eliminated and venture capital encouraged and rewarded. Japan cannot compete in the future by merely offering products that are also made in the developing Asian countries at a lower price. Tokyo must concentrate on commodities and services that have a high added value, and this means the rapid development of information-intensive industries.

Finally, the labor market represents a concern, given that Japan's population has not grown to match its economic growth. According to a recent UN study, Japan will need to import 609,000 immigrants yearly to maintain its 1995 working population level of 87.2 million through 2050. Whereas only 1.2 percent of the Japanese population were foreigners in 1998, such immigration would bring the figure up to 30 percent by 2050.[3] The rapid aging of the Japanese population, with nearly 27 percent being 65 years of age or older by 2015, poses a series of challenges that extends beyond the economic sphere. In this context, it is not difficult to appreciate the importance that Japan attaches to economic issues in its foreign policy.

Three broad efforts characterize Japanese economic policies on the regional and global fronts. First, a series of financial assistance measures has been advanced to alleviate Asian economic problems and promote development in the region. The New Miyazawa Initiative, launched in October 1998, committed about $30 billion to training, research, and development. A more recent proposal, set forth at the G-8 meetings in Okinawa during the summer of 2000, pledged $15 billion to narrow the information-technology gap between advanced and developing economies. As always, Japanese leaders are prepared to extend aid to those markets that are critical to their country's future. Such a policy is not unprecedented; Japan's aid during the 1980s and much of the 1990s served as a key agent of its economic strategy.

Second, Tokyo has demonstrated a renewed interest in Asian-centered economic and financial operations, based this time upon multilateral coordination rather than unilateral control. An early proposal was for an Asian Economic Fund, led by Japan. This was strongly opposed by the United States, which feared it would compete with the Asian Development Bank and the International Monetary Fund. The idea was dropped, but remains a subject of discussion. Japan has also assumed an active role within the Association of Southeast Asian Nations (ASEAN), particularly in the ASEAN Plus Three (Japan, China, and South Korea) meetings that have focused on regional economic issues. Various proposals to make the yen the key regional currency have been circulated in these circles. Also of

---

[3]The Federation of Economic Organizations posits a less-dramatic picture, asserting that, depending upon its own human resources and rapid innovation, Japan can grow at an average annual rate of 2.7 percent through 2025. But with foreign workers, the rate can be raised.

note, Japan has played an active role in the loosely knit group known as Asia-Pacific Economic Cooperation (APEC).

Finally, a related form of Asian economic regionalism is to be seen in the form of Natural Economic Territories (NETs), economic entities involving states or portions of states that are geographically contiguous and have reciprocal assets. The NETs could result in the merging of labor, natural resources, capital, technology, and management. Japan has participated in ongoing discussions regarding a Sea of Japan (East Sea) NET that would involve western Japan, the Russian Far East, the Korean peninsula, and portions of northeast China. Through such ventures, the vital economic importance of northeast Asia to Japan is further revealed.

These Asia-oriented commitments, however, have not been allowed to reduce the importance of Japan's economic relations with the industrialized West, particularly the United States. As noted earlier, Japan has reduced some of the barriers to foreign investment and has shown special interest in combined ventures with high-tech companies from the United States and other industrialized nations. There can be no doubt that a growing number of officials and members of the business community see Japan's future closely related to its adjustment to the information-technology revolution, and hence are receptive to all methods of advancing progress in this realm. Thus, the Japanese are engaged in intensive dialogues with major trading partners, showing greater receptivity to openness than in the past and working more actively within such bodies as the World Trade Organization. Though hesitantly, Japan is nonetheless adapting to the free-market pressures of globalization.

In sum, having achieved a prominent economic position globally and in the Asia-Pacific region, Japan will seek to use every means to protect and advance that position. Its leaders are well aware that this represents a major challenge, given the rise of such competitors as the PRC, the continuing scientific-technological prowess of the United States, and the fact that some Asian societies are now seeking to reach postmodernity before they are modern. Moreover, future trends with respect to the U.S. economy will have a profound effect on the Japanese economy as well as the economies of other East Asian nations.

RETHINKING NATIONAL SECURITY

In the security realm, the revival of nationalism in Japan as elsewhere in Asia is much in evidence. Nationalist movements have been expressed in drives for Japan to achieve the status of "a normal state" and to receive the full range of rights accorded a sovereign nation. Japanese leaders have also sought greater acceptance as a partner, not a client, of the United States. A top priority within Japan is permanent membership on the United Nations Security Council, a goal that has propelled Tokyo's ongoing efforts to establish itself as a model "citizen" in global diplomacy. On various occasions, however, nationalist leaders have riled the waters by promoting the assertion of Japanese military power or being insufficiently remorseful for Japan's imperialism of the past (see Chapter 4).

The concerns about a restoration of the prewar type of Japanese militarism are largely unwarranted. Only a combination of two developments would make a major thrust in the direction of militarism possible: a greatly increased perception of external threat, and the loss of the United States as a reliable ally in maintaining regional security. Recent *Diet* discussions regarding a possible revision of Article 9 of the Japanese Constitution, however, testify to an interest in legitimizing Japan's security options. Even within the constraints posed by Article 9, Japan in 2000 boasted the world's second-largest defense budget, which totaled almost $50 billion. While nearly one-half of that budget meets personnel and related costs, and while logistical support amounts to another 40 percent of the total, the military assets acquired in recent years have been significant. Major acquisitions include state-of-the-art antisubmarine and combat aircraft, surface warships and submarines, and an array of weapons for land combat (Baker and Morrison 2000). Given its technical and financial capacities, Japan could advance further into a military enhancement program very quickly.

Japan has moved cautiously with respect to security commitments. Nevertheless, the revised guidelines governing the U.S.–Japan Security Treaty, enunciated in 1998 and approved by the *Diet* in 1999, provide for an expansion of Japanese assistance in "areas surrounding Japan"—a deliberately vague designation—should conflicts break out. Such assistance, however, does not include overt military participation. In its concern about North Korea, and more discreetly about China, Japan has moved cautiously to increase its strategic commitments in ways not spelled out in the revised guidelines. The Japanese government has decided to build its own intelligence satellites, to join with the United States in research on a Theater Missile Defense system, and to engage in military-to-military exchanges with other governments in the region. Tokyo has also proposed sending Coast Guard ships to Southeast Asia to cooperate with others in combatting piracy. In sum, the climate with respect to strategic issues is undergoing a change in Japan, but not one affirming the "Japan threat" thesis advanced by some Asian neighbors.

With respect to strictly political considerations, Japan takes a strong stand at the UN and in such regional organizations as the ASEAN Regional Forum (ARF) in support of democracy and human rights. However, in general, Tokyo does not make these issues a precondition for political and economic interaction. Japanese leaders have occasionally applied economic sanctions—toward China after the 1989 Tiananmen Square crackdown, for example, and toward North Korea after its missile-satellite launch over Japan in August 1998. But this has not been Japan's preferred approach. Rather, Japanese leaders have supported the notion that, through economic and political engagement, authoritarian states are more likely to evolve toward greater openness.[4]

JAPAN'S PRINCIPAL BILATERAL RELATIONS

Despite its active participation in multilateral forums at the global and regional levels, Japanese foreign policy remains concentrated principally upon its bilateral relations. These relations are reviewed briefly in this section, after which this chapter concludes with some cautious speculation regarding Japanese foreign policy in the future.

THE U.S. LINCHPIN

Most important to Tokyo are its relations with the United States, which remain strong despite trade tensions and cultural differences. Both countries have overriding common interests stretching from economic interdependence to political coordination and strategic alignment. The economic ties between the two nations, combining trade and foreign investment, are massive and still growing. Japan is gradually opening its doors to U.S. investors, with jointly owned enterprises increasing in number. As noted earlier, however, the trade imbalance remains very high, with the negative balance for the United States running about $5 billion per month in 2000. Thus, despite modest Japanese reforms, the trade frictions will not go away. A weakening U.S. economy in 2001 threatened to strain these relations further.

On the strategic front, the revised guidelines for the Mutual Security Treaty have strengthened military ties between Tokyo and Washington. The United States has wanted Japan to undertake greater security obligations, without being certain of precisely what it wanted Japan to do. The new guidelines pleased Washington as a step in that direction, with research cooperation on missile defense providing added evidence of the alliance's strength. The pact retains the strong support of the citizenry of both societies, although some critics have called for U.S. withdrawal from Japan or, on the U.S. side, for Japan's greater financial responsibility for its own defense. Specific problems persist, such as the conduct of U.S. personnel in Okinawa and more recently the extent of Japanese funding of U.S. base costs. But these issues show no signs of disrupting the security pact.

---

[4]Japanese leaders have concurred with Washington on this point, particularly as it regards the engagement of China through closer commercial relations.

Relocation as well as reductions of certain U.S. forces may well take place at some point. Moreover, further advances in military technology, including the potential for rapid deployment and intercontinental warfare, may reduce the need for in-country deployment of U.S. forces abroad. It is clear, however, that the abandonment of U.S. bases at present would greatly heighten tensions throughout the region and unleash an Asian arms race. Hence, the great majority of Asian states want the U.S. presence in Japan—as well as in South Korea—to continue.

Perhaps the most complex aspect of the U.S.–Japan relationship lies in the cultural gulf that inhibits genuine closeness at the personal level. Throughout its modern history, Japan has featured a largely homogenous civil society, deeply conscious of its separatism despite imperialist thrusts. Among younger generations, cultural infusion from external sources, especially the United States, is now taking place at an unprecedented pace. In the United States, moreover, Japanese culture has made inroads, and tourism by both peoples has expanded knowledge concerning each other. Further, unofficial dialogues are taking place on many levels. Yet the fear of "Japan passing," which assumed full force when President Clinton skipped Japan in the course of his visit to the PRC in 1998, is exhibited on occasion.

Despite this concern, the most profound trend in U.S.–Japan relations is the movement from patron–client relations to that of partnership. Japanese officials insist upon higher stature and greater independence from the United States (see Green and Cronin 1999; and Cossa 1997). Such an assertive stance is likely to be tolerated by Washington so long as Japan's government does not succumb to nationalist fervor.

FRAGILE RELATIONS WITH CHINA

Turning to Japan's relations with China, fragility continues to be the predominant characteristic despite growing economic ties between the two Asian giants. As noted in the previous chapter, Japan's trade and investment in the PRC constitute a huge stimulus for Beijing's economy, although Chinese entrepreneurs often complain about Japan's reluctance to share its technology more fully. It is primarily in the political–strategic realms, however, that problems remain. As President Jiang Zemin's 1998 controversial visit to Tokyo graphically illustrated, China's repeated efforts to secure a more comprehensive apology from Japan for its past behavior creates strongly negative reactions from many Japanese, who feel they have sufficiently apologized and provided adequate compensations to the PRC and other East Asian states.

Chinese leaders and citizens have also expressed concern about the perceived resurgence of Japanese militarism. They pay special attention to statements by some government leaders that Japan should consider the possession of all modern weapons, including nuclear weapons. Also of concern to Beijing have been the visits of top Japanese officials to the Yasukuni Shrine, which commemorates Japan's war dead. Proposals to revise Article 9 of the Japanese Constitution, which has thus far prohibited large-scale military rearmament, have further troubled Chinese leaders. Aware that Japan has the technological and financial capacity to expand armed forces rapidly, Chinese leaders openly warn of the risks of a militarily powerful Japan. Their apprehensions are evident in frequent warnings that Tokyo should "not forget the lessons of history" and in Beijing's reluctance to see Japan attain a permanent seat on the UN Security Council. Territorial disputes over the Senkaku (Diaoyutai) islands add to the tensions between Tokyo and Beijing.

Although Japan's more recent worries have involved North Korea and its missile program, the specter of an economically advanced PRC, strongly nationalistic and with growing military strength, is not absent from the worries of a number of Japanese. In this connection, Taiwan is a focus of attention, as detailed in the previous chapter. Taiwan, once a part of the Japanese empire, is the one former colony that retains a generally favorable impression of Japan, a troublesome fact for Beijing. Moreover, Japan's security alliance with the United States risks Japan's involvement should a military conflict over Taiwan erupt.

The Japan–China relationship thus remains marked on both sides by a lack of trust that only time and events—and new generations of citizens in both countries—can mitigate. Fortunately, military-to-military contacts between the two countries have recently been instituted, enabling greater openness. Japan and China have also been parties to multilateral dialogues involving general security issues in East Asia and on a global scale. Among various scenarios for the future, the most promising would be a PRC prepared to accept Japan as a major power and willing to work with Tokyo and other regional powers toward a peaceful resolution of existing bilateral and multilateral issues. The least promising would be that of a rising China that insists on its leadership in Asia and a declining Japan that is growing more fearful of its larger, more populous, and more economically and militarily advanced neighbor.

OVERCOMING DISTRUST OF MOSCOW

Russia constitutes another uncertainty for Japan. The eastern-most region of the Russian Federation lies directly to the north, geographically close but culturally and politically distant. In a 1999 poll, fewer than 8 percent of the Japanese people felt close to Russia, mirroring a century of recurrent animosity and conflict.

The primary problem at present blocking a Japan–Russia peace treaty, which would formally end World War II, is the disposition of the Northern

Territories (south Kurils), a small cluster of islands that was captured by Japan early in the twentieth century and then returned to the Soviet Union after World War II. Recent progress on this issue has been stymied by political infighting within both states, despite the earlier pledge to reach an agreement by the end of 2000. With high-level visits having now taken place and intensive discussions underway, some acceptable solution may be found. Or possibly, Japan will agree to sign a peace treaty and set the issue aside for later resolution. But strong nationalist sentiments on both sides make a final solution difficult.

On the economic front also, progress in Japanese–Russian relations has been slow due chiefly to the dismal economic conditions in Russia, a problem that has hindered other aspects of Russian foreign policy (see Chapter 3). This is especially the case in the Russian Far East. The vast resources of this region, and particularly its gas and oil deposits, offer significant opportunities for the future if Russian leaders can reverse the decline of the national economy. Indeed, plans for a pipeline from Sakhalin to Japan have been under discussion. As noted earlier, the creation of a Sea of Japan NET that would involve the Russian Far East among others is being promoted. To bring this plan to fruition, however, will require advances in both the economic and political realms.

For the present, Japan's effort will be to engage Russia more actively, especially on economic matters. While there is not great concern in Tokyo over the proclaimed "strategic partnership" between China and Russia, there is no desire to see the two great powers enter into close alignment. Japan will thus seek to advance its ties with Moscow within limits, cognizant of the fact that at some point in the twenty-first century, the Russian Federation is very likely to regain its power and global influence.

OTHER REGIONAL PRIORITIES

Among the smaller nations of Asia, none are of greater significance to Japan than the two Koreas. The Korean peninsula has been important to Japan throughout recorded history as a bridge for cultural transmission and, periodically, as an invasion route both to and from the Asian mainland. In modern times, Korea became a vital part of the Japanese empire. Today, it serves as a source of both opportunity (primarily South Korea) and perceived threat (North Korea). Moreover, the Korea tangle is intertwined with the domestic scene since some 700,000 individuals of Korean ethnic origin live in Japan. These ethnic Koreans are equally divided politically among pro-North, pro-South, and neutral groups.

Unlike in Taiwan, the post-1945 reverberations of Japanese colonialism have not been positive in the Koreas, and the legacy of history still looms despite ongoing initiatives to change this situation. However, Japan's relations with South Korea have improved recently. The visit of President

Kim Dae-jung to Tokyo in 1999 resulted in a fulsome Japanese apology for the past by Prime Minister Keizo Obuchi. This in turn led to Kim's pledge to open South Korea to some Japanese cultural imports and produced a fisheries agreement between the two neighbors. Moreover, Japan has remained a part of the U.S.–Japan–South Korea security triangle, with regular consultations on strategic and related matters taking place.

With respect to North Korea, Japan has been a financial supporter of the ongoing program, cosponsored by the United States and South Korea, to provide Pyongyang with light-water nuclear reactors for energy. This initiative, although not without problems, has been seen as an important means to discourage North Korean leaders from developing nuclear capabilities with potential military applications. Japan has also provided substantial food aid in recent years to North Korea, which has been plagued by a devastating drought and famine. Prompted by South Korean and U.S. policies, moreover, the Japanese government has repeatedly proclaimed its desire to establish formal relations with North Korea. Toward this goal, high-level talks were renewed at intervals in 2000.

Tokyo has no interest in seeing Korea reunified, however, since Korean antipathy to Japan remains strong. Further, Japan would probably face very heavy pressures for economic assistance should reunification come through North Korea's collapse or renewed military conflict. The status quo on the Korean peninsula, occasionally acrimonious but peaceful, best serves Japan's interests. Japan, meanwhile, supports the ongoing efforts to improve and deepen relations between the two rivals.

Japanese leaders, furthermore, are showing an increasing interest in other parts of Asia. Japan's economic relations with Southeast Asia have greatly expanded in the past decade. While the Asian economic crisis temporarily damaged economic ties, these are again advancing. Japan contributed large volumes of economic aid to the ASEAN states during the economic crisis of the late 1990s, despite the economic troubles that also confronted Tokyo. Active involvement in such organizations as ASEAN Plus Three and APEC reflect Tokyo's interest in being a major player on the Asian front. Its involvement has been political as well as economic, with a Japanese proposal regarding a resolution of the bloody civil war in Cambodia having played a key role in resolving that crisis.

Similarly, the Japanese government has raised its profile beyond Asia by contributing humanitarian aid and assistance to Kosovo, Albania, and Macedonia during the Balkan conflict, as well as making available its medical specialists as staff members of nongovernmental organizations. Similar contributions have been made to African states such as Sierra Leone and the Democratic Republic of the Congo that have been torn apart by civil war and worsening poverty. The United States and Japan have together been paying more than half the costs of UN peacekeeping operations, which grew far more numerous after the Cold War. The deployment of Japanese military forces to such trouble spots, however, has been limited by the requirement that they not be involved in combat operations. Their involvement thus far has been confined to small units in Cambodia, Mozambique, and the Golan Heights area along the Israeli–Syrian border. One of the issues being actively discussed is whether the Self-Defense Forces should be permitted to participate more fully in UN peacekeeping activities. If so, the move would likely require an amendment to Article 9 of the Japanese Constitution and would therefore provoke controversy both within Japan and in some foreign capitals.

Finally, Japan has shown a stronger interest in what is often termed "human security." This broad term relates to issues ranging from environmental degradation and resource depletion to the host of social and economic problems confronting people in failing states such as Rwanda and Haiti. Given Japan's limitations as a military power, its active involvement in such issues provides Tokyo with an important opportunity to enhance its profile and credibility beyond its borders.

CONCLUSION

As observed earlier in this chapter, Japan's leaders grasped the essentials of Western strength in the nineteenth century and applied these with certain modifications, adding Japanese characteristics. By 1900, Japan was clearly the rising power of Asia and quickly built an empire that extended from the western Pacific Ocean to the Asian mainland. Japanese imperialism, however, ended abruptly with its defeat in World War II. In the decades that followed that war, Japan had to adapt to its new role as a ward of the United States, which assisted Tokyo in rebuilding its economy and creating a democratic political system.

Once again, Japan adapted to the new circumstances without abandoning many of its cultural attributes. Indeed, some of these proved to be assets in the difficult years of the Cold War. By the 1970s, Japan was again the major Asian power—not militarily, but in terms of its dynamic economy. With its security assured by a bilateral defense treaty with the United States, Japan could concentrate on economic reconstruction and regional economic integration. Its earlier goal of a Greater East Asian Co-Prosperity Sphere now seemed close to achievement, but without its military and political costs. By the turn of the millennium, Japan seemed established not simply as the catalyst of East Asia's economy, but as a credible power on the world stage.

Given its international contributions, Japan feels that it is entitled to being recognized unequivocally as a great power. Yet much will depend upon its future domestic conditions. If the country returns to the path of robust economic growth, having carried through the market-friendly reforms required in the era of globalization, and if it achieves the political coherence essential to enable necessary reforms to be undertaken in a timely fashion, Japan will have attained two critical prerequisites for major-power status. At present, however, there are currents of pessimism running through both public and official channels. Can the lengthy period of slow growth and political weakness be reversed? If so, within what time framework will this take place? In confronting these questions, Japan must shed the excessive reclusiveness and introversion of the past, a step that would enable its leaders to make a much greater contribution to global peace and prosperity.

Unquestionably, the twenty-first century will witness significant changes in Asia's strategic picture. China is likely to achieve greater power and influence despite continuing domestic problems of substantial dimensions. The Russian Federation, now geared to a Eurasian policy of enhancement, will inevitably regain its global stature, although the precise shape and effectiveness of its economic and political systems in the post-Yeltsin era remain to be seen. The United States will likely remain the only truly global power, at least for the next several decades. But with a slowing economy and deep political divisions stemming from the controversial 2000 presidential elections, Washington, too, will face new problems.

The other major Asian power likely to increase in influence and status is India, whose relations with Pakistan and China will be crucial concerns to stability in South Asia, a region of growing interest to Tokyo. Elsewhere, Japan's future will likely be closely linked to the middle powers of East Asia. Whether Southeast Asia can achieve greater cohesion through ASEAN or by some other means remains to be seen. If the regional organization does take on a more potent role, however, Japan may benefit by becoming actively engaged with ASEAN and ASEAN Plus Three.

For all of these reasons, Japan will need to refine its capacity to adapt rapidly to the dynamic environment of which it is a part. This poses many challenges, but also presents important opportunities for Japan to shape, as well as adjust to, the regional revolution now underway.

European Union Foreign Policy: Still an Oxymoron?[1]

James Sperling

University of Akron

The European Union (EU) is a curious actor in international politics. It is difficult to speak of an EU foreign policy, let alone trace its evolution since the founding of the European Economic Community (EEC) in 1957. To some observers, the EU is simply a clearinghouse for aligning national preferences. To others, the EU is a work in progress toward an "ever-closer union" of the European peoples. The debate over the existence and success or failure of the EU's foreign policies is linked to the larger conceptual problem of finding a place for the EU in the study of foreign policy. Unlike the other great powers discussed in this book, the EU is not a sovereign state, the traditional focus of foreign-policy analysis. Defining foreign policy as the sole prerogative of the state would deny the existence of an EU foreign policy.

It has long been clear to many that international institutions play an important role in shaping and changing state preferences over time (see Keohane 1984). While the role and importance of international institutions has not been accepted unconditionally by everyone (Waltz 2000; Mearsheimer 1994), a consensus has emerged that institutions play a significant role in the international system today. This consensus, however,

---

[1]The author would like to thank the following individuals for their comments and clarifications on portions of this chapter: David Anderson, Haruhiro Fukui, Mary Hampton, Wolfgang-Uwe Friedrich, Steven W. Hook, Michael Huelshoff, Emil Kirchner, Martin Smith, and Graham Timmins. A debt is also owed to the *Deutsch-amerikanischer Arbeitskreis* for facilitating off-the-record interviews in Bonn and Frankfurt in May 1999.

has not resolved the conceptual problem posed by the EU, which is less than a nation-state but more than an international institution. What kind of actor is it?

Unfortunately, there is not a clear-cut or definitive answer to this question. The EU falls far short of the attributes of the state since its viability depends upon the willingness of states to support it and remain contractual members. There are no powers that have been given the EU by its fifteen member-states that cannot be revoked, even if the costs far exceed the material benefits of doing so.[2] At the same time, the EU has a greater impact on the preferences and actions of its member states than do other international institutions such as the North Atlantic Treaty Organization (NATO) or the International Monetary Fund. Unlike those international institutions, the EU "commands resources, distributes benefits, allocates market shares, and adjudicates between conflicting interests" (Kirchner 1992, 28; Wallace 1982).

But treating the EU as if it were a state is also problematic. The union remains dependent upon its member states for its existence and direction, but its members will act independently of the EU when it is in their national interest to do so. This constitutes an absence of *de jure* (legal) and *de facto* (effective) sovereignty, essential elements of "stateness." Yet those who favor treating the EU as a state can point to issue areas where the EU has virtual sovereign prerogatives—international trade and monetary policy, for example. But it still remains the case that any of the EU member-states can "opt out" of the European monetary union, and EU trade policy remains the sum of national bargaining positions (Sperling and Kirchner 1997a, 143–146). Thus, the EU may best be described as a hybrid organization that pursues both its "own" collective interests in foreign affairs while also serving the national interests of its members. In this regard the adaptation of EU foreign policy to changing circumstances is doubly difficult.

This chapter is divided into five sections. The first section examines the conceptual debate that has shaped our understanding of EU foreign policy. The second section explores the foreign-policy objectives of the major EU members—Great Britain, France, and Germany. This context is helpful in understanding the EU as a foreign-policy *objective* and in coming to terms with the constraints facing the EU as a foreign-policy *actor*. The third section examines the evolution of the EU as a foreign-policy objective in two substantive issue areas: European monetary union and the search for a "common foreign and security policy." The fourth section investigates

---

[2]The current members of the EU are Austria, Belgium, Denmark, Finland, France, Germany, Greece, Ireland, Italy, Luxembourg, the Netherlands, Portugal, Spain, Sweden, and the United Kingdom.

two issue-areas that reflect the emergence of the EU as a foreign-policy actor: the eastward enlargement of the EU, and the EU's relationship with an important member of the international community, Japan. Finally, in the conclusion, we return to the central questions regarding EU foreign policy: Are there elements of identity formation present that will contribute to further development of the EU as an effective actor in international politics? Has the EU made the transition from a foreign-policy objective to a foreign-policy actor? How are we to assess the EU as a great power in world politics?

THE CONCEPTUAL TANGLE

Several theories have been developed to cope with the conceptual problem posed by the EU. The first and most influential approach to the problem was *neofunctionalism*, which was based upon the simple but important insight that regional cooperation in one area would likely lead to "spillover" effects that would require cooperation in other areas (Haas 1964; Lindberg 1963). The stalling of the regional integration process, particularly during the 1970s and early 1980s, led scholars such as Robert Keohane and Stanley Hoffmann (1991, 18–25) to amend neofunctionalism. They argued that spillover only occurs when previous bargaining between states is "successful" for all the participants, when the external environment compels or encourages states to pool their sovereignty to achieve common objectives, or when there is a convergence of national preferences. This variant of neofunctionalism reinforces the continued importance of the nation-state as we approach the problem of understanding the foreign policy of the EU.

A second body of theory relies upon state preferences to understand the founding and evolution of European integration since 1945. Its adherents adopt a straightforward approach that focuses on the Franco–German relationship. In this view, tensions between France and Germany that vexed European politics since at least the Napoleonic Wars were a major barrier to regional cooperation after World War II. The initial postwar settlement, which hindered Franco–German cooperation, transferred the Saar region of Germany to France and left the Ruhr under international control. German sovereignty over the Ruhr was partially restored in 1951 with the Treaty of Paris that established the European Coal and Steel Community (ECSC). The ECSC, which created a supranational governance structure controlling the coal and steel production of its six member-states, was the first step in tempering Franco–German enmity. Importantly, the ECSC also provided the basis for the political and economic recovery of Western Europe. The founding of the EEC in

1957 is likewise attributed to the economic and political self-interests of the Western European states rather than to the logic of spillover. From this conceptual vantage point, the origins of the EEC and its subsequent emergence as a foreign-policy actor are best explained by reference to the national interests of its member-states (see Moravcsik 1993; Milward 1992; and Hanrieder 1989).

A third body of literature assumes that there is an interaction between the preferences of states and the preferences of the EU. Robert Putnam (1988) argues that there are at least two bargaining "games" that are played in the formulation of foreign policy: the domestic game, which defines the set of domestically viable policy preferences; and the international game, which identifies those national policy preferences compatible with the external environment. This approach has been fruitfully employed to understand the interplay between state preferences and the constraints imposed on the state by the EU (see Huelshoff 1994). While this approach provides a gateway to understanding the bargaining that goes on between the members of the EU and the role that the EU plays as an actor in bargaining negotiations, it still does not tell us to what extent the EU qualifies as an independent foreign-policy actor.

This chapter adopts a largely state-centric approach to understanding EU foreign policy. As will become clear, the foreign-policy activities of the European Economic Community (EEC) and its successor, the European Community (EC), were severely constrained by conflicting national interests and the member-states' desire to retain their prerogatives in the area of foreign policy. The creation and expanding roles of the EEC and EC were, in this respect, important elements of the members' foreign-policy agendas. In the area of foreign policy, the EEC and EC functioned at best as a clearinghouse for reconciling the national preferences of their major members, particularly France, Germany, and the United Kingdom. Since the transformation of the EC into the EU under the 1991 Maastricht Treaty on European Union, the EU was granted only a limited ability to initiate foreign policies independent of the interests of its member-states. Foreign policy thus remained, in an important sense, a key *objective* of the EU's members.

These limitations on the EU's autonomy in foreign policy, however, were relaxed in response to the profound changes in the international system after the Cold War. During the Soviet–U.S. competition for dominance over the European continent, progress toward a more politically cohesive and economically integrated Western Europe reinforced the U.S. position. The Western Europeans (with the possible exception of France) had no option other than a sophisticated obsequiousness to U.S. foreign-policy preferences. After the Soviet Union dissolved in December 1991, Europe was pushed to seek an independent foreign policy, for three primary reasons. First, Europe now had the option of pursuing an independent foreign policy less tainted by U.S. interests. Second, the absence of a common threat brought to the surface conflicts of interest between Europe and the United States that had been suppressed during the Cold War. Third, the deepening of a "European identity" increasingly conflicted with the "trans-Atlantic identity" fostered by the United States since 1945. The altered international system thus removed an important barrier to an independent EU foreign policy and provided greater incentives to craft a truly *European* foreign policy.

Two individuals personified the EU's "arrival" as a foreign-policy actor during this crucial period of transition. Jacques Delors, the past president of the European Commission, worked vigorously to deepen the organization's foreign-policy role through the Maastricht Treaty, his primary accomplishment. This momentum was further symbolized in October 1999 by the naming of Javier Solana, the former Secretary General of NATO, as the first "high representative" for the EU's common foreign and security policy. Through this latter move, Europe finally answered Henry Kissinger's famous lament in the 1970s that Europe had no foreign-policy "address."

BRITISH, FRENCH, AND GERMAN FOREIGN POLICY

The end of the Cold War freed Europe from the constraints of the bipolar competition. The EU became the focal point for those who saw the end of the Cold War as an opportunity to make good on the promise of an "ever-closer union" of the European peoples. For others, the EU became a mechanism for creating a third pole of power in the international system that could finally withstand U.S. foreign-policy pressures in Europe. And for still others, the EU became the only institution capable of reining in Germany, which was reunified in 1990 after being divided for nearly half a century along Cold War lines. These diverse motivations forced Great Britain, France, and Germany to craft new strategies to cope with the opportunities offered by the new geostrategic context. The convergence and divergence of their foreign-policy agendas will largely define the role the EU eventually assumes.[3]

---

[3]Our discussion is restricted to these countries for several reasons. First, no progress toward the grand objective of political union, or even the more modest objective of a common foreign policy, is likely without their active involvement. Second, analysis of the central themes in this chapter would not be strengthened by adding other countries. Finally, the foreign-policy agendas of these three countries span the spectrum of ambitions held for the EU by its member-states. For a broader perspective of the foreign policies of all three countries through the end of the Cold War, see Macridis (1992).

GREAT BRITAIN'S QUEST FOR REGIONAL BALANCE

The initial British response to the Soviet Union's collapse was cautious and conservative. The newly formed Russian Federation was assumed to pose the primary threat to British security. There was a related concern that a potential threat to European stability arose from the inability to integrate the western, central, and eastern portions of the European continent. In London's view, the independence and integrity of these countries were essential elements of the British national interest. Threats to the central and eastern European states had two sources: internal disorder and external pressure from Russia. Of the major EU states, Great Britain was perhaps the most skeptical of Russian intentions in Central and Eastern Europe and the most preoccupied with the Russian ability to upset the European balance.

The British fought what proved to be a rearguard action, not only against its major partners in the EU but against the United States as well. The conservative governments of Margaret Thatcher and John Major were reluctant participants in any effort to strengthen a European defense identity (Croft 1991). For prime ministers Thatcher and Major, British security interests suggested a strategy similar to that adopted during the Cold War: The United Kingdom should play a decisive security role within Europe and in the wider world, but only in tandem with the United States. In this respect, the British eagerly sought to sustain the link between European and U.S. security. Until the late 1990s, the British attitude toward NATO remained largely unchanged: NATO primacy and the Anglo–American connection were the paramount objectives of British foreign policy.

Until the New Labour government of Tony Blair arrived in 1997, British support for a European defense identity reflected the narrow objectives of preventing U.S. withdrawal from Europe due to corrosive burden-sharing debates, and of extending British influence over the security policies of its major European allies, particularly France and Germany. This preference reflected Britain's ability to project military power and its privileged position within the Western alliance system, which in turn were by-products of German political disabilities, France's preoccupation with its autonomy in foreign affairs, and Britain's special relationship with the United States. Any change in a NATO-dominated security order would, from the British perspective, erode the country's privileged position and weaken British influence in areas not directly related to security (Hutton 1992, 619–632). Consequently, a common EU foreign policy would necessarily reduce British visibility and influence.

Great Britain, like France, reserved the right of sovereign control over its defense policies. Nonetheless, London also recognized that British policy would be increasingly shaped within a multilateral context. From that perspective there was considerable common ground among France,

Germany, and Great Britain. Many of the differences on the future institutional shape of a common European foreign policy that existed between Paris and London were resolved at the Anglo–French Saint Malo summit in 1998. However, the British still clung to a starker institutional hierarchy than France and Germany and believed NATO remained the core security institution for Europe. In comparison with their European partners, British leaders adopted a different stance toward the roles and aspirations of subordinate security institutions such as the Organization for Security Cooperation in Europe (OSCE). Their primary goal was not to create a mechanism for "escaping" U.S. influence, but to strengthen and deepen the U.S. commitment to Europe, or to allow the Europeans limited autonomy when Washington chose not to act.

British leaders today are loathe to entertain any architectural design that appears to diminish the primacy of NATO or threatens a looser connection between the United States and Europe. A continued dependence upon NATO reflects both political and military calculations. The political dimension reflects the disproportionate influence wielded by the British on security matters within NATO. This influence is derived from London's contribution to NATO, its status as the only other nuclear power within the integrated military command, and its privileged relationship with the United States for most of the postwar period. With this influence, British leaders have been able to counter French pretensions to European leadership and offset the clear economic advantages possessed by Germany (Coker 1992, 407–421). The enduring preference for NATO embodies the British calculation that only U.S. power can thwart the hegemonic designs of any continental European power, a long-standing British concern.

British leaders acknowledge that some European autonomy from the United States is desirable, but they want to ensure that the trans-Atlantic security order is not a casualty of European autonomy. The Major government recognized that the development of an independent European capability *within* NATO was essential if an autonomous European security actor *outside* of NATO were to be avoided. The British concern, once again, was to prevent the loss of British influence vis-à-vis France or Germany, and more importantly, to forestall a premature abdication of U.S. responsibility for European stability and balance. The Maastricht Treaty of 1991 committed the EU to a common foreign and security policy that "might in time lead to a common defense." The conditional "might" in the Maastricht language reflected the British preference to leave open the question of a centralized European defense system. The language in the Amsterdam Treaty of 1997, however, removed any doubts that the EU was moving in that direction. Until the Anglo–French meeting at Saint Malo in 1998, the British insisted that the Western Europe Union (WEU), the designated defense arm of the EU, retain its intergovernmental (rather than supranational) character and remain subordinate to NATO.[4]

The NATO alliance, therefore, remains the centerpiece of British security policy. It not only provides the best guarantee of British security, but also offers an alternative to a Franco–German dominated Europe. The British still function within a security universe dominated not only by the two world wars, but also by a traditional statecraft designed to ensure a balance on the European continent. It is clear that Britain can no longer play the role of balancer in Europe. It is equally clear that the United States can play such a role, but is not inclined to continue doing so. Consequently, British efforts have been directed at guaranteeing the U.S. commitment to the European balance, meeting U.S. demands for the creation of a stronger European "pillar" of the alliance, and ensuring that the European pillar remains constrained by and subordinated to NATO.

FRANCE'S QUEST FOR AUTONOMY

The parochial language of *national interest* remains the dominant idiom of French foreign policy. Yet the Cold War's collapse has altered not only the content of French interests, but enhanced France's weight in the European and global balances of power. While French leaders today acknowledge a new security agenda, they share the British view that the primary threat to European stability rests with the Russian Federation.

French security policy has three interlocking elements. The first seeks the development of a credible European security identity. The second element seeks a continuation of the trans-Atlantic link to assure a long-term U.S. commitment to Europe. The third element seeks Russia's inclusion in a comprehensive European security order. Paris wishes to avoid the revival of antagonistic military blocs that would divide Europe anew and throw the Western Europeans once again upon the mercies of the U.S. security guarantee.

France anticipates the development of a European security identity within the EU that gives political substance to the EU's common foreign and security policy. Until the late 1990s, Paris relied upon a Franco–German axis to achieve that objective. Once the Anglo–French agreement at Saint Malo broke the institutional impasse on the relationship between EU and the WEU, Paris could look to London rather than Berlin on security matters.

---

[4]Under an *intergovernmental* framework, national governments retain a decisive role in decision making. By contrast, a *supranational* framework shifts such authority toward a centralized body that could override the preferences of national governments.

A closer Anglo–French relationship may provide the foundation for the eventual creation of an independent European nuclear deterrent that would be an essential component of a truly autonomous Europe. Thus, the European dimension of French security policy combines the old and the new: The French still presume a leadership role in shaping a European security identity, and the EU will fashion a common European security policy (Moïsi and Mertes 1995, 132–133).

The French preference for a European security identity reflects an abiding concern with German power in Europe, but also a perceived gap between the EU's competence in economic and security policy, respectively. Security policies remain located in national ministries of defense, while economic policy is increasingly made by the EU. For France, the interdependence of economic and security policies suggests the need for a strong EU role in both policy areas if the policies are to be compatible.

France has actively participated in the reshaping of NATO. Toward that end, France nearly reconciled itself to the integrated military command of the alliance but balked when the United States refused to grant France a regional NATO command. The French acknowledge that NATO has emerged as the most important security institution of post–Cold War Europe. Paradoxically, NATO remains the guarantor of France's ambitions in Europe despite its role as the mechanism legitimizing U.S. hegemony in Europe. An autonomous Europe depends upon the long-term health of NATO, which provides a forum in which Europe and the United States can fashion a common security policy jointly and as equals. But the French have not abandoned the position that the long-term viability of NATO requires an equal Europe acting in concert with the United States.

The French security architecture places the EU at the center of a French-led European security order. The EU is to forge the primary connection between the Western, Central, and Eastern Europeans. A WEU incorporated into the EU would provide the basis for a European defense identity. While the French have been unable to prevent the continuing dominance of NATO and the United States on security affairs, France has finally convinced participants on both sides of the Atlantic Ocean that European autonomy on security affairs is in the interest of all concerned.

GERMANY'S QUEST FOR STABILITY

The content and direction of German security policy during most of the Cold War was largely dictated by the Federal Republic's membership in NATO, its dependence upon the U.S. security guarantee, its desire to contain Soviet power in Europe, and its membership in the EEC/EC. The preoccupation with guaranteeing Germany's territorial integrity has largely evaporated thanks to unification in 1990 and the dissolution of the Warsaw Pact. The Germans have refined and broadened their concept of security to exploit the opportunities offered by the evolution of the European state system. Today, German security is threatened not by an invasion of the Russian army, but by the challenges of the new security agenda: controlling the flow of unwanted refugees, threats to the economy emanating from outside its borders, drug trafficking, environment decay, and pandemics of untreatable and deadly diseases.

This redefinition of German security interests reflects a redefinition of the German state. Germans have embraced the notion that Germany must play the role of a *civilian* power in Europe since the role of *military* power has been proscribed by history, conscience, treaty, self-interest, and, until recently, constitutional interpretation (Maull 1990/1991). The Germans thus remain hesitant contributors to the military requirements of regional and global stability. Instead, Berlin has played a leading role in financing the political and economic reconstruction of Eastern Europe and has championed the eastward expansion of the EU and NATO. Until the Kosovo crisis in 1999, which required troop deployments by several NATO members and later by the Europe-based OSCE, Germany was satisfied to contribute primarily to the economic requirements of security.

Germany, the key continental European partner of the United States in NATO, faced a choice in the procurement of its security after 1989. Whereas NATO had the character of a compulsory alliance during the Cold War—the Germans had little choice but to support NATO in exchange for a place under the U.S. nuclear "umbrella"—the collapse of the Warsaw Pact had the unsettling effect of providing Germany with choice. While it appeared in the early 1990s that NATO faced a longer-term challenge from the OSCE as the core security institution of the future, institutional innovations within NATO and political uncertainty in Russia ensured that NATO would remain at the center of German security calculations. The alliance remains attractive to German leaders for several reasons. First, NATO stabilizes the periphery of western Europe. Second, NATO provides an institutional mechanism for integrating all the countries of Europe into a single European security order. Third, the changes in NATO strategy promise a more secure Germany with a greatly diminished exposure to nuclear war. Finally, NATO serves as a hedge against neoisolationism in the United States and the "renationalization" of European defense policies.

The German foreign-policy agenda has five objectives: (1) to create a pan-European security structure that integrates Germany into Europe as an equal, if not a leading, state; (2) to accelerate the demilitarization of Europe in order to create an environment favoring German economic interests; (3) to retain the U.S. presence in Europe as insurance against the failure of a demilitarized pan-European security structure; (4) to ensure the full participation of the Russian Federation in the institutions of the European security order; and (5) to convince Germany's neighbors that it has renounced any hegemonic ambitions in Europe.

The German preoccupation with the institutional configuration of the post–Cold War security order reflects two lessons of history. The first is that peace and stability in Europe are only possible if Germany is closely tied to its neighbors in a manner that benefits each reciprocally. The second lesson is that NATO provided Germany and the other European democracies with the longest period of peace and prosperity in their modern history. Germany has sought to strike an implicit bargain with its European partners similar in design to the post-war bargain that restored German sovereignty in the 1950s. The most influential state in Europe by virtue of geography, demography, economic capacity, and potential military power has offered to enmesh itself more tightly within the EU and NATO. In exchange, Germany seeks the right to lead Europe on economic affairs and to set the framework conditions of the post–Cold War European economy. This bargain yields tangible economic returns to the Germans while the Europeans are left with the intangible gain of resolving the "German problem" through the full and irreversible integration of a Germany satisfied with the status quo in Europe anchored by the EU.

THE FOREIGN-POLICY STRATEGIES COMPARED

The foreign policies of Great Britain, France, and Germany with regard to European security exhibit elements of convergence and divergence. The key dimensions of comparison are the definition of threat, the roles of NATO and EU in the European security order, and the relationships between those institutions. The French and British still consider the prospect of a revived Russia as the explicit and primary threat to the European security order. The importance of the transition process in Central and Eastern Europe explains the priority Berlin has placed on the economic requirements of security. While successive German governments have been aware of the military threat that Russia could pose to German security, they have sought to construct a new partnership that would bind Russia as closely to Europe as Germany was bound to Western Europe after World War II.

A second divergence reflects different assessments of the geographic source and reach of security threats. The British have been content with an Atlantic conception of security. The French are as concerned with the Mediterranean Sea region as they are with Central and Eastern Europe. For their part, the Germans are preoccupied with the evolution of the European system beyond their eastern border. These geographic orientations do not generate irreconcilable differences of interest, but they do lead to different reactions to the same security threat. The absence of an immediate threat, which the Soviet Union once posed, and a creeping parochialism in foreign-policy calculations, may yet discourage them from cooperating even when common interests are clearly at stake.

None of the major European powers is yet willing to abandon NATO. Britain, reading off the Atlanticist script, prefers a perpetuation of NATO predominance and is comfortable with continued U.S. dominance of the alliance. The British, however, have overcome their skepticism that an autonomous European defense capability is inherently incompatible with U.S. leadership in NATO, or with NATO dominance in the European security system. They now accept the proposition that an independent European security identity would enable the Europeans to act in concert with the United States and that NATO can become the forum for reconciling the security interests of the United States and Europe. France, meanwhile, has become more accepting of NATO so long as it does not preclude other security arrangements based in Europe, and Germany remains committed to NATO for the reasons outlined earlier.

The points of convergence and divergence between these states must not obscure the extraordinary level of security cooperation that has existed since 1989. The Pact on European Stability, for example, established a network of bilateral treaties and multilateral programs connecting the EU and the states of Central and Eastern Europe. The pact has contributed to greater cooperation in economic areas, to the creation of a common sense of destiny, and to the identification of common interests. Likewise, the EU-sponsored Stability Pact for Southeastern Europe has emerged as an exemplar of security cooperation in Europe and has demonstrated Europe's ability to act constructively and in common.

THE EU AS A FOREIGN-POLICY "OBJECTIVE"

Upon its inception, the EEC served first and foremost the national interests of its member-states. The community in this respect was a foreign-policy *objective* of the six founding states: France, Germany, Italy, and the three "Benelux" countries (Belgium, the Netherlands, and Luxembourg). Each viewed European integration as a mechanism for resolving common problems, exploiting the gains to be achieved by an integrated market, and overcoming the chronic problem posed by Germany for European peace and stability. Cooperative ventures in two issue areas—the pursuit of European monetary union and a common foreign and security policy—illustrate the continuing role that today's EU plays as a foreign-policy objective of its member states.

CREATING A EUROPEAN MONETARY UNION

The driving force behind European integration has been the economic self-interests of its members. European leaders understood that by forming a more integrated internal market, Europe could rise from the ashes of World

War II, rebuild its political and social institutions, and compete against the United States in world markets. Furthermore, an integrated economic bloc would render the European states politically dependent upon each other, a development that could only contribute to peace and stability. The progress toward European monetary union (EMU) is thus central to the evolution of a politically and economically integrated Europe. Every step toward monetary union promoted greater balance in the U.S.–European relationship, helped establish a European financial center capable of competing with New York, and enhanced European autonomy in the dollar-dominated international monetary system.

Monetary cooperation in Europe long preceded the Treaty of Rome in 1957. The European Payments Union, established in 1950, facilitated the coordination of trade and payments within Europe. Monetary cooperation intensified after 1957 with the establishment of the Committee of Central Bank Governors to monitor financial and monetary developments. More than a decade later, the more ambitious goal of monetary union was placed on the EEC agenda at the Hague Summit in 1969.

The initial rationale for European monetary union reflected a number of concerns, including the desire to move toward political union. While this objective remained a rhetorical constant, two other concerns drove the efforts to find some alternative to the dollar-dominated Bretton Woods system.[5] The most immediate concern was the threat that monetary instability in the late 1960s posed to Franco–German relations. Monetary instability threatened the Franco–German bargain, making the EEC possible in the first place: In exchange for the unimpeded access of German industrial goods, Germany agreed to the closure of the European agricultural market to the outside world and to the opening of the German market to French agricultural goods. Monetary instability could nullify the Franco–German bargain by undermining the only "common" policy that the EEC possessed at that time, namely the highly protectionist agricultural price-support system of the common agricultural policy (CAP).

The responsibilities for adjustment within Europe represented the second facet of the Franco–German monetary wrangle. The chronic balance of trade surpluses enjoyed by Germany since the early 1950s placed unrelenting upward pressure on the value of the Deutsche mark vis-à-vis the U.S. dollar and the currency of its most important trading partner, France. The German central bank, the Deutsche Bundesbank, was dedicated to an anti-inflationary policy which, in its view, largely accounted for the postwar "economic miracle." Moreover, German leaders believed that

---

[5]Under the Bretton Woods monetary system, which was created by U.S. and British negotiators in 1944, exchange rates had a fixed value against the U.S. dollar. The dollar, in turn, was fixed to the value of gold.

the chronic payments deficits plaguing France and the United States reflected their lack of fiscal and monetary discipline. This assertiveness in German monetary diplomacy became a centerpiece of German foreign policy and remains in evidence today.

Despite the currency competition between Germany and France, it was clear to both that the Bretton Woods system was responsible for the currency crises that occurred after 1958. Until then, there was a dollar "shortage" because all trade was settled in dollars. After 1958, the convertibility of European currencies transformed the dollar shortage into a dollar *glut*. Europe could only force the United States to restore an equilibrium between the supply of and demand for dollars with the highly disruptive policy of redeeming U.S. dollars for gold. France availed itself of that policy, in part to strengthen its own reserves and in part to serve French President Charles de Gaulle's larger objective of freeing Europe from U.S. domination (see Calleo and Rowland 1973). The French policy had two consequences. First, it disrupted the international monetary system without correcting the problem. Second, the United States forced Germany to hold dollars in exchange for the U.S. security guarantee. The Johnson administration only made things worse when it decided to pay for the Great Society programs and the war in Vietnam with deficit spending rather than taxation. European monetary union was one way of escaping dollar dominance.

The quarrel over monetary matters was rendered moot by the disturbances of the early 1970s that included the closing of the U.S. gold "window" in August 1971 and the resulting "float" of the dollar in currency exchange markets. During this period of monetary instability, the Europeans maintained relatively fixed rates of exchange between their currencies. The oil crisis in October 1973 made European monetary cooperation more important, but such cooperation also became less likely due to the clashing economic strategies adopted by the European states, particularly France and Germany, in response to spiraling oil prices.

Weak U.S. leadership and the "benign neglect" of the dollar prompted the reconciliation of the French and German positions on European monetary cooperation. While EC Commission President Roy Jenkins proposed the creation of a European Monetary System (EMS) in 1977, French President Valery Giscard d'Estaing and German Chancellor Helmut Schmidt together exploited the post-Nixon leadership *malaise* that made progress toward EMS possible. The formal decision to create the EMS in 1978 at the Bremen Summit represented a Franco–German declaration of monetary independence from the United States and the dollar. The EMS, which began operation in 1979, had the initial objective of creating a "zone of monetary stability" in Europe. In addition to exchange-rate stability among the European currencies, the EMS established the economic foundations for European monetary union.

Three important developments took place during the 1980s that laid the political foundation for monetary union. First, European leaders agreed that anti-inflationary economic policies were the best means of ensuring long-term economic growth and low unemployment. Second, the European governments committed themselves to stable exchange rates in Europe and macroeconomic policies consistent with that objective. Third, the political independence of central banks became accepted as "best institutional practice" in the management of national currencies (Ungerer et. al. 1990; Deutsche Bundesbank 1989, 30).

The Maastricht Treaty gave constitutional status to European monetary union. The agreement by the participating governments to abandon a key element of sovereignty—the national control of currencies—reflected an understanding that the single European market had to be promoted through monetary integration. Such cooperation offered a number of economic benefits. It reduced the currency transaction costs of trade among EU states and promised not only an inflation-averse European economy managed by a politically independent European central bank, but also a more fiscally conservative EU. Further, creating a "zone of monetary stability" would perform the double task of insulating the European economy from external economic shocks while providing Europe the ability to negotiate as an equal with Japan and the United States. The political rationale for monetary union flowed from the overarching objective of an "ever-greater union" among the European states—the pooling of monetary sovereignty would, in principle, complement the pooling of sovereignty in general. A final rationale for monetary union was the fear that a unified Germany, untethered to the EU by monetary union, could emerge as an unconstrained and dominant European power.

Despite the attractions of monetary union, Europeans were in varying degrees wary of Maastricht. The psychological importance of the national currency as a source or symbol of national identity is deeply rooted. Most Germans, for example, were uneasy with the prospect of bidding farewell to either the mark or the Bundesbank. Likewise, the British and Danes were unwilling to abandon their national currencies or the symbolic sovereignty invested in them. For the Danes, the unwillingness to abandon the kroner reflected a desire to underline their cultural and political independence from Germany. For the British, the surrender of the pound sterling would signify, perhaps, a psychologically unacceptable abandonment of sovereignty and acknowledgment of Britain's postwar decline. The EMU participants, particularly those in Northern Europe, gained more than they lost from monetary union: With the creation of an independent European central bank, their loss of nominal sovereignty would be compensated by effective participation in the making of European monetary policy.

The Maastricht Treaty specified five "convergence criteria" for membership in monetary union. First, national inflation rates must be within

1.5 percent of the average of the three EU states with the lowest rates of inflation. Second, long-term interest rates must be within 2 percent of the three-country average. Third, national budget deficits cannot exceed 3 percent of gross domestic product (GDP). Fourth, total public debt cannot exceed 60 percent of GDP. Finally, national currencies must be free from realignment within the European Monetary System for two years.

Remarkable progress was made by the applicants in lowering inflation rates.[6] Their progress in fiscal policy, however, was not as notable. Unlike monetary policy, the Maastricht Treaty did not provide a mechanism for the coordination of fiscal policies (Masson and Taylor 1993). The fiscal criteria, which involved taxing and spending by national governments, appeared to create an insurmountable barrier to monetary union. Only Austria and Germany had budget deficits under the 3-percent ceiling shortly after signing the Maastricht Treaty. Whether by threat, conviction, or fear of being left behind, the majority of EU states were able to sneak under the 3-percent standard by 1999, even though it took a little bit of creative accounting to do so. But only five countries (Austria, Finland, France, Luxembourg, and Portugal) that eventually participated in EMU reduced their central government debt to the level specified in the treaty (European Central Bank 1999, 35). Even Germany, which had insisted upon including this criterion, failed to meet it, an unanticipated consequence of national unification. While Germany initially insisted on a strict interpretation of Maastricht, its own budgetary problem required a more elastic reading of the treaty.

This reading of the treaty made possible the transition to the third stage of EMU and the introduction of the *euro* as the system-wide currency. All the EU countries except Denmark, Great Britain, Greece, and Sweden joined in 1999. Due to its economic problems, Greece did not initially qualify for EMU membership, and the other three states did not express a keen desire to join immediately. The prospects for British entry improved, however, in June 2001, with the lopsided victory of Blair's Labour Party in national elections.

Several factors made this historic pooling of monetary authority possible. These factors included France's need to tether a unified Germany to the EU, Germany's desire to ease French fears of German economic and political dominance, a shared interest in creating a "zone of monetary stability" in Europe, and the desire for a currency that could compete with the

---

[6]While only four EU states (Belgium, Germany, Ireland, and the Netherlands) met the inflation criterion prior to Maastricht, thirteen qualified in 1999. There was also a significant narrowing of the gap between the countries with the highest and lowest levels of inflation. Overall, the rate of inflation in "Euroland" fell from 5.6 percent in 1990 to 1.1 percent in 1998 and 1999 (Deutsche Bundesbank 1989, 30; European Central Bank 1999, 29).

U.S. dollar and Japanese yen on international markets. The apparent irreversibility of monetary union represented an important surrender of national sovereignty that made the logic of political union all the more compelling. While political union probably remains a long way off, monetary union compelled the Europeans to think more seriously about a common foreign and security policy as well. It is to this vital area that we now turn our attention.

PURSUING A COMMON FOREIGN AND SECURITY POLICY

As noted earlier, the Maastricht Treaty provided a constitutional basis for a "common foreign and security policy" (CFSP). Two previous attempts to do this failed, and a third effort was largely ineffectual. The first attempt was the French-inspired European Defense Community (EDC), which was established with the Paris Treaty of 1952 and signed by the six members of the coal and steel community. The EDC not only proposed the creation of a European army, but required complementary supranational political institutions. Its call for a European "executive" accountable to a directly elected European Parliament proved too ambitious and was the EDC's undoing.

The EDC reflected not only the federalist aspirations of leading European politicians but strong U.S. pressure for an acceptable solution to the problem of German rearmament. The United States considered this essential due to the twin outbreaks of the Cold War in Europe and the Korean War in Asia. The failure of the EDC led U.S. Secretary of State John Foster Dulles to undertake an "agonizing reappraisal" of the U.S. role in Europe. European fears that the United States might abandon Europe led to the creation of the Western European Union (WEU), an institution that facilitated German rearmament and its eventual membership in NATO. Thus the initial failure of a supranational approach to the problem of defense cooperation was followed by a more modest approach that left a core element of sovereignty largely untouched.

French leaders were also behind the second attempt to craft a common European foreign and security policy. Their proposals represented de Gaulle's "twin challenge to American hegemony and to the supranational pretensions" of the EEC (Forster and Wallace 1996, 413). While the proposals did not move toward a supranational solution to the problem of European weakness vis-à-vis the United States (or the Soviet Union), they did raise important questions: What institutional form should foreign-policy cooperation take? Where should the secretariat, or central office, be located within the organization? What type of defense role should the organization seek? What relationship should it have with NATO? While de Gaulle asked the right questions, answers have only been forthcoming since the 1990s.

The rudiments of foreign-policy cooperation emerged at the Hague Summit of 1969. At that time, the Europeans recognized political cooperation in security policy as an important step toward reconciling their growing economic power with their relative inability to shape their common strategic and diplomatic destinies. The creation of the negotiating framework known as European Political Cooperation in 1970 began the transition to a common EEC foreign policy within an intergovernmental framework. The 1970s, however, proved unkind to this third effort to build the foundations of a common foreign policy. Europe was unable to maintain even the semblance of unity in response to the oil crisis in 1973–1974, which revealed conflicts of interest that were not easily papered over.

European interests were again threatened as Soviet–U.S. antagonisms intensified in the early 1980s. Again, Europe sought to reconcile its relative economic power with its relative diplomatic weakness. The major initiative during this period was the Colombo-Genscher proposal, which called for "the coordination of security policy and the adoption of common European positions in this sphere" (Nuttal 1992, 186). While this proposal failed to gain acceptance, the commitment to foreign-policy cooperation was incorporated into the 1986 Single European Act. A legal basis for European foreign-policy cooperation was thus established and became the second "pillar" of the 1991 Maastricht Treaty on European Union.[7] The treaty committed the EU states to "safeguard the common values, fundamental interests and independence of the Union; to strengthen the security of the Union and its Member States in all ways; to preserve peace and strengthen international security, in accordance with the principles of the United Nations Charter as well as the principles of the Helsinki Final Act and the objectives of the Paris Charter; to promote international cooperation; to develop and consolidate democracy and the rule of law, and respect for human rights and fundamental freedoms." Article B of the Treaty expressed the desire that the EU "assert its identity on the international scene, in particular through the implementation of a common foreign and security policy including the eventual framing of a common defense policy, which might in time lead to a common defense."[8]

While the treaty specified five broad objectives for the common foreign policy, the process remained strictly intergovernmental rather than supranational, meaning that the national governments retained a strong role in the process.[9] Another significant innovation occurred under the

---

[7]The Maastricht Treaty included three "pillars" to accommodate the different demands and levels of integration found in the earlier treaties. These pillars included monetary union, common foreign and security policy, and justice and home affairs.

[8]The full text of the treaty can be found by consulting the EU's official Web site (www.europa.eu.int).

[9]This lack of centralized authority was partially remedied in the 1997 Amsterdam Treaty.

Maastricht accord, which described the WEU as "an integral part of the development of the Union." Nonetheless, the treaty maintained an arm's-length distance between the WEU and the EU in deference to the Anglo–Dutch desire to sustain the primacy of NATO and to prevent the "denationalization" of defense policies.

Maastricht spurred the WEU to reclaim a meaningful defense role for itself. At the June 1992 summit, the WEU reserved for itself a set of limited security tasks, the so-called "Petersberg tasks," which included peace-keeping, humanitarian intervention, rescue tasks, crisis-management, and conflict prevention. Around the same time, NATO embraced the European Security and Defense Identity (ESDI) and the Combined Joint Task Force (CJTF) programs. The former was an alliance effort to complement the EU's mandate to create a common foreign and security policy. The latter promised Europeans access to NATO military assets in cases where the United States chose not to act. Both programs temporarily transformed the WEU into a "hinge" institution linking NATO and the EU, and they served the interests of both the EU states and the United States (Kirchner 1999). For the Europeans, the new programs promised greater autonomy in defense that would lend credibility to CFSP. For the United States, the programs encouraged the Europeans to assume a greater share of the responsibility for low-intensity conflict and crisis-management in Europe without direct U.S. participation. Moreover, the two programs linked NATO to the EU via the WEU and thereby removed the need for an autonomous European security program *outside* NATO.

The Amsterdam Treaty continued this momentum. Indeed, the language of the treaty put the EU "only one step away from a mutual-defense guarantee" (Cameron 1999, 70). Amsterdam also moved the EU away from strict intergovernmentalism; the EU states agreed that while "common strategies" would be adopted unanimously, they would be implemented via "common positions" and "joint actions" that would be adopted by qualified majority voting (see Missiroli 2000). The cumulative effect of these changes may be the progressive pooling of a core element of sovereignty and the emergence of a common foreign policy worthy of the name.

The Amsterdam Treaty also introduced three substantial changes in the relationship between the WEU and the EU. First, the treaty acknowledged that the EU would one day have a common defense policy. Second, the treaty incorporated the Petersberg tasks of the WEU into the legal framework of the EU. Third, the WEU emerged as the clear institutional address of any EU defense ambition. Yet the full integration of the WEU into the EU was blocked by the different foreign-policy aspirations of Britain and France. The impasse was finally overcome at the Anglo–French meeting at Saint Malo in December 1998, where the two countries agreed on the future shape and purpose of a common European security policy. The British accepted that the EU "must have the capacity for autonomous action, backed up by credible military forces, the means to decide to use them, and a readiness to do so in order to respond to international crises." The subsequent European Council Declaration at Cologne in June 1999 settled the question more clearly: The WEU would eventually be subordinated to and subsumed by the EU. The French and British met again in November and agreed that the EU required an "autonomous capacity to make decisions" and the EU should be able to deploy between 50,000 and 60,000 troops for crisis-management tasks. These recommendations were endorsed by the European Council in December.

Through this long and tortuous process, the Europeans have met the U.S. challenge to assume greater responsibility within Europe. In so doing, they have established a new division of labor within NATO. Europe is now responsible for the Petersberg tasks, while the United States and NATO are responsible for the traditional task of territorial defense. The WEU is no longer the "hinge" institution mediating the relationship between NATO and an EU with foreign and defense policy ambitions, a development underlined at the December 2000 Nice Summit. Instead, the EU and NATO are now direct partners. Rather than talking of a European defense "identity" within NATO, the focus will increasingly shift to the creation of a European defense policy compatible with NATO. All of this promises a changed balance of power within NATO and may herald the beginning of EU defense autonomy, with uncertain consequences for the trans-Atlantic relationship.

THE EU AS A FOREIGN-POLICY "ACTOR"

The changed European context after the dissolution of the Soviet Union in 1991 provided both an opportunity and incentive for a common EU foreign policy. While the origins and scope of EU foreign policy are rarely independent of its member-states' interests, the European Commission (the executive arm of the EU) has had some latitude in shaping the *content* of EU policy. In those cases where there are high costs attached to independent national policies, the EU can emerge as a viable actor with its "own" foreign policy. On occasion, the EU has acted with a clearly defined agenda detached from the specific interests of its members.

Beyond the institutional refinements, however, the EU's experience during the 1990s in regional conflicts did not provide reassurance that the union would soon emerge as an effective foreign-policy actor. National interests continued to prevail over collective interests in these cases of armed conflict outside the EU's immediate territory. For example, the EU played virtually no role in the Persian Gulf crisis of 1990–1991, which followed Iraq's invasion of Kuwait. The German government wrote a check to cover U.S. expenses incurred during Operation Desert Storm and later demanded a rebate. France, Great Britain, and the other European states, meanwhile, contributed troops under national flags rather than as part of a joint contingent.

A second and even more direct challenge to the EU's capacity as a foreign-policy actor involved the dissolution of Yugoslavia in the early 1990s. While the EU was able to hammer out a compromise that acknowledged the secessions of Slovenia and Croatia from Yugoslavia, Germany preempted the EU by recognizing the countries unilaterally and ahead of schedule. Subsequently, the NATO-led interventions in Bosnia (1995) and Kosovo (1999) revealed the EU's inability to manage European security either within or outside the EU. In both cases, U.S. leadership and *matériel* rather than EU declarations ended the ethnic bloodlettings in the Balkans.[10]

These failures, however, should not obscure the EU's growing stature as an independent foreign-policy actor. The EU has played an increasingly meaningful and independent role in world political and economic affairs. The eastward enlargement of the EU illustrates a case where the Commission has provided the content of the EU's policy toward central and eastern Europe. The EU's bilateral relationship with Japan illustrates a case in which the member-states have been satisfied to allow the EU to find areas of common interest between two of the most important economic powers in the international system. Both cases are detailed in the following sections.

ENLARGING THE EUROPEAN UNION

Enlargement—or expansion of membership—has been a crucial and perennial foreign-policy issue since the founding of the EEC in 1957. The first enlargement took place in 1973 when Great Britain, Ireland, Denmark, and Norway joined the original group of six member states.[11] Britain had earlier abstained from joining and instead founded the European Free Trade Association. British leaders did apply for EEC membership twice in the 1960s, only to be rejected by de Gaulle's France. The country's eventual entry in 1973 reflected changes both internal and external to Europe. Within Europe, Paris recognized that growing German power could only be balanced with the addition of Britain; Bonn understood that the exercise of German power required a reassured France; and London finally realized that its future was in Europe, not in the former empire or in North America. Outside Europe, the faltering U.S. management of the international

---

[10]In July 1999, the OSCE was given the task of overseeing the postwar settlement in Kosovo. Toward that end the OSCE assumed the lead role in attempting to build a democratic order in the Yugoslav province, promoting the rule of law, and monitoring human rights.

[11]The Norwegian electorate subsequently rejected membership in a national referendum. The same outcome followed a second referendum in 1994.

monetary system, the Vietnam war, and uncertain U.S. leadership created the need for a more unified Western European bloc.

The second enlargement occurred in the 1980s with the additions of Greece in 1981 and Portugal and Spain in 1986. This was primarily an effort to shore up new democratic governments in three countries that suffered various forms of authoritarian rule for most of the postwar period. Adding these three states also broadened the EC's geographical focus to include Southern Europe and states with less advanced economies. The third enlargement of the EU occurred after the Cold War. Austria, Sweden, and Finland were able to join in 1995 because their neutrality during the U.S.–Soviet struggle no longer complicated domestic debates over EU membership.

The anticipated eastward enlargement of the EU, which may take in more than ten countries by 2020, began with the signing of the Europe Agreements in 1992 with the Visegrad states (the Czech Republic, Hungary, Poland, and Slovakia) along with Bulgaria and Romania. Subsequent agreements were signed with Slovenia and the Baltic states (Estonia, Latvia, and Lithuania). While the primary purpose of those agreements was the promotion of free trade between the EU and the Central and Eastern European signatories, the preamble to the agreements identified them as a preparatory stage for those states' entry into the EU.[12] In the 1993 Copenhagen summit declaration, European leaders declared the Europe Agreements to be the first step toward EU membership. In a single stroke, six countries (Bulgaria, Romania, and the Visegrad states) were promised eventual membership in the EU, and four others (Slovenia and the Baltic states) subsequently signed similar agreements. The enlargement decisions were made at the level of "high" politics: EU membership was seen as the best way to end permanently the division of the European continent. The EU saw itself as the institution best suited to the tasks of consolidating the transitions to democracy and market-driven economies in Central and Eastern Europe. The EU also viewed itself as the least obtrusive mechanism for creating a European security identity (Ruggie 1997, 110–112; Kaiser 1996, 137–142; Baldwin 1995, 474–481).

At Copenhagen, the EU established a broad set of membership requirements, including the consolidation of democratic institutions, respect for human rights, the protection of minorities, a functioning market economy, and the fulfillment of the Maastricht criteria for monetary union. With the 1997 Treaty of Amsterdam, it became certain that conformity to the entire body of EU legislation (the *acquis communautaire*) would be the key to accession. A subsequent report, *Agenda 2000*, detailed the accession requirements. The EU later required that the new states possess the administrative and judicial capacity to apply the *acquis*.

---

[12]For a review of early EU policies toward Central and Eastern Europe, see Sedelmeier and Wallace (1996).

Two questions arose during this process: Would enlargement leave the new states better off? Would the current EU members be worse off after enlargement? As to the first question, EU membership was attractive to potential new members as the EU offered them significant opportunities, including a vast internal market for products made in Central and Eastern Europe. Moreover, membership would lower the cost of capital for investment given an implicit EU promise to guarantee development loans (it would be awkward for an EU member state to default on its loans). The new states would also receive an agricultural subsidy and their infrastructure needs would be met in part by access to EU funds. Politically, the EU offered an opportunity for the new states to play a more effective role in international affairs through their input into a common foreign and security policy. Finally, the prospect of EU membership provided potential new members the political cover they needed for implementing difficult and necessary domestic reforms.

It remains unlikely that any of the EU applicants will be admitted before 2004 at the earliest. The pace of EU enlargement has been hindered by institutional, political, and financial considerations. Although the Nice Summit in December 2000 made some progress in clearing up the institutional barriers to enlargement, the central problems remain (see Peterson and Jones 1999).

Increasing the number of EU members has several drawbacks. First, the EU faces the difficult task of integrating a group of economically and politically diverse states into the EU framework. Second, the new member-states would probably not be capable of joining the European monetary union any time soon. Finally, the entry of new states may also make the "deepening" of EU foreign policy—the acceptance of new powers and roles—more difficult (Stubb 1998). Enlargement is also vexed by the clashing objectives that the major powers have for the EU (Sperling and Kirchner 1997b; Jopp 1994). The most persuasive arguments against EU enlargement center around the propositions that "widening"—admitting additional members—would come at the expense of deepening the EU's powers and roles, or that hasty expansion could precipitate the unwinding of the EU itself.

The potential enlargement of the EU reveals four themes that illuminate the barriers to a more integrated EU. First, enlargement has brought to the fore several issues that have been festering within the EU since 1966: the need to reform the Common Agriculture Policy, the need to rewrite the rules governing the disbursement of EU funds, and the need to improve and reform the EU decision-making process. Second, enlargement has (paradoxically) revealed the continuing force and vitality of the European nation-state. For most students of the EU, it has become an operating assumption that multilevel governance has largely displaced the sovereignty principle (see Marks, Hooghe, and Blank 1996, 341–368). Yet the process of widening and deepening is accompanied by fears of lost cohesion and growing regional discord.

Third, it remains uncertain whether EU enlargement will actually contribute to collective identity formation between the two halves of Europe. It is just as likely that an overly ambitious enlargement agenda will undo the emerging common identity within Western Europe. So far, the EU has successfully created a community of interest in many policy areas where member-states have initially had conflicting interests. It remains to be seen, however, whether the EU can continue to forge common policies as it grows in size and becomes more diverse politically and socially. Finally, there is an imbalance between the supply and demand for enlargement of the union. The applicant states have many reasons for desiring membership, but it is also clear that the EU's demand for new members is hedged and limited. The EU offer of membership remains suspect in this regard due to its inability to address fully the barriers to enlargement. In any event, the prospect of enlargement will remain a central element of any EU foreign policy and may determine the future roles and capabilities of the EU in foreign affairs.

GLOBALIZING THE EUROPEAN UNION: RELATIONS WITH JAPAN

The EU's bilateral relationship with Japan illustrates both the significant potential and limits of the EU as a global actor. Until the end of the Cold War, both the EU and Japan were happy to allow the United States to assume a leadership role whenever issues of common concern emerged. This arrangement proved less workable, however, in the Cold War's aftermath. The full diplomatic engagement of the EU and Japan in 1991 was spurred by growing bilateral economic disputes, strategic concerns in Asia, and a belated recognition that the United States could no longer be depended upon to referee their relationship.

The EU–Japanese relationship has turned on three axes: political dialogue, trade liberalization, and cooperation on global challenges. The Europeans engaged Japan in order to facilitate a more balanced trading and investment relationship, not out of a desire to foster global stability. In a series of bilateral meetings between 1991 and 1996, the economic dimension of this relationship overshadowed any effort to find political common ground. Nonetheless, the EU and Japan formally recognized that each had a role to play in the international system commensurate with its economic clout. Despite this important step toward defining a common geopolitical interest, their relationship was largely defined by the knotty trade issues of market access, the reform of the Japanese economy (see Chapter 5), the promotion of a multilateral trading system, and a host of other trade and financial issues.

The challenges of security and stability eventually found their way into the EU–Japanese agenda. In 1996, the EU sought Japanese diplomatic support and financial contributions to preserve the fragile peace in Bosnia following the signing of the U.S.-brokered Dayton Accords. Japan in turn sought European support in heading off North Korea's acquisition of nuclear weapons. These issues, along with the common desire to gain global acceptance of the Comprehensive Test Ban Treaty and the Chemical Weapons Convention, formed the basis of the Euro–Japanese contribution to international stability. A confluence of security interests, combined with the growing importance of Southeast Asia to Europe and Japan, produced a change in the tenor of EU policy toward Asia. The Europeans recognized the importance of multilateral cooperation in Asia, particularly through the Asia–Europe Meetings, the Association of Southeast Asian Nations (ASEAN), and the ASEAN Regional Forum. The need for multilateral cooperation framed the EU–Japanese dialogue on outstanding and common problems in the Asia-Pacific, particularly the need to integrate China into the international trading system. In these respects, Europe and Japan moved beyond the narrow trade disputes that hindered their relationship until the mid-1990s.

This effort to stabilize the international economy was tested as the Asian financial crisis unfolded in 1998 (see Chapters 5 and 9). Both Japan and the EU recognized that the crisis had not only regional but global implications and that both had an important role in containing the crisis. Nonetheless, their common response produced a lopsided division of labor. Japan was expected to minimize the global impact of the crisis, while Europe was expected to work within the various international financial institutions that were also seeking to foster recovery. The primary responsibility for providing the solution to the Asian financial crisis was clearly left on the Japanese doorstep. At the same time, the EU sought Japanese support in addressing the problems posed by the faltering reform effort in Russia (see Chapter 3) and the 1999 NATO-led war in Kosovo. Only the recurring problem posed by the North Korean nuclear program engaged Japan and the EU in equal measure.

By 2000, the key elements of the EU–Japanese relationship had been largely defined. The relationship remains one-sided in obligation and overwhelmingly economic in content. In most cases, the EU has defined the intersection of Japanese and European interests. It is also the case, however, that both Japan and the EU have a common interest, along with the United States, in fostering global stability in the post–Cold War world. But the incentive for a stronger bilateral relationship between the EU and Japan reflects regional rather than global security concerns. The mutual engagement of Japan and EU on various threats to international stability looks less like a joint resolution of common problems than a simple tit-for-tat exchange of financial and diplomatic support in problem areas that affects one of the partners directly and the other virtually not at all. The postcolonial European interest in East Asia has been driven by the concern that a "Pacific Century" not pass by Europe. The Japanese interest in a dialogue with the EU has been largely driven by its desire to avoid the closure of the European market to Japanese goods and to meet European demands that the Japanese market better accommodate European trade and capital.

European monetary union had important ramifications for Japan that the Europeans were happy to overlook. Japan made a concerted effort after 1998 to engage Europe as Tokyo sought to transform the yen into an international currency. Those efforts, however, were met with European indifference. The Japanese found themselves in the position of unwelcome suitors in their effort to elicit the cooperation of European monetary authorities. The Japanese, with good reason, have feared the emergence of a "euro-zone" that would cover most of Europe and the Mediterranean basin and a "dollar-zone" that would encompass the Americas. The emergence of such zones would hamper the yen in international monetary markets because the Japanese have assumed that the creation of a "yen-zone" in Asia is unlikely due to the comparatively low level of integration among the Asian economies.

The EU–Japanese agenda has been driven by factors external to each rather than by a set of agreed-upon goals that reflect a set of common interests, or even a shared concern for global stability and prosperity. Put simply, Japan and Europe lack a common strategic vision. There is no EU–Japanese equivalent of NATO or even a limited bilateral security relationship patterned on the U.S.–Japanese guidelines for defense cooperation. There has been no articulation of what would constitute a common security threat to either partner that would fully engage the interests or involvement of the other.[13] Nonetheless, the EU and Japan have made great strides in the 1990s toward repairing the underdeveloped state of their relationship. It is equally clear that the evolution of the EU–Japanese relationship is the product of a post–Cold War world in which the United States can no longer be depended upon.

CONCLUSION

The evolution of the EU as reviewed in this chapter has contributed to a common European identity. The institutional framework of the union makes it possible for the major European states to contemplate common foreign policies in many areas. Cooperation has been aided by the transformation of the historic enmity between Great Britain, France, and Germany into the post–Cold War amity these states enjoy today. The depth of economic interdependence and the convergence of values within the EU

---

[13]For more detailed discussions of the security interests shared by the EU and Japan, see Stares and Regaud (1997–1998), Mahncke (1997), Shin and Segal (1997), and Funabashi (1996–1997).

states have likewise provided the basis for the reconciliation of national preferences, if not their transformation into collective preferences. Finally, differences between EU leaders and U.S. President George W. Bush on a variety of issues—including nuclear missile defense and global warming—have reinforced unity within the EU.

The EU, however, has yet to make a complete transition from foreign-policy *objective* to foreign-policy *actor*. Recent experience suggests that the EU can be independent of its member-states only after they decide that a collective solution is superior to one hammered out at the state level, when the costs of conducting separate policies are too high, or when the stakes are low enough that a foreign-policy "failure" can be easily rectified by national exertions. More importantly, the EU remains a foreign-policy objective of the three major states. For Germany, a unified Europe within a federal framework remains a long-term goal. For France, the EU promises the basis for a European and French-led challenge to the United States and Russia. And for Great Britain, the EU remains a channel for wielding global influence and for preventing regional mischief.

How then are we to assess the EU as an actor in international politics? As Christopher Hill (1993) noted, the EU faces a "capabilities-expectations gap." Simply put, the economic wealth and diplomatic presence of its member-states has not been converted into a workable and effective EU foreign policy. While the constitutional and institutional innovations introduced by the Maastricht and Amsterdam treaties promised greater cooperation in foreign affairs, the absence of a truly "common" foreign and security policy has been often cited as the major failing of the EU (see Gordon 1998; Smith 1996; and Hill 1992). Yet the more the EU achieves in the area of foreign policy, the more will be expected of it. The EU will continue to disappoint those unwilling to acknowledge that the European nation-state is undergoing fundamental change. Conversely, the EU will disappoint those who are unhappy with the limited progress made by the EU in eroding the self-interests of its member-states. The future possibilities of the EU in foreign policy, therefore, are likely to remain qualified by its hybrid status in the international system.

To call EU foreign policy an oxymoron today would be both unfair and inaccurate. Despite the many problems noted in this chapter, significant progress has been made in forging a common foreign policy. A commitment to further progress was firmly expressed at the Cologne summit in 1999 and reaffirmed at Nice in 2000. Indeed, as Samuel Johnson remarked to James Boswell on a different matter, EU foreign policy is not unlike "a dog walking on its hind legs. It is not done well; but you are surprised to find it done at all."

PART II

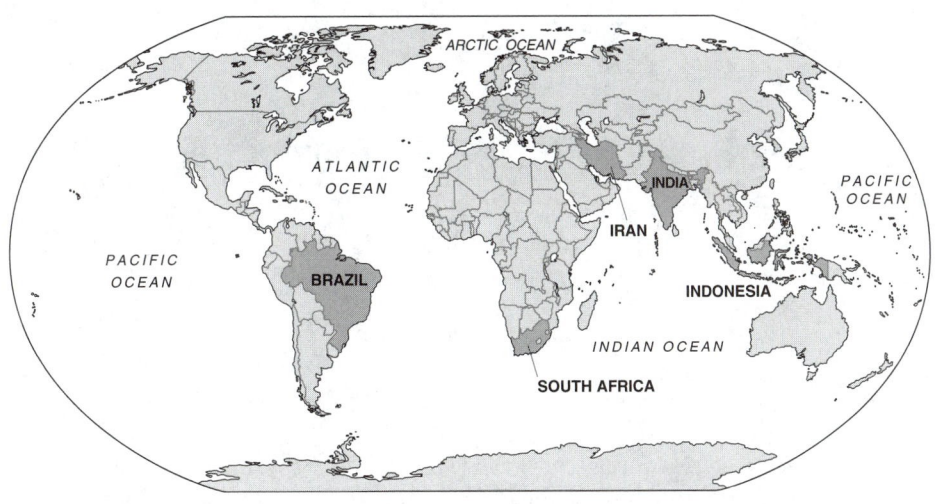

ADAPTATION STRATEGIES OF THE EMERGING POWERS

THE FOREIGN POLICY OF MODERN BRAZIL

Andrew Hurrell

Oxford University

This chapter examines the foreign policy of Brazil, Latin America's largest, most populous, and most economically productive country. Our primary emphasis is on the period since the late 1980s, a key turning point in the evolution of Brazilian domestic and foreign policy. Our focus is on the many ways Brazil's government has adapted to the changes unleashed by two major developments: the end of the Cold War, and the accelerating pace of economic and social globalization.

There is little doubt that the late 1980s witnessed a series of profound changes in Brazilian foreign policy. These changes, in turn, modified Brazilian understandings of the country's place in the world. For at least the previous two decades, Brazil had placed great emphasis on the pursuit of national autonomy, inequities in global economic relations, and the perceived "freezing" of the international power structure in favor of the great powers. By the end of the 1960s, the close alignment with the United States that followed the military coup of 1964 had given way to a broader and more pragmatic policy and relations with Washington varied between cool and distant. Brazil sought to diversify its foreign options during this period and expanded ties with Western Europe, Japan, the socialist and communist states, and, increasingly, other developing countries.

The "developmentalist" and nationalist foreign policy of this period was closely tied to economic policy, which relied heavily on a strategy of *import substitution* in contrast to the *export-led* growth strategies that were adopted during this period by the industrializing countries of East Asia. The strategy of import substitution involved large-scale state investment in public-sector enterprises, a high degree of state regulation of

146

the economy, and the pursuit of national technological development (in the nuclear, computer, and arms industries, for example). This led to massive subsidies to domestic industries, restrictions on imports of foreign goods and services, direct investments in state-owned enterprises, and strict controls on technology transfers. There was a deep-rooted belief in the imperative of continued economic growth, even at the expense of high inflation. Brazil's developmentalist ideology was embedded within and around the state; it was backed by a relatively high degree of elite consensus and a wide array of powerful interest groups.

Developmentalism, however, came under sustained attack in the 1980s, a decade that witnessed a simultaneous debt crisis in Latin America and rapid economic growth in East Asia (see Chapters 4 and 5). As a result, there was a marked move away from Brazil's inwardly oriented development policy and toward trade liberalization, privatization, and the easing of government regulations. Externally, there was a recasting of Brazilian attitudes toward closer integration in the world economy and a greater willingness to accept dominant international economic norms. Relations with other South American countries improved greatly as Brazil granted a higher priority to regional economic integration and the creation of a South American common market, Mercosur.

As this new approach set in, Brazil became more accepting of dominant international norms in other issue areas. These included arms exports and nuclear proliferation, important issues given the significant development of the Brazilian arms industry in the 1970s. In the environmental field, there was a shift away from the nationalism and defensiveness of the 1960s and 1970s toward an acceptance of international concerns about environmental degradation, especially regarding deforestation in the Amazon River area. Brazil thus played a key role in environmental issues, especially in the process leading to the 1992 Earth Summit in Rio de Janeiro. There was also a change in the area of human rights, with Brazil taking a much more activist stance at the 1993 Vienna Conference on Human Rights. Its government became far more willing to acknowledge the seriousness of its own record on human rights.

The first section of this chapter raises some of the central questions that are involved in the analysis of foreign-policy change and adaptation as it applies to Brazil. The second section provides the historical background against which this adaptation process has taken place in recent years and reviews the major features of Brazilian foreign policy between World War II and the 1980s. The third section examines current Brazilian foreign policy in three areas of primary concern: Brazil's role in international institutions, its engagement with other South American states, and its crucial bilateral relations with the United States. As we will find, a combination of domestic and international pressures have led to important changes in the pattern of Brazilian foreign policy. And yet change has been balanced by important elements of continuity and has been much less dramatic than in other Latin American countries.

FOUR QUESTIONS ABOUT POLICY ADAPTATION

We begin this analysis by raising four questions about foreign-policy adaptation in Brazil. These questions, and the tentative answers provided, help create a foundation for understanding the evolution of Brazilian foreign policy during the turbulent period of the past two decades. Moreover, it is hoped that exploring these questions promotes our general understanding of foreign-policy adaptation and may thus be useful in considering the other chapters in this volume.

ADAPTATION TO WHAT?

The first and most important of these questions considers what exactly Brazilian leaders have adapted to in recent years. Which aspects of the international system have been important for Brazil?

Realist theories of international relations place primary emphasis on patterns of conflict and the balance of power within the interstate system. This is because foreign policy is believed to be heavily influenced, if not determined, by the necessity of seeking security in an anarchical international system (Rose 1998; Waltz 1979). Foreign policy from this perspective is explained by looking from the "outside in" and tracking the ways in which states are "pushed and shoved" by the international system to act in particular ways.

From this perspective, the end of the Cold War is undoubtedly the most important driving force for change. It has altered the distribution of global power and the nature of the international power hierarchy, leaving the United States as the "lone superpower" (see Chapter 2) and, very critically for Brazil, reinforcing U.S. hegemony across the Western Hemisphere.[1] In addition, the end of the Cold War has led to a decentralization, or "regionalization," of the international security system. The disappearance or weakening of great-power involvement in many areas has exposed or liberated regional security dynamics. As a result, instability and conflict have less to do with the meddling and intervention of the great powers and need to be understood within a regional or national context.

---

[1]"Hegemony" in this context refers to the preponderant and pervasive assertion of foreign influence that falls short of formal occupation or colonial control. This is a vital concern to Latin American scholars given the disproportionate power of the United States in the Western Hemisphere.

However, in addition to the international *political* system—the world of nation-states and diplomacy—states are embedded in an *economic* arena—the world of firms, markets, production, and trade. Further, there is what has come to be called *transnational civil society*—the world of non-governmental organizations (NGOs) such as Greenpeace and Amnesty International. All three domains must be considered in assessing the adaptation of all countries' foreign policies in recent years.

Throughout Brazil's history as a Portuguese colony from 1500 until 1822, the global economy played a major role in shaping its pattern of economic development. After Brazil became an independent country, it remained highly vulnerable to external economic forces. The successes and failures of its own economic development were therefore central to framing its foreign-policy options. From this perspective, we should look to the debt crisis of the 1980s as a major potential factor in explaining change in recent Brazilian foreign policy. The 1980s witnessed a dramatically worsening external economic environment, the deepest recession in Latin America since the 1930s, and a protracted fiscal crisis of the Brazilian state that forced a profound rethinking of its development and foreign-policy goals.

Yet there is much more at stake in regard to the global economy. The end of the Cold War also witnessed, and not coincidentally, an upsurge of writing on "globalization." Scholars have highlighted the growing interdependence that results as money, people, images, values, and ideas flow ever more swiftly across national boundaries (see Scholte 2000). In this respect, globalization involves dramatic increases in the density and depth of economic, ecological, and societal interdependence.[2] The globalization of economic life affects national economic management as states face powerful pressures to align economic policies in order to attract foreign investment and technology and to compete in the more closely linked marketplace. From this perspective, we should expect to see globalization playing a critical role in pushing such emerging powers as Brazil and India toward market-friendly economic policies. We should also expect to see a more general revision of their foreign-policy goals, especially toward the major Western states. Indeed, we have witnessed exactly this pattern of behavior, as the other chapters in this section aptly describe.

To many analysts, globalization is not simply about economics, but involves a broader shift in the character of world politics. Thus, for example, military power becomes both less useable and less relevant. International institutions, meanwhile, expand in order to deal with global economic management and draw attention to urgent problems that cross national borders. As institutions such as the UN and the World Trade Organization

---

[2]"Density" in this context refers to the increased number, range, and scope of cross-border transactions. "Depth" refers to the degree to which that interdependence affects, and is affected by, the ways in which societies are organized domestically.

(WTO) expand in membership and administrative capacity, new norms on trade and investment, human rights, collective security, and "sustainable development" emerge and traditional conceptions of sovereignty are recast or jettisoned. Further, globalization opens the door to new political actors operating within transnational civil society—for example, knowledge-based networks of economists, lawyers, or scientists (Haas 1989), or NGOs such as Greenpeace, Amnesty International, and Freedom House that demand changes in the domestic and global conduct of states (see Keck and Sikkink 1998; and Risse-Kappen 1995).

Two points are clear with respect to Brazilian foreign policy. First, Brazilian *perceptions* of globalization have been extremely important in the process of foreign-policy change that is examined in the following sections. Second, globalization has definitively changed the *agenda* of Brazil's foreign policy. Although traditional issues of security have not gone away, the foreign-policy agenda of countries such as Brazil now includes a much broader range of issues, including regional economic integration, the environment, drugs, human rights, and democratization.

WHAT ARE THE DOMESTIC SOURCES OF CHANGE?

A second question relating to foreign-policy adaptation involves placing external developments in the context of domestic pressures for change. This is especially important in the case of Brazil, which underwent an extraordinary process of economic development and modernization in the twentieth century, especially in the post–World War II period. Its population grew from 51 million in 1950 to 168 million in 1997. Brazil moved from being a predominantly rural and agricultural society to an industrialized and urbanized society in little more than a generation.[3] The urban population increased from 36 percent in 1940 to 86 percent in 2000—very close to the levels of the United States and the EU. The share of nonagricultural employment, meanwhile, rose from 40 percent in 1940 to more than 70 percent by the 1980s. These developments were comparable in their rapidity and intensity to the similar transformation that occurred in Germany and the United States a century earlier. Thus, from whatever theoretical perspective one looks, we would expect change of this magnitude to have some effect on a country's foreign policy.

Importantly, Brazil has also undergone important political changes during this period. The country was ruled by a military government from 1964 to 1985. A gradual process of liberalization began in 1974, however, in the midst of the major socioeconomic changes that were gaining

---

[3]In 1964, coffee accounted for more than half of all export earnings in Brazil with manufactured exports only accounting for 5 percent of exports. By 1988, coffee's share had declined to 6 percent and manufactured goods accounted for 58 percent of its exports.

momentum. Civilian government was reestablished in 1985 and direct presidential elections took place in 1989. Moreover, the character of politics was changing, with new patterns of political mobilization and an increasingly vibrant civil society (Stepan 1989). Liberal theories of international relations would lead us to expect two possible consequences. First, democratization would affect the formulation of foreign policy, with increased pluralism of the foreign policy-making process and a greater role for societal actors (e.g., firms, political parties, and social movements). Second, democratization would shift the objectives and priorities of foreign policy and, in particular, would increase the prospects for cooperation with other democratic states.

WHAT ARE THE MECHANISMS OF CHANGE?

A third question concerns the mechanisms through which external pressures have influenced foreign-policy change and the overall character of the process of adaptation. We explore this question by highlighting two possibilities. Liberals would characterize the process as one of *progressive enmeshment*. This builds upon the Kantian notion of a gradual diffusion of liberal values as a result of growing interdependence, a more democratic legal order, and the successful examples set by republics. Dominant international norms are seen as not just practically beneficial, but also morally legitimate in such areas as political liberties, human rights, and ecological sensitivity.

More critical analysts, by contrast, see the process of foreign-policy change in terms of *hegemonic imposition*. They stress the degree to which countries such as Brazil had little option by the late 1980s but to change course. Indeed, Brazil's range of foreign-policy options had been narrowed by the end of the Cold War, the reassertion of U.S. regional dominance, and the absence of alternative options. The liberal agenda of the "new world order," in this view, reflected not shared global values, but rather the preferences of the dominant Western countries, especially the United States. Moreover, Washington was increasingly prepared to use its power to press its own values and policy preferences through military intervention, economic sanctions, and the imposition of an expanding range of conditions tied to the flows of foreign assistance and private investments.

The case of Brazil illustrates that external pressures and constraints have been very important. But it also demonstrates that we cannot understand foreign-policy change solely in terms of a simple model of hegemonic imposition. On one side, the character and intensity of liberalization pressures depends on geopolitical position, level of development, size, and state strength. The intensity and the character of the pressures faced by Brazil have been very different from those facing Mexico and Chile. On the other side, liberalization pressures come up against powerful inherited domestic structures and historically embedded modes of thought. To understand the Brazilian case we need to trace how the external world has been understood along with the complex domestic processes of adaptation that occur within individual societies. What is crucial in the Brazilian case is the combining of old themes and old values with the new policy options in the face of a changing external environment.

What emerges from this analysis is that change has been balanced by important elements of continuity. Foreign policy in Brazil has changed to a lesser degree than that of other states in Latin America, such as Mexico, Argentina, and Chile. Brazil is distinctive in the extent to which it has applied its own particular understandings to the dramatic changes in economic policies and foreign relations that have transformed Latin America since the 1970s. Brazil has adopted widespread reforms, but they remain incomplete. Its government has adopted a new approach to foreign relations, yet its concern with power and autonomy has by no means disappeared. Brazil is increasingly prepared to join international institutions and to accept many emerging international norms, but its leaders still seek a greater role for themselves in the reshaped institutions. Brazilian leaders have sought to avoid confrontation with the United States, but they are reluctant to become too closely involved with many aspects of Washington's regional agenda—on drugs and democracy promotion, for example. In particular, Brazil seeks to use Mercosur rather than U.S.-dominated bodies to negotiate the terms of a possible hemispheric economic zone.

WHAT IS THE IMPACT OF CHANGE?

The final question concerns the impact of change on the power position of Brazil. This book is concerned with the adaptation strategies of great and emerging powers. But in what sense can Brazil be included in the latter group? Predictions that Brazil is destined to play an influential role in world affairs have a long history inside Brazil (see de Carvalho 2000, 65–68). The intensity of such predictions has varied across time. At times, such ideas have been no more than a vague aspiration and not tied to practical political action. At other times, they have assumed a much more direct role in the shaping of foreign policy. Such a view became most pronounced during the 1970s, when the high growth rates of the so-called "economic miracle" seemed to establish the country as an upwardly mobile middle power that was moving steadily toward great-power status.

The success of economic stabilization in the 1990s, combined with a greater degree of international self-confidence, has led to a revival of this perspective. Recent commentators have identified Brazil as one of the primary emerging markets. As Garten (1997, xxv) observed, "Countries like China, India, and Brazil ... are acquiring enough power to change the face of global politics and economics." Others (e.g., Chase et al. 1999) identified

Brazil as one of the "pivotal states" that will dominate U.S. policy toward the developing world. The mood surrounding the Brasilia Summit of South American leaders in September 2000 reinforced this perception of Brazil as an emerging power.

In one sense, such claims about Brazil are intuitively plausible. Accounts of Brazilian foreign policy routinely include lists of its "power resources." With approximately 170 million citizens, Brazil is the fifth-most populous country in the world—after China, India, the United States, and Indonesia, and ahead of Russia and Japan. It has the world's eighth-largest level of economic output, estimated by the World Bank at $760 billion in 1999. Brazil is by far the largest country in South America, covering nearly 3.3 million square miles and neighboring every country on the continent except Chile and Ecuador. It is also not difficult to show that what happens in Brazil matters to those outside (see Krasno 1999). The size of its foreign debt means that a financial crisis in Brazil has major implications for the stability of the global financial system. Further, what Brazil chooses to do with its vast Amazon rain forests will profoundly and permanently affect the global environment.

And yet Brazil has long provided an important illustration of the complexities of power analysis. Discussion of power and influence cannot be separated from the analysis of motives. It may be true that all states seek power and security, as realists claim, but the real questions concern what sorts of power they seek, and for what purposes. Although power has mattered for Brazilian policymakers and continues to do so, a simple power-maximization model does not fit the Brazilian case. Its leaders have not played the game of "power politics" in the way that realist theories would lead us to expect. When we look more closely at its motives, objectives, and strategies, the picture is a complex one. The other major lesson of power analysis is that power and influence cannot be understand in isolation. To paraphrase the political scientist Robert Dahl, "When you hear that Brazil is an emerging and increasingly influential power, the proper question is: Influential over which actors, during which period, and with respect to which issues?"

When we put all this in its proper context, we see that Brazil *does* matter in world politics today and that it is in many respects becoming more formidable. We also see, however, that the constraints on Brazilian power and influence continue to be very real.

FOREIGN POLICY DURING THE COLD WAR

The central feature of the early postwar period was the "closing of the hemisphere" and the establishment of a hegemonic system built around the U.S. role as the major source of trading opportunities, foreign investment, and economic and military assistance to less-developed countries in the region. The system was also based upon U.S.-dominated regional institutions mobilized as part of the Cold War—in particular the Organization of American States (OAS), with its headquarters in Washington. Within its sphere of influence, the United States was able to maintain its position as the essential political and economic link between the countries of Latin America and the rest of the world. U.S. leaders were able to set down and enforce limits on what was permissible in Latin American foreign as well as domestic policies.

Brazil responded to this situation in three ways. First, as both common sense and realist theory would expect, Brazil sought to diversify its foreign relations in order to reduce its dependence on Washington. As Western Europe and Japan recovered economically in the 1950s, so Brazil sought to expand its economic relations. Brazilian leaders looked to Africa, the Middle East, and Asia for trading partners. The policy of diversification also included the development of relations with socialist and communist countries. One should note, however, that Brazil's relations with the USSR, China, and their respective allies revealed the degree to which Brazil's policy was one of "constrained balancing." Despite its efforts to broaden its diplomatic horizons, Brazil fell short of establishing close and direct alignments with major U.S. antagonists. This revealed the high direct and indirect costs of such a move and reflected the substantial dangers of radicalization within the country.

Second, Brazilian foreign policy took on an increasingly nationalist and "Third Worldist" stance. Many of the major themes of *terceiro-mundismo* (Third Worldism) appeared in the so-called "independent" foreign policy of the period from 1961 to 1964 and reappeared forcefully in the 1970s. Thus Brazil played a prominent role in such Third World forums as the Group of 77 (G-77) and was heavily engaged in the proposed creation in the 1970s of a New International Economic Order (NIEO). Primarily through the UN, whose General Assembly was dominated by developing countries in the wake of African and Asian decolonization, the G-77 countries demanded greater economic equality between the industrialized North and the largely impoverished South. A common theme was that the North's domination perpetuated the "dependency" of the world's poorest countries.[4]

The third Brazilian response concerned the United States. Relations with Washington varied considerably across the period. The military government that took power in 1964 actively tried to build its foreign policy around a "special relationship" with Washington. Its leaders supported the U.S. government on several important issues in the hope that a special

---

[4]See Chilcote (1984) for an informative review of the *dependencia* school of thought and its place in North–South economic relations of the Cold War.

relationship would produce both direct benefits as well as ideological support. But this close alignment unraveled and by the time of the foreign policy of "responsible pragmatism" under the leadership of General Ernesto Geisel (1974–1978) many of the themes of Third Worldism were firmly reestablished. From the mid-1970s, Brazil's relations with Washington were plagued by friction over human rights, nuclear issues, and, most importantly, Brazil's proclaimed solidarity with the developing world.[5] As the 1980s began, Brazil was ever more reluctant to be drawn into Washington's Cold War policies.

At the same time, South America was viewed in ambiguous ways by Brazilian officials during this period. On the one hand, South America was a potential source of solidarity and support in the face of an uncertain and unwelcoming world and the locus for attempts at economic integration. But, on the other hand, Brazil's disproportionate size and its political ambitions led to persistent tensions with its neighbors, most notably Argentina.

Brazilian foreign policy in this period was heavily shaped by the character of its economic and development policy. As noted earlier, this policy was dominated by the strategy of import-substitution, which developed partly as a pragmatic response to the successive external shocks of the Great Depression and World War II. It was in the postwar period, however, that the model took the form of a coherent doctrine and was embedded in government institutions. Its core provisions included the protection of national industries, the creation of state enterprises, and government subsidies to strategic sectors. Domestically, the most important assumption concerned the central role of the state in coordinating economic policy. Externally, there was a powerful sense that global economic structures possessed far more constraints and snares than opportunities. It was also widely held that conflict with the capitalist countries was likely, if not inevitable.

In addition to the importance of development policy, there were two historically rooted factors that shaped Brazilian understandings of its place in the world. The first of these related to the complex origins of Brazil's international identity (see Lafer 2000). Brazil was formed as part of the process of European colonial settlement that involved the wholesale subjugation of indigenous peoples. Brazilian elites saw themselves as part of the West in cultural and religious terms, and there was a strong tradition of liberalism, including Western ideas about international law and society. Brazilian society was also shaped by the African slave trade, which emerged in the early stages of the anticolonial revolution, and has faced great obstacles in its struggle for economic development. It is not necessary

---

[5]Brazil's recognition of the Marxist government in Angola in 1975, which greatly frustrated the U.S. government, was an example of "Third Worldism" in practice.

to accept a civilizational view of the world to appreciate how this duality has remained an important element of Brazilian debates of where the country "fits in." Certainly running through the post-1945 period is a persistent set of debates and arguments as to whether Brazil was part of the West in its battle against communism and the Soviet Union or a member of the Third World in its struggle for development and a greater role in international affairs.

The other great historical legacy derives from the character of state formation and from Brazil's geopolitical location. As Latin America's postcolonial states were formed during the course of the nineteenth century, they were generally able to escape the destructive link between state-building and war-making that was such a feature of the Westphalian nation-state system. Brazil secured its (relatively remote) frontiers with its neighbors in the late nineteenth and early twentieth century on successful terms and became a "satisfied," status-quo power. With the exception of its relations with Argentina, Brazil avoided serious conflicts with its neighbors. This left its leaders free to develop an ideology of national development that was largely inner-directed, responding to domestic failures and aimed at upholding order and promoting economic development.

This distinctive security framework was reinforced by the degree to which the region as a whole was relatively cut off from major international tensions. There was no convincing need for Brazil to develop an elaborate military capability against foreign powers beyond Latin America. This would have upset the regional balance of power and led to the destructive regional and extraregional conflicts that so bedeviled the Middle East and the Indian subcontinent. This is especially relevant for understanding why Brazil—unlike, say, India and China—is a country whose governments have not placed a high priority on expanding regional influence, especially in the military arena.

Of course, we must not oversimplify. There was significant variation of foreign policy across the period from 1945 to 1982. Debates raged fiercely with clear extremes, particularly the strong Third Worldism of the so-called "independent" foreign policy of 1961–1964 versus the anticommunist zealotry of the first post-1964 military government. Nevertheless, developmentalism provided a cohesive framework for the formulation and conduct of Brazilian foreign policy during the heyday of the Cold War. Four unspoken assumptions shaped the model and were rarely, if ever, challenged. These included the intrinsic value of national autonomy, the importance of defending economic and political sovereignty, the need to gain a more prominent role for the country overseas, and the belief that the capitalist international economy contained more dangers than opportunities.

Neither the economic crisis of the 1980s nor the democratic transition of 1985 led to major foreign-policy changes under the leadership of José Sarney (1985–1990). The core premises of the developmentalist model did not change under his rule. In terms of foreign policy, the Sarney period witnessed several points of friction between Brazil and United States, particularly over economic issues (see Muñoz and Tulchin 1996). There was much resentment in Brazil over U.S. policy toward the Latin American debt crisis. The two countries also clashed over a wide range of trade-related issues, including the liberalization of services, intellectual property rights, and Brazil's attempt to develop an independent computer industry. These issues generated a considerable nationalist backlash and fueled the widespread belief that the United States was attempting to exploit Brazilian weakness in order to compound its domination over the country.

Beyond economics, there was a resistance to many of the international norms that were evolving in this period. Brazil upheld the norms of sovereignty and nonintervention in the face of increasing international concerns over human rights and environmental destruction. In the latter case, there was a striking similarity between the strident environmental nationalism of the Sarney government and the influential language and positions adopted by Brazilian delegates at the 1972 Stockholm Conference. The 1980s witnessed an upsurge in protests against deforestation in the Amazon River area and against government policies that fostered mineral development, road-building, and large-scale development projects in the region. Brazilian officials responded in traditional fashion. For example, Foreign Minister Abreu Sodré in early 1989 declared that "Brazil does not want to transform itself into an ecological reserve for humanity. Our greatest duty is with our economic development." Or, as Sarney stated, "Brazil is being threatened over its sovereign right to use its own territory." To Paulo Tarso, head of the Brazilian foreign ministry, there was an international "campaign to impede the exploitation of natural resources in order to block Brazil from becoming a world power" (see Hurrell 1992).

By far the most important exception to this general pattern of foreign-policy continuity concerned Brazil's relations with other South American states, particularly Argentina, which had been plagued by a long tradition of rivalry and competition. Tensions with Argentina had centered on its influence in the buffer states of Bolivia, Paraguay, and, to a lesser extent, Uruguay, over the use of the hydroelectric resources of the Paraná river and over the nuclear programs in the two countries. The latter followed the 1975 Brazilian–West German nuclear agreement that led to the largest-ever transfer of nuclear technology to a developing country.

By the end of the 1980s, however, a dramatic shift had taken place in the enduring rivalry between Brazil and Argentina. In the economic sphere, moves toward regional economic cooperation gathered steam. In 1985, leaders from the two countries signed an agreement that covered nuclear issues and energy cooperation and established a commission to examine economic cooperation. In 1986, the two countries launched the Economic Cooperation and Integration Program. Two years later, a Treaty of Integration, Cooperation and Development was signed that called for a free-trade area within the two countries. In the security field, improved bilateral ties led to arms-control agreements, shifts in military doctrines toward a defensive orientation, and declining levels of military spending. All of this presaged the moves toward deeper regional integration that was to come in the 1990s.

BRAZIL'S EMBRACE OF INTERNATIONAL NORMS

Awareness of the need to rethink policy had been growing across a number of areas through 1988 and 1989, including the beginnings of trade liberalization and privatization, and shifts in policy toward multilateral trade and human rights. But it was the inauguration of the government of Fernando Collor de Mello in March 1990 that increased the centrality of reform. For all the inconsistencies and failures of the Collor government, the increased pace of economic reform and the rhetoric of modernization acted as an important catalyst, disturbing the existing orthodoxy and fueling a new cycle of intellectual adjustment.

Collor's reform agenda included the standard elements of economic liberalization: tariff reductions, the removal of import quotas, the privatization of state enterprises, and the easing of restrictions on foreign investment. Closely allied to economic reform was a broader recasting of Brazilian attitudes toward closer integration in the world economy, a greater willingness to accept widespread international norms, and important changes in several substantive areas of foreign policy. In September 1990, for example, the government drastically reduced the scope of its restrictions on intellectual property that had caused so much friction with the United States. Brazil also became much more receptive to the General Agreement on Tariffs and Trade (GATT) and, later, the WTO, further demonstrating its shifting of loyalties from the NIEO to the *Liberal* International Economic Order (LIEO).

Outside the sphere of economics, Brazil began to accept international norms controlling missile and arms exports and nuclear proliferation. Previously, Brazil had refused to embrace the Nuclear Nonproliferation Treaty (NPT) and had refused to become a full member of the Treaty of Tlatelolco that prohibited nuclear weapons in Latin America. Improved relations with Argentina stabilized the bilateral nuclear relationship and pushed Brazil closer toward acceptance of the safeguards established by the International Atomic Energy Agency (IAEA). In 1995, Brazil placed export controls on nuclear materials and joined the Missile Technology Control Regime. In 1996, Brazil became a member of the Nuclear Suppliers Group and in 1998 Brazil signed the NPT.

A similar pattern is visible in the environmental field. There was a sharp move away from the defensiveness of the 1980s toward an acceptance of the legitimacy of international concern for environmental matters. The government became more receptive toward the environmental NGOs it had previously denounced as subversive. Brazil's growing engagement in this area led to the selection of Rio de Janeiro as host of the 1992 UN Conference on Environment and Development (the Earth Summit). Collor's environmental policy was characterized by several dramatic gestures and concessions that were clearly intended to court international public opinion.

In addition, Brazilian leaders became more willing to acknowledge the seriousness of previous human rights abuses within their own borders. Brazil had previously adopted a defiant stance stressing nonintervention in internal affairs and the illegitimacy of NGO involvement. By the 1990s, Brazil moved to an active human rights policy in the international arena and acknowledged the importance of human rights domestically. In June 1990, for example, the foreign minister received a mission from Human Rights Watch investigating rural violence. In August 1990, Brazilian leaders met with representatives of Amnesty International and formally accepted the right of the international community to monitor human rights and promote reforms. In July 1992, Brazil ratified the International Covenant on Civil and Political Rights. Under the leadership of Fernando Henrique Cardoso, a prominent Brazilian intellectual who was elected in 1994, the government established a human rights bureau in its foreign ministry and drew up a national plan for protecting human rights in the country. In December 1998, Brazil announced that it would recognize the Inter-American Human Rights Court, and in 1999 it agreed to support the rulings of the International Criminal Court.

Domestic economic difficulties played a major role in this reform process. Although Brazil had recovered in some measure from the debt crisis of the 1980s, the resurgence of inflation and the difficulties of stabilizing the economy meant that the costs of putting off more radical structural reforms grew ever higher. A renewed fiscal crisis and the repeated failures of subsequent "stabilization plans" undermined the pillars on which the previous development model had rested. In addition to domestic pressures, changes in Brazil's external environment worked against the continuation of old economic ideas and policies and powerfully reinforced the need for more ambitious reforms. The conviction that the developmentalism of the 1960s and 1970s had run its course was powerfully reinforced by accelerating changes that were occurring in domestic politics and the global economy.[6]

---

[6]Brazil's economy had long been relatively closed and had become more so in the years before the reform movement began. Imports fell from 14 percent of GNP in 1974 to 6 percent in 1994. Exports, meanwhile, dropped from 9 percent of GNP in 1974 to 8 percent in 1994. Moreover, Brazil's share of world trade fell from 1.4 percent in 1985 to 0.9 percent in 1990. Most dramatically, its share of private credit to developing countries plummeted from 61 percent in 1974 to 9 percent in 1994, and its share of foreign direct investment to developing countries dropped from 24 percent in 1974 to 3 percent by 1994.

A new view of the international economy took shape in Brazil. Its leaders came to believe that fundamental economic change and globalization were real and inevitable, that dynamic economies were internationalized economies, and that economic growth depended on successful participation in the world economy. Increased foreign investment was viewed as vital to the effective importation of modern technology. In this latter respect much of the move toward liberalization reflected a consensus that the "information revolution" had shifted the ground rules of international commerce and that Brazil had to be more efficient and competitive in this area.

In addition, international political support for previous foreign economic policies was crumbling. In a broad sense, this followed from the increasing fragmentation of the South and the obvious failure by 1990 of any chance of pressing for a New International Economic Order. But, more importantly, the shift in policy reflected the failure of more narrow international coalitions. Thus, within the GATT, a "Group of 10" led by Brazil and India failed in its opposition to the expansion of the GATT agenda. In the absence of meaningful coalitions, the Latin American debtors failed to develop a common political position and to maximize their potential bargaining advantages. In the environmental area (along with foreign debt, a key source of Southern "power" in the late 1980s), major Southern states came to reject any radical challenge and settled instead for maximizing advantages within the ground rules and on the agenda set by the North. There was also increased recognition that successful bargaining, above all with the United States, depended on internal recovery and on the restoration of international economic credibility.

The process of change and adaptation in Brazil is best characterized not by images of progressive enmeshment, nor of hegemonic imposition, but rather as an ongoing process of *coercive socialization*. Under this process, interaction within a highly unequal international system leads to the adoption and incorporation of external ideas, norms, and practices. Deeply rooted conceptions of national interest shift as political leaders reevaluate their options and revamp organizational structures. The changing institutional context, in turn, provides the framework for an evolving set of bargains between state and society. This conception highlights the ways in which developments within the international political system, the global economy, and transnational civil society interacted to shape and reinforce the process of change in Brazil.

It is clear, then, that the recent past has witnessed significant and continuing changes in the pattern of Brazil's foreign policy. There was a greater willingness to accept many of the dominant norms of the new liberal order of the post–Cold War period. As many prominent Brazilians proclaimed, their country (and Latin America more generally) was an integral part of the West and shared such core values as democracy, human rights, and market-based economic competition.

But there are also important limits to change. First, there is still a clear concern for Brazil's national interests, and power and autonomy continue to form a central element of how these national interests are defined. In this respect there is still a hard-nosed view of the international system and of the ways in which that system constrains Brazil's options. Liberal norms may be genuinely shared, but they may still reflect the particular interests of the United States and Europe. Emerging powers such as Brazil or India may agree with the *objectives* of the "new world order" that were espoused by U.S. leaders in the early 1990s, but they may also reject the *means* by which those objectives are pursued. There is also a continued desire to develop a more influential role for Brazil in which it is neither a status-quo power nor a deeply revisionist state. Its leaders no longer express serious grievances toward the international system, but they are far from satisfied. Many of their goals are defensive and continue to reflect Brazil's economic interests and its continued economic vulnerability. Others involve a more direct effort to increase its international influence.

CURRENT PRIORITIES IN FOREIGN AFFAIRS

In order to ascertain the balance between change and continuity and to explore the prospects for Brazil as an emerging power, the remainder of this chapter looks at three critical arenas of Brazilian foreign policy (in ascending order of importance): Brazil's role in international institutions, its regional engagement in South America, and its relations with the United States.

AN ACTIVE ROLE IN INTERNATIONAL INSTITUTIONS

As we have seen, Brazil is an important player in a growing number of international institutions that benefit emerging states by constraining the freedom of the most powerful global actors through established rules and procedures.[7] In addition, these institutions provide political space for their members to build new coalitions in order to affect emerging norms in ways that are congruent with their interests. International institutions are now widely seen as useful agents to counterbalance, or at least deflect, the preferences and policies of the most powerful states by opening up "voice opportunities" for smaller states to express their interests and gain political support in the broader marketplace of ideas.

Among other initiatives, Brazil has sought to enhance its role within the United Nations. It has been on the UN Security Council eight times,

---

[7]The WTO's mechanisms for settling trade disputes are a good example of this.

more than any other nonpermanent member other than Japan.[8] The 1990s also saw increased Brazilian involvement in UN peacekeeping and election-monitoring activities. Since 1991 Brazil has been involved in various multilateral operations in the African countries of Angola, Liberia, Mozambique, and Rwanda; the European states of Croatia and Macedonia; and the Central American countries of Guatemala and Nicaragua. Brazil also participated in peacekeeping efforts in Cambodia, and more recently it played an active role in the political transition of newly independent East Timor (see Chapter 9).

At the same time, Brazilian leaders have continued to place emphasis on the importance of state sovereignty and on the need to constrain interventionism, even for humanitarian purposes. They have provided only lukewarm support for the role of regional organizations in collective action, especially that of NATO in the Bosnia and Kosovo conflicts. They have also resisted moves toward more coercive forms of peacekeeping and toward an active UN role in peace *making*. In this latter case Brazil supported the UN intervention in Kuwait but did not send troops. Elsewhere, Brazil supported peace operations in Somalia and Rwanda but abstained over the proposed UN intervention in Haiti.

Within these institutions Brazil has employed the two classic strategies for exerting influence. The first may be called "insider activism." This involves working intensively within international institutions by encouraging diplomatic efforts, organizing negotiations and follow-up meetings, assembling regional experts to consider peaceful solutions, and clarifying the normative issues that establish the basis for outside intervention. Brazil's assertive diplomacy at the Vienna Human Rights Conference in 1993 provided a good example of this strategy. At Vienna, its leaders sought to play a central role as a "bridge builder" and were heavily involved in forming committees and networking on an informal basis.

The second strategy involves the formation of coalitions and continues to be an important source of influence. In the discussions on a "millennium trade round" within the WTO, Brazil sought to reassemble a broad coalition of developing countries in favor of pressing the industrialized countries to fulfill their commitments on market access before any new economic reforms were undertaken. Brazil also resisted the imposition of environmental and labor standards in the trade agenda. Taken together, its efforts highlighted the increasing complexity of forming coalitions. Within the WTO, for example, issues regarding agricultural

---

[8]In 1993, Brazil formally applied for permanent membership in the Security Council, which continues to reserve this status for just five countries: China, France, Great Britain, Russia, and the United States. As we have seen elsewhere in this volume, the governments of India, Indonesia, Japan, and South Africa have also sought permanent seats on the UN Security Council, which provide greater influence—as well as prestige—for their occupants.

trade, service industries, foreign investment, intellectual property, and bioengineering frequently produce overlapping, but distinct, lobbying coalitions. A natural ally on agricultural trade, for example, may take a very different line on trade in genetically altered products. This pattern of cross-cutting coalitions, however, is far different from the rigid North–South blocs of the Cold War era.

REGIONAL ENGAGEMENT IN SOUTH AMERICA

By the 1990s, South America was well established as a critical arena for Brazilian foreign policy and a central focus for any analysis of Brazil as an emerging power. In this respect there has been important progress in the regional security and arms-control fields. In September 1990, Collor formally renounced any Brazilian desire to acquire nuclear weapons and, in a symbolic gesture largely intended for U.S. consumption, closed the weapons testing facility at Serra do Cachimbo and approved greater civilian oversight of continuing nuclear research. The 1990 Joint Declaration on a Common Nuclear Policy created a system of jointly monitored safeguards. This system provided the basis of the December 1991 agreement between Brazil, Argentina, the IAEA, and a newly formed bilateral agency for controlling nuclear materials. This agreement, in turn, opened the way for full implementation of the Treaty of Tlatelolco that rendered South America a nuclear-free zone. Finally, the 1991 Mendonca Agreement (which included Chile) extended arms control to cover chemical and biological weapons.

The primary focal point of regional cooperation in the 1990s was in the area of economic integration (see Roett 1999). The 1991 Treaty of Asunción creating Mercosur was signed by Brazil, Argentina, Paraguay, and Uruguay and entered into force in November of that year. Mercosur has since emerged as an important force for regional economic cooperation and a potential rival of the North American Free Trade Area (NAFTA) and the European Union.[9] Mercosur is seen as a "regional laboratory" for modernization and global competitiveness and provides a means for aligning the internal and external aspects of liberal economic reform. As a result of parallel moves toward liberalization on both fronts, Mercosur was able to implement a common external tariff (with significant exceptions) that came into effect in January 1995.

Contrary to many expectations, Mercosur developed successfully through the 1990s, becoming the third-largest regional economic bloc in the

---

[9]Like the EU and NAFTA, Mercosur is much more than a trade agreement. Its related treaties cover a wide range of issues, including investment flows, dispute settlement, labor issues, and energy security. It also has an explicit political agenda, with a formal commitment to the consolidation of democracy in Latin America and overseas.

world (after the EU and NAFTA). Total intraregional trade grew from $5 billion in 1991 to more than $20 billion in 1997. By the latter year more than 30 percent of Argentina's exports were going to Brazil while nearly 13 percent of Brazil's exports went to Argentina. Both trends represented a significant upswing in the level of commerce between South America's two largest economies. Mercosur also emerged as a major target for foreign direct investment and sought to divert much of the investments that had previously been destined for East Asia before its economic crisis of 1997 and 1998.

Brazilian policy toward Mercosur has two faces. On the one hand, Brazil's status as the largest regional economic player gives it the means to press its own interests. Thus Brazilian leaders have consistently refused to allow regional economic integration to threaten their own key industrial sectors, and certainly not to constrain their autonomy in managing economic policy. Pressed both by powerful domestic industrial lobbies and by the external vulnerability that followed the East Asian economic crisis, Brazil has adopted unilateral protectionist measures. Its government has shown a penchant for unilateralism, believing that Argentina (with a GNP less than half the size of Brazil's) is economically vulnerable and has few options in foreign economic policy. This tendency to play economic hardball was visible in the disputes of 1999 and 2000 concerning the development of an automotive industry in South America and the respective roles to be played in the endeavor by the Brazilian and Argentine governments.

On the other hand, Mercosur is extremely important to Brazil's economic and foreign-policy goals. In three respects, this provides Brazil a major incentive to solve problems, often by means of intense, high-level presidential diplomacy. First, the direct costs of any reversion to rivalry with Argentina would be very high. Second, a prolonged souring of regional relations would undermine the strategic advantages of regional integration, which include a stronger international bargaining power and a united front in capturing export markets and attracting private investment from overseas. Third, Mercosur is critical to Brazil's relations with Europe. This is important given that the South American countries continue to favor the development of interbloc trade between the EU and Mercosur, their growing competition in key industrial and agricultural sectors notwithstanding.

Also of significance, Mercosur provides a political and economic framework for Brazil's broader foreign-policy goals in South America. In recognizing this fact, President Itamar Franco proposed in 1993 that Mercosur be expanded into a South American Free Trade Area. Association agreements were signed three years later with Chile and Bolivia. At the Brasilia Summit of South American leaders in August 2000, plans were announced for negotiations between Mercosur and South America's other regional economic bloc, the Andean Pact. Finally, and very importantly,

Mercosur is central to Brazilian relations with the United States. The idea of Mercosur as a counterweight, and as a negotiating instrument with the United States, has never been far beneath the surface. Brazil, then, has a powerful self-interest in managing the economic and political problems that arise within the grouping, even when these involve concessions to the weaker members.

So what kind of power is Brazil regionally? In keeping with its traditions, it has little interest in developing a strong military role within South America. Brazil's military power is very limited, particularly compared to other regional powers such as India. Its military forces are heavily concentrated in the Amazon region, where concerns remain strong regarding a possible spillover from the drug wars in Colombia. Brazilian leaders have learned from the past that talking too loudly about regional influence would only create opposition from Spanish-speaking South America. (As citizens of a former Portuguese colony, Brazilians continue to speak Portuguese.) Brazilian "self-containment" in the region therefore makes good geopolitical sense.

One measure of national power concerns the extent to which a country cannot be ignored when important international issues have to be determined. On this basis Brazil is certainly a major (perhaps *the* major) regional actor. The foreign policies of South American countries have increasingly come to take "the Brazilian factor" into account. But what of the more positive, managerial side of being a regional leader? Here the situation has undoubtedly changed significantly over the past two decades. For a long time there was an ambivalence toward Brazil's regional presence, a sense that Brazil was "in South America but not of South America," and a view that the region played a relatively minor part in its overall foreign policy. The "South Americanization" of Brazilian foreign policy goes back to the late 1970s, took a decisive turn with the rapprochement with Argentina in the 1980s, and was reinforced by the development of Mercosur. As a result Brazil has been pressed into a more activist role in South America. It has a clearer sense of its own regional interests and is steadily becoming more involved in shaping regional developments and in fostering a cohesive South American understanding of important international issues.

RELATIONS WITH THE UNITED STATES

Finally, we turn to Brazil's key interregional bilateral relationship. In contrast to past patterns, current relations between the United States and Brazil are not marked by overt tensions and crises. And yet, despite the rhetoric of a "mature dialogue," this bilateral link is far from close, and the 1990s witnessed recurrent conflicts over economic issues and fundamental differences in overall foreign-policy outlooks. Perhaps most notable is the absence of intense bilateral engagement. The United States has not sought to build its regional policy around close relations with Brazil, nor even to give any particular priority to South America's major regional power. Indeed, it is remarkable just how little Brazil has figured in Washington's policy statements of the post–Cold War era. Equally, Brazil has not sought to develop a powerful role for itself by means of a "special relationship" with Washington, as happened during the World War II or under the military government after 1964. Thus Brazilian pronouncements have continued to place emphasis on the idea of "universalism" and of the country as a global trader whose fundamental interests lie in multilateral coordination and political diversification.[10]

While Brazilian leaders have been unable to resist the need to redefine and improve their relations with the "lone superpower," they have sought to maintain their freedom of action by strengthening the viability of subregional options. For most of the 1990s Brazil chose to place itself at a distance from the rhetoric of a new liberal hemispheric community based on the shared values of democracy and free markets (see Corrales and Feinberg 1999). Their approach toward Washington has in this respect been markedly different from that of Mexico, which has become deeply enmeshed in North America as a result of NAFTA. There is also a contrast with Argentina, which sought extremely close relations with Washington in the 1990s under President Carlos Menem. This divergence reflected a deep-rooted belief that Brazil is different and is powerful enough to stand apart—not in radical opposition, but more cautious and more keen to preserve a considerable degree of freedom.

There have been several notable occasions on which Brasilia and Washington have collaborated politically and effectively. The two countries, for example, combined efforts to secure a peaceful settlement to the recent Peru–Ecuador border conflict and to support democracy in Paraguay. But there have also been important instances in which Brazil has sought to oppose or limit democratic interventionism, as in the case of Haiti and in response to the U.S. push for multilateral sanctions against Peruvian President Alberto Fujimori after he clamped down on the country's democratic institutions and suspended the Peruvian constitution. Brazilian leaders have also expressed doubts about escalating U.S. military involvement in Colombia and have maintained a strongly noninterventionist position on that conflict.

In terms of economic relations, there is a high level of economic interdependence between Brazil and the United States, but it is one-sided. Brazil certainly matters to the United States. For example, the United States exports more to Brazil than to China, Russia, or India. Of the top

---

[10]As described in Chapter 11, South Africa's government has also adopted a posture of "universalism" that is not unlike that espoused by Brazil in recent years.

500 U.S.-based multinational corporations, 420 currently operate in Brazil. Total U.S. investment in Brazil, currently around $40 billion and concentrated in the financial and manufacturing sectors, is larger than that in China, Russia, India, or even Mexico.[11] The United States is economically central to Brazil as a source of foreign investment; as a market, especially for its manufactured goods (the top three Brazilian exports to the United States in the late 1990s were aircraft, automobile parts, and shoes); and as a source of support during financial crises. However, the United States continues to dominate this economic relationship. The pattern of financial crises that recurred in the late 1990s has made Brazil intent on maintaining the confidence of foreign investors and dependent on the willingness of U.S.-dominated financial institutions to provide crisis support. This represents a major and enduring structural factor that limits Brazil's bargaining power in bilateral relations.

There are three sets of economic issues over which friction has arisen recently between Washington and Brasilia. First, U.S. leaders believe the Brazilian government has dragged its feet on economic reform in ways that directly harm U.S. interests. Second, continuing a pattern that goes back to the 1970s, Brazil has complained about the high levels of U.S. restrictions on the import of Brazilian products in such areas as steel, ethanol, sugar, shoes, textiles, orange juice, and meat. Within the WTO, Brazil has taken six cases against the United States, and the United States has presented three against Brazil. Third, and perhaps most importantly, there is the larger question of hemispheric economic integration, a point that deserves some elaboration.

By the mid-1990s, two subregional economic arrangements had been created: NAFTA in North America and Mercosur in South America. Reversing its past policy, the United States launched the idea of a hemispheric free-trade area—first with U.S. President George Bush's 1990 Enterprise for the Americas initiative, and more forcefully with the 1994 Miami Summit at which the Clinton administration proposed that a Free-Trade Area of the Americas (FTAA) be negotiated by the end of 2005. On many issues related to the substance and process of negotiations, the United States and Brazil have been far apart.

Mercosur and NAFTA represent distinct models of regional economic integration, so there are many important and difficult questions about the terms of a future hemispheric arrangement. Should the hemispheric pact be based on NAFTA? Should it be negotiated on the basis of existing agreements within NAFTA and Mercosur? How would this pact relate to regional cooperation in noneconomic areas? As the prospect of a free-trade area grew, Brazil placed primary emphasis on Mercosur rather than the

---

[11]For further details and a Brazilian perspective, see Barbosa (2000).

possibility of joining an expanded NAFTA (a position that clashed with that of Chile and Argentina). As the FTAA process gained momentum after 1994, Brazil adopted a defensive agenda, stressing the need for gradualism and respect for national positions.

After the Santiago Summit in 1997, Brazil assumed a more overt leadership role in defense of the Mercosur position and negotiated successfully on establishing the procedural ground rules for the FTAA process. These ground rules included the following provisions: Mercosur should negotiate as a single bloc, consensus of all member-states should be obtained, all economic sectors should be included in negotiations, trade rules should be compatible with WTO norms, the FTAA should coexist with other regional trade arrangements, and negotiations should continue until 2005.

The economic difficulties that arise between the United States and Brazil reflect the concrete interests of both sides. In this regard it is vital that the differences be understood through the prism of past history and through the mutual images that have been created over time. The U.S. government's frustration with Brazil is reinforced by Washington's unwillingness to forgo its "hegemonic presumptions," the idea that it is the natural leader in its own "backyard" with special rights and an expectation that regional states will fall into line. On the Brazilian side, there remains a persistent degree of resentment that the country is not taken more seriously in Washington.

The U.S. government's preponderant influence rests on three pillars: its relative strengths and its capacity to force Latin American states to follow its wishes through the use of a wide variety of carrots and sticks; its disproportionate ability to set the regional agenda and to ensure that the dominant norms of regional behavior reflect key U.S. principles and priorities; and the cultural and ideational power of its political system, civil society, and the "American way of life." As the dominant power in the region, Washington is significantly unconstrained and enjoys wide discretion in its statecraft. It is free to play economic hardball in pursuit of its short-term interests, and it does not need to soften its goals in order to appease potential regional rivals, as it does in its global relations (see Mastanduno 1999). Ultimately, despite the significant degree of economic ties, Brazil matters much less to the United States in terms of overall foreign-policy interests than Mexico, the Caribbean, or even the Andean region of South America.

What conclusions can we draw from hemispheric relations about Brazil's position as an emerging power? In one respect the continued reach of U.S. hegemony acts as a major constraint on Brazilian foreign policy. Yet the situation is more fluid and more complex than this picture of stark hegemony portrays. In the first place, to be sustainable, hegemony requires three things: power resources (both material and ideational), a clear hegemonic design, and firm domestic political support. While the enormous asymmetry of U.S. power toward the region remains self-evident, the other two factors are less clear-cut. The need to maintain U.S. long-term global preponderance does not necessarily press Washington toward deep engagement in Latin America. Moreover, economic integration with Mexico remains contentious in U.S. domestic politics and there remain domestic obstacles to hemispheric integration. It is precisely this fact that provides Brazil with the diplomatic and economic space to influence the ways in which the hemispheric political and economic agenda is played out in the future and to carve out a constrained but still autonomous and wide-ranging foreign policy.

Secondly, as noted earlier in this chapter, if we define power not just in terms of aggregate resources but in terms of the ability to achieve desired outcomes, the idea of U.S. hegemony looks less secure. For all its power Washington has been unable to find a solution to the problems of drug trafficking, illegal immigration, and the continuing instability and conflict in the Andean region. Furthermore, coercive pressure is a blunt instrument for promoting democracy and upholding human rights, two proclaimed priorities of the U.S. government. As liberal writers on hemispheric affairs insist, solving many of the most serious problems on the regional agenda (e.g., drugs, immigration, environmental decay, and threats to democratic transitions) requires deeper involvement and more cooperative policies. This, in turn, suggests the need for active engagement with major regional players such as Brazil and opens up a wider range of policy options for such players.

How Brazil's international role develops depends partly on its own objectives and on the degree to which it seeks a higher profile. This depends in turn on the country's continued economic and social progress and on whether domestic problems dominate the government's agenda or create external vulnerabilities that undercut activism in foreign policy.[12] But, as with so many aspects of the post–Cold War era, a great deal will hinge on the future direction of U.S. foreign policy, particularly as the administration of President George W. Bush redefines the nation's global strategy and regional priorities. The central U.S. role will depend largely upon the continued power and dynamism of the U.S. economy, whose robust growth of the 1990s slowed in the first years of the twenty-first century. How U.S. policy toward Latin America develops is not preordained amid such uncertainty, but it will remain the major factor shaping Brazil's future options in foreign affairs.

---

[12]This point was underscored in June 2001 when the Brazilian government, in the face of an acute energy crisis, imposed at least six months of obligatory electricity rationing.

THE SHIFTING LANDSCAPE
OF INDIAN FOREIGN POLICY

Raju G. C. Thomas
Marquette University

As other chapters of this volume have noted, the growing importance of economic issues has been a central reality in the adaptation of states' foreign policies to the world politics of the post–Cold War era. The case of India, whose population recently jumped past the one-billion mark, is no exception to this rule. Indeed, developments in the economic realm have profoundly influenced India's regional and global diplomatic and security policies.

The adaptation of Indian foreign policy may be summed up as a revolutionary shift from a situation in which ideology determined its economic system to the current situation in which market economics shape national politics and foreign policy. Former Prime Minister Jawaharlal Nehru's socialism and the foreign policies that flowed from it are now history. While many chronic regional and global security concerns remain, India now looks ahead to the integration of its rapidly growing economy within the global marketplace. In this respect, Indian leaders expect to play a constructive role in the statecraft of the twenty-first century.

Economic globalization has particularly cast its shadow across India through the growth of intergovernmental organizations, the spread of multinational corporations (MNCs), the expansion of computer industries, and rapid advances in Internet communications. Economic reforms begun in 1991 have transformed the old Indian socialist system into a market-oriented economy based largely on the private sector. This has resulted in a flurry of new MNCs into India, which has become one of the largest software developers in the world. India's rapid entry into the global market economy has positive as well as negative ramifications for policymakers. Political and strategic policies now need to be adjusted or modified by economic pressures, while economic conditions are more affected by political and security problems than ever before.

A related trend has been the transformation of the world economy into a U.S.- or Western-dominant system, which has further prompted New Delhi to adjust its foreign policies. For example, India's condemnations of the 1999 U.S.-led bombings of Yugoslavia over Belgrade's crackdown on its Muslim population in Kosovo had much to do with the precedent this set for the similar situation in India's northern region of Kashmir, which has an overwhelming Muslim majority population. These condemnations, however, and the urge to accept Russia's call for a Russian–Chinese–Indian "strategic partnership," were tempered by India's growing economic and technological ties to the West in general and the United States in particular. A key reason for this: The threat of war with Pakistan, which also claims control over Kashmir, undermines the confidence of foreign investors.

A similar case involved India's controversial nuclear weapons tests of 1998, which promptly led to Western economic sanctions and the denial of low-interest loans from the World Bank, the IMF, and Western governments. India's nuclear weapons and missile policies are at odds with Washington's nuclear nonproliferation policy and the Missile Technology Control Regime promoted by the United States. Defiance of these international regimes and the resulting imposition of Western technological sanctions have deprived India of Western technology for its nuclear energy and space programs and the development of domestically produced weapons for its armed services.

Yet traditional concerns, including military security and border disputes, remain crucial. Along these lines India's bilateral relations with neighboring Pakistan and China have continued to preoccupy New Delhi since the Cold War, along with its relations with the conflict's primary antagonists, the United States and the former Soviet Union. The interaction between regional and global politics over time is significant in shaping foreign policy. India's relations with Pakistan, for example, have drawn special attention to its broader policies toward the Islamic world, especially in the Middle East and Central Asia. India's relations with China, meanwhile, have required greater attention toward Eastern Asia, where India has sought to rival China as an Asian great power.[1]

THE RISE OF LIBERATED INDIA

Before we undertake a detailed examination of India's foreign policy since the Cold War, some historical perspective is in order. The following section briefly reviews the key developments in Indian foreign policy since

---

[1]India's relations with Africa and Latin America, by contrast, have tended to be largely apolitical, emphasizing economic cooperation and cultural exchanges with these regions.

its independence from Great Britain shortly after World War II. As we will see, India struggled throughout the Cold War to assert itself as a rising world power. This struggle, which produced mixed results as India found itself caught in the Cold War cross-fire, continues in the twenty-first century.

NEHRU'S NONALIGNMENT POLICY

Three months after India gained independence in 1947, its first prime minister, Jawaharlal Nehru (1961, 24), declared the following:

> [U]ltimately foreign policy is the outcome of economic policy, and until India has properly evolved her economic policy, her foreign policy will be rather vague, rather inchoate, and will be groping.... Whatever policy we may lay down, the art of conducting the foreign affairs of a country lies in finding out what is most advantageous to the country.

The above linkage between domestic economic policy and foreign policy carried four interrelated arguments (see Thomas 1978, 29–53). First, the primary task of newly independent India, which possessed the world's second largest population, was rapid industrialization and social development. Second, Nehru believed that from both the political and economic standpoints, the most acceptable means of attaining this objective was through a policy of democratic socialism.[2] This meant that India's parliamentary system, which was based on the British model, would implement a variant of the five-year economic plans launched by Soviet leader Joseph Stalin, but through voluntary and democratic means. This development model, which poured scarce resources into heavy public-sector industries, led to the neglect of agriculture and serious food shortages. Famine conditions in the 1960s were averted only through a large-scale food-aid program provided by the United States. The Indian government subsequently channeled more resources into agriculture, leading to the "green revolution" that greatly boosted food production.

The third argument that informed Nehru's development strategy was based on his view that the urgency of domestic economic transformation required a minimal diversion of resources to military defense. Finally, Nehru concluded that the best way to accomplish his objectives was through a policy of friendship with all states. The last point was translated into a foreign policy of nonalignment and "peaceful coexistence." From

---

[2]Indian socialism did not embody the "welfare state" model of many Western European states in the 1950s, such as Sweden, because India could not afford to provide free social services to its impoverished masses such as secondary education, medical care, unemployment compensation, and pensions. Compared to some of the mixed economies of Western Europe, the Indian government owned and operated a much larger proportion of heavy industries while it excluded or restricted private Indian and overseas competition.

the U.S. standpoint, however, this nonalignment policy was unsatisfactory. The most critical U.S. response to India's refusal to join Western military blocs was the decision to arm Pakistan unilaterally through the Southeast Asian Treaty Organization (SEATO) and the Central Treaty Organization (CENTO). The distinct and direct threat to India now appeared to come from a U.S.-armed Pakistan. The Indian government was convinced that Pakistan's reasons for joining these groups was to seize Kashmir by force, not to contain the spread of global communism. In any event, the Cold War quickly penetrated the regional subsystem of South Asia, creating bitter antagonisms both between India and the United States, and between India and its primary regional rival, Pakistan.

THE SOURCES OF INDO–PAKISTANI CONFLICT

The Kashmir issue is the legacy of the partition of India in August 1947, when British India was divided into the two newly independent states of India and Pakistan. The roots of this crisis go back to different interpretations and expectations regarding the underlying basis of that partition. In particular, India rejected the "two-nation theory" propounded by the leader of the All-India Muslim League and founder of Pakistan, Mohammed Ali Jinnah. He claimed that Hindus and Muslims, by virtue of their religions, constituted two separate nations. Thus, Punjabi, Bengali, and Tamil Muslims—three distinct linguistic and racial groups based at the three corners of the subcontinent—were theoretically all part of Pakistan. Their Hindu counterparts, according to this logic, belonged in Hindustan (see Thomas 1994, 11–22).

The Indian National Congress, led by Nehru and Mohandas Gandhi, and all subsequent Indian governments have consistently rejected this theory. They have claimed that, while they accepted the inevitability of a separate Pakistan to avoid a bloody Hindu–Muslim civil war, the formation of the two states could not be determined by Jinnah's "two-nation theory." Religion did not constitute the basis of nation or state, and accordingly, India declared itself a secular state after independence, albeit with an 80-percent Hindu majority.

Eventually, an agreement was reached to separate the Muslim majority areas of British India to become part of the new state of Pakistan. The new Muslim state was to be formed only in two large areas, in the west and the east, although concentrations of Muslims were to be found scattered in pockets throughout India amidst Hindu majorities. The main force of the "Pakistan" movement among Muslims arose in these Hindu-majority areas that remained in India because it was they who most feared Hindu domination once the British left India. Except for about seven million of the Muslims who migrated to West and East Pakistan (now Bangladesh), most Muslims were left behind in India after the creation of Pakistan.

After the 1947 declaration of a separate state of Pakistan, some 600 "native" Indian states ruled by Hindu and Muslim princes were asked to join either India or Pakistan. Some of these states were the size of a private university campus, and others the size of France. Their accession to either India or Pakistan was to be determined by two conditions: the religion of the majority of their population; and whether the state bordered East or West Pakistan, if the ruler wished to join Pakistan.

Three princely states provided problems. Hyderabad, a large state in the Southern Indian peninsula had a Hindu majority and was ruled by a Muslim ruler. This territory, however, was located far from Pakistan. The Muslim Nizam of Hyderabad wanted independence, but the state was seized by Indian forces. Junagadh, a much smaller state, faced a similar situation of Muslim ruler and Hindu population. It was close to Pakistan but not territorially contiguous. The Muslim Nawab of Junagadh formally acceded to Pakistan and the accession was duly accepted by Jinnah, but the Nawab was overthrown spontaneously by his Hindu population. Finally, Jammu and Kashmir was a geographically large, but sparsely populated state that bordered both India and Pakistan. The population of this state in the valley of Kashmir—the bone of contention between India and Pakistan—was 90 percent Muslim and 10 percent Hindu. Thus, Pakistan's claim to Kashmir was based on the two conditions of majority religion and territorial contiguity that had been fulfilled. India's claim to Kashmir was based upon the rejection of the "two-nation theory" and the acceptance of the legal rights of the ruler to accede to India or Pakistan.

The Hindu leader of Kashmir, Hari Singh, was considering independence when Pakistani forces invaded the state in order to annex it to Pakistan. As the state was about to fall, the leader acceded to India, whose forces then moved in to repel the Pakistani attack. Nehru took the issue to the UN with a complaint of Pakistani aggression. The UN arranged for a cease-fire, which has since divided Kashmir along the current "Line of Control" between India and Pakistan, the former holding two-thirds including the prized Kashmir Valley, and the latter one-third in the northwest.[3]

Under the terms of the UN-sponsored cease-fire, a plebiscite was to be conducted among the peoples of Kashmir. But this was to be held only after Pakistan withdrew all of its forces from Kashmir, to be followed by India, which was to withdraw the bulk of its forces, leaving some contingents behind to maintain order. Pakistan, however, never took the first step. India withdrew the offer of a plebiscite in 1954 when Pakistan joined the U.S.-led SEATO alliance. India alleged that Pakistan's motive was not to contain communism, SEATO's stated objective, but to obtain U.S. arms in order to seize Kashmir by force, which it attempted to do in September 1965.

---

[3]China, meanwhile, occupied the Aksai Chin plateau, a small sector in the northeast Buddhist region of Kashmir called Ladakh.

In 1971, following the massacres of Bengalis in East Pakistan by Punjabi and Pashtun forces from West Pakistan, the Bengali population arose in revolt. With the help of Indian military forces, Pakistani forces were defeated and the new state of Bangladesh was created. This, however, failed to create a stable environment on the subcontinent. As a result, tensions between India and Pakistan festered along religious, political, and geographical lines. All of this was aggravated by the regional designs and interventions of the Cold War superpowers.

TENSIONS ON THE SINO–INDIAN FRONTIER

In its first fifteen years of independence, the Indian government's perceptions of threat were almost exclusively focused on Pakistan. Among other results of this preoccupation was the neglect of India's northern borders along the Himalayan Mountains. India's relations with China, which was transformed into a communist state in 1949 (see Chapter 4), had worsened after Chinese forces seized control of Tibet the following year (Thomas 1978, 40–45). However, for Nehru, there was no question of approving or disapproving of the communist revolution led by Mao Zedong. From Nehru's perspective, it was most noteworthy that an Asian nation had shed a century of European interference and domination. While India and Pakistan had already gone to war over Kashmir, in the recorded history of Asia there had never been any conflict between various Indian and Chinese empires. Thus, India became one of the first countries to recognize communist China and was one of its most ardent supporters.

Yet the seeds of conflict between India and China existed from the outset over China's occupation of Tibet, a vast and mountainous region just across India's northern border. Nehru's solution came in an agreement with Chinese premier Zhou Enlai on April 29, 1954. The Sino–Indian treaty on Tibet was governed by a preamble that came to be known as *Panchshil*, or the Five Principles of Peaceful Coexistence. These called for (1) mutual respect for each other's territorial integrity and sovereignty, (2) mutual nonaggression, (3) mutual noninterference in each other's internal affairs, (4) equality and mutual benefit, and (5) peaceful coexistence.

The treaty, however, had virtually signed away the Indian position regarding the autonomy of Tibet. During the debate in the Lok Sahba (lower house of parliament), Nehru tried to justify the agreement by pointing out the strategic inevitability of the situation. In his view, peace between India and China, which now had 1,800 miles of common frontier, would guarantee peace in Asia. As Nehru (quoted in Thomas 1978, 42) argued, "Several Honorable Members have referred to the 'melancholy chapter of Tibet.' I really do not understand. What did any Honorable Member of this House expect us to do in this regard to Tibet at any time? Did we fail, or did we do a wrong thing? The fact is, and it is a major fact of the middle of the twentieth century, that China has become a great power, united and strong."

The Tibetan revolt and Chinese crackdown, and the flight of the Dalai Lama and thousands of Tibetans to India in 1959, increased tensions between India and China. India now discovered that China had occupied the Aksai Chin plateau in the Ladakh sector of Kashmir, while the communist regime laid claims to the region between Nepal and Bhutan occupied by India. The Indian government's policy toward China came under intense criticism in the Indian parliament and in the press. The result was an outpouring of war-mongering rhetoric in India against China regarding the territorial integrity of the Indian state. In China, all of this rhetoric in the freewheeling Indian democracy was taken seriously and eventually descended into war in October 1962 (see Whiting 1975, 42–62).

The problem was further aggravated at this time by the nuclear confrontation between Washington and Moscow over the installation of Soviet missiles in Cuba. While this crisis was quickly diffused in the Americans' favor, the two superpowers were unwilling to risk another nuclear confrontation over the Sino–Indian border war. The war finally ended in December with a unilateral withdrawal of Chinese forces from territory it had seized. In this war, which was confined to ground operations by both sides, the ill-equipped and ill-prepared Indian forces were crushed. The territorial situation has remained unchanged since 1962 with both sides occupying the areas of strategic importance to themselves. However delicately, peaceful coexistence has been maintained between the two regional powers.

BILATERAL RELATIONS SINCE THE COLD WAR

The developments highlighted earlier defined India's foreign relations during the Cold War period. Despite the many conflicts that occurred during this period, India maintained its territorial integrity, along with a foreign policy that refused to accede to the demands of either superpower. Yet with its economy seeking to keep up with its immense and rapidly growing population, India struggled as an emerging world power. It is to the impact of this long struggle on India's current foreign relations that we now turn our attention.

NEW ECONOMIC TIES WITH THE UNITED STATES

The end of the Cold War, marked by the collapse of the Soviet Union in December 1991, transformed the global security environment. This sudden change generated a catharsis in India's security perspectives and policies. However, even before 1991, India's security problems were not directly related to Cold War politics. The primary sources of Indian security fears were regional, not global, but these fears were compounded by great-power intrusions into the region emanating from the intrigues of the Cold War. Rivalry between the United States and the Soviet Union, and later between China and the Soviet Union, enabled Pakistan to obtain U.S. and Chinese military assistance in order to counter Indian military capabilities. Meanwhile, India had turned increasingly to the Soviet Union for weapons to counter or preempt Pakistani arms procurement from the United States and China.

Following the end of the Cold War, nonalignment, the one-time fulcrum of India's foreign and security policy, became irrelevant (see Thomas 2000). With no competing global power blocs, India has recognized that the West in general, and the United States in particular, is militarily and economically dominant. Russia can be of little assistance to India, as compared to the situation during the Cold War, in countering Washington's regional ambitions.

Immediately after the Cold War, India sought greater military cooperation with the United States but soon ran into several obstacles. These included India's refusal to protect U.S. pharmaceutical patents, its decision to buy engines from Russia for India's rocket program and two nuclear reactors for its energy program, and the testing of the Prithvi and Agni missiles despite U.S. warnings. Most importantly, the underground detonation of five nuclear devices in May 1998 triggered U.S. bilateral as well as multilateral sanctions against India. The Indian government rejected these efforts to control its missile program and strongly defended its right to maintain its status as a nuclear power. Taken together, such disputes produced growing suspicions in India about its presumed friendship with the United States.

While Indo–American military ties have not progressed as well as both sides would have liked, economic ties between the two countries have been booming as never before. The United States had been India's main trading partner during the latter stages of the Cold War and became the leading foreign investor in India. Following a series of economic reforms in 1991, several U.S. corporations rushed into India with new investments. During 1997–1998, the Indian government approved more than 2,500 foreign investment projects from the United States, nearly 20 percent of the total approved for that year. Indian exports to and imports from the United States were 23 percent and 12 percent of its total trade, respectively, making the United States India's largest trading partner.[4]

---

[4]India's relations with the governments of Europe and East Asia (other than China), meanwhile, are now almost strictly economic, based upon trade and investments. There are no serious political disputes of any kind with the countries of Europe or East Asia beyond the ongoing disapproval from governments in both regions of India's nuclear policy.

More importantly, the United States is the only major country with which India has had a favorable trade balance in recent years. A further rise in bilateral trade and investments was expected between the two countries following President Clinton's visit to India in March 2000.

The 1971 Indo–Soviet Treaty, renewed in August 1991 without change, was one of the major casualties of India's post–Cold War foreign and defense policies. The utility of forging a treaty between India and Russia along the lines of the old treaty had become dubious. Russia had little strategic interest in South Asia except as a potential market for arms and missile technology sales in exchange for hard currency. However, a new vigor emerged in Indo–Russian relations as Indo–American strategic ties failed to make progress. Russia may feel the need to assert greater independence of action from the West, and both India and Russia may perceive common concerns in dealing with problems that may arise in Central Asia.[5]

Indian and Russian leaders met repeatedly in 1996 and 1997 to explore these mutual ties further. However, planned visits by President Boris Yeltsin failed to materialize, first because of the Russian president's ill health in 1997, and then because of the fall of the Indian government in January 1998. Following NATO's 1999 assault on Yugoslavia without sanction from the UN Security Council, Indian politicians, defense analysts, and journalists endorsed a plan to accept Russian Prime Minister Yvgeny Primakov's call for a triangular alliance among Russia, China, and India. All three countries fiercely condemned the NATO attacks as an illegal and unprovoked aggression against a sovereign independent state. Notably, all three countries faced similar problems as Yugoslavia in their own Muslim-majority provinces of Chechnya (Russia), Xinjiang (China), and Kashmir (India). In China's case, the Tibet question was also relevant, although rarely stated in Sino–Indian communications.

While Russia had few economic benefits to offer India, military collaboration between the two countries was revived in the mid-1990s. Indeed, the positive trends in Indo–American relations that ushered in Clinton's visit to India in 2000 were overshadowed in October by the visit of Russian President Vladimir Putin. The visit led to the declaration of an Indo–Russian "strategic partnership." Indian Prime Minister A. B. Vajpayee declared bilateral understanding between the two countries to be "essential to peace and stability in Asia and the world." In return, Putin shared India's concern on terrorist violence in Jammu and Kashmir and

---

[5]In May 1992, Russia's foreign minister noted during his visit to India that the potential rise of Islamic fundamentalism and the ongoing changes in the Central Asian republics showed that Russia and India were on a geopolitical axis, sharing common goals and perceived dangers.

asserted that these border conflicts should be resolved bilaterally between India and Pakistan. The substantive part of the Indo–Russian strategic partnership was a $3-billion arms agreement that included the licensed production in India of 140 Sukhoi SU-30MKI fighters, the purchase of 310 battle tanks, and the acquisition of the Russian aircraft carrier *Admiral Gorchkov*.[6] Beyond this, Russia agreed to sell India three more nuclear reactors in addition to the two already being installed at Kudankulam in Tamil Nadu.

Meanwhile, China was also relying heavily on purchases from Russia to bolster its conventional military capabilities. It was probably no coincidence that the visit of Indian Prime Minister Deve Gowda to Moscow in March 1997 was followed almost hours later by the visit of Chinese Foreign Minister Qian Qichen to prepare the visit of Chinese President Jiang Zemin to Russia in April. President Zemin had already visited India in November 1996, and was warmly received by Indian leaders. The visit recalled the days of Sino–Indian friendship in the early 1950s.

One interpretation of these high-level visits to Moscow is that Russia, upset by its failure to prevent NATO enlargement (see Chapter 3), is seeking new partnerships with India and China in the post–Cold War world. Indeed, as noted earlier, there have been voices in both India and Russia that a new triangular defense relationship should be established between India, Russia, and China to counter NATO expansion and the military dominance of the West. Such a triangle, however, is unlikely to go beyond a loose and informal relationship since all three countries are dependent on their economic ties with the West. The rapid rise of India's trade with the United States, and the even more spectacular rise of U.S. investments in India, place upper limits on the type of Indo–Soviet strategic cooperation that emerged during the latter half of the Cold War.

INDIA'S OPENING TO CHINA

Relations between India and China, meanwhile, also took center stage in the aftermath of the Cold War. There was a steady thaw in Sino–Indian relations since 1990, marred only by Indian concerns about the transfer of Chinese nuclear technology and the sale of M-11 missiles to Pakistan. Underlying the Sino–Indian thaw is a greater convergence of strategic interests than is readily apparent. Although nothing was said on the Kashmir question, there may be increasing sympathy for the Indian position given China's own separatist movement among the Tibetans and among the Ugyur Muslims of Xinjiang. In December 1991, Chinese premier Li Peng

---

[6]Some $5 to $7 billion worth of additional arms deals were also reported to be in the pipeline following Putin's visit. Predictably, Pakistan protested the Indo–Russian strategic partnership and the arms deals as destabilizing for the region.

visited India, the first Chinese prime minister to do so since Zhou Enlai visited India in 1962 prior to the outbreak of the Sino–Indian war. Li Peng's visit reciprocated the earlier visit to China in 1988 by Indian Prime Minister Rajiv Gandhi. Significantly, this was the first prime ministerial visit of its kind since Gandhi's grandfather, Jawaharlal Nehru, visited China in 1962.

The 1991 communiqué between the Indian and Chinese governments condemned the rise of "international oligarchies," an apparent reference to the military dominance of the West in the post–Cold War era. Later, during a second high-level summit meeting in May 1992, Chinese leaders declared that cooperation between India and China was essential in order for both countries to avoid being "left behind" and "bullied by others." These visits were significant largely in terms of adding to the ongoing gestures of Sino–Indian reconciliation.

Much is made of the fundamental differences between India and China—for instance, that their political systems are radically different, that they are economic competitors at both the regional and global levels, and that they are possibly even military antagonists in Asia. Yet the only serious potential for friction between the two Asian giants has been the Himalayan border dispute, noted previously, which led to war in 1962. This problem was addressed through a series of meetings of the India–China Joint Working Groups that began negotiations following Li Peng's visit. It culminated in the implementation of the Border Peace and Tranquility Agreement of 1994. The two countries also celebrated the fortieth anniversary of the Five Principles of Peaceful Coexistence signed by Nehru and Zhou Enlai in 1954. A high point of these growing ties was reached in November 1996 when Jiang Zemin paid an official visit to India, the first Chinese head of state to visit India. During this visit, both sides agreed to significant troop reductions along the border, although no formal treaty was signed settling the dispute. The Tibetan question was not addressed—Tibetan refugees who turned up in New Delhi to protest were ignored—and China did not raise the Kashmir question on behalf of Pakistan.

There was, however, some deterioration in Sino–Indian ties following India's nuclear tests in May 1998. These tests were justified by the Indian government as a necessary response to the growth of Chinese economic and military power and the U.S. political and economic preference for closer ties with China than with India. Perhaps spurred by NATO's assault on Yugoslavia during which time Russia, China, and India took up a common stance of opposition, Sino–Indian relations have shown improvement. On the Pakistani attempts to seize parts of Kashmir on the Indian side of the "Line of Control," China has endorsed the Indian position against Pakistan. Meetings between Indian and Chinese officials in October 1999 resolved many other contentious issues between the two countries, which agreed to maintain a "security dialogue" on issues of mutual interest.

INDIA AS A NUCLEAR POWER

The question of whether India should become a nuclear weapons power initially became a critical issue in response to the first Chinese atomic test in October 1964 (see Thomas 1998, 284–309; and Thomas and Gupta 2000, 1–12). That test was conducted just two years after the Sino–Indian war of 1962, when the Indian army was crushed by Chinese forces along their Himalayan frontiers. Thereafter, India participated in the negotiations leading up to the 1968 Non-Proliferation Treaty (NPT) but then refused to sign because of the discriminatory clauses between the nuclear "haves" and "have-nots."

The Indian policy of maintaining the nuclear option was perceived to be a strategic middle ground between the extremes of action and inaction. The formal renunciation of nuclear weapons by signing the NPT was considered unacceptable. From India's view, the potential threat from a nuclear China during times of crisis on the subcontinent required flexibility in terms of future nuclear policy (Thomas 1986, 28–30, 44–50, 174–181). Following the Sino–Indian war and the Chinese atomic test in 1964, arguments for countering the growth of Chinese nuclear weapons capability were strong. China's ultimatum to India during the 1965 Indo–Pakistani war strengthened the claims of the pro-bomb lobby in India at the time. This position was primarily upheld by the pro-Hindu party, Jan Sangh, which later became the Bharatiya Janata Party (BJP) that assumed power in March 1998 and quickly turned India into a nuclear power.

Pressures within India to acquire nuclear weapons intensified during the East Pakistani revolt against West Pakistan and the ensuing civil war that began in March 1971. That crisis, as noted earlier, ended with the Indo–Pakistani war of December 1971 and the creation of the new state of Bangladesh. During this prolonged crisis, which kept India and Pakistan on the brink of war, efforts by U.S. President Richard Nixon and his national security adviser, Henry Kissinger, to seek normalized U.S. relations with China suddenly raised doubts about the credibility of external nuclear guarantees against China. The signing of the Indo–Soviet Treaty of Peace and Friendship in August 1971 may be interpreted as the immediate Indian reaction to these global realignments among the major powers. The treaty was intended to negate Chinese threats to intervene in the looming Indo–Pakistani conflict by formalizing Indo–Soviet ties, thereby increasing the risk of Soviet military intervention against China on behalf of India.

In spite of the treaty, doubts remained about the long-term effects of the new Sino–American relationship on India's nuclear security. The nuclear insurance provided by the hostility of both superpowers against China before 1971 had been reduced to a more dubious Soviet nuclear guarantee alone. Because the United States and the Soviet Union were perceived to neutralize each other with their retaliatory strike capabilities, potential Chinese nuclear threats would appear more credible. The intrusion of the U.S. nuclear-powered carrier, the *USS Enterprise*, into the Bay of Bengal in a show of force against India during the Indo–Pakistani war of December 1971 further strengthened the case for nuclear weapons. An Indian decision was therefore made in 1972 to go for the bomb, and the 1974 atomic test may be seen as the delayed response by Prime Minister Indira Gandhi to the evolving global realignments. However, the decision to detonate in May 1974 may also be interpreted to be primarily directed at a domestic Indian audience to shore up the prime minister's sagging prestige.

Pakistani military defeat and its dismemberment produced a similar decision in 1972 on the part of Prime Minister Zulfikar Ali Bhutto to acquire nuclear weapons. This program was accelerated following the Indian atomic test in 1974. While the Western outcry against India's "peaceful nuclear explosion" appeared to end the prospect of an Indian nuclear program, Pakistan vigorously pursued many avenues for acquiring a nuclear capability. These developments climaxed in 1988 and 1989, when Indian reports claimed that Pakistan had produced a few bombs based on the uranium enrichment process, or at least had acquired the capability to assemble the bomb on short notice.

Herein lay the case for the bomb in India (see Subrahmanyam 1987, 51–122; and Thomas and Gupta 2000, 87–122). While it was one thing to accept the risk of a Chinese nuclear threat all these years without an Indian response, it was quite another to expect India to ignore a nuclear China as well as a Pakistan with "bombs in the basement," Israeli-style. With further allegations that India's two traditional adversaries had colluded in the design and development of the Pakistani nuclear program, the pressure to go nuclear was great.

The acquisition of nuclear weapons in itself would have provided no security value unless India could establish and manage a stable, two-way nuclear-deterrent relationship with China and Pakistan. This, too, was perceived to be a feasible proposition with the development and deployment of the Indian missiles. Assessments in the 1990s of the number of nuclear warheads that India could produce from its plutonium stockpile ranged from 80 to 300.

The Indian argument in May 1998 for discarding the policy of "No Bombs and No NPT" was that this ambiguous stance provided no deterrence or defense against a Chinese, Pakistani, or other nuclear threat from the Middle East (Thomas and Gupta 2000, 13–36, 87–122). Yet the primary justification for India's decision to acquire an independent nuclear deterrent may have been global rather than regional. India's traditional ally and nuclear guarantor, the Soviet Union, was succeeded by a weak Russia dependent on the West for economic survival. When Western economic assistance is dangled before Moscow, Russian protests or threats to take action against U.S. military actions against its allies tend to evaporate quickly. If Russia could not deter NATO's attack on Serbia during the Kosovo crisis, it would hardly be able to deter a Western attack on India over human rights abuses in Kashmir.

Under these new global strategic conditions, Indian security analysts now argued that nuclear deterrence had become more essential than before if India's sovereignty were to be maintained. However, the motive and timing of the BJP government to conduct five nuclear tests in May 1998 did not appear to be based upon some immediate or distant strategic imperative. As noted earlier, the Hindu nationalist party had declared since the mid-1960s that India should become a nuclear power. It repeated this objective during the 1998 election campaign and then felt compelled to fulfill the campaign promise.

Meanwhile, the prospects of India signing the Comprehensive Test Ban Treaty (CTBT) dimmed following the U.S. Senate's refusal to ratify the treaty in 1999. Even if India did sign the CTBT, there is no indication that India would reverse its policy of maintaining nuclear forces through the simulated tests of nuclear weapons in labs and continued development of missile capabilities. In demonstrating its pronuclear stance, the BJP-led Indian government in March 1999 endorsed a major program for missile development that would eventually give India an intercontinental capability.[7]

In an August 1999 document entitled "India's Nuclear Doctrine," the government clarified the objectives, composition, deployment, and control of India's nuclear weapons. In its preamble, the document stated that the use of nuclear weapons and other weapons of mass destruction constituted the "gravest threat to humanity and to peace and stability in the international system." The report, however, drew a distinction between nuclear weapons, on the one hand, and biological and chemical weapons, "which have been outlawed by international treaties." In the Indian government's view, nuclear weapons "remain instruments for national and collective security." The nuclear doctrine went further. First, it argued that the country's "credible and survivable nuclear deterrent" would be safeguarded through appropriate command-and-control facilities. Second, India would maintain a no-first-use nuclear policy and would use such weapons only for retaliatory purposes. Finally, nuclear weapons would never be used to threaten nonnuclear-weapons states that were not aligned with existing nuclear-weapons states.

Critics have alleged that the doctrine's release was a political ploy on the part of the BJP government to improve its chances of winning a clear

---

[7]Despite their profound differences on regional security issues, India and Pakistan have signed and ratified the multilateral 1972 Biological Weapons Convention, which went into effect in 1974, and the 1993 Chemical Weapons Convention, which went into effect in 1997.

majority in parliament during the September 1999 elections. However, there was no indication from the rival Congress Party that it disapproved of the doctrine in principle. Concerns have also been raised that this seemingly irreversible decision by the National Security Advisory Board would lead to a nuclear arms race between India and Pakistan, at a very high economic price that neither country could afford. This criticism, however, was widely dismissed by BJP officials as India's nuclear status became a fact of life.

ONGOING CONCERNS IN SOUTH ASIA

An Indian nuclear doctrine alone appears to be quite meaningless unless it is linked to other serious problems that India faces in the areas of conventional security, cross-border insurgency, and terrorism. The problem is reflected in Kashmir, where terrorist tactics and guerrilla warfare sponsored by Pakistan could escalate to an Indo–Pakistani conventional war that could, under current circumstances, then escalate to nuclear war. Conversely, the three-way Indian, Pakistani, and Chinese doctrines of mutual nuclear deterrence may prevent India from resorting to conventional war for fear of escalation to nuclear levels. This could allow Pakistan to conduct insurgency and terrorism through its proxies. All of these factors have greatly complicated the security environment in South Asia, a subject to which we now turn.

MILITARY BRINKMANSHIP WITH PAKISTAN

Unlike past crises over Kashmir between India and Pakistan that provoked conventional wars between the two states, the ongoing prolonged crises since 1989 involve terrorism, insurgency, and a proxy war (see Bose 1997; Kadian 1993; Akbar 1991; and Lamb 1991). There is also a fundamental difference in the nature of the current Kashmir crisis. As noted previously, past differences between India and Pakistan concerned the acceptance and validity of the "two-nation theory" of Hindu and Muslim nations in an undivided India. The current Kashmir crisis is far more international and broadly "Islamic" in character. Various Kashmiri insurgent groups have adopted the Islamic fundamentalist beliefs of Iran, learned from the insurgency tactics of the Afghan rebels during the Soviet occupation, and have assumed the style and approach of the Palestinian *intifada* ("uprising").

Tensions between India and Pakistan were revived following the Indian nuclear tests and Pakistan's tests in May 1998. The result has been to revive and internationalize the Kashmir issue. However, belligerent rhetoric in the aftermath of the tests gave way to greater efforts to promote peace and cooperation in South Asia, culminating in the bilateral Lahore Declaration of February 1999. While the declaration was welcomed in India by almost all parties except a small minority on the Hindu nationalist fringe, it was not accepted by Pakistani opposition groups. Indo–Pakistani relations plummeted in June 1999, when Pakistani-supported *mujaheddin* backed by regular forces seized the Kargil sector of Indian-held Kashmir across the Line of Control. India called the Pakistani actions a betrayal of India's offer of friendship and a broken promise of a new beginning between the two countries.

The military coup in Pakistan in October 1999 caused further alarm in New Delhi. The December 1999 hijacking, hostage-taking, and release of an Indian Airlines plane en route from Khatmandu to New Delhi by Pakistani militants highlighted once again the terrorist problem faced by India over the Kashmir issue. After an eight-day standoff, mainly on the tarmac at Kandahar airport in Afghanistan, the Indian government finally met the minimum condition for the release of jailed Pakistani cleric, Maulana Masood Azhar, and two other Pakistani members of an Islamic militant group who were engaged in violent efforts to separate Kashmir from India and annex it to Pakistan. This crisis brought Indo–Pakistani relations to the all-time low since the two countries went to war over Kashmir following India's independence in 1947.

RELATIONS WITH BANGLADESH, SRI LANKA, AND NEPAL

As noted earlier, India's military intervention in East Pakistan in December 1971 during the Bengali struggle for independence from West Pakistani military rule brought about the new state of Bangladesh (see Sisson and Rose 1990). Early relations between India and Bangladesh were generally cordial until the assassination in 1975 of Shaikh Mujibur Rahman, the country's first prime minister, who led the struggle for independence. Much of his family was also massacred except for a daughter, who happened to be visiting India at the time. Indo–Bangladeshi relations soured thereafter.

A central problem was the unresolved question of India's decision to build a dam on the Ganges River to control flooding and other problems that were affecting the West Bengal port of Calcutta. Bangladesh complained that the dam would deprive its impoverished people of much-needed irrigation water in the other Ganges tributaries that flowed into East Bengal. The issue became a source of bitter contention between India and a series of military and civilian governments in Bangladesh. In January 1997, however, Indian Prime Minister Gowda met with his counterpart in Bangladesh, Shaikh Hasina Wazed, and signed an agreement on the sharing of the waters of the Ganges.

Relations between India and neighboring Sri Lanka have also been complex and contentious. The main source of political friction between India and Sri Lanka concerned the status and the treatment of the Tamils. About 13 percent of Sri Lanka's population of 18 million is composed of the original Tamils, an ethnic group that migrated to the island more than 2,500 years ago. Other Tamils in modern times were indentured labor brought to Sri Lanka from India by the British to work in the tea plantations. Initially, disputes between India and Sri Lanka (then known as Ceylon) arose from the status of "Indian" Tamils following the departure of the British. Sri Lankan officials wanted the Indian Tamils, numbering about one million, to be repatriated back to India. A compromise was reached in 1964 whereby India would repatriate approximately half of these Indian Tamils to India, and Sri Lanka would give citizenship to the rest. The "plantation Tamils," as they are now called, are not involved in the violent struggle by other Tamils for secession from Sri Lanka. Cooperation between India and Sri Lanka has weakened the Tamil struggle for independence but has not ended the uprising.

Although Nepal is the only other Hindu majority state in the world apart from India, occasional tensions have occurred between the two countries. Sandwiched between India and China, Nepal is anxious not to alienate either Asian giant. However, as a landlocked state, all of Nepali trade travels through India, and questions regarding customs and transit facilities have caused differences. Nepal has claimed interference in the rights of passage for goods to and from Nepal, while India has complained about goods that are not subject to Indian customs and end up in Indian black markets. Nepal's monarchy has also complained at times of Indian interference in its domestic politics.

PROMOTING REGIONAL COOPERATION

In addition to its bilateral relations, the Indian government has sought to advance its interests through regional cooperation. Prominent among other regional groups, the South Asian Association for Regional Cooperation (SAARC), launched in 1983, was intended as a confidence-building system in South Asia by encouraging the growth of economic and social cooperation among India, Pakistan, Bangladesh, Nepal, Sri Lanka, Bhutan, and the Maldives. The organization has endured the transition from the Cold War to the post–Cold War era, and new roles for it have been openly debated. One conceivable direction that SAARC could take would be to move toward a large confederation of states, roughly along the lines of the European Union. The less ambitious but more feasible agenda for SAARC would be to emulate the Association of Southeast Asian Nations (ASEAN), which thus far has proved to be an effective consultative body concerned with regional economic and security issues.

The 1983 New Delhi Declaration that formalized SAARC made it clear that this was essentially an intergovernmental organization. It was not intended to become a supranational organization along the lines of some EU bodies (see Chapter 6). The South Asian group confines its discussions to the economic and social arenas only. As a matter of policy, it excludes all contentious security and political issues that might reduce meetings to accusations and recriminations. Mainly under India's insistence, SAARC also attempts to keep the military forces of major external powers away from the region. This is quite unlike the ASEAN approach, which has seen the role of external military powers (primarily the United States) in the region as essential to the maintenance of strategic stability.

The strategy of excluding all contentious political issues from the deliberations of SAARC was adopted in large part to isolate the dispute over Kashmir between India and Pakistan. Inclusion of the Kashmir dispute almost certainly would have paralyzed the organization and led to its early demise. Issues regarding the Ganges River dispute between India and Bangladesh, the Tamil secessionist struggle in Sri Lanka, and Indo–Nepalese disputes regarding overland trade routes through India were also left off SAARC agendas. As noted previously, India's differences with these countries over such issues have been addressed primarily through bilateral negotiations.

Another major concern among the smaller members of SAARC is India's natural economic dominance. After all, India is a country whose population of more than one billion is about seven times larger than that of the next most populous state in South Asia. India's level of economic output, estimated at nearly $2 billion in 1999, also overshadows its neighbors. It has thus been argued by the smaller states within SAARC that any attempt at regional economic integration through the removal of trade barriers would cause the other economies to be overwhelmed by the Indian economy.[8] At the same time, Bangladesh, Nepal, and Sri Lanka are eager to penetrate the large Indian market and have pushed for a South Asian Free Trade Association (SAFTA), a customs-free union that would resemble the North American Free Trade Agreement (NAFTA) that includes the United States, Canada, and Mexico.

A TILT TOWARD SOUTHEAST ASIA

India and Pakistan are looking now in different directions to define the central aspects of their foreign and security policies. While Pakistan looks westward toward the Islamic world (Central Asia, Iran, and Turkey) to foster closer political, economic, and perhaps military ties, India has been

---

[8]In this respect, comparisons have been made to the impact of the Indonesian economy within ASEAN (see Chapter 9).

seeking economic cooperation with ASEAN and the economically vibrant East Asian states.

Over the past fifty years, Pakistan has regularly sought economic and political support from the Muslim world for its disputes with India, while India has sought to offset these moves with diplomatic measures of its own. Thus, India was steadfast in its support for the Palestinians against Israel, recognizing Israel only in 1992 shortly after China did. This one-sided, pro-Arab policy may have been partly due to sincere convictions regarding the Palestinian cause. The policy, however, was also dictated by India's need to offset Pakistani efforts to isolate India in the Muslim world over the Kashmir issue. The situation has now changed. In early 1997, President Chaim Weizman of Israel visited India, the first Israeli leader to do so. Various opportunities for Indo–Israeli military cooperation are now being explored, especially Indian arms purchases from Israel and technological cooperation in the joint defense production of major weapons systems. Thus far, this bilateral tie has developed without generating much adverse reactions in the Arab or Muslim worlds.

India established cordial ties with Iran during the 1990s in spite of U.S. allegations that Iran was a "rogue state" that sponsored terrorism abroad. In 1993, Indian Prime Minister Narasimha Rao became the first Indian prime minister to visit Teheran since the Iranian revolution of 1979. In February 1997, Indian Foreign Minister Inder Kumar Gujral was warmly received by Iranian officials in Teheran, where a tripartite economic agreement was signed by Iran, Turkmenistan, and India. Correspondingly, there was a setback in relations between Iran and Pakistan following the February 1997 attack by Pakistani mobs on an Iranian cultural center in Multan, in which seven people were killed. Meanwhile, India has maintained cordial political and economic relations with Iraq under the regime of Saddam Hussein despite the severe constraints imposed by international economic sanctions against Iraq. India's ability to maintain cordial ties and close economic cooperation with Israel, Iran, and Iraq—all mutually antagonistic states—demonstrated remarkable diplomatic creativity.

Finally, India's relations with the ASEAN group of countries have generally been good. In 1996, India was admitted as a member of the Asian Regional Forum within ASEAN. In early 1997, the Prime Minister of Malaysia, Maathir Mohammed, was awarded the Nehru prize for international understanding by the government of India. This was followed by the visit of President Fidel Ramos of the Philippines to India. There have also been several high-level political and cultural exchanges between India and Thailand. More recently, an important exchange of visits took place in January 2001 between Prime Minister Vajpayee and Indonesian President Abdurrahman Wahid. In the communications that followed, both India and Indonesia supported the other's territorial integrity. This amounted to Indonesian support for the Indian position on Kashmir. Finally, India's relations with Vietnam have always been cordial, both during the Vietnam War and thereafter.

INDIA'S ECONOMIC POLICY

After forty years of pursuing a socialist economic policy, India turned aggressively toward capitalism in the 1990s. There was little disagreement among the major political parties that the market reforms, first introduced in 1985 by Prime Minister Rajiv Gandhi, were essential (Thomas 2000). The only substantial differences of opinion concerned the extent and pace of these reforms.

Overall, India's economic reforms have been threefold. First, there would be no more new economic enterprises launched by the public sector. Second, industrial privatization would occur through a slow process of government disinvestment whereby the shares of public-sector firms would be auctioned periodically, thereby diluting government ownership. Third, India would remove all obstacles to foreign and domestic private-sector investment and industrial expansion through the elimination of licenses and permits.[9]

Some concerns in India were raised regarding the degree to which the government would endorse the agenda of the World Trade Organization (WTO). Opposition members of parliament charged that India had virtually sold out to the U.S. economic and trade agenda that called for linkages between trade, investments, and industry on the one hand, and labor standards and environmental issues on the other. In the view of critics, these linkages were likely to jeopardize Indian economic interests. The government, however, reassured critics that imbalances in the existing WTO agreements would be addressed, that labor and environmental issues potentially harmful to India would not be placed on the WTO agenda, and that multilateral agreements on foreign investments would be avoided.

Compared to past socialist and bureaucratic obstacles to foreign investments, the economic reforms have made India's business environment more friendly to investors. With most regulatory restrictions removed, state governments competed with each other for foreign investments by offering the easiest and fastest access to their economies. In a survey of 274 Japanese companies conducted by Japan's Export-Import Bank in 1998,

---

[9]Dozens of foreign-based MNCs now operate in India, including AT&T, British Telecom, Citicorp, Coca-Cola, Ford, Fujitsu, General Electric, General Motors, Hewlett Packard, Hitachi, Honda, Microsoft, Mobil, Nestle, Sony, and Xerox. As this partial list demonstrates, these MNCs are based in many countries and are engaged in many sectors of the Indian economy.

India was ranked third after China and Vietnam as among the most promising Asian countries for long-term foreign investment. More evidence of India's improved investment climate came in 1995 from Great Britain's Economic Intelligence Unit, which rated India as a lower investment risk than China, Russia, and several newly industrialized countries, including Mexico and the Philippines.

India has experienced phenomenal growth in the field of software and information technology since the early 1990s. India has the most vibrant "Silicon Valley" outside of California. Software exports from India grew at more than 50 percent a year in the 1990s as Indian businesses discovered the profitability of employing high-skilled, low-wage computer engineers in India to write computer codes and software programs for businesses abroad, especially in the United States. There is also a mutual business advantage in the 12-hour time difference between India and the United States. Computer problems are sent by software companies in the United States to India via the Internet at the close of U.S. business hours. Software engineers in India then resolve these problems and send them back to the United States to be received first thing on the next business day. According to the New Delhi–based National Association of Software and Service Companies, the software industry in India employed about 280,000 people early in 2000 and was expected to earn $4 billion in 2000, most from sales and services provided to U.S.-based firms.

Comparisons between the economic reforms of China and India, the two most heavily populated countries in the world, have often been made. In these studies, China, operating under an authoritarian political system, often appears to have outclassed India, which is governed by a parliamentary democracy with much greater private influence, including a free press. Annual GDP growth rates since 1980 averaged about 10 percent in China compared to about 5 percent in India. These comparisons, however, are misleading for a variety of reasons. China introduced its reforms in the mid-1970s while India embarked on its economic reforms more than a decade later. Since 1992, China's economic growth rate has slowed considerably while the growth of India's economy has accelerated to nearly 7 percent annually.[10]

Despite these positive economic trends, several criticisms remain to be voiced regarding the Indian economy. These include the exclusion of the masses in India's economic growth; rising prices for food and other necessities; a lack of information regarding the privatization of government-owned enterprises; growing MNC control over the power, petroleum, and

---

[10]These measures tend to underestimate India's economic growth given that much of its economic activity remains underground, in the form of a black market that constitutes as much as one-third of the country's output. Thus Indian growth rates may be even higher than revealed in its own government reports.

telecommunication industries; and overly generous trade concessions to foreign countries without reciprocal benefits. Other critics have denounced reductions in government spending for public health and education. Taken together, these criticisms have questioned the principle that "markets know best," a principle that remains widely embraced within the Indian government.

FOREIGN-POLICY DECISION MAKING

It is appropriate at this point to consider briefly the process of making Indian foreign policy, a vital dimension that has a strong effect on the government's actual behavior overseas. Unlike the nonalignment doctrine that shaped much of Indian foreign policy during the Cold War, no long-term vision has emerged as yet to replace this doctrine. The emphasis instead has been on short-term policy formulation, especially crisis management, along with a growing emphasis on economic rather than security affairs.

From India's independence in 1947 until after the 1962 Sino–Indian war, Nehru made foreign policy in consultation with a small circle of close advisors. It was only after the 1962 war that a formal foreign and defense policy-making structure began to emerge. Under this structure, the prime minister has assumed a critical role in foreign policy, often assuming the role of Minister of External Affairs and relinquishing this post only when it has become clear that handling both responsibilities is burdensome and is leading to the neglect of urgent foreign problems. Notably, Prime Minister Vajpayee assumed both roles upon taking office in March 1998.

In other aspects of foreign policy, however, decision making is not fundamentally different from that of other Western democracies, especially that of the British parliamentary system that still serves as a role model for the Indian government. The formulation and conduct of Indian foreign policy flows from the prime minister through the ministers of External Affairs, Defense, and Home Affairs. These three key ministries are augmented by the Finance and Commerce ministries when issues of international trade and finance are involved. These issues have become more vital in recent years following the implementation of economic reforms in India that include greater involvement in world markets and increased penetration by foreign-based MNCs.

During much of the Cold War, security decision making was directed at threats from external powers, especially China and Pakistan. The Defense Committee of the Cabinet, the Defense Minister's Committee, and the Chiefs of Staff Committee constituted a three-tier hierarchy of committees to assess the security environment of India. By the mid-1970s,

significant changes were made in this structure. Most importantly, the
Cabinet Committee on Political Affairs took on the entire range of external and internal political and security issues (see Thomas 1996, 60–63;
and Thomas 1986, 119–134). Two rationales were offered for this change.
First, Indian policymakers felt that the problems of external threats could
not be separated from the problems of internal strife and domestic political stability. Second, it was felt that questions involving defense spending
should involve an assessment of the total resources available to the Indian government. In the government's view, excessive defense allocations
that might hamper development or economic stability could prove disastrous for long-term national defense and for maintaining political stability at home.

As for military command, the Indian army proposed the creation of a
centralized administrative structure along the lines of the Chief of Defense Staff in Britain and the Joint Chiefs of Staff in the United States. But
this proposal was rejected by Indian politicians, who were concerned about
potential military takeovers. Such a strong and centralized military command, they felt, represented a potential threat to democracy in India. Indeed, as the military grew more powerful in terms of capabilities, the
tradition of decentralized civilian control over the military became all the
more essential.[11]

Although the structure and process of foreign-policy making have
been institutionalized and formalized, "the whole process ... is much
more informal than any 'flow chart' would suggest" (Hardgrave and
Kochanek 2000, 413). In practice, there is often little coordination among
the various ministries, which conduct their own foreign policies with
little oversight. As in the case of the State and Defense departments in
the United States, the ministries of External Affairs and Defense in
India sometimes act as competitors rather than the main coordinators
of foreign policy. This situation has not improved under coalition governments, in which government ministers routinely come from different
political parties.

CONCLUSION

Regional and global problems aside, the most serious threat to India's territorial integrity arises from problems of *internal* security, many of which
are abetted from beyond the country's borders. These problems include

---

[11]There was a sudden reversal in this policy in May 2001, when the Indian government
declared that it would soon establish a centralized strategic command to manage its nuclear
forces (under civilian control), a defense intelligence agency, and a Chief of Defense Staff to
provide a central command post for India's army, air force, and navy.

secessionist movements and ethnic conflicts that have occurred at various times over the decades in several territories. Except for Kashmir, however, most of these problems have subsided, receded, or been resolved. The Indian political system has shown a remarkable capacity to respond and cope with such issues. Given India's ethnic diversity, however, such problems appear inevitable and are likely to resurface periodically.

The second ongoing concern relates to the threat of conventional war with India's neighbors over disputed border territories. As noted earlier, Sino–Indian border disputes were mainly resolved in a 1994 agreement that clarified the mutual borders. The Indo–Pakistani dispute over Kashmir has not been resolved, although India unilaterally adheres to the UN-brokered cease-fire line. But tensions between the two countries remain acute. The recent overthrow of Pakistan's civilian government by the military has further set back relations and has produced a high level of anxiety on both sides of the border.

The third and related Indian challenge involves nuclear weapons in China and Pakistan. These two threats are compounded by China's transfer of nuclear and missile technology to Pakistan. India, which has not signed the 1970 Non-Proliferation Treaty or the 1996 Comprehensive Test Ban Treaty, responded to this security concern in May 1998 by becoming a nuclear power. The Indian rationale for maintaining an independent nuclear deterrent includes not only the threats from China and Pakistan, but the broader potential threat from an expanding NATO that includes three nuclear-weapons states (the United States, France, and Great Britain). India's nuclear program has aggravated its relations with the United States, whose drive for global nonproliferation was set back by the emergence of India and Pakistan as nuclear states.

The primary challenge for India is to balance its security and economic policies. At the regional level, this tension would appear to be best addressed through the continued promotion of the regional SAARC, which calls for open markets and economic benefits for all the countries while advancing peace and regional stability. At the broader level, the process of marketization and economic globalization has been tempered by domestic fears of foreign takeovers and economic dependence. While economic liberalization has benefitted the rapidly expanding Indian middle class, it has also widened the gap between a minority business class of extremely wealthy people and the impoverished masses. More than 350 million Indians still live below the poverty line, a crucial fact with obvious implications for the government's domestic and foreign policies. As in the past, the key to Indian foreign policy in the future may well be found within its own borders.

INDONESIA: FROM PIVOT TO PROBLEM

Donald E. Weatherbee
University of South Carolina

A half-century ago, James Michener wrote a book entitled *Voices of Asia* in which he reflected on his travels through the continent's newly emerging nations. In Indonesia, Michener (1951, 159) found that "every shred of sympathy and identification in my body allied me with this new nation. Spiritually I became an Indonesian.... (I)f I were a young man in Asia today I would prefer being an Indonesian." Michener was particularly impressed with the country's enormous potential that drew from its vast human and natural resources. Indonesia, Michener (1951, 175) observed, held the geostrategic key to the future of Southeast Asia, and the U.S. government "must understand this mighty nation. We must work patiently with it on Indonesian terms."

The question not only for Washington, but for all major powers as the Cold War set in, concerned what the appropriate terms of engagement with Indonesia would be. President Sukarno, who ruled from 1950 until 1965, had quickly established himself as a formidable leader. He successfully resisted a fundamentalist Islamic revolt, which was a major accomplishment given the fact that Indonesia was home to the world's largest Muslim population. Sukarno also overcame separatist uprisings among the dozens of ethnic groups that inhabited the country. Finally, he had to quell widespread regional dissent within Indonesia, a vast chain of nearly 14,000 islands spanning 3,200 miles, or one-eighth of the circumference of the globe.

Sukarno managed to preserve the integrity of the newly independent state, but at a high political and economic cost. The Indonesian Communist Party prospered during this period as the national economy collapsed.

Parliamentary rule was dismantled and replaced by martial law and "guided democracy," Sukarno's term for his own authoritarian rule. Relations with the West plummeted as Sukarno's radical anti-imperialist stance led to undeclared war against Malaysia and to alignment with communist movements elsewhere in East Asia. Many Western observers saw Sukarno turning Indonesia into a socialist republic, not by revolution but by populism. This prospect changed in 1965, when after a failed coup attempt the Indonesian military wrested political leadership from Sukarno and crushed the communists.

After General Suharto replaced Sukarno as Indonesia's president in 1967, his government turned to Western-trained technocrats to rescue the economy.[1] The dramatic reorientation of Indonesian policy was a critical turning point, with important political ramifications for Asia and beyond. Suharto's Indonesia was staunchly anticommunist; its relations with the People's Republic of China were frozen along with military links with the Soviet Union. Although officially nonaligned, Indonesia's security interests were compatible with the U.S. grand strategy of "containing" communism (see Chapter 2). Under Suharto's "soft" authoritarian rule, the Indonesian economy became one of Asia's success stories and seemed to be a remarkable validation of the global market-driven, export-led growth strategies espoused by the IMF and the U.S. government. Indonesia joined its neighbors in the Association of Southeast Asian Nations (ASEAN), allowing it to pursue its national interests in a nonthreatening multilateral context.

By the end of the 1980s, the Suharto regime began to project an image of regional leadership. Indonesia's new role was widely viewed as one of "regional entitlement" (Leifer 1983, 173). The country emerged in the 1990s as a "pivotal state" (Bresnan 1999), defined as a country whose future was poised at a critical turning point and whose fate would strongly affect regional and even global security. Indonesia had become the dominant power within Southeast Asia, a major player in the East Asian and Pacific regions, and a leader in the developing world.

Despite its growing political and economic importance, Indonesia's image in the West was tarnished by the authoritarian nature of its political system. Suharto's record of widespread human rights abuses gained notoriety at a time when other developing countries were undergoing democratic transitions. In particular, Suharto was condemned for his refusal to grant self-determination to the people of East Timor, who were forcibly incorporated into the country in 1976. Misgivings about Indonesia's repressive political order still could not override its regional significance in the 1990s as East Asia adapted to the post–Cold War environment. With

---

[1]Many Indonesians, including Sukarno and Suharto, have or use only one name.

210 million people, Indonesia ranked as the fourth most populous country in the world, with 85 percent of its people identifying themselves as Muslims. The archipelago nation still possessed vast natural resources, and its deep-water straits provided vital commercial and military access between East Asia and the Indian Ocean. Not only had Indonesia soundly adapted to the post–Cold War environment, its relative power was enhanced by the greater autonomy it achieved once it was freed from the regional constraints posed by the clash between the United States and its communist rivals in the Soviet Union and China.

To be categorized as a "pivotal" state implied that Indonesia could make important, positive contributions to progress and stability beyond its shores. Conversely, domestic upheaval and conflict would have significant and highly negative spillover effects that would threaten regional stability. This latter possibility became all too real as the East Asian economic crisis of 1997 laid waste to Indonesia's economy. Years of real economic gain were wiped out in months. The Suharto government imploded, a victim of the economic crisis, government corruption and incompetence, and democratic opposition. In the turbulent year that followed Suharto's downfall, the country wrestled with the problem of establishing democratic succession as the government tried to convince the IMF, major aid donors, foreign investors, and multinational corporations of its real commitment to reform.

In its first year in office, the new Indonesian government led by Abdurrahman Wahid failed to demonstrate that it was capable of bringing about economic recovery and political stability, the requisites of regional leadership. The territorial integrity of the republic itself was again at risk after the internationally backed secession of East Timor (detailed later). Indonesia's partners in the Association of Southeast Asian Nations (ASEAN) became deeply concerned that, rather than representing the core of regional stability, Indonesia's problems could *destabilize* the region and threaten regional economic recovery. Singapore's Prime Minister Goh Chok Tong put it bluntly when he warned that, if Indonesia unraveled, "the consequence for the entire region will be horrendous." With Indonesia's leadership role in jeopardy, the direction of its fragile government remained unclear (see Clad 2000).

Doubts about Indonesia's future come into play as all Southeast Asian states continue to adapt to the shifting balance of power in the region. The complex dynamics of the relations among China, Japan, and the United States have replaced the Cold War face-off between the superpowers. In the new environment, Indonesia and its neighbors are fashioning foreign policies designed first and foremost to promote their national interests. In this respect, self-determination has assumed a new dimension.

Viewing Indonesian foreign policy only in terms of the upheavals noted earlier should not obscure the underlying continuities in the country's foreign relations. In many respects, the successive managers of Indonesian foreign policy had similar understanding of Indonesia's national interests. This fact tends to be overlooked when attention is drawn to the dramatic contrasts between Sukarno's wielding of revolutionary ideology, Suharto's authoritarian rule, and Wahid's more recent emphasis on democratic principles. Although every government has managed affairs differently, their underlying goals have been consistent since independence.

This distinctive Indonesian approach begins from a premise of political and economic vulnerability, a fact remarked upon in nearly every analysis of Indonesian foreign policy (see, for example, King 1990; Leifer 1983; and Weinstein 1976). A principle goal of Indonesian foreign policy from the founding of the republic to the present has been national security, defined largely in terms of the political and territorial integrity of a multiethnic, geographically fragmented state. This embraces Indonesia's far-flung maritime zones as well, which are seen as an indissoluble part of Indonesia's territorial space. Foreign policy has also consistently been utilized to promote a unifying sense of national identity and to spur economic growth and development.

All of these aspects of Indonesian foreign policy remain evident today. But their impact on the country's role in the twenty-first century remains highly uncertain. Only one fact is clear: The outcome of Indonesia's domestic and foreign struggles will be "pivotal," not only for the country's future, but also for peace and prosperity far from its borders.

INDONESIA'S RISE AS A REGIONAL POWER

An examination of Indonesia's foreign-policy record since independence demonstrates the continuity of foreign-policy interests even as regimes changed, the Cold War ended, and a new great-power constellation of forces emerged. In this section, the succession of political regimes in Indonesia is reviewed in greater detail. As we will find, each regime faced daunting challenges in building a viable nation-state at home while fending off foreign threats, real and imagined. The cumulative effect of this struggle remains palpable today.

THE SUKARNO ERA (1945–1965)

Indonesia proclaimed independence on August 7, 1945, as the last act in the Japanese occupation of the Dutch East Indies and the first act in the eventually successful struggle to throw off Dutch rule. Armed revolt accompanied a vigorous diplomatic campaign in the newly established United Nations. After two "police actions" against the Java-based republic drew international condemnation, the politically isolated Dutch were forced to transfer sovereignty to a new Federal Republic of Indonesia on December

27, 1949. Eight months later, the federal republic became the unitary Republic of Indonesia, which became the UN's sixtieth member on September 28, 1950.

The struggle for independence left a "distinctive imprint" on Indonesian foreign policy (Leifer 1983, 1). Indonesian nationalism was forged in a bitter anticolonial war, giving it a militant edge shared in the region only with Vietnam. The struggle also helped shape Indonesian ambivalence toward the West in general, particularly toward the United States, which provided lukewarm support for the new state.[2] The revolutionary ideals proclaimed by the Sukarno regime quickly clashed with the geopolitical realities of the East–West conflict. In 1948, Vice-President Hatta asked, "Have the Indonesian people fighting for their freedom no other course of action open to them than to choose between being pro-Russian or pro-American?" He went on to prescribe an "active and independent" foreign policy that would inform Indonesia's view of its international role for the rest of the century (see Sukma 1999).

After independence, the disparate political forces that previously united in the revolution struggled for dominance of the new state. Fundamentalist Muslims, secular nationalists, democratic socialists, communists, and ethnic traditionalists jockeyed for power in a Western parliamentary framework that deepened elite divisions. From the outset, the integrity of the new state was threatened by revolt, and the military was soon mobilized to combat insurgencies in West Java (see van Dijk 1981), Aceh (see Nazaruddin 1985), and East Indonesia (see Chauvel 1985). The problems faced by the Indonesians were similar to those of other newly independent states: coming to terms with the former colonial ruler, defining a role in the international system, and searching for external resources for economic development. The many divisions in domestic politics only complicated matters and were echoed in attitudes toward foreign policy (Agung 1973).

Normalization of relations with the Netherlands was hampered by the festering problem of sovereignty in Dutch New Guinea. Although the colony was administered separately from the Netherlands East Indies, the Indonesian government saw itself as the ruler of all Dutch territory in the archipelago. The issue was not resolved in the negotiations leading up to the transfer of sovereignty, nor did the Dutch accept the Indonesian position. The campaign to bring the territory into the fold became a unifying nationalist cause. Sukarno, initially relegated to a symbolic presidency in the parliamentary system, assumed a much stronger political role.

Indonesia's "independent and active" stance in the Cold War was tested early by its desire to have an economic relationship with the United

---

[2]Gardner (1997) provides a thorough analysis of the conflicted interests and personalities involved in the formulation of U.S. policy toward Indonesia during this period.

States. American leaders soon overplayed their hand by trying to link economic aid to a mutual-security framework that would declare Indonesia a part of the "free world." The difficulty in this plan was in the linkage between foreign-policy interests and the contentious reality of domestic politics. Leftist forces within the Indonesian government, which strongly opposed the linkage strategy of the U.S. government, soon gained the upper hand as Jakarta defied Washington and established diplomatic relations with the Soviet Union and China.

Indonesia fully emerged on the international stage as host of an African–Asian conference in Bandung in April 1955. Twenty-nine countries from Asia, the Middle East, and Africa were represented at the conference, whose agenda was driven by the twin themes of anti-imperialism and nonalignment. The final communiqué set forth "Ten Principles of Peaceful Coexistence." Although compromises were made to accommodate the Philippines and Thailand, which had security agreements with the United States, the general tenor was reflected in the principle of "abstention from the use of arrangements of collective defense to serve the particular interests of any of the big powers." The Bandung conference was the antithesis of the 1954 Manila Pact that produced the U.S.-backed Southeast Asia Treaty Organization (SEATO).[3] As one U.S. analyst (Colbert 1977, 291, 311) observed, SEATO "symbolized confrontation" while Bandung "exalted coexistence." The Nonaligned Movement, with its Asian core (including India), was formalized and internationalized at the September 1961 Belgrade Conference.

The last parliamentary cabinet resigned in March 1957, a victim of a deadlocked party system, military threats, and governmental incapacity in the face of regional challenges. Sukarno declared martial law and reinstated, by decree, the 1945 Constitution that provided for a strong presidential system. Sukarno had claimed a role on the international stage during the parliamentary period, unconnected to either his constitutional or parliamentary role. Now his rhetorical posturing was linked to real power in the state, the essential component of "guided democracy." The conceptual framework for foreign policy articulated by Sukarno elaborated on well-established themes: an "active and independent" foreign policy that was anti-imperialist, nonaligned, and distrustful of the West. Sukarno, however, gave his foreign policy a radical ideological spin in which the "new emerging forces" of the world were pitted against the "old established forces" of domination and exploitation (see Weatherbee 1966). In East Asia, the "new" forces were exemplified by Sukarno's vaunted "axis" that included Indonesia, China, North Vietnam, Cambodia, and North Korea.

---

[3]Thailand and the Philippines were the only Southeast Asian members of SEATO. The other signatories to the Manila Pact were Australia, France, Great Britain, New Zealand, Pakistan, and the United States.

The government's first challenge was internal, as Sukarno quickly faced insurrection and rebellion in the disparate regions that sought to link Islamic fundamentalism with ethnic separatism. Underpinning the unrest were grievances about shared revenue between Jakarta and the outer islands. American leaders saw an opportunity to topple Sukarno, whom they feared was opening the possibility of a communist takeover. In support of anticommunism, the Eisenhower administration decided in September 1957 to provide covert support to anti-Sukarno dissidents (Gardner 1997, 140). The U.S. government's role, managed in large part by the Central Intelligence Agency, was exposed when a U.S. pilot was shot down during a bombing run in East Indonesia (see Kahin and Kahin 1995). This confirmed to even noncommunist Indonesians the aggressive face of U.S. policy toward the republic. The regional uprisings were eventually suppressed by Sukarno, but the grievances that prompted them remained unresolved.

Sukarno made the region of West Irian the touchstone of Indonesian nationalism, both domestically and internationally. When, in November 1957, the UN General Assembly failed to provide the Indonesian position the necessary two-thirds majority, the government moved unilaterally against Dutch interests in West Irian, a large territory that borders Papua New Guinea. Dutch enterprises were expropriated, economic relations were frozen, and Dutch nationals were expelled. Although damage was inflicted on Indonesia's own economy, this was viewed as the cost of cleansing the country of the last vestiges of Dutch colonialism. Encouraged by closer political ties to China and a new military supply line to Moscow, Sukarno threatened war. In December 1961, a military command was established to liberate the territory, after which guerrilla infiltration began. The command was entrusted to Major General Suharto, who was charged with planting the Indonesian national flag in West Irian by August 17, 1962.

The Indonesian escalation came as the U.S. involvement in Vietnam was deepening. To head off a real war the Kennedy administration offered to mediate the dispute. The Dutch, who had become politically isolated, were forced to accept an agreement that transferred authority of the region to the United Nations. The agreement ultimately affirmed Indonesian sovereignty over the region, which was renamed Irian Jaya and became Indonesia's twenty-sixth and largest province. Resistance to Indonesian rule persisted among indigenous forces, however, in a low-intensity guerrilla war (see Osborne 1985).

This struggle strengthened the legitimacy of Sukarno's radical nationalism and proved the efficacy of his military threats. These two elements combined again in Indonesia's effort to "crush" the newly created Federation of Malaysia in the mid-1960s (see Mackie 1974).[4] The causes

---

[4]Malaysia's independence resulted from a comprehensive agreement in 1962 by which Britain decolonized Singapore, Sabah (North Borneo), and Sarawak in association with Malaya, independent since 1957.

of this confrontation were complex, in part an expression of the pan-Malay element in Indonesian nationalism. If they prevailed in the conflict, the fragmented territories of Malaysia "could not be anything but satellites of Indonesia" (Modelski 1964, 20). Moreover, the conflict with Malaysia shifted national attention from Indonesia's failing economy and polarized political environment. Given many of the same elements that made Indonesia a "pivotal state" in the 1990s—its large size, vast resources, and strong economic potential—Sukarno's demand to have a voice in regional affairs, particularly as they affected the regional balance of power, resonated widely.

Indonesia's domestic and international slide toward the communist bloc accelerated during this confrontation. Communist leader D. N. Aidit (1964, 10) captured the mood: "It cannot be denied that the development of the political situation in Indonesia in the past ten years, in particular during the past few years and months, has been continuously shifting to the left." Indonesia's estrangement from the nonsocialist world climaxed when, in the name of the "new emerging forces," the country withdrew from the UN, charging that the world body had become a tool of the West. The economic consequences of Sukarno's foreign policy were disastrous as Indonesia cut itself off from international assistance and investment. By 1965, the country's "possible dream" (Jones 1971) was turning into a nightmare.

Sukarno fell in September 1965 amid violent clashes between communist forces and the military. Suharto, the senior officer left in a command position, mobilized a political and physical assault on the communists and other pro-Sukarno factions. The military forced Sukarno to give acting authority to Suharto, who officially took power in 1967. Sukarno's "old order" was terminated and Suharto's "new order" began.

THE SUHARTO ERA (1967–1998)

Suharto's regime lasted for more than three decades. Although its ultimate political foundation was the military, its foreign policy cannot be analyzed on that basis since there was nothing "militaristic" or regionally aggressive about it. The development of Indonesia's pivotal role was not based on the military's institutional interests, but rather on the government's effort to build a peaceful regional Southeast Asian order and link it to a wider framework (see Suryadinata 1996). During his stewardship, Suharto became ASEAN's senior statesman. Jakarta became not only ASEAN's official headquarters, but also a source of continuity within the regional association.

As in the Sukarno period, control of Indonesian foreign policy was firmly held by the president. Suharto's initial strategy was informed by two guidelines. First, he sought to prevent alterations in the regional status quo that might inhibit the realization of Indonesia's full potential. Second, Suharto attempted to gain multilateral support for his policies in ways that would increase Indonesia's capabilities without limiting its options. The new Suharto government was faced with the immense task of rescuing the economy and overcoming the political legacy of Sukarno. To do this, Indonesia had to reconnect to the West. The government thus suspended relations with China and cut its military links to the Soviet Union. Through these measures, Suharto sought to demonstrate that Indonesia was neither a threat to international stability nor a menace to its neighbors.

The first step was to end the confrontation with Malaysia. The restoration of normal relations across the Straits of Malacca was part of a wider outreach in which Indonesia became a founding member of ASEAN. The stated goals of the August 1967 Bangkok Declaration, which brought ASEAN into existence, were to promote cooperation among the five signatory states in a number of functional areas.[5] Underlying this new regionalism were the political commonalities of anticommunism and threat perceptions stemming from the escalating Vietnam conflict. Importantly, the ASEAN countries were economically engaged with the industrialized economies of Japan, the United States, and Western Europe. Through ASEAN, Indonesia had a vehicle through which it could pursue its regional interests and economic goals in a nonthreatening way. Indonesian policy through ASEAN "was designed to undo the damage" that confrontation with Malaysia and the West had done to the country (Anwar 1995, 57).

Suharto turned to technocrats to formulate and implement economic policies designed to turn the economy around. An international consortium of twelve donor states, led by Japan and the United States, provided ample support for these policies and approved massive volumes of aid for Suharto. The grouping, called the Intergovernmental Group on Indonesia, met throughout the Cold War and served as a crucial instrument of Suharto's drive to become an "emerging" economic power.

In 1976, ASEAN's security objectives became more concrete after the communist victories in Vietnam, Cambodia, and Laos. Suharto hosted the first ASEAN summit in Bali, where the member countries approved the Declaration of ASEAN Concord and signed the Treaty of Amity and Cooperation in Southeast Asia. Both documents reflected deep, widely shared concerns about the future ambitions of post-war Vietnam, concerns that seemed justified when Vietnam invaded Cambodia in December 1978. As the stalemate in Cambodia continued through the 1980s, ASEAN became, for all intents and purposes, a single-issue body fixated on forcing Vietnam out of Cambodia (see Weatherbee 1985). What came to be called the "Third Indochina War" functioned as a kind of political cement holding ASEAN together.

---

[5]The original members of ASEAN were Indonesia, Malaysia, the Philippines, Thailand, and Singapore. Brunei became a member at its independence in 1985. Vietnam was admitted in 1995, followed by Myanmar (formerly Burma) and Laos in 1997. Cambodia became the newest ASEAN member in 1999.

Indonesia's goal during this period was to find a *modus vivendi* that would accommodate Vietnamese security concerns and ASEAN's insistence on a peaceful, independent Cambodia (Weatherbee 1986). From Jakarta's vantage point, prolongation of the war opened a strategic window into Southeast Asia for the Soviet Union and China. A weakened Vietnam, it was assumed, would be a frustrated Vietnam that would be a permanent source of threat in Southeast Asia. Furthermore, a weakened Vietnam would not be an effective partner in resisting Chinese pressure throughout the region.

As a result, Indonesia approached Hanoi with a carrot and a stick. The stick was continued support for Cambodian forces that Vietnam could not defeat. (In this regard, Cambodia ironically became Vietnam's own "Vietnam.") The carrot was the prospect of ASEAN membership for Vietnam. Indonesia's dual approach led to two Paris International Conferences on Cambodia, capped by UN Security Council resolutions calling for a Transitional Authority for Cambodia. Indonesia, however, did not hold the key to peace. The United States, China, and the Soviet Union turned that key by decoupling their bilateral relationships from their Cold War clients in Southeast Asia. Importantly, however, Indonesian foreign policy had started the peace process by asserting its leadership role within ASEAN. Indonesia was able to do this and have the regional organization follow since it was clear that ASEAN needed Indonesia more than Indonesia needed ASEAN.

By the mid-1980s, Indonesia was secure in a new regional identity forged by Suharto's foreign policy, which itself was bolstered by robust economic growth and sustained political stability. Indonesia's achievements in attaining rice self-sufficiency and its effective family-planning initiatives were widely recognized as models of development. From its now firm domestic base, Indonesian foreign policy moved to a higher profile in which Suharto himself became a recognized global actor (Vatikiotis 1993). Suharto became the quiet but implicit leader in ASEAN and emerged as a subtle mediator of regional disputes. For example, when political insecurity threatened to scuttle the December 1987 ASEAN Summit in Manila, Suharto prevailed on ASEAN to show support for the new government of President Corazon Aquino, who had recently defeated and replaced the Marcos dictatorship in the Philippines. As Singapore's Prime Minister Lee Kuan Yew observed, "It was the president of Indonesia who set the example."

Even as Indonesia was raising its regional profile, it carefully cultivated relations with its immediate non-ASEAN neighbors. In particular, Jakarta was conscious of the concerns left by the confrontation with Malaysia. In its province of Irian Jaya, Indonesia shares a 1,300-mile border with Papua New Guinea that was regulated by a 1986 Treaty of Mutual Respect, Cooperation, and Friendship. This was unique in Indonesia's bilateral relations as it served as a mutual nonaggression pact.

Good relations with Indonesia made it possible in 1987 for Papua New Guinea to become the first non-ASEAN country to accede to the ASEAN Treaty of Amity and Cooperation in Southeast Asia.

Australia served as an additional problem in Indonesia's bilateral relations during the Suharto era. The unease felt on both sides of the Timor Sea was inherent in the geostrategic setting, with a densely populated Indonesia sitting just above a thinly populated northern Australia. Ever since the confrontation with Malaysia, Indonesia was viewed as a potential threat by Australian leaders. Indonesian–Australian relations improved, however, after the signing of a 1989 agreement that provided for shared revenue from the exploitation of underground oil reserves in an area of boundary overlap. Although unstated in specific terms, a post–Cold War convergence of views was developing on common strategic interests in the security and stability of the region.

The unspoken stimulus to the closer relations between Indonesia and Australia were apprehensions about China's long-range ambitions and the staying power of the United States as an economic, political, and military presence in Southeast Asia. An Australian–Indonesian security partnership, the first of its kind ever approved by Jakarta with any foreign government, was later cemented in a December 1995 defense cooperation agreement calling for consultations in the event of "adverse challenges." The pact revealed the extent to which middle powers felt compelled in the Cold War's aftermath to fill the power vacuum left by the demise of superpower competition.

The clearest indicator of Indonesia's growing self-confidence during the final stages of the Cold War was Suharto's decision in August 1990 to normalize relations with China, which had been frozen since 1966. As the Cold War wound down, the relatively stable terms of U.S.–Soviet bipolarity had given way in East Asia to a multipolar subsystem in which China became a more significant player as Soviet and U.S. influence waned. To maximize its own evolving role, Jakarta had to be able to relate to Beijing (see Sukma 1999). For its part, the Chinese government renewed its pledge not to interfere in Indonesia's domestic politics. Suharto responded by promising closer economic ties and opening the ASEAN door to China as a formal dialogue partner through the grouping known as ASEAN Plus Three (including the ten primary members plus China, Japan, and South Korea).

The intertwining of "stability" and "economic progress" telegraphed Suharto's convictions about the domestic economy. The linkage was also consistent with the U.S. government's vision for the region, particularly since Suharto looked to Washington as a major contributor to regional stability and economic progress. As Gardner (1997, 298) summarized the dominant view in the late 1990s, "Indonesia and the United States now share more goals and are separated by fewer fears than ever."

The congruence of U.S. and Indonesian economic interests was most clearly demonstrated when Indonesia brought an initially reluctant ASEAN into the framework of the loosely knit regional economic grouping called Asia–Pacific Economic Cooperation (APEC).[6] At APEC's second summit in Indonesia in 1994, the Bogor Declaration spelled out the goal of "free and open trade" throughout the vast region by 2020. Suharto's perspective on trans-Pacific relations and globalization was in sharp contrast to that of Malaysian Prime Minister Mahathir, who promoted the idea of an East Asian economic bloc that excluded Australia, New Zealand, the United States, and Canada. Importantly, it was Suharto who prevailed on this issue.

Indonesian and U.S. interests—which coincided on most Cold War–related issues during Suharto's reign—were not always parallel. For example, since 1987 Indonesia was the major proponent within ASEAN of a Southeast Asian Nuclear Weapons Free Zone that was considered to be a natural follow-up to the 1970 ASEAN declaration of a Southeast Asian Zone of Peace, Freedom, and Neutrality. The United States lobbied vigorously against the nuclear-free zone, seeing it as an impediment to the free movement of U.S. strategic forces. For Indonesia, however, support for the zone validated its "nonaligned" credentials and its independence of action. Also, to the degree that the great-power presence could be reduced in the region, Indonesia's relative power would be increased. The United States and Indonesia also frequently disagreed on the navigation rights of U.S. naval vessels through Indonesian waters.

Suharto's efforts to consolidate Indonesia's gains as a regional power came to a crashing halt with the sudden onset of economic crisis across East Asia in 1997. The economic bubble burst on July 2, 1997, when the Thai central bank floated its currency, the baht. The plunge in the baht's value led to speculation against other Asian currencies, including Indonesia's rupiah. The rapid depreciation of these currencies exposed the underlying softness of the debt-ridden financial structures that were built across the region during the economic boom of the 1980s. (The private foreign debt "overhang" in Indonesia alone was an astounding $65 billion.) The problem of servicing these debts led to widespread defaults, and the unavailability of new capital led to factory closings and soaring unemployment. By January 1998, Indonesia had fallen into a financial abyss comparable only to the economic chaos of the late-Sukarno period. As an Australian analyst (Forrester 1999, 11) noted in 1999: "Certainly, no country has in recent times experienced the economic collapse experienced by

---

[6]APEC is a Pacific Rim grouping committed to regional cooperation based upon trade and investment liberalization, business promotion, and economic and technical cooperation. It links the economies of the NAFTA nations, Japan, China, Russia, South Korea, Taiwan, Hong Kong, eight ASEAN nations, Australia, New Zealand, Chile, and Peru.

Indonesia in the past year." He pointed out what is now generally realized even in Indonesia, that "it could take a decade for Indonesia to recover from a shock of these proportions, and the social and economic consequences could be felt for years to come."

Indonesia's financial plunge occurred as a political crisis gripped the country. There was mounting democratic opposition to Suharto's bid for a seventh five-year term. Suharto doggedly resisted the controls and restructuring demanded by the IMF as the price of financial support. Defenders of the regime were quick to paint the IMF as a tool of Western capitalism and its recovery strategy a new form of imperialism. In fact, the reforms would have primarily undermined the vested interests of Suharto's family and cronies. The parallel between the ousted Marcos regime in the Philippines and Suharto was often raised in this regard.

As students protested in the streets against "corruption, collusion, and nepotism," Suharto believed his presidency could outlast the economic crisis. The Suharto forces were politically in command of the People's Consultative Assembly that reelected him by acclamation on March 10, 1998. But Suharto's reelection prompted even greater and more widespread opposition, with establishment figures joining the attack. Their demand was for sweeping political and economic reforms against which Suharto was seen as the main obstacle. Elite support began to melt away as it became clear that Suharto stood between Indonesia and full access to the resources of the international financial community that were vital to Indonesia's rescue. Finally, when the military faced the possibility of a Tiananmen Square crackdown in Jakarta, its chief announced it was time for Suharto to step down. This left Suharto no choice. On May 21, 1998, 72 days into his seventh term, Suharto resigned and was succeeded by his handpicked vice president, B. J. Habibie, himself a target of democratic opposition and student wrath.

FOREIGN POLICY AFTER SUHARTO

The caretaker Habibie regime was immediately plagued by its fateful decision to offer self-determination to East Timor, which in 1999 led to a referendum, violence, and international intervention. After a free and fair direct parliamentary election in June 1999, the 700-member People's Consultative Assembly indirectly elected a new government headed by President Abdurrahman Wahid, a prominent Islamic scholar who had overseen Indonesia's largest Islamic social movement. Wahid officially became Indonesia's fourth president in October 1999.

Wahid was one of the most respected public figures in Indonesia—a moderate Muslim leader, an opponent of Suharto's rule, and a self-proclaimed democrat and defender of a pluralist state. Even though his election was marked by opportunism and did not fully reflect the popular will, it was generally considered a victory for democracy when compared to the previous thirty years of Suharto. The battle cry was *reformasi*: democratic reform of the political and economic systems by ending the corrupt and repressive practices that had become firmly entrenched facts of life.

Foreign policy was not a major issue in the transition of power. During the East Timor uprising, Wahid joined other nationalists in criticizing Habibie's capitulation to international pressure. Once in office, however, Wahid quickly became subject to the same kinds of pressure from Western governments, including the United States, which insisted that he punish the military forces responsible for the post-referendum violence in the territory. It was even suggested by human rights groups that the Indonesian military leaders be brought before an international war crimes tribunal. Wahid responded by wielding his democratic credentials and promising that the Indonesian Human Rights Commission would be diligent in recommending for prosecution anyone who might have been involved in the crackdown.

By early 2000 the basic outlines of the foreign policy of the Wahid government had emerged. Although differing in details and emphases, there was no real break with its predecessors that would distinguish it as a "democratic" foreign policy in contrast to the "authoritarian" foreign policy of Suharto. Within the ranks of ASEAN, Wahid made it clear that Indonesia would not allow issues of domestic governance (including human rights) to interfere with state-to-state relations. The government's first major foreign-policy statement reaffirmed this long-standing basic principle of Indonesian foreign policy and sounded the alarm about what it called the "new internationalism" of democratic and humanitarian intervention.

The vital interests that preoccupied Indonesia since independence had not changed. If anything, the country's historic sense of vulnerability had only been heightened. As in the past, foremost among foreign-policy concerns was defending the territorial and political integrity of the state. The separatist struggles noted earlier were not isolated events; weaknesses at the political center and the example of East Timor unleashed regional and ethnic dissension throughout Indonesia that threatened the "unitary" republic. Sectarian violence in East Indonesia, for example, claimed hundreds of lives and displaced thousands. The government's inability, or unwillingness, to intervene decisively to stop the violence between Muslims and Christians in the Malukus region was particularly condemned. In an ironic twist, Indonesian leaders claimed that Western economic sanctions had forced the government to curb its military forces, a move that precluded an intervention to stop the bloodshed.

Wahid actively sought support for Indonesia's territorial integrity and noninterference in the troubled regions. At his first ASEAN Summit Meeting in Manila in November 1999, his counterparts pledged their "full support for the sovereignty and territorial integrity of Indonesia." Similar statements were elicited from Indonesia's major aid donors, including the United States. Of greatest concern to Jakarta was that the same coalition of nongovernmental organizations that mobilized in support of self-determination in East Timor would bring pressures on Indonesia to support self-determination elsewhere in the archipelago.

The continuation of political turmoil and perceptions of instability hindered the Wahid administration's ability to entice the return of foreign capital that had "fled" the country during the economic meltdown. Not since the early days of the Suharto era had Indonesia been so dependent on international assistance, public and private. Because of its diminished geostrategic significance and the depth of its crisis, the Wahid government had less wiggle room than Suharto. Wahid's flirtation with capital controls, and his threatened retreat from banking reform, elicited ominous threats from the IMF. Politically, the linkage of economic support with democratic governance complicated the government's attempt to suppress internal unrest. Even if the military still had sufficient capabilities, its harsh methods of internal control used for more than two decades had become unacceptable in the twenty-first century.

In the face of these problems, Wahid quickly became a visible spokesman for Indonesia, taking on a high-profile, globe-trotting role. In his first eight months in office, he took ten foreign trips and visited thirty-five countries. Indeed, he became subject to increasing criticism for neglecting domestic problems. For example, in June 2000, Wahid left for an eight-nation trip just after a Sumatran earthquake without visiting the devastated region. Wahid defended the travel as necessary to reassure Indonesia's friends of the country's stability and to seek further assistance and foreign investment. In August 2000, after a secret meeting with Israel's Regional Cooperation Minister Shimon Peres, and ahead of a visit by Palestinian President Yassar Arafat, Wahid tried to inject himself into the Middle East peace process by suggesting a form of split sovereignty over Jerusalem. In his formula, Israel would maintain "administrative" sovereignty and a seven-member committee composed of Israel, Egypt, Jordan, Lebanon, Syria, the United Nations, and the Palestinian Authority would hold "political" sovereignty. In general, Wahid promised even greater direct involvement in foreign affairs. In August 2000, he answered the rising chorus of criticism of his administration's domestic policy record by saying that he would assign the day-to-day tasks of running the government to Vice President Megawati Sukarnoputri while he concentrated on foreign policy. Coupled to this was the announcement of a new round of foreign visits.

If the Wahid foreign policy had a strategic vision, it involved the placing of Indonesia more squarely within the East Asian environment. This was heralded in his speech at Beijing University in December 1999 during his first official visit as head of state.[7] In his speech, Wahid called for a closer relationship between the two regional powers despite their ideological differences. This theme was repeated in January 2000 by Foreign Minister Alwi Shihab, who said that in order to balance the domination of the West, a common stance among Asian states was needed. In particular, Alwi stated, a "strategic partnership" should be forged with China and India while at the same time intensifying East Asian regional cooperation. Such rhetoric was accompanied by bilateral agreements designed to forge closer links between three of the four most populous states in the world. It was no coincidence in this regard that Indonesia, China, and India shared the same aversion to the hectoring tone of the Western social and human rights agenda.

The new political warmth in Sino–Indonesian relations could be attributed to a number of factors. In announcing in October 1999 that he would make Beijing his first official foreign destination, Wahid hailed China as a loyal friend and a consistent supporter of Indonesia in its international diplomacy. In making this statement Wahid reasserted Suharto's "active and independent" foreign policy that sought to balance the country's economic dependency on the West with political independence *from* the West. In terms reminiscent of the old North–South confrontations, Indonesia insisted that the domination of the West could only be resisted by Asian solidarity.

Wahid also seemed to enjoy tweaking the eagle's beak by going out of his way to show political independence from the United States. In Havana in April 2000, Wahid rejected pleas from Washington that he not visit other "rogue states" such as Libya, Iran, Iraq, and North Korea. Wahid defended his freedom of travel and made it clear Indonesia would not be "colonized" by the United States. In Iran two months later, and just three days after he had met with President Clinton, Wahid repeated this statement. By "looking East," Wahid struck a nationalist note that resonated widely in Indonesia, even among his political opponents. Indonesian–U.S. relations reached their lowest point in years in October 2000. Anti-U.S. sentiments fueled by violence in the Middle East and resentment against the U.S. ambassador's criticism of corruption and human rights abuses led to demonstrations and threats against U.S. citizens. Due to acute security concerns, the U.S. embassy was closed for more than a week.

Indonesia's opening to China demonstrated that Jakarta had other options in the post–Cold War, post-Suharto world, no matter how limited

---

[7]Wahid had earlier visited the United States for a medical examination and an informal meeting with President Clinton. He stopped over in Tokyo on his return from Washington to meet Japanese leaders. The fact that China was his first official state visit was accorded great significance in Indonesia and elsewhere in East Asia.

these options were in real economic terms. The notion of an Asian "axis" was not just a defensive political reaction to Indonesia's economic dependence on the West. It also responded to the new geostrategic realities in East Asia. China and India were politically and militarily proximate to Jakarta; the United States was viewed as increasingly distant. From this perspective, Indonesian leaders viewed their own foreign-policy options as more flexible than ever.

ONGOING FOREIGN-POLICY CONCERNS

Now that we have reviewed Indonesia's historical experience, we shift our attention to a series of foreign-policy concerns that emerged during the Cold War and remain vital today. Of most immediate concern to Jakarta is the transformed status of East Timor, which achieved its long-sought independence only after a period of violent struggle and foreign intervention. The ongoing effort to maintain stability in the South China Sea is then assessed, as is Indonesia's continuing relationship with other developing countries. Finally, the possibilities and limitations of Indonesia's stature as an emerging power are considered in this section.

SECESSION AND INTERVENTION IN EAST TIMOR

From its forced incorporation into Indonesia in 1975 to its sudden and violent separation in 1999, the problem of East Timor epitomizes Indonesia's conflicting interests and vulnerabilities. It also illustrates the geostrategic divide between Indonesia's Cold War security linkages and the post–Cold War regional environment. As previously noted, Suharto's image was tarnished by the persistent issue of East Timor. Once described by Indonesian leaders as a "pebble in the shoe," East Timor was better likened to an albatross around the neck that made it impossible for Indonesia to fully realize its foreign-policy aspirations.

Indonesia had incorporated the former Portuguese colony, the eastern half of an island that also included Indonesian Timor, as its twentyseventh province in 1976. This followed a coup, countercoup, and civil war produced by the vacuum of Portugal's retreat in 1974. Indonesia's military intervened in December 1975 and managed the political process leading to annexation.[8] In the circumstances of the time, Indonesian intervention was a rational, if ultimately counterproductive, response to a threat that any Indonesian government might have perceived. Indeed,

---

[8]There is a copious bibliography on East Timor and Indonesia, most of it highly critical. These include Taylor (1991), Hiorth (1985), and Jolliffe (1978).

the annexation of East Timor gained the tacit approval of U.S. leaders, who feared the spread of communism in East Asia through nationalist groups such as the East Timorese. For their part, Indonesian leaders insisted that control over such territories was vital to the security of the Indonesian state.

Indonesia's *de jure* (legal) sovereignty in East Timor was never accepted by the international community, which demanded a free expression of East Timorese self-determination under UN auspices. International concern was heightened by the human disasters that took place in East Timor between 1974 and 1978 (see Weatherbee 1981). A continuing low-intensity insurgency by East Timorese separatists prompted harsh repression by Indonesian military forces and human rights abuses that further fueled opposition to Indonesian rule. Human rights groups around the world mobilized behind exiled East Timorese activists to keep their struggle for independence alive.

International pressure on Indonesia mounted after the November 1991 Dili massacre in which Indonesian troops fired on separatists, killing hundreds. The event had far-reaching consequences, prompting greater international scrutiny of human rights abuses in East Timor than ever before. Global condemnations and sanctions made it clear that Indonesia's behavior would be a critical determinant in its future bilateral relations and its influence in multilateral settings. In 1993, the United States voted for the first time in the UN Human Rights Commission to censure Indonesia for its actions in East Timor.

The post–Cold War international environment clearly altered the geostrategic parameters for Indonesia. The concerns that had prompted U.S. and Australian acquiescence to Indonesian rule in East Timor no longer muted criticism. Issues of human and political rights became priority items in the normative shifting of the winds. Still wedded to integration, Indonesia was forced into UN-mediated negotiations with Portugal for an internationally acceptable transfer of sovereignty.

Before the talks could be concluded, however, the Suharto regime collapsed. Indonesia's dire economic circumstances, and the growing linkage of human rights conditions to aid packages, moderated Indonesia's intransigence on East Timor. Upon assuming power, Habibie announced in January 1999 that the East Timorese would be offered a referendum on autonomy, as opposed to outright independence. Habibie may have felt that the gesture would gain him international legitimacy and open more channels for badly needed foreign assistance. Along with most Indonesians, he may also have truly believed that the East Timorese had become "Indonesians" and would settle for autonomy rather than independence.

The referendum was held on August 30, 1999, and was monitored by the UN mission in East Timor along with hundreds of foreign observers. Autonomy in Indonesia was rejected by 78.5 percent of the voters, who decisively opted for independence. After the results were announced, Indonesian militia groups went on a violent rampage, destroying much of the infrastructure that had been built up over a quarter century of Indonesian rule and uprooting more than a quarter of the population of 800,000. With its own security forces unable or unwilling to restore order, and with the Indonesian government under threat of crippling international sanctions, Habibie was forced to accept international intervention. The UN Security Council approved an International Force for East Timor under Australian command. In February 2000, the peacekeeping task was turned over to the UN Transitional Authority in East Timor, whose military force of 10,000 was assigned to provide the security framework necessary to rebuild East Timor and move it toward independence.

It was left to the government of President Wahid to fashion a new relationship with East Timor. In February 2000, Wahid made a symbolic visit to East Timor with a conciliatory message, even apologizing for the Dili massacre. The baggage of East Timor, however, continued to burden Indonesian foreign policy. Indonesian nationalists chafed under the international scrutiny given to East Timor and the demands that those responsible for the violence be punished. In January 2001, pro-Indonesian militia terrorism against the 120,000 East Timorese refugees still encamped in West Timor underscored the serious challenges still facing Jakarta.

Any benefits of the separation of East Timor from Indonesia were domestically offset by the spillover of the East Timor precedent elsewhere in the archipelago and emerging separatist demands. Indonesia had been able to hang onto East Timor due to its strong central government that wielded wide authority and was backed by the coercive force of a disciplined military. Now a weak central government was challenged by the emboldened peripheral regions. Jakarta's ability to defend the political and territorial integrity of the state was seriously compromised, a problem that continues to plague the Indonesian government today.

THE SOUTH CHINA SEA INITIATIVE

The South China Sea is an area of prolonged competition centered on a collection of rocks and reefs known as the Spratly Islands. Five countries—Brunei, China, Malaysia, the Philippines, and Vietnam—have claims in the region, with China's claims overlapping all of the others (Valencia 1996). As a regional zone of conflict, the South China Sea ranks in East Asia just behind the Korean border and the Taiwan Straits (see Chapter 4). At stake, besides national pride, are the potentially vast oil fields in the region. Indonesia has no territorial claim of its own in the South China Sea, but Chinese claims would intrude on the Indonesian continental shelf and oil fields north of its Natuna Islands. Moreover, conflict in the South China Sea between China and an ASEAN member, or between ASEAN members, would be destabilizing for all of Southeast Asia and pose serious security problems for Indonesia.

In its boldest diplomatic initiative, Indonesia in 1990 offered to host "unofficial" discussions on areas of possible multilateral cooperation in the South China Sea zone. Its mediating role in Cambodia and the successful outcome of the Timor Gap negotiation with Australia had bolstered its negotiating confidence. With no claim of its own in the disputed zone, Indonesia could provide a neutral venue. This was the beginning of what has become an annual series of Indonesian-hosted Workshops on Managing Potential Conflicts in the South China Sea. In 1991, only Indonesia coming off the Cambodian settlement could have gotten China and Vietnam to sit down at the same table to discuss potential conflicts in the region.

The "workshop" process created a pattern of regular exchange among government officials, think-tank academics, scientific experts, and military leaders, all of whom acted unofficially but with the backing of their governments. The idea was to create a framework of confidence building focused on technical and scientific subjects without confrontation over sovereignty. The Indonesian approach was influenced by the Antarctic Treaty that was made possible by freezing unilateral claims. Indonesia's role was to keep the exchange open, nudge it along, and to continue to insist on its regional character. Implicit in the Indonesia approach was the notion that solutions had to be sought in a multilateral setting. China, on the other hand, has insisted that the problems are bilateral and has not allowed the workshop process to chip away at its sovereign claims.

The Indonesia-sponsored workshop process, frustrating as it has been for its managers, has been an important part of the wider effort of what Foreign Minister Ali Alatas called "parallel processes seeking solutions to the disputes in the South China Sea." One measure is "first-track" government diplomacy in ASEAN ministerial dialogues with China, along with closer contacts with Beijing through the ASEAN Regional Forum and through the ASEAN Plus Three grouping noted earlier.[9] The other measure is the more informal "second-track" process. The hope is that the two tracks can reinforce one another.

The eleventh workshop on the South China Sea was held in the Wahid government's first months. Even without substantive results, the Indonesian effort has been endorsed by ASEAN and the regional forum as a "positive contribution." At the very least, the Chinese government has been engaged in discussion rather than confrontation on the regional dispute. Importantly, China's ultimate reaction to Indonesia's and ASEAN's appeal

---

[9]The ASEAN Regional Forum is an annual foreign ministerial–level dialogue on issues of regional peace and security among ASEAN and its dialogue partners, including Australia, Canada, China, the European Union, India, Japan, New Zealand, Papua New Guinea, Russia, South Korea, and the United States.

for a peaceful resolution of the problems of conflicting sovereign claims in the South China Sea will be viewed from Jakarta and the other ASEAN capitals as a critical indicator of the role China sees for itself—whether as a cooperative partner or a threat to regional security.

INDONESIA IN THE "SOUTH"

In its last decade, the Suharto government determinedly sought to expand the leadership role it had assumed in Southeast Asia into a larger sphere of influence. It was in the developing world of the "South" that Jakarta could most freely articulate its "active and independent" foreign-policy stance. As noted earlier, Indonesia was instrumental in recasting the political, economic, and social agendas of the organizations that claimed to speak for the "South," a shorthand term used to describe the diverse range of developing countries in southern Asia, Africa, and Latin America. In the 1960s and 1970s, these forums had served as global Cold War megaphones for radical anti-Westernism and anti-capitalism. Indonesia's emergence as a major player in the South was signaled in April 1985, when it hosted a gathering of eighty developing countries to commemorate the thirtieth anniversary of the Bandung Conference. This provided Suharto his first significant extraregional platform to project Indonesia as a leader in the nonaligned developing world. The Indonesian goal was to reenergize the so-called "North–South dialogue" and to fashion new cooperation among the developing countries themselves.

After the Cold War ended, Indonesia was selected to chair the deliberations of the Nonaligned Movement between 1992 and 1995. Indonesian leaders eagerly stepped to center stage in this forum, now with 113 members, at a critical moment in the movement's history. Indonesia's vision for the future was made clear as it wrenched the movement from its Cold War past by refocusing its agenda on economic and social security. The 1992 "Jakarta Message," a summary of the movement's new objectives, served as Indonesia's call for a constructive North–South dialogue based on genuine interdependence. Suharto personally carried the "Jakarta Message" to the UN General Assembly in his first address to the world body. He also became the first leader from the Nonaligned Movement to meet with the Group of 7 industrialized powers.

The watchwords for Indonesia in South-based organizations are *pragmatism* and *flexibility*. Jakarta carried these themes into the Group of 77 developing countries when it assumed the group's coordinating role in January 1998.[10] In such roles, Indonesian leaders reject the linking of the West's so-called "social agenda" to issues of trade and economic cooperation.

---

[10]The Group of 77, now including 133 developing countries, is the South's primary caucus within the UN and seeks to enhance the group's negotiating position on major economic and social issues affecting the South.

Indonesia is also a member of the G-15, which was created in 1989 as a core grouping of the nonaligned states.[11] Finally, in 1998 Indonesia joined in the founding of the "Developing 8," whose stated purpose was to promote cooperation among Islamic countries.

Also noteworthy in this regard was Indonesia's role in 1995–1996 as a nonpermanent member of the UN Security Council. Deliberately reversing Sukarno's condemnation of the organization, Suharto proclaimed Indonesia's support for the principles and purposes of the world body. "Since it proclaimed independence more than fifty years ago," he stated, "Indonesia has endeavored to work for the achievement and maintenance of international peace and security through the UN." Indonesia's commitment to the UN was tested during the Gulf War, when, unlike Malaysia, it reluctantly supported the UN resolutions supporting intervention even though it disapproved of the sanctions imposed on Iraq. Within the UN, Indonesia emerged as a staunch defender of the "sacrosanct principles" of states' sovereignty and territorial integrity. In this respect, Indonesian leaders questioned the legitimacy of UN-sponsored peacekeeping operations that were launched after the Cold War in the name of humanitarianism or democracy. Such missions were criticized by Jakarta, and by leaders elsewhere in the developing world, as unwarranted interference in domestic affairs. In Jakarta's mind, of course, was East Timor and other potential breakaway republics.

Indonesia has been a strong, vocal supporter of UN reforms that would make the organization more representative of the global realities of today, as opposed to those that existed during its founding just after World War II or during the heyday of the Cold War. Specifically, Jakarta has called for the appointment of new permanent members to the Security Council, suggesting criteria that would fit an Indonesian candidacy. In all of these ways Indonesia has sought to maintain its stature as a leader of the developing world.

MANAGING THE ISLAMIC DIMENSION

Although the great majority of the Indonesian population are Muslims, the promotion of Islam or the articulation of a specifically Islamic-tinged image has never been an important foreign-policy interest of Indonesia (Suryadinata 1996, 158–169). Indonesia has embraced many Arab causes, particularly those of the Palestinians, but this was characteristic not just of Islamic foreign policy but of Third World nationalism in general. What Libya or Syria might view as Islamic issues were situated by Indonesia within the framework of the Nonaligned Movement.

---

[11]The G-15 members in 1989, in addition to Indonesia, were Algeria, Argentina, Brazil, Egypt, India, Jamaica, Malaysia, Mexico, Nigeria, Peru, Senegal, Venezuela, Yugoslavia, and Zimbabwe. Since then Chile, Kenya, and Sri Lanka have been added and the old Yugoslavia has disappeared.

This commitment to a secular, religiously pluralistic state distinguishes Indonesia from most other primarily Muslim nations. Although Indonesia participated in the Organization of Islamic Conference (OIC), it was not a signatory of the OIC Charter that stated that the members were "Islamic states." Sukarno and Suharto, nominal Muslims, had long opposed backward linkages from the international Islamic community, particularly from radicals such as Libya's Mu'ammar Qaddafi, fearing that they could penetrate and possibly co-opt the potent domestic Islamic community. In contrast to Malaysia, Indonesia has not used Islam in foreign policy to garner domestic support, but has tried instead to insulate domestic politics from Islamic influence.

The election of an avowed Islamic leader, Wahid, as president of Indonesia, and the parliamentary dominance of Muslim political parties, led to speculation that Indonesian foreign policy in the future might become more "Islamic." Leaving aside the question of what an "Islamic" foreign policy might be, the record does not suggest any break with the "non-Islamic" policies of Wahid's predecessors. The January 2000 proclamation of Indonesia's foreign-policy priorities did not even hint at an infusion of Islamic values or goals. In this respect, Wahid exhibited the same pragmatic flexibility that was characteristic of the Suharto years. In looking for South Asian partners, he selected India, not Pakistan, with whom Indonesian Islam shares a great deal. Wahid even made an opening toward Israel with an eye toward eventual recognition.

More problematic, however, would be the role of Islam in the foreign policy of a post-Wahid government that might represent more strident voices within Indonesia's huge Muslim community. This could lead to a breakdown of the unitary secular state, and the replacement of a pluralistic nationalism with an appeal to religious fundamentalists. In this respect, the tensions remain strong—and almost overwhelming—between Indonesia's profound internal problems and its capacity to assert its interests beyond its borders.

INDONESIA'S FOREIGN-POLICY FUTURE

Given its many internal problems, Indonesia has stepped back from its status as a regional leader in Southeast Asia. Its role within ASEAN has recently been limited to cutting its losses. Given that current Indonesian leaders have no personal or bureaucratic interests in the organization, they have effectively ceded regional leadership to Malaysia. It may even be argued that, in the absence of a strong Indonesian pivot, ASEAN has outlived its utility in the regional subsystem. This means that ASEAN's external partners must rethink their relations with the region.

The intensification of Jakarta's bilateral relations with China and other Southeast Asian states suggests that a new form of regionalism is emerging. Even though ASEAN remains the official cornerstone of Indonesia's foreign policy, Jakarta's disenchantment with ASEAN has become obvious. From the government's standpoint, the regional grouping has become centered in *mainland* Southeast Asia. President Wahid proposed in November 2000 the creation of a West Pacific Forum to include Indonesia, East Timor, Papua New Guinea, Australia, New Zealand, and, perhaps, the Philippines. His initiative clearly expressed the government's shifting regional strategy.

More generally, Indonesia's foreign-policy stance at the beginning of the new millennium is not unlike that of the mid-century days of early independence. Again Indonesia has a weak central government beset by internal divisions and disunity in an international environment that is viewed as menacing. The primary threat to Indonesia today is no longer imperialism from the West, but dissolution. The country's claim to an "active and independent" foreign policy, therefore, must be seen within the real context of its diminished capabilities.

What sets Indonesia's problems apart from those of a half-century ago is that they are embedded in a far different regional strategic environment. In the 1950s, the United States was the preponderant power with many hegemonic characteristics. That preponderance is questioned today, even contested. China has emerged to challenge the long-established hierarchy of regional power. The Cold War interests that led Washington to eventual partnership and strategic support of Indonesia no longer exist to such a great extent. Although President Clinton reaffirmed to Wahid that "a strong and stable and prosperous and democratic Indonesia is very much in our interest," it is doubtful that this interest can any longer be considered "vital" in terms of U.S. national security. This fact will act to limit Indonesia's capability to influence U.S. policy and behavior, particularly since the coming to power in January 2001 of U.S. President George W. Bush, who promised to restrict the U.S. conception of its national interests.

If a contemporary observer were to travel in Indonesia today, he or she would be impressed by the great potential of the country. All of the possible elements of real power that impressed James Michener in 1951 still exist today, and many have been enhanced. As during the 1950s, however, political incapacity, instability, and disarray hinder the realization of this potential. Yet Indonesia's proud nationalists still aspire to be recognized as significant international actors, and they have sound reasons for commanding attention.

Wahid's global ambitions kept Indonesia highly visible. As demonstrated by his assertive stance toward Washington, he was able to demonstrate independence, a core element of Indonesia's foreign policy. But his failure to confront fully the nation's economic problems, bring the military under civilian control, or establish a cordial working relationship with the parliament ultimately proved his undoing. He was impeached by legislators and replaced in July 2001 by Vice President Megawati Sukarnoputri, daughter of Indonesia's founding leader, Sukarno.

While Wahid's dismissal brought new uncertainties to Indonesia, the peaceful and constitutional manner in which he was removed showed promise for the political reforms undertaken since Suharto's departure just three years earlier. Sustained progress must be made toward economic recovery in order for Sukarnoputri to attain real regional leadership and heightened global status. And she must find some way to unify the fragmented nation politically and socially.

Even if Wahid's successors are able to regain momentum in healing Indonesia's wounds, the country's foreign-policy role will not be the same. Its "active and independent" foreign policy of the past will likely be deployed in a new distribution of power, one in which China will be the principal political concern even as access to Western economic markets and private investors remains critical. Indonesia's global capacity as a "pivotal state" will likely remain muted given the domestic convulsions of the recent past. But even in this case, the success or failure of Jakarta's foreign policy will have major consequences for regional stability, economic growth, and political development. Given its large size and population, and given its still-vast economic and military potential, Indonesia will remain a key player in the world politics of the twenty-first century.

CHAPTER 10

IRAN'S AMBIVALENT WORLD ROLE

Mohsen M. Milani

University of South Florida

Iran is one of the world's oldest countries, and no stranger to diplomacy. During its long and turbulent history, it has adapted to a variety of roles in international affairs. Iran represented the core of the Persian empire in ancient times and was a formidable world power for more than six hundred years.[1] Invaded and ravaged many times over, the country demonstrated a remarkable ability to rise again. More recently, Iran represented the Great Prize in the Great Game played by the Great Powers—primarily Great Britain and Russia—which imposed their colonial policies on the country but ultimately could not subdue it.

In the era since World War II, Iranian foreign policy has oscillated from reluctant cooperation with the Western powers to neutralism to confrontation with them. Specifically, Iranian foreign policy shifted during the Cold War from strategic collaboration with the United States to an uncompromising opposition to Washington and its Western allies. Situated on the underbelly of the Soviet Union, Iran in the 1950s became a strategic ally of the United States, which relied upon Teheran to "contain" Soviet influence in the Middle East. This partnership ended abruptly, however, when Iranian dissidents overthrew the U.S.-backed monarch (shah) in 1979 and created the Islamic Republic of Iran. The United States and Iran have since been engaged in a process of mutual demonization, although an opening for renewed goodwill has emerged in recent years.

---

[1]Persia is the Greek word for Iran. In 1936, the Iranian government requested that foreigners use *Iran*, the name its indigenous population has used for millennia. This designation, therefore, is used throughout the chapter.

These shifts and confrontations may appear irrational on the surface. To the contrary, they reflect the varying adaptation strategies of an old country in search of a new role in international affairs. They also reflect the desire of Iranian leaders to use foreign policy to consolidate their rule, protect Iran's territorial integrity and independence, preserve the country's religious heritage, and reassert Iran's role in international affairs. Considering Iran's weakness relative to the foreign powers drawn to it, Iranian leaders have shown considerable cunning as they have played one power against another, forged alliances, and asserted their interests at the regional and global level. Iran's status as a major oil producer has added greatly to its influence, which it has wielded effectively in recent years along with other members of the Organization of Petroleum Exporting Countries (OPEC).

Iran today is a highly independent country with a population of nearly 63 million and a gross national product (GNP) approaching $100 billion. Life expectancy, just fifty-five years in 1970, is now close to seventy years. Iran is the strongest indigenous power in the Persian Gulf and a major player in the Islamic world. Political reforms currently underway are designed to empower Iran's population within a more stable, pluralistic governmental system, albeit one that retains its rigid adherence to Islamic principles and customs. Economic reforms, meanwhile, seek to integrate Iran into the market-driven world economy. In this context, Iran is an emerging power in world politics that cannot be ignored.

This chapter provides a broad overview of Iranian foreign policy. I adopt a largely historical approach that illustrates several recurring patterns in the country's past that remain evident and vital today. In particular, three aspects of Iranian foreign policy are given emphasis. First, Iran's frequent, though reluctant, role in the intrigues of great-power politics has been an inescapable fact of life for Iranian foreign-policy makers. Second, although Islamic principles have played an important role in shaping Iran's politics, they have become a decisive force in the country's domestic and foreign policies since the 1979 Islamic revolution. Finally, Iran's status as a major oil producer in the heart of the Persian Gulf region has given its leaders a crucial voice in the international political economy throughout the past century. Today, each of these factors informs the calculations of Iranian leaders as they continue to adapt to changes at home and abroad.

THE VITAL DOMESTIC CONTEXT

As other chapters in this volume have noted, the formulation and conduct of foreign policy are intimately linked to the dynamic interactions between domestic and external factors. This essential fact certainly applies to Iran, whose foreign policy has long been shaped by actors far from its borders. Since World War II, Iranian foreign policy has been formulated mostly in reaction to the policies of the United States, and to a lesser extent to those of the former Soviet Union and Great Britain. However, several internal factors have also influenced Iran's policies and given them some degree of continuity.

The first internal factor is Iran's geostrategic location and its enormous oil reserves. A bridge between East and West, Asia and Europe, and Asia and Africa, Iran was rightly called the "bridge to victory" during World War II. During the Cold War, Iran shared long borders with the Soviet Union. Today, it connects the natural gas–rich Caspian Sea to the Persian Gulf, the location of some two-thirds of the world's proven oil reserves. For this reason alone Iran inevitably plays a pivotal role in global affairs.

A second factor is Iran's acute sensitivity about protecting its territorial integrity, a function of an ethnically diverse population. Although Persians represent the majority in Iran, five other ethnic groups are significant, most of them located in specific provinces. Iran's leaders have continually feared that if one province broke off, it would create a domino effect that could lead to Iran's disintegration. Some ethnic groups have been supported by foreign powers whose aim was to enhance their own interests and weaken the central government. Iran has certainly not been unique in this regard—a similar pattern was described in the previous chapters on India and Indonesia—but this concern for internal as well as external security has been particularly strong among Iranian policymakers.

Other internal pressures have driven Iran's external relations, including the frequent manipulation of foreign policy by various leaders to consolidate their rule. During the Cold War and prior to the 1979 revolution, for example, massive arms transfers from the United States were used not simply to bolster the "containment belt" around the Soviet Union, but to strengthen the shah against potential domestic opponents. Also of note has been the strong desire among Iranians to remain independent after many years of foreign domination. Iran's determination to play an active role in world affairs has manifested itself in nationalistic, imperialistic, and Islamic robes. Inspired by the glory of pre-Islamic Iran and the crucial role the Persians played in building Islamic civilization, Iranians consider it their historical destiny to be a major player on the world scene. We will better recognize the importance of all these factors as we review the key developments in Iran's diplomatic history.

Iran's Struggles against Foreign Domination

A central theme of Iranian foreign policy throughout its long history relates to the country's ongoing struggle against foreign powers. Long before the industrial revolution, Iran was coveted by European imperialists, primarily the British, for whom Iran represented a vital segment of their "passage to India." Russian leaders, meanwhile, found Iran attractive as a stepping stone to the Persian Gulf. And in the twentieth century, Iran's rich oil deposits became the object of fierce competition among Western oil companies and governments. The key question, therefore, for Iranian leaders throughout their volatile history has been: How would they resist such intense foreign pressure while retaining their cultural integrity, political freedom, and economic well-being?

The roots of Iranian foreign policy extend deep into antiquity. Under Achaemenid rule (about 546–334 B.C.), the far-flung Persian empire and the Greek city-states were in constant contact and involved in occasional wars. After Iran's conquest by Alexander from Macedonia, the Sassanids (A.D. 226–642) created another empire and "a brilliant society that reflected a cultured and luxurious civilization" (Ghirshman 1979, 347). Iranian leaders of this time maintained complex diplomatic relations with Rome and the Byzantine Empire, both of which were often considered Iran's adversaries. Iran and the West profoundly affected each other, but their contact virtually ended after Iran was invaded by the Arab Muslims in 637. Although Iranians played a critical role in transforming Islam from the religion of a tribal city-state based in Mecca to that of a global empire, and although small Iranian dynasties still had limited contact with Europeans, it was not until the early sixteenth century that a unified Iran met the West again.

In 1501, the Safavid dynasty unified Iran, restored its sovereignty, and championed a remarkable renaissance in Iranian arts, architecture, and handicraft industries. The Safavids (1501–1722) imposed Shiism as the state religion to distinguish the Iranians from the Sunni Turks and Arabs.[2] The Ottoman Turks, who controlled most of the Middle East and threatened Europe, were the Safavid's main enemies. Their hostilities with the Safavids prevented the Ottomans from focusing exclusively on Europe and may have saved some European countries from domination by the Turks. Cognizant of this important schism within the Islamic world, the Europeans became more interested in developing close relations with Iran.

The momentous events of eighteenth-century Europe significantly tilted the balance in the Europeans' favor (Stavrianos 1981, 224–229). While the irresistible forces of secularization, democratization, and industrialization were creating a new social order in Europe, Iran's renaissance of the previous two centuries was abruptly halted. The country bled through three dynastic changes, ferocious civil wars, a foreign invasion, and fruitless foreign conquests by ambitious Iranian shahs. By the time this long nightmare ended in 1796, Iran found itself on the periphery of international politics, with its independence in jeopardy.

---

[2]Shiism is a minority sect of Islam but the dominant religion in Iran. Sunnism is the majority sect of Islam.

Iran's foreign policies in the nineteenth century were shaped by the rivalry between two great powers of the era, Russia and Great Britain. For decades, Russia under Tsar Peter the Great sought to make Iran obedient so that landlocked Russia could gain access to the Persian Gulf. The British strategy, meanwhile, was to exploit Iran's riches and use the country as a buffer zone that would protect India, its "crown jewel." Iran's decline accelerated after its first devastating war against Russia, which lasted from 1803 until 1814. In this struggle Iran adopted the first of many "third-force" strategies, seeking help from Napoleonic France. With his eyes on India, Napoleon sent a French military mission to Iran in 1807, but this had little impact. When Napoleon was driven from Egypt in 1814 and his invasion of Russia failed, Iran's strategy proved futile. In 1828, Iran again went to war with Russia and again lost. As a result of the two wars, Iranian leaders were forced to cede two large provinces to Russia and grant Moscow territorial rights and favorable tariff rates (which were also granted, under duress, to the British). For the rest of the century, Iran's rulers continued to auction off parts of their country to the highest bidder.

The dawn of the twentieth century found Iran's economy in shambles, its despotic government bankrupt, and its population desperately crying for reform. The Constitutional Movement of 1906–1911 was launched to throw off foreign domination and create a constitutional monarchy that would define and constrain the power of the shah. A written constitution and a parliament (the Majles) were the results. The Majles and the Iranian prime minister were empowered to deal with some aspects of Iran's foreign policy, the first time in Iran's history that a governmental force besides the shah was granted such power.

As Iran was about to have its first encounter with constitutional democracy, however, the great powers concluded an agreement in 1907 to partition the country into three zones of influence—one for Russia, one for Great Britain, and one neutral. Iranian leaders, who naturally opposed this scheme, turned to the United States for support. But this reapplication of the third-force strategy only provoked a real threat of Russian invasion and the suspension of Iran's constitutional reforms. Ironically, "democratic England" supported Russia against Iranian democrats in this struggle. Henceforth, Iran became even more dependent upon the great powers and was challenged internally by popular movements in the provinces. Although it declared neutrality in World War I, Iran was invaded by both sides.

Iran's strategic and economic value grew enormously when oil was discovered in the country in 1908. The British oil explorer William D'Arcy created the Anglo–Persian Oil Company (APOC), which later became the Anglo–Iranian Oil Company and eventually British Petroleum (BP). The British government purchased 51 percent of the company just weeks before the British navy changed its source of fuel from coal to oil. To further solidify their position, the British secretly negotiated the Anglo–Persian

Treaty of 1919 that would have turned Iran into a virtual British protectorate. The infamous treaty, however, was never ratified by the legislature. British leaders then pressured Iran to sign a new oil agreement with APOC in 1920 and supported a coup in 1921 that was designed to strengthen Iran's central government and prevent communism from spreading in and through Iran. (The Bolshevik revolution had occurred just four years earlier in neighboring Russia and Iranian leaders were mindful of Soviet leader Vladimir Lenin's call for a Communist International.)

The main agent of the coup was Reza Khan, commander of the British-controlled Cossack Brigade. He forcefully restored order and convinced the Majles to promote him as shah and founder of the Pahlavi dynasty in 1925. Reza Shah was a passionate patriot and a ruthless dictator who crafted his foreign policy to modernize Iran, obliterate foreign influence, and consolidate his dynasty. He reduced the power of foreign countries in Iran, ended the Belgian control of customs, and nationalized some foreign banks. Under his rule, which lasted from 1925 until 1941, Soviet influence in Iran declined. While Reza Shah remained friendly with the Soviet Union, he violently suppressed Iranian communists. As for London, the Iranian leader could not break the British monopoly of the oil industry.

Reza Shah's boldest foreign-policy initiative was to develop close ties with Germany. His primary goal was to use Germany as another "third force," in this case with a mission to modernize Iran and check the influence of London and Moscow. For its part, Germany saw in Iran the potential to make lucrative profits and gain access to Persian Gulf oil. Hundreds of German advisors, technicians, and businessmen came to Iran, and by 1939 Germany was Iran's main trading partner. Unlike the Soviet Union and Great Britain, Germany shared technological knowledge with Iran. Reza Shah's greatest economic achievement, the construction of the 850-mile Trans-Iranian Railroad, was completed with German assistance.

When World War II began, Iran quickly declared neutrality. The shah refused to comply with British demands that Iran expel the "German spies," although he agreed to place the suspected Germans under surveillance. When Germany attacked the Soviet Union in June 1941, the Soviets joined Great Britain in demanding the immediate expulsion of the Germans (Ramazani 1975, 28). Before the shah could respond, the allied powers invaded Iran on August 25, 1941. Their goal was to use the Iranian railroads to transport military equipment to the Soviet Union and install a more obedient regime in Iran (Ramazani 1975, 258). Three weeks after the invasion, Reza Shah was forced to abdicate in favor of his twenty-two-year-old, Western-educated son, Mohammad Reza Shah Pahlavi.

Iran's occupation had two contradictory consequences. On the one hand, a new parliamentary democracy emerged as previously suppressed domestic groups became active. On the other hand, foreign interference in Iran's affairs reached such a level that Great Britain claimed the right to "modify the Iranian cabinet at will" (Alexander and Nanes 1980, 96). Under such conditions, Iran's foreign policy was primarily aimed at evacuating foreign troops and neutralizing the influence of the great powers. Toward that end, Iran, the Soviet Union, and Great Britain signed a Tripartite Treaty that ensured Iran's territorial integrity, independence, and the withdrawal of all foreign troops after the war. Justifiably suspicious of London and Moscow, Iran turned to the United States as yet another "third force" to ensure that the treaty would be implemented.

As some 30,000 U.S. troops entered Iran through the Persian Gulf in December 1941, the U.S. government became more active in Iran's domestic affairs. In return for U.S. military aid and other forms of assistance, Iranian leaders invited U.S. oil companies to obtain oil concessions in their country. The growing U.S. power alarmed the Soviet Union, however, which in late 1943 demanded its own oil concessions in Iran's northern provinces. While the British retained their monopoly over the oil industry, the American Standard Oil Company requested an oil concession in northern Iran in March 1944. All three occupying forces demanded oil concessions, placing Iran in a delicate situation. The Majles, led by Mohammad Mossadeq, forbade the government to grant any concessions while Iran remained occupied. When Iran rejected its request for an oil concession, the Soviet Union refused to withdraw its troops from Iran. This sparked the Azerbaijan crisis, the unofficial start of the Cold War.

The Cold War in Iran

The occupying Soviet forces in Iran were supposed to withdraw their troops by March 1946. But the Soviet troops, which had helped establish two puppet republics in northern Iran, showed no signs of leaving. This was a calculated move to solidify the Soviet Union's foothold in a weak Iran and to counter the growing U.S. involvement in Iran. The Soviet Union had all the winning cards in this standoff. Its troops controlled the two northern provinces and enjoyed the loyalty of the Tudeh Party, the largest party of the time. Through skillful diplomacy and U.S. support, however, Prime Minister Ahmad Qavam handed the Soviet Union its first defeat of the Cold War era.

Qavam, a quintessential Iranian diplomat, took office in January 1946 and negotiated directly with Soviet leader Joseph Stalin. After two weeks of negotiations in April, Stalin agreed to withdraw his troops by May. Qavam pledged to deal with the renegade republics peacefully by addressing their concerns and proposed the formation of an Iranian–Soviet oil company, with Moscow controlling 51 percent of the shares. The Soviet Union withdrew its troops from Iran but continued to support the northern republics. The shah then stepped in and launched a military intervention to liberate the territories from Soviet interference. When the new Majles convened, Qavam's proposal for a joint oil company with the Soviet Union was soundly defeated, and Qavam himself was removed from power.[3]

The unfolding of the Cold War had an immediate impact in Iran. Mossadeq, a Western-educated legislator, skillfully combined the potent forces of Iranian nationalism with anticolonialism to formulate his foreign policy in the Majles. He aimed to eradicate the influence of foreign powers in Iran while maintaining friendly relations with the West and the Soviet Union. Mossadeq saw no compelling national interest to justify entangling Iran in the Cold War. In his view, the Anglo–Iranian Oil Company (AIOC) posed the greatest menace to Iran's sovereignty, and he prompted the Majles to pass a bill in 1951 nationalizing Iran's oil fields. Nationalization became so popular that a reluctant shah, under heavy pressure from the legislature, appointed Mossadeq prime minister in April 1951. The liberal Mossadeq gave freedoms to rival political parties and made good on his vow to nationalize the oil company (see Katouzian 1999).

Having "lost" India in 1947, Great Britain vehemently opposed the nationalization of Iran's oil industry. After all, the AIOC was London's largest foreign investment, a major contributor to its economic growth, and a source of cheap oil for its navy. Having failed to undermine Mossadeq, Britain turned to the United States for help. Ironically, Mossadeq also sought support from Washington, applying his own variant of the third-force strategy. In mid-October 1951, Mossadeq reached a tentative agreement that included a 50-50 profit-sharing scheme with the United States, similar to the agreements U.S. oil companies had reached with Saudi Arabia. But the pact was rejected by British leaders, who were encouraged by the growing collaboration between the British and U.S. oil companies. Indeed, as early as May of 1951, the major U.S. oil companies declared they would neither buy Iranian oil nor help its oil industry. That decision started the collusion against Mossadeq by the Anglo–American oil companies, which feared his nationalizations would spread to other developing countries.

What drastically changed the U.S. policy was the 1952 election of President Dwight D. Eisenhower. Unlike President Truman, who believed that Iranian nationalism could be consistent with U.S. interests, Eisenhower strongly resisted Iranian nationalism and Mossadeq's "neutralism" as dangerous trends that could be manipulated by the Soviet Union (Cottam 1979). It mattered not that Mossadeq was anticommunist, that he sought

---

[3]Although the United States played a major role in this event, there is no evidence, as has been suggested, that President Harry Truman threatened Stalin with a nuclear ultimatum to get out of Iran (see Ramazani 1975).

to improve relations with Washington, and that he had extended the U.S. military-aid program to Iran in 1952 despite Soviet opposition. In the end, Washington could not resist the temptation to increase its influence in Iran and prevent it from "going communist." Nor could it suppress its rapacious appetite to profit from Iran's huge oil markets. Thus the United States and Great Britain agreed on a covert operation, code-named AJAX, to overthrow Mossadeq (Gasiorowski 1991). The shah, who had fled the country before the start of the coup in August 1953, returned home after Mossadeq was captured and arrested. Iranian nationalism was defeated for the sake of oil and the Cold War.

FOREIGN POLICY UNDER THE SHAH

Mohammad Reza Shah Pahlavi, like his father, used Iran's foreign policy to consolidate his rule, modernize the economy and security forces, and increase Iran's stature in international affairs. His relations with the two superpowers, the pivotal components of his entire foreign policy, went through three distinct phases.

In the first phase (1941–1953), which preceded his return to power in place of Mossadeq, the shah laid the foundation of an alliance with the United States. He saw Great Britain as a declining power with a colonial legacy that he could neither trust nor forgive for having mistreated his father, and he viewed the Soviet Union as Iran's traditional adversary with imperialistic ambitions. It was the United States that he admired and trusted. He asked Washington to recognize Iran's vital strategic importance in containing the Soviet Union and argued that, while Greece was the "left flank" of the anti-Soviet front in Eurasia and Turkey its center, Iran was its "right flank." Thus the shah requested the same level of U.S. assistance provided to Greece and Turkey. Washington rejected this request but signed a mutual-defense agreement that made ample "equipment, materials, and services" available to Iran.

In the second phase, the shah became the sole architect of Iran's foreign policy. This phase began after the coup against Mossadeq in 1953 and ended in 1962, when the shah pledged not to turn Iran into a military base of the United States to use against the Soviet Union. The 1953 coup transformed the shah into an autocrat who alone changed the country's foreign policy. His prime minister, General Fazollah Zahedi, restored order, and the United States provided him with $45 million in emergency financial assistance. Mossadeq and many of his associates were jailed or exiled, and hundreds of opposition leaders were executed or imprisoned. In 1954, the United States reorganized the Iranian national police and later helped create the shah's most powerful and feared organ of command, the SAVAK. Accountable to no one but the shah, SAVAK gathered information, arrested and tortured dissidents, and acted as a "government within the government." The shah banned political parties, muzzled the press, and packed the Majles with obedient servants, turning it into an instrument of his will.

Secure on the home front, the shah now focused on improving his relations with the United States. He supported the three major U.S. goals in the Middle East: contain the Soviet Union, protect Israel, and gain free access to inexpensive oil from the Persian Gulf. Immediately after the coup, the shah endorsed an agreement with a newly formed oil consortium, effectively "denationalizing" the Iranian oil industry. The British and U.S. oil companies each controlled 40 percent of the shares of the consortium, and the Dutch and French companies controlled the other 20 percent.

The shah also supported other pro-Western regimes in the Persian Gulf and a British naval presence in the region. In addition, he had such special relations with Israel that the Israeli intelligence unit, MOSSAD, trained SAVAK's second generation of cadres, and the two agencies, like the two nations' armed forces, maintained close working relations. Trade between the two countries flourished and Iran, in defiance of the Arab world, sold oil to Israel and purchased agricultural and military products from the Jewish state.

The shah was willing to play the strategic role Washington had assigned to Iran. In the early 1950s, the United States developed its "Perimeter Defense Strategy," which called for security alliances with countries bordering the Sino–Soviet bloc (see Keddie and Gasiorowski 1990). The anti-Soviet Baghdad Pact of 1955 was a key component of the strategy. Iran joined the alliance, which included Iraq, Turkey, Pakistan, and Great Britain.[4] Eisenhower explicitly declared that, if requested, the United States would use any means necessary, including force, to protect any country in the Middle East from foreign attack. Under the terms of the 1959 U.S.–Iran Joint Defense Agreement, the U.S. government significantly increased its military presence in Iran and stipulated that, in case of aggression, the United States would take "appropriate action" on behalf of Iran.

The shah and the United States also shared the common goal of modernizing the Iranian armed forces, although their intentions were not always identical. The United States supported a modernized Iranian armed force primarily because it wanted a force that could delay any Soviet advance into Iran in case of war. While the shah did not oppose this policy, he had his own ambitions to become a major regional power. Therefore, throughout the 1950s and early 1960s, he pressed for more military rather than economic assistance. In the first decade after the coup, Iran received

---

[4]When Iraq's monarchy was overthrown by a coup in 1968, Iraq left the pact and the other four members renamed it the Central Treaty Organization (CENTO).

about $122 million annually in U.S. aid, much of it for military purposes (Keddie and Gasiorowski 1990, 149). Through this process, Iran became overtly pro-American and fully integrated into the U.S. global network for containing Moscow.

Contrary to the conventional wisdom about Soviet regional ambitions, Moscow's policy toward the shah was rather defensive and was designed largely to prevent the United States from turning Iran into an anti-Soviet military base. Although the shah was thoroughly anticommunist and deeply suspicious of the Kremlin, he was determined not to antagonize the Soviets. From the coup of 1953 until the early 1960s, Iran and the Soviet Union were engaged in a mini–Cold War. The Soviets condemned the shah for joining the Baghdad Pact and signing the U.S.–Iran Joint Defense Agreement. What Moscow wanted was a nonaggression treaty with Iran; what it eventually got was the Mutual Nonaggression Agreement, signed in 1962, in which Iran pledged not to allow missiles, rockets, or nuclear weapons to be deployed from its territory against the Soviet Union. The United States, though clearly unhappy with the agreement, did not actively oppose it because its recently improved missiles could hit Soviet targets from the seas. Still, the agreement was a major victory for Teheran and Moscow; thereafter bilateral relations improved and Soviet leaders never tried to destabilize the shah.

In the final phase of prerevolutionary Iran's foreign policy (1962–1979), the shah's relations with Moscow became friendlier even as he maintained close relations with the United States. Recognizing the constantly changing patterns in the relationship between the superpowers, the shah always suspected them of pursuing secret agreements that involved Iran. Therefore, he skillfully flirted with Moscow with the dual objectives of getting more concessions from Washington and appeasing the Soviets not to engage in subversive activities against him. As Iran's oil revenues increased in the late-1960s and 1970s, the shah ensured that the Soviets would benefit. Economic, military, and technical exchanges increased between the two countries. The Soviet Union completed two major projects: a large steel mill in Isfahan, and the Trans-Iranian Gas Pipeline, designed to carry gas from Iran to the Soviet Union. The shah even bought arms from the Soviet Union, although on a very modest scale.

While his relations with the Soviet Union remained friendly, the shah grew closer than ever to U.S. leaders. He faced tensions in this regard, however, as he tried to decrease his dependence on Washington and pursue a more independent posture domestically and internationally. The first strain developed in the relationship when President John F. Kennedy pressured the shah to support land reform, a move Kennedy considered an effective deterrent against communism. The shah reluctantly allowed a limited opening of the political process and approved a series of reforms that included land reform and women's suffrage.

It was during this period of reform that Ayatollah Ruhollah Moussavi Khomeini gained national prominence. When the ayatollah (a leading Shiite scholar) harshly criticized the shah, his arrest precipitated antigovernment protests that were violently crushed by the police (Milani 1994a, 37–56). After serving a six-week jail term, Khomeini condemned the shah's collaboration with the United States. What infuriated Khomeini was the U.S. pressure on the government to sign the Status of Forces Agreement, which Iranians called the "capitulation laws." In October 1964, the shah succumbed to pressure and the Majles approved the bill, which gave U.S. military personnel and their dependents full immunity in Iran. Khomeini denounced the agreement for turning Iran into a "U.S. colony." Unable to silence the ayatollah, the shah exiled him to Turkey, and then to Iraq. The ruptured relationship between the two Iranian rivals would prove fateful in the years to come.

OPEC AND THE OIL WEAPON

As global demand for petroleum soared, the shah enthusiastically pushed for higher oil revenues within OPEC, the cartel of oil exporters formed in 1960 to gain more income from the Western-based oil companies. The 1973 OPEC oil embargo against the United States and the pro-Israeli European states quadrupled the price of oil. Although the shah refused to participate in the embargo, he pushed for even higher prices that created a phenomenal economic boom in Iran and transformed the shah into a major player in international affairs. Thus, when President Gerald Ford warned the oil-producing countries of dire consequences after increasing oil prices again in 1976, the shah retorted, "We can hurt you as badly, if not more, than you can hurt us" (Milani 1994a, 95).

While the oil boom fueled the fastest economic growth in Iran's history and increased the living standards of most Iranians, its impact on Iran's relations with Washington was equally profound. Iran became a new business center for U.S.-based corporations eager to cash in on the "oil rush." In 1973 and 1974 alone, U.S. companies signed contracts and joint ventures with Iran totaling almost $12 billion. In 1975, the two countries signed an economic agreement in which Iran pledged to buy $15 billion worth of goods and services from the United States over the next five years. American companies also agreed to build eight nuclear power plants in Iran. By 1978, some 47,000 Americans were living in Iran. At the same time, some 56,000 Iranian students were studying in the United States. The shah gave generous gifts to major U.S. universities and used his ample "petrodollars" to strengthen his ties with members of the U.S. government, the news media, and the business community.

The oil boom also changed the nature of military relations between the two countries. Using petrodollars, the shah armed Iran to the teeth by purchasing more than $20 billion worth of modern U.S. weapons. The Nixon administration encouraged the shah to buy whatever armaments he desired, except nuclear weapons. By 1975, Iran was the world's leading buyer of U.S. weapons and military equipment. Other Western countries, especially Great Britain and France, also made considerable fortunes from the shah's military spending, much of which was designed to consolidate his power at home.

The most drastic consequence of the oil boom and Iran's massive militarization was the emergence of the shah as a regional superpower, or the "policeman of the Persian Gulf" (Milani 1994b). A highly militarized Iran with an ambitious shah and strong support from the United States thus quickly established its regional hegemony. Most other Persian Gulf states were pro-Western and close to the shah; only Iraq and, to a much lesser extent, the Republic of Yemen, championed radical pan-Arabism and developed friendly relations with the Soviet Union. Flexing his muscle, the shah sent Iranian troops to Oman to crush a Marxist movement supported by Yemen and encouraged ethnic Kurds in Iraq to destabilize the government in Baghdad. The shah appeared so invincible that President Jimmy Carter, who was visiting Teheran in 1978, praised the shah for creating an "island of stability" in the troubled region. Soon after Carter's visit, however, the shah's straw house was torn apart and he was overthrown. His close relations with the United States played a major role in his demise.

The shah's troubles began when he loosened his controls over the government in 1977, a decision linked to Carter's call for greater protection of human rights among U.S. allies. Many Iranian citizens considered the new policy a signal that Washington would no longer support the shah unconditionally. The shah himself became suspicious that Carter's real intention was to undermine him. That perception, and his losing battle with cancer, paralyzed the shah. Once he relaxed his grip on power, the autocratic system he created quickly crumbled. Not only did Islamic fundamentalists resent the shah's cozy relations with the West, Iran's emerging middle class demanded an end to the shah's repressive rule.

Carter did little to lift the shah out of confusion and inaction. On the one hand, his commitment to human rights compelled Carter to pressure the shah to undertake domestic reforms. On the other hand, Carter was unwilling to terminate the U.S. government's lucrative economic and military ties with the shah. Once the revolutionary movement began, Zbigniew Brzezinski, Carter's national security adviser, favored an iron-fisted policy in favor of the shah while Secretary of State Cyrus Vance recommended a peaceful resolution of the growing crisis. Amid this impasse the shah departed Iran in January 1979 for medical treatment overseas. In his absence, the Iranian armed forces melted like snow and the Islamic Revolution assumed full force.

REVOLUTIONIZING IRAN'S FOREIGN POLICY

From his triumphant return to Iran in February 1979 until his death in June 1989, the Ayatollah Khomeini was the newly proclaimed Islamic Republic's undisputed leader. His old age and austere lifestyle contrasted sharply with the shah's lavish ways. This factor, combined with the ayatollah's confrontational policies, decisive leadership, approval of revolutionary violence, and genius in communicating with the lower classes, transformed Khomeini into a titanic force for radical change in Iran and across the Islamic world. Unlike the shah, who suffered from an inferiority complex toward the West, the secure Khomeini regarded Islam and his mission as divinely inspired and superior to the ideologies of the West, particularly that of the "great Satan" in the United States.

In revolutionizing Iranian foreign policy, the Islamic government proceeded cautiously in response to shifting domestic and international challenges. Its foreign policies passed through moderate, radical, pragmatic, and conciliatory phases, each of which was intimately linked to the evolution of the Islamic revolution itself, to the ideological orientation of the faction that controlled the government, and to key changes in the international system. These phases also reflected the Islamic Republic's effort to reconcile Iran's national interests with broader Islamic goals. Often the Islamic Republic, which proudly declared itself a defender of the Islamic faith, was torn between strengthening Islam and promoting Iran's more narrow, but substantial, national interests. It is in this context that the four phases are briefly detailed in this section.

THE MODERATE PHASE AND THE HOSTAGE CRISIS

The first, relatively brief, phase of the foreign policy of Islamic Iran began when the shah was overthrown in February 1979 and ended when militant students seized the U.S. embassy in Teheran in November of that year. Iran's foreign policy was reoriented during this period to promote nonalignment. With the shah gone, the revolutionary coalition soon dissolved and a bloody struggle for power began in which the pro-Khomeini forces—the Islamists—prevailed. To create his version of an Islamic republic, Khomeini moved in two different directions. He appointed Mehdi Bazargon, an old associate of Mossadeq, to head the Provisional Revolutionary Government, and he created a ministate within the government that he effectively used to suppress his opponents. The main components of the ministate included the *Komites*, which were armed vigilantes, the Revolutionary Guards, his private army, and the Revolutionary Courts, which prosecuted "counterrevolutionaries." Bazargon was the first to challenge this ministate and became its first victim.

Bazargon was an Iranian patriot first and a Muslim second, and his foreign policy reflected this priority, based on "nonalignment." Iran was no longer prepared to stay in the Western camp as an agent to contain the Soviet Union but was prepared to maintain good relations with both superpowers. Bazargon's most sensitive task was dealing with the United States, a country that strongly opposed the revolution. While he talked of decreasing Iran's military dependence on Washington, he opposed expelling U.S. military advisors. The United States failed to reciprocate Bazargon's overtures, however, and refused to recognize Khomeini's leadership. Washington was slow to recognize that real power resided not in the government, but in Khomeini.

Carter precipitated the cataclysm in U.S.–Iranian relations by admitting the ailing shah to the United States for medical treatment on October 22, 1979. His decision fed the revolutionaries' fears that Washington was planning to reinstall the shah, as it did in 1953. In early November, nearly five hundred students stormed the U.S. embassy in Teheran and took sixty-six staff members hostage.[5] While Khomeini blessed the takeover as "Iran's Second Revolution," Bazargon called for the unconditional release of the hostages. When the students defied Bazargon, he resigned. Khomeini masterfully used the hostage crisis and vitriolic anti-Americanism to create a new, radical order in Iranian politics and foreign policy.

THE RADICAL PHASE AND THE IRAQ–IRAN WAR

This second phase began with the hostage crisis and ended when Ayatollah Khomeini died in June 1989. During this phase, an Islamic theocracy was established, all opponents of the Islamic Republic were eliminated, and a cultural revolution was launched to "Islamicize" all aspects of life in Iran and eradicate all vestiges of Western influence. Driven by inexhaustible idealism, the new Islamic leaders transformed the purpose and orientation of Iran's foreign policy. They adopted a pan-Islamic posture, placing the "export of the Islamic Revolution" at the top of their agenda. Iran de-linked from the West and severed its diplomatic relations with the United States.

Khomeini used the hostage crisis to destroy his opponents, ratify the new Islamic constitution, and radically reorient Iran's foreign policy. With much fanfare and careful timing, the militants used the documents they had captured from the U.S. embassy to accuse hundreds of Iranians of spying for the United States. Some of the suspects were tried and imprisoned;

---

[5]Fourteen of these hostages were soon released, leaving fifty-two to be held by their captors for 444 days.

others were forced into exile. The new constitution created an Islamic Republic and granted extraordinary power to the *Faqih*, the system's supreme political and religious authority who must be a qualified Shiite cleric. Among his other powers, the *Faqih* commanded the armed forces and determined the general policies of the Islamic Republic.

The new government held its first presidential election in January 1980. President Abolhassan Bani Sadr, like Bazargon, was a nationalist who was gradually suffocated by the ministate Khomeini controlled. When he unsuccessfully challenged Khomeini, he was forced to leave Iran in March 1981. With his exile, the Islamists were in complete control of both the regular state and the ministate.

The Islamists were determined not to release the hostages until they had first secured their own power. Carter's decision to force a dying shah out of the United States only made the students more belligerent. Carter responded by severing diplomatic relations with Teheran, freezing Iranian assets in the United States (estimated at between $8 billion and $15 billion), imposing economic and military sanctions on Iran, and seeking to isolate Iran internationally. When his diplomatic initiatives failed, Carter took military action to rescue the hostages, but one of the helicopters collided with a transport plane, killing eight American servicemen. The aborted mission further energized the Islamists.

While the Islamic Republic was preoccupied with the hostage crisis, Iraqi leader Saddam Hussein invaded Iran in September 1980. His main objectives were to stake Iraq's claim as the dominant power in the Persian Gulf, impose Iraqi sovereignty over the disputed Shatt al Arab waterway, and destroy the Islamic revolution, which Hussein feared threatened his own power. But Iraq's aggression unified all Iranians behind Khomeini and solidified the rule of the Islamists. With no prior experience in the subtle world of diplomacy, they believed God and history were on their side and they could change the landscape of the Islamic world. Once Hussein started the war, Khomeini was determined to punish Iraq and spread his revolution to the fragile countries of the region and beyond. This obsession compelled him to continue the war in 1982 even after Iran had gained the upper hand.

Hussein and Khomeini were guided by misleading assumptions. Hussein's ambitions blinded him both to the source and magnitude of Western support for his regime, which was designed to make Iraq sufficiently strong to contain Iran, but not to make it a regional superpower. For his part, Khomeini's idealism kept him from recognizing that the United States and the West would never allow Iran to win the war. Such a victory would have been detrimental to their interests and would have radically changed the balance of power in the Middle East.

Although the United States was officially neutral in the Iraq–Iran war, it saw Iraq as the lesser of the two evils despite its close relations with

Moscow. Washington saw Iran as a greater threat that was determined to export its revolution and destabilize pro-Western governments in the Persian Gulf region. As the war intensified, the hostage crisis became less of a boon to the Islamists, who signed the Algiers Agreement with the United States, pledging, among other things, to release all the hostages. The United States, in turn, agreed not to interfere in Iranian affairs in the future. The agreement was approved by the Majles hours before Carter left office on January 21, 1981, and the hostages were released as President Ronald Reagan was inaugurated.[6]

By the middle of the 1980s, all factions in Iran were publicly embracing the slogan of "war, war, war until victory." Washington, which did its best to stop the flow of arms to Iran, was getting closer to Iraq. The Reagan administration, concerned about the Soviet occupation of Afghanistan, was also alarmed about the possible subversion of Iran by Moscow and the disintegration of Iran after the aging Khomeini's death. Officials from the Islamic Republic and the Reagan administration began a series of secret talks that were first revealed in a Lebanese newspaper in November 1986. The Iran–Contra scandal involved secret arms transfers to Iran, the release of three Americans held hostage in Lebanon, and the transfer of funds from the weapons sales to U.S.-backed Contra rebels who were trying to overthrow the Marxist Sandinista regime in Nicaragua. Reagan's aides claimed their goal was to create a "strategic opening" by strengthening "moderate elements within and without the Government of Iran" (Milani 1994a, 211). Once the secret deal was exposed in 1986, however, it created Reagan's most serious constitutional crisis and showed the hypocrisy of his policy that pressured others not to negotiate with Iran while his aides were doing just that.

The scandal did nothing to resolve Iran's problems in continuing the war against Iraq. It did, however, tilt U.S. policy in favor of Iraq and became an excuse for an increasing U.S. naval presence in the Persian Gulf. Further complicating matters, in July 1988 the *USS Vincennes* downed a commercial Iranian aircraft, killing all 290 of its passengers. The U.S. government acknowledged that the ship accidentally fired upon the passenger jet, fearing that it was an attacking warplane. The incident, however, further strained relations between Washington and Teheran. Internationally isolated, Khomeini finally accepted the UN cease-fire resolution. In the end, Iraq did not become the dominant regional power or destroy the Islamic Revolution; nor did Khomeini export his revolution and overthrow Saddam. The war, whose staggering costs

---

[6]According to Gary Sick (1985), representatives of the Reagan campaign had covertly struck a deal with the Iranians in 1980. The Iranians allegedly promised not to release the hostages during the presidential race in return for a pledge by Reagan to provide Iran with weapons after he took office.

were estimated to exceed the total oil revenues of both Iran and Iraq for the entire century, devastated the two countries and resulted in the death and injury of millions of people.

After the war ended, Iran focused on improving its relations with Europe in order to rebuild its shattered economy. But once again ideology prevailed, this time over the publication of *The Satanic Verses* by Salman Rushdie (1988). Without even reading the book, Khomeini issued a religious decree that legitimized the killing of Rushdie for writing a "blasphemous book." The decree outraged European leaders, who recalled their ambassadors from Iran. The Rushdie affair was another vivid example of how ideology intervened to complicate and damage Iranian foreign policy during this radical phase. Only after the Ayatollah's death in June 1989 did Iran begin to liberate itself from the ideological prison Khomeini had created and to formulate its foreign policy based less on ideology and more on national interests.

THE PRAGMATIC PHASE AND THE COLD WAR'S DEMISE

Ali Akbar Hashemi Rafsanjani became president shortly after Khomeini's death and engineered the drive toward moderation in Iran's foreign policy. Internally, the succession was completed peacefully and Ayatollah Seyyed Ali Khamenie became the new *Faqih*. Rafsanjani successfully reduced the power of the hard-liners who were influential under Khomeini's rule. While Iran's support for Islamic movements continued, "exporting the revolution" was no longer a priority.

The Iran that Khomeini inherited from the shah was vastly different from the one he left his successors. The latter was an isolated country with a tarnished international image, exhausted from the tumultuous experiences of a revolution and a debilitating war in the same decade. Real percapita income in Iran had fallen by half, making economic reconstruction all the more urgent. Rafsanjani's development plan was based on attracting foreign capital and borrowing on international markets. To succeed in his plan, he would have to reorient Iran's foreign policy.

Rafsanjani had four specific goals in pursuing his foreign policy: to end Iran's international isolation, to neutralize the U.S. containment of Iran, to attract foreign investment, and to acquire modern weapons to revitalize Iran's armed forces. Developing close relations with Moscow was a top priority, designed to show the United States that, in reaction to its hostile policy, Iran would improve relations with its former nemesis. Rafsanjani also saw in Moscow, as well as the People's Republic of China, reliable and cheap sources of arms to rebuild Iran's shattered military forces. In the early 1990s, Iran and Russia signed a nuclear cooperation agreement in which Russia pledged to help Iran develop peaceful nuclear technology and complete the construction of two German-supplied reactors the shah had purchased (Ehteshami 1995, 187–191). Chinese officials, meanwhile, signed an agreement to build a light-water nuclear reactor in Iran and sell Teheran two research reactors. Moscow, Beijing, and Teheran stressed that these nuclear agreements would be implemented under the strict guidelines established by the International Atomic Energy Agency (IAEA) and that Iran's nuclear program was only for civilian purposes.

Iran's close relations with Moscow and Beijing alarmed the West, which accused it of having a "crash program" to build an Islamic bomb. Rumors abounded that Iran had purchased three tactical nuclear warheads from Russia and that scores of Russian nuclear scientists had been employed by the Iranian government. Three facts, however, can be stated with certainty. First, Iran was one of the first signatories of the Nuclear Non-Proliferation Treaty. Second, the IAEA repeatedly confirmed that Iran's nuclear program was designed for peaceful purposes. And third, Iran supported the creation of a "Middle East nuclear-free zone." Although strong arm-twisting by Washington forced China to reduce its nuclear cooperation with Iran, Moscow resisted U.S. pressure and agreed in 1995 to build two nuclear reactors in Iran.

The collapse of the Soviet Union strengthened Iran's ties with Moscow, but it also created instability on Iran's northern borders as many of the former Soviet republics became immersed in ethnic and religious conflicts that could easily spread to Iran. Here, too, Iran's objective was not to export its revolution in a predominantly Islamic area, but to protect its national interests. In the conflict between Armenia, a Christian country, and Azerbaijan, an Islamic one, Iran did not side with the latter because it feared the possible unification of the Republic of Azerbaijan with Iran's province of Azerbaijan, noted previously in this chapter. Instead, Iran successfully brokered a cease fire between the two countries.

Iran pursued other goals in Central Asia that could be realized only by promoting stability and cooperation (Hunter 1994). Although eager to establish good relations with Moscow, Iran also feared a revived Russian domination of the region. Consequently, Teheran developed good relations with the former Soviet republics to counter potential Russian expansionism and create a safe buffer zone between Iran and Russia. Moreover, Iran saw in the region potentially lucrative markets for its exports. Finally, Iran hoped to convince the regional players and the Western powers that oil pipelines from the Caspian Sea through Iran to the Persian Gulf represented the cheapest, safest, and shortest route to transport gas and oil to world markets, a plan strongly opposed by Washington.

The second pillar of Rafsanjani's foreign policy was a cautious rapprochement with Western Europe. To neutralize Washington's policy of containing Iran, he tried to drive a wedge between the United States and other industrialized countries by strengthening commercial ties with the European Union and Japan. In a symbolic move, the revolutionary graffiti on city walls in Teheran was replaced by huge billboards advertising European and Japanese products. American pressure and ill will from the Rushdie affair, however, prevented the development of friendly relations with Europe. Still, the European powers and Japan countered Washington's hard-line policy toward Iran, maintaining that their "constructive engagement" with Teheran would be more effective diplomatically than trying to isolate the republic indefinitely.

In the Persian Gulf, too, Iran's pragmatism and its desire to reassert itself were visible. Iran's goals were to reestablish its leadership role, contain Iraq, persuade the pro-Western governments to distance themselves from Washington, and maintain regional stability. The champion of radical change during the Khomeini era, Iran became an advocate of stability and regional economic cooperation. Rafsanjani recognized that without stability in the region, Iran could neither rebuild its damaged oil refineries nor increase production and reestablish its leading role in OPEC. Rafsanjani publicly stated that Iran must refrain from intervening in the internal affairs of others, a clear signal that the export of revolution was no longer a policy objective.

Iran's new policy faced a major challenge when Saddam Hussein invaded Kuwait in 1990. Hoping to prevent the massive entry of U.S. troops into the region, Iran was the first country in the region to condemn Iraq's aggression, demand Iraq's withdrawal, and propose a peaceful resolution of the conflict. Saddam's attack prompted the deployment of 500,000 (largely U.S.) troops into the region under the United Nations flag, placing Rafsanjani in an unenviable position. Iranian hard-liners warned that the U.S. military posed a more serious threat to Iran than Iraq ever could. While some proposed siding with Islamic Iraq against the UN coalition, the more adventurous talked of a holy crusade against both Saddam and the United States.

Rafsanjani prudently determined Iran's policy based on national interests. In adopting a posture of "active neutrality," he chose to stand on the sidelines without antagonizing either Baghdad or Washington. Iran did, however, observe the UN-imposed sanctions against Iraq. Most revealing was Iran's inaction during the ensuing Iraqi civil war. After Iraq was expelled from Kuwait, there were popular uprisings by Kurds in the north of Iraq and Shiites in the south. While Iraqi troops ruthlessly massacred the Shiites and damaged some of their holiest shrines, Rafsanjani merely expressed deep sympathy for the suffering of his fellow Shiites and called for Hussein's resignation. Clearly, the days of adventurism were over.

Moderation was also evident in Iran's policy toward other Islamic movements and the Arab–Israeli conflict. Iran continued to support radical Islamic movements, many of which had offices in Teheran, including the Palestinian groups that opposed the U.S.-sponsored peace process. Nor did Iran soften its harsh denunciation of Israel. In Lebanon, however, Iran moderated its policy while keeping intact its alliance with Syria. Rafsanjani continued to support the *Hezbollah*, an organization Iran had helped create, but he also established closer ties with mainstream Shiite organizations. Moreover, he secretly negotiated, with the support of the UN, the release of some Western and U.S. hostages in Lebanon.

Iran's neutrality during the Gulf War and Rafsanjani's role in the release of Western hostages improved Iran's image and strengthened its relations with Western Europe. Washington was also encouraged by the ascendance of the pragmatic faction and moderation in Iran's foreign policy. Rafsanjani was willing to begin a dialogue with the United States if Washington would release Iran's frozen assets. At the same time, he recognized the strong opposition in both Iran and the United States against normalized relations. Therefore, he sought to improve commercial ties with the United States. President George Bush, insisting that "goodwill by Iran will beget goodwill by the United States," supported this approach, and a few U.S. companies made small investments in Iran. American exports increased from zero in 1989 to $1 billion in 1993. In the early 1990s, U.S.-based oil companies purchased up to $4 billion worth of Iranian oil on the open international market (Gerges 1999, 120–121).

The collapse of the Soviet Union, followed by Bill Clinton's election as president, tilted U.S. policy toward Teheran in a more hostile direction. With the end of the Cold War, the United States lost its nemesis, the Soviet Union. The only obvious replacement for the Soviet threat was militant Islam, with Iran as its heart and soul. Iran was again demonized and labeled a "rogue state." The more confrontational U.S. approach to Teheran was underscored in May 1994, when Assistant Secretary of State Martin Indyk outlined the new U.S. policy of "dual containment." The stated objectives of the new policy were to change the regime in Iraq and to force changes in Iran's behavior through a series of political, economic, and military sanctions and covert operations. The United States accused Iran of undermining the peace process in the Middle East, sponsoring international terrorism, acquiring weapons of mass destruction, and destabilizing pro-Western governments. In this spirit, the Central Intelligence Agency asked Congress for $19 million to undermine the regimes in Iraq and Iran (Gerges 1999, 122).

The tough U.S. policy persuaded neither the Europeans nor the Russians to modify their policies toward Teheran. Nor did it stop U.S.-based oil companies from pursuing lucrative deals with the Islamic Republic. In March 1995, Teheran signed a $1-billion oil deal with Conoco to explore for oil in the Persian Gulf. Mostly because of the pressure from pro-Israeli lobbyists, who argued that Iran intended to use its oil revenues to acquire weapons of mass destruction, and partly because of pressure by the Republican-controlled Congress, Clinton issued an executive order that forced Conoco to withdraw its agreement with Iran. In April 1995 he announced a total ban on all U.S. trade with and investments in Iran. These actions were reinforced by Congressional legislation that prohibited U.S. companies and their subsidiaries from doing business with Iran and imposed heavy penalties on foreign companies that invested more than $40 million in Iran. As if these sanctions were not sufficient, Secretary of State Warren Christopher, whose fixation with the ayatollahs was legendary, openly called for the overthrow of the Iranian government in January 1996.

The new policy proved counterproductive and undermined U.S. business interests. Instead of with Conoco, Iran made bigger deals elsewhere, including a $2-billion oil agreement with French-based Total and two smaller Russian and Malaysian companies. The Europeans regarded the new U.S. sanctions policy as violating their sovereign right to establish commercial relations and insisted that the United States could not impose its laws on the rest of the world. Not even Turkey, a member of NATO, would be constrained by Washington as it signed a massive natural gas deal with Iran. The new sanctions ultimately failed to deprive Iran of its oil revenues. Its oil production actually increased and was sold on the international markets with little difficulty.

IRANIAN FOREIGN POLICY TODAY

Today, Iran's foreign policy is based on establishing dialogue and normalizing relations with most foreign countries. This continues Rafsanjani's approach at an accelerated pace, with greater emphasis on Iran's national interests and rapprochement with the West. This new policy is the result of the landslide electoral victory of President Mohammad Khatami in May 1997, which confirmed that some two-thirds of the electorate warmly embraced his goals of increasing political transparency and accountability, giving more personal freedoms to people, improving the stagnant economy, and ending Iran's international isolation. His foreign policy was based on what he called "civilizational dialogue," which he believed would reduce international tension and create a more peaceful world order.

While other countries in the Middle East remain stifled by petro-despots, autocratic monarchs, old-fashioned authoritarian dictators dressed as presidents, and generals camouflaged as democrats, Iran has been energized by the refreshing breeze of democracy. The country whose Islamic Revolution for more than two decades sought to transform Islam into a formidable force for revolutionary change by any means necessary is now the champion of the principle that Islam and popular sovereignty are compatible and complementary.

Khatami belonged to a small group of ruling clerics in Iran that believed interaction between Iran and the West could be mutually beneficial.

He maintained that the principle tenet of Western political liberalism—the contractual basis of a relationship between the rulers and the ruled—was a noble notion that Islam and Iran could embrace. Internally, Khatami began several reforms to open up the political process and popularize the notion that the government was the servant rather than the master of the people. Still, one must remember that Khatami's conservative opponents held more power than he did. They controlled the judiciary, the armed forces, the security and intelligence agencies, and many other governmental units. Therefore, the space for Khatami's reforms was limited. Yet despite these internal obstacles, Khatami improved Iran's tarnished image, reduced its isolation, restored diplomatic relations with Great Britain, and improved relations with other European countries and, to a lesser extent, the United States.

Under Khatami, Iran accelerated its reintegration into international organizations. In December 1997, Iran hosted the Islamic Conference Organization meeting that was attended by fifty-four Islamic countries. Khatami was elected as its head, a move that provided evidence of his popularity among Islamic nations. Within the UN, the same organization Khomeini denounced as a puppet of the superpowers, 2001 was proclaimed the year of "Dialogue Among Civilizations," an extension of Khatami's goal to reach out to non-Islamic states.

Khatami's most successful initiative within the Islamic world was the close relationship he established with Saudi Arabia, whose monarchy Khomeini had declared incompatible with Islam. This necessary cooperation helped both countries harmonize their opposing policies on Afghanistan and Central Asia and on oil prices. The resolution of the Salman Rushdie affair was another major achievement. Khatami declared in 1998 that the Rushdie chapter was closed and that Iran would not support efforts to kill the author. Since this statement, relations between Iran and Great Britain have improved. Indeed, British oil companies are again bidding to reenter the Iranian market. Khatami, meanwhile, continued with his fence-mending with Europe by visiting France and Germany.

In making similar overtures toward the United States, Khatami praised "the great American people" and spoke of the many cultural and historical commonalities shared by the two former allies. He also expressed his regrets for the pain the hostage crisis inflicted on the United States and he called for increased educational, cultural, and scientific exchanges between the two countries. Clinton and Secretary of State Madeleine Albright responded positively to these overtures. Clinton acknowledged that prerevolutionary Iran had long been exploited by the Western powers and that Iran had suffered under foreign domination. In March 2000, Albright acknowledged the U.S. role in overthrowing Mossadeq, regretted the U.S. support for Iraq during the Iraq–Iran war, and welcomed Iran's developing democracy. The United States lifted its ban on exports of agricultural products and medicines to Iran and renewed its imports of Iranian carpets, dried fruits, and caviar.

In short, for the first time in two decades, U.S.–Iranian relations seemed to be moving in a more cooperative direction. Each country prudently lessened its accusatory rhetoric toward the other, and unofficial contacts increased markedly. In 2000, for example, the Speaker of the Iranian Majles, Hojatolislam Mehdi Karubi, visited Washington and unofficially met with government officials. Equally encouraging were the growing contacts between U.S. and Iranian scientists, academics, entrepreneurs, and athletes. The road to normalizing diplomatic relations is understandably difficult and complicated, but the stakes are simply too high for both countries not to overcome the obstacles.

CHALLENGES IN THE NEW CENTURY

The most important goals of the Islamic Revolution were crystallized in the popular slogan chanted by millions of revolutionaries as they sought to overthrow the Pahlavi dynasty in 1979: "*Esteqlal, Azadi, Jomhuri-e Islami*" ("Independence, Freedom, Islamic Republic"). Today, after two decades of rule, through a combination of coercion and religious legitimacy, the ayatollahs have institutionalized the Islamic Republic. Despite the intense and sometimes bloody rivalry between the pro-reform and conservative forces, the young republic faces today no imminent danger of collapse. Thus, the goal of establishing the Islamic Republic has been realized, albeit at an exorbitant cost.

However we may judge the failures and successes of the Islamic Republic, Iran under the ayatollahs has enjoyed considerable independence in the conduct of its foreign policy. Of course, the country has paid dearly for this independence: international isolation, a tarnished image as a "rogue state," the inability to attract foreign investments and buy the most modern technologies, and a decline in most people's standard of living. Still, Iranian foreign policy today is not determined in, or dictated by, Washington, Moscow, or London. For good or ill, Iranian foreign policy is made in Teheran. Moreover, despite eight years of war against Iraq and Iran's open defiance of the United States, the Islamic Republic has protected the country's territorial integrity. For a country obsessed about protecting its independence, the achievements of the past two decades are striking.

But establishing an independent Islamic Republic without allowing Iranian citizens to enjoy the fruits of freedom is not only the betrayal of the very spirit of the Islamic Revolution, it is also a perfect recipe for longterm disaster. It was the combination of the three goals of the Islamic Revolution—independence, freedom and Islamic republic—that energized millions of Iranians in 1979 to support the revolution. Of the three goals, freedom was elusive despite the stated goal of President Khatami to expand freedom and make the people the masters of their own destiny. In a way, Khatami was implicitly confessing, much to the chagrin of his conservative rivals, that the Islamic Revolution had failed to deliver its sacred promise of enriching people's lives with the precious gift of freedom.

On the surface, the struggle between the pro-Khatami reformists and the conservatives, which revolved around the pivotal issue of freedom, appeared to be completely internal, with no ramifications for the nature and direction of Iranian foreign policy. In reality, however, the struggle was intimately linked to the future orientation of Iran's world role. Khatami decisively defeated his rival in the 1997 presidential election—and he was reelected in 2001 by a wide margin—because he promised to make the Islamic Republic more transparent and tolerant and end Iran's debilitating international isolation. As the print media enjoyed a greater degree of freedom during Khatami's first years in power, Iranians repeatedly expressed their aspirations to end Iran's isolation, improve their standards of living, and develop friendly relations with the Western countries, including the United States.

Iranian reformists are aware that, in this age of mass information and globalization, Iran cannot close its borders and refuse integration into the new global economic system. They are cognizant that Iran will not be able to deal effectively with these new international challenges until they enjoy freedom at home. Every step of the way, however, Khatami's major foreign-policy initiatives were neutralized by the recalcitrant forces of conservatism. The policies of allowing people only limited access to the Internet and forbidding the use of satellite dishes with the ostensible goal of stopping Western cultural imperialism—policies the conservatives strongly endorsed—hampered Iran's entry into the new age of information and its integration within the world economy.

In the eighteenth century, the forces of industrialization and democratization were transforming and empowering Europe. But Iran, ignorant of or oblivious to those changes, was debilitated by internal chaos. When internal order was at last established by a brutal Qajar king in 1799, Iran was relegated to the periphery of international politics and its very independence was in jeopardy. That sad state of affairs lasted for almost two centuries. Iran cannot afford to repeat this mistake today. It cannot afford to silently sit on the sidelines and watch the new global economy and the information age change the nature of international affairs. The two greatest challenges of Iran's foreign policy, therefore, are to prepare the country and its population for the emerging and irresistible global economy and the information age and to secure a favorable position for itself, one that prevents it from being marginalized in the future while ensuring the prosperity of its large population. Without freedom at home, the Islamic

Republic will fail to deal with these challenges and Iran's global stature will diminish significantly.

Iran will have enormous difficulty achieving its long-term goals unless it normalizes relations with the United States, which so profoundly affected Iran in the previous century. Unlike the reformists, the conservatives generally oppose any rapprochement with the United States, the world's only superpower, the leading force of information technology, and the dominant economic force in the global economy. Iran would pay dearly, as it already has, by ignoring this reality. Nor can the United States ignore Iran. Although each country has legitimate grievances against the other, they also share many common goals. Only through dialogue can the grievances be addressed and their common goals be used to establish new relations based upon reciprocity and mutual respect.

For Iran, the ultimate challenge of its foreign policy is to establish normal relations with the Western powers without endangering its cherished political independence. This is indeed difficult, but possible—and essential. Iran has a rich and ancient civilization, an invaluable geostrategic location, abundant natural resources, a huge and relatively educated population, and sizable markets. If Iran can meet this challenge, it can build on those resources to play a more influential and constructive role in world politics during the twenty-first century and beyond.

SOUTH AFRICA: FROM THE SHADOWS

Peter J. Schraeder

Loyola University–Chicago

T he Republic of South Africa has emerged from the shadows of its past to become a respected and formidable regional power. In this chapter, the linkage between South Africa's fundamental internal reforms and its growing international stature is explored in detail. As we will find, democracy in South Africa has brought with it a democratic revolution in the formulation and conduct of its foreign policy, a pattern that has become evident in other emerging powers of the post–Cold War era.

From 1948 until 1994, South African leaders maintained an authoritarian political system known as *apartheid* (apartness). Under this system, the white minority imposed racial segregation on a disenfranchised black majority. The cost of this strategy was South Africa's branding as a pariah within the African continent and the wider international community. Continued adherence to apartheid policies amid the rising chorus of domestic and international condemnation virtually guaranteed South Africa's "diplomacy of isolation" during the Cold War (Geldenhuys 1984).

South Africa's pariah status ended in 1994, when Nelson Mandela was elected president in his country's first multiracial and multiparty elections. South Africa emerged as the embodiment of the political–military and socioeconomic changes sweeping Africa that are often referred to as the "African renaissance." This status was further strengthened in 1999, when Mandela's anointed successor, Vice President Thabo Mbeki, emerged victorious in presidential elections (Vale and Maseko 1998). An important aspect of this newfound status has been the determination of both administrations to redesign the South African foreign-policy apparatus, a measure that would presumably lead to alterations in foreign-policy practices and relationships. These internal changes have solidified South Africa's ongoing transformation from international pariah to leader of the African renaissance.

South Africa constitutes an excellent case study for understanding foreign-policy adaptation in the post–Cold War era. Often referred to as a "regional superpower" (Butts and Thomas 1986), South Africa is without question the leading power on the African continent. It possesses Africa's most industrialized economy whose annual gross national product of more than $130 billion accounts for nearly 30 percent of the continent's economic output. South Africa also boasts the largest and best-trained military in Africa, including air and naval forces capable of projecting military power far beyond South African territory. Politically, South Africa serves as the embodiment of the democratic changes that have swept across Africa since the fall of the Berlin Wall in 1989. Dubbed the "rainbow nation," South Africa is also a leader in the cultural realm as its leaders strive to create a civil society that is capable of resolving internal conflicts through the rule of law. This case, therefore, illuminates the promise and potential foreign-policy implications of far-reaching social and political reforms in Africa. More generally, South Africa offers important insights into the adaptation strategies being pursued by other emerging powers throughout the world.

THE ROOTS OF SOUTH AFRICAN FOREIGN POLICY

As other chapters in this volume have aptly demonstrated, the foreign policies of great and emerging powers alike cannot be understood without reference to their historical context. South Africa is certainly no exception to this rule. Indeed, it may be argued that, more so than the other countries featured in this volume, South Africa's primary challenge today at home and abroad is to escape from the shadows of its past. The shadows include not only the apartheid era, but the previous and longer period in which South Africa was established and subsequently dominated by foreign powers. Both periods, therefore, deserve attention in this section of the chapter.

EARLY SETTLEMENT AND FOREIGN CONTROL

The first white settlers arrived at the Cape of Good Hope in southern Africa in 1652 to create a "refreshment station" for the Dutch East India Company. As time went by, this settler population began to speak a unique language (Afrikaans) and think of itself as a unique people (Afrikaners) with permanent roots in the coastal areas of southern Africa. Yet, when faced with the imposition of British colonial rule early in the nineteenth century, approximately 20 percent of the Afrikaner population undertook the so-called "Great Trek" into the hinterland, establishing independent Afrikaner provinces known as the Transvaal and the Orange Free State. Under pressure from both the migrating Afrikaners and the imperial conquests of the British colonial army, the indigenous black populations of the region, such as the Xulu, the Xhosa, and the Swazi, were subjugated and placed under white rule.

The Afrikaners' determination to forestall the encroachment of the British was soon dashed by the discoveries of diamonds near Kimberly in 1867 and of gold in the area of Witwatersrand in 1886. Intent on adding these resources to an expanding imperial colonial order, Great Britain annexed the Transvaal in 1877. This contributed to rising British–Afrikaner tensions and culminated in the Boer War of 1899–1902. The defeat of the Afrikaners in this war cemented the supremacy of British colonial rule over the region. It also fueled the unification in 1910 of Afrikaner territories within a self-governing, British-controlled state known as South Africa. This was followed in 1931 by London's recognition of the country's legal sovereignty within the British Commonwealth. The Afrikaners were granted full political franchise within the South African political system. Nonetheless, they were dominated by an English-speaking elite of British origins. The indigenous African nations that comprised the majority of the region's population were largely stripped of their lands and political rights.

This newest member of the British Commonwealth enjoyed a positive international image early in the twentieth century. This was in part due to the influential role of South African diplomats in the creation and activities of the League of Nations and the United Nations (Geldenhuys 1984; Munger 1965). Jan Christian Smuts, a decorated hero of the Boer War who ruled South Africa from 1939 to 1948 as the head of the relatively moderate United Party, was credited with playing a major role in the peace conference following World War I (Noer 1985, 18). South Africa was also praised for its active military participation on the side of the Western allies during World War I and World War II. In the latter conflict, South Africa received more than $100 million in U.S. aid that was repaid by the South African government in 1947. In exchange for this assistance, the U.S. War Department was granted the right to establish several air bases on South African soil as part of the allied war effort (Lake 1974, 49).

Several aspects of South Africa's political system foreshadowed future problems within the international community. First, a fragile political monopoly of the English-speaking political elite was threatened by the emerging power of splinter Afrikaner parties. Their leaders believed the government had "betrayed" Afrikaner culture, most notably by placing South Africa on a path that eventually would lead to "destructive" black rule (Noer 1985, 18–19). In World War II, for example, several National Party leaders openly praised and admired Adolf Hitler's fascist brand of "national socialism" and opposed entry into the conflict on the side of Great Britain in favor of giving support to Nazi Germany.[1] As the April 1948 parliamentary elections approached, Daniel Malan, dubbed the "Boer Moses" by both critics and supporters, campaigned on a National Party platform of white supremacy and strict segregation of the races. The platform included a proposal for an apartheid system in which nonwhites would be stripped of any remaining legal, political, and economic rights.

Another dilemma in foreign policy revolved around the discriminatory practices directed against Indian ethnic groups in South Africa. Despite the conclusion of an agreement with India in 1927 that guaranteed Indian minority rights, South Africa's parliament restricted Indian property rights and provided for separate political representation. An ensuing diplomatic conflict between India and South Africa prompted India to bring the issue before the UN General Assembly, foreshadowing many future debates over the treatment of nonwhite groups in South Africa.

A final problem resulted from South Africa's occupation during World War I of the German colony of South West Africa (currently Namibia). Rather than acceding to UN demands to place the territory under trusteeship status in preparation for eventual independence, South Africa announced in 1946 its intention to incorporate Namibia as an integral part of South Africa. This act reflected a growing consensus of the South African foreign-policy establishment that the country was destined to play a leadership role throughout southern Africa, not unlike that of the northern industrialized countries in other parts of Africa.

GLOBAL ISOLATION DURING THE APARTHEID ERA

A new era in South African foreign policy began in May 1948, when the Afrikaner National Party achieved an upset victory in parliamentary elections. Despite receiving only a minority of the popular vote, the Afrikaner-based National Party obtained a working majority within the parliament by allying itself with the smaller Afrikaner Party. In a series of legislative actions, the National Party consolidated its power and carried out an electoral promise to institutionalize a political system based on apartheid. Three laws passed in 1950 served as the cornerstones of this political system. First, the Population Registration Act mandated the classification and registration of all South Africans according to race. Second, the Group Areas Act formally divided South Africa into racially segregated living areas. Finally, the Suppression of Communism Act banned the South

---

[1]Consider the following 1942 statement by B. J. Vorster (quoted in Laurence 1979, 41), future prime minister of South Africa: "We stand for Christian Nationalism, which is an ally of Nazism."

African Communist Party and allowed the government to suppress any criticism of the National Party or its apartheid policies. The system of apartheid was further strengthened in 1951. In the aftermath of the extension of parliamentary representation that accompanied Namibia's annexation, the National Party achieved an absolute majority within parliament and further exerted its control over the black majority.

The abhorrent nature of South Africa's racially based political system not surprisingly generated a rising chorus of domestic and international condemnations and attacks. This led to perceptions within the South African policy-making establishment of the emergence of a "total onslaught" against South Africa by the beginning of the 1980s. Internal protests had been growing in both scope and intensity since the Sharpeville massacre of March 21, 1960, when demonstrators against the so-called "pass laws," which limited the movement of nonwhites throughout South Africa, were fired upon by South African security forces. This incident resulted in the deaths of 69 and the wounding of more than 180 blacks. The protests reached their peak in the mid-1980s, when a series of rebellions throughout the country pitted blacks against the South African security and police forces over a period of two years. When the dust settled, more than 2,000 blacks had died and nearly 30,000 others were detained for political reasons, including nearly 3,000 children under the age of 18 (Lodge et al. 1991).

Pretoria's fear of a "total onslaught" was strengthened by the emergence of guerrilla organizations that sought to overthrow the apartheid regime. The three largest guerrilla movements—the African National Congress (ANC), the Pan-African Congress (PAC), and the South-West People's Organization (SWAPO)—enjoyed varying degrees of safe haven within neighboring countries. They could also count on generous amounts of financial support from abroad. Afrikaner policymakers, who were vehement anticommunists, were particularly alarmed by the substantial amount of support the Soviet Union and other communist countries provided to antiapartheid guerrilla forces. In the case of the ANC, South Africa's oldest political party that was established in 1912, early support for nonviolent change was altered in the aftermath of the Sharpeville massacre. Under Mandela's leadership, the ANC in 1961 formed a military wing, *Umkhonto we Sizwe* (Spear of the Nation), which carried out a sustained guerrilla struggle against the apartheid system. The ANC evolved into a formidable political actor with an impressive diplomatic network that paralleled that of the "official" South African government (Thomas 1996). But the ANC suffered a devastating blow when Mandela was captured by South African police in 1962, receiving a life prison sentence.

Increased isolation, culminating in the imposition of a wide range of internationally mandated sanctions, served as the final component of the "total onslaught" perceived by South African policymakers. Many foreign countries refused to recognize South Africa and severed diplomatic ties with the country after the emergence of the Afrikaner-dominated regime in 1948. International organizations quickly followed suit, further compounding South Africa's isolation. The British Commonwealth of Nations forced South Africa to withdraw in 1961, after which South Africa declared itself an independent republic. The Organization of African Unity (OAU) refused to consider membership for South Africa, and the UN General Assembly passed a series of sanctions resolutions. These sanctions included a prohibition on the sale of military goods to the South African regime and a ban on South African involvement in international sporting events, including the Olympic Games. In other cases, foreign countries prohibited all forms of trade and investment with the apartheid regime. "Divestment" from multinational corporations doing business in South Africa became widespread in the 1980s. The global anti-apartheid movement, with affiliates in almost every country of the world, was one of the strongest international efforts directed against a single country during the twentieth century.

South African policymakers responded to their growing isolation by launching a series of related initiatives that became collectively known in the 1980s as the "total national strategy." This strategy underscored the necessity of using all tools available to the South African state to protect the viability of the apartheid system and the Afrikaner way of life. The government's response to rising domestic protests greatly militarized South Africa's civil society (Cock and Nathan 1989). The South African Defense Force (SADF) doubled in size to 85,000 soldiers from 1975 to 1989 and could count on nearly 400,000 reserve forces with military training. The SADF oversaw the military training of white children in a cadet program that expanded from 56,000 members in 1975 to 250,000 in 1987. The South African Police, which exceeded 100,000 officers in 1994, received extensive military training and maintained a large arsenal of military equipment.

As painstakingly documented by South Africa's Truth and Reconciliation Commission, created after the abolition of apartheid, these and other components of the state security apparatus routinely violated the human rights of all opponents of apartheid. Extensive documentation has now become public, for example, describing how state security officers extracted confessions through a variety of grisly techniques. These included use of the "black bag," a tightly wrapped cloth designed to bring a prisoner to the brink of asphyxiation (Truth and Reconciliation Commission 1999).[2] The apartheid regime responded to the threat of guerrilla attacks by relying

---

[2]Former officials of the apartheid state have similarly confessed to human rights violations, including the execution of informants by the use of "necklacing," in which an automobile tire doused in gasoline is wedged around the informant's body and set on fire.

on a host of military tactics that culminated in a policy of destabilizing neighboring countries that provided safe havens to guerrilla groups (Barber and Barratt 1990). In Angola, military raids ranged from a March 1981 bombing of refugee camps to Operation Askari, a December 1983 invasion that involved thousands of troops and led to South Africa's long-term occupation of Angolan territory. Similar military operations against Mozambique included commando raids against suspected ANC safe havens in Maputo to paramilitary support for a guerrilla organization known as the Mozambique National Resistance (RENAMO).[3]

The policy of regional destabilization was particularly effective and forced the leaders of Angola and Mozambique to sign nonaggression pacts with South Africa in 1984 (the Lusaka and Nkomati accords). Indeed, regional destruction wrought by South African destabilization policies prompted the so-called "frontline states" to seek unity in numbers by creating the Southern African Development Coordination Conference (SADCC). Despite its official title, the regional organization was initially formed on the basis of shared threat perceptions of South Africa (Khadiagala 1994). The SADCC stood in sharp contrast to the ill-fated, pro-South African Constellation of Southern African States envisioned by apartheid leaders.

The final element of South Africa's total national strategy sought to reverse the trend toward diplomatic isolation and mitigate the impact of mounting international sanctions. Periodic diplomatic offensives at best delayed the inevitable. In the case of the United States, for example, the imposition of economic sanctions was long delayed by a White House sympathetic to South Africa's diplomatic overtures, anticommunist credentials, and hospitable treatment of U.S.-based corporations. Successive presidential administrations were reluctant to act against Pretoria despite mounting public protests on college campuses and elsewhere in the United States. The nonresponse by the White House continued until Congress in 1986 passed the Comprehensive Anti-Apartheid Act by such a large margin as to make it veto proof (Schraeder 1994).

In other cases, such as the Côte d'Ivoire under the administration of President Félix Houphouët-Boigny, the South African diplomatic corps was able to convince foreign leaders of the necessity of allowing an official visit by the South African president. Such cases, however, represented a rare exception to the general rule of official diplomatic isolation. Informal ties and visits, however, were not only tolerated but encouraged as a useful means of fostering change in South Africa.

---

[3]Originally created by the Rhodesian security services to weaken Mozambique's support for anti-Rhodesian guerrillas, RENAMO became a willing client of South Africa's security services when Zimbabwe's independence in April 1980 terminated its only source of support.

Success was much more evident in South Africa's determination to mitigate the worst effects of internationally mandated sanctions. Like many pariah states that find themselves cut off from access to international arms markets, South Africa was forced to pursue a high level of economic and military self-sufficiency (Geldenhuys 1990). The apartheid regime successfully developed a domestic arms industry—the Armaments Corporation of South Africa (ARMSCOR)—that made South Africa largely self-sufficient in armaments by the end of the 1980s. This was an impressive feat when one realizes that the country previously relied on foreign imports for nearly 70 percent of its defense needs in 1963 (Crawford 1995). By the early 1980s, ARMSCOR employed 28,000 people and was responsible for at least 100,000 jobs within the private sector (Geldenhuys 1984, 142).

The authoritarian nature of the Afrikaner regime exerted a significant impact on the formulation and conduct of South African foreign policy (see Munger 1965). The shift from a parliamentary system based on the Westminster model to a presidential system with a strong executive in 1983 did little to change the repressive nature of the political system. The majority black population still remained politically disenfranchised. It was noteworthy, however, that the foreign-policy role granted to the president was much stronger than that accorded the prime minister under the previous governmental design. Since South Africa became an independent republic in 1961, four Afrikaner leaders—Hendrik Verwoerd (1958–1966); B. J. Vorster (1966–1978); Pieter W. Botha (1978–1989); and Frederik W. DeKlerk (1989–1994)—have left their personal imprints on South African foreign policy.[4] In sharp contrast, the legislature, historically weak in South Africa, was reduced to a "rubber stamp" role by the 1983 constitutional reforms.

The State Security Council (SSC), established by the Security Intelligence and State Security Council Act of 1972, played a leading role in the formulation of foreign policy, not least of all because it included the heads of the major bureaucracies. Originally conceived as an advisory body with little formal power, the SSC became highly influential under the leadership of President Botha, who ensured that the committee met on a regular basis. The SSC's rising fortunes were related to the perceived threat of "total onslaught" and the necessity of coordinating a response that included domestic and international components (Barber and Barratt 1990, 252). The SSC also served as an important arena of bureaucratic debates over foreign policy and in this sense offered insights into the evolving impact of the various foreign affairs bureaucracies. One of the most noteworthy trends was the gradual deterioration throughout the 1970s and

---

[4]Chris Heunis served as acting president (January–September 1989) during the transition from Botha to DeKlerk.

the 1980s in the preeminence of the Ministry of Foreign Affairs in favor of the rising influence and power of the Ministry of Defense and the intelligence services (Geldenhuys 1984, 107–158). As was the case with the SSC, the rising fortunes of the defense and intelligence services were directly related to the perceived necessity of countering greater levels of internal insurrection and externally based guerrilla activities.

In this regard, it should come as no surprise that an authoritarian regime would favor military over diplomatic options. Indeed, the fact that many diplomats within the Ministry of Foreign Affairs favored a more "enlightened" foreign-policy approach did not endear them to a national elite intent on vigorously implementing the total national strategy (Barber and Barratt 1990, 213). Unfortunately, the enhanced bureaucratic power of the generals and intelligence officers effectively marginalized the diplomatic option. This contributed to an ever increasing spiral of violence between the apartheid regime and its opponents. Faced with a seemingly endless military operation and mounting international sanctions, however, the government finally opted for a negotiated settlement in September 1993. Under the agreement, free elections would be held in 1994, opening the door for the first time to majority rule in South Africa.

FOREIGN POLICY AFTER APARTHEID

South Africa's national elections in April 1994 serve as one of the most heralded examples of African democratic transition. Voters of all races cast ballots in free and fair elections that ushered in South Africa's first multiracial, multiethnic, and multiparty democracy. Mandela, who was released after spending nearly twenty-eight years in prison under the apartheid system, was elected president. The party he represented, the ANC, won 63 percent of the popular vote, 252 of 400 seats in the National Assembly, and a majority share of seats in seven of the nine provincial legislatures.[5] This so-called South African "miracle" was repeated five years later when, as promised, Mandela stepped down from power and his vice president, Thabo Mbeki, became president after free and fair elections.

Most observers have focused on the domestic impact of South Africa's transition to democracy, most notably the dismantling of its apartheid political system. This process, however, also entailed a complete reexamination and restructuring of South African foreign-policy practices and relationships. As Mandela (1993, 86) aptly explained in the influential U.S. journal *Foreign Affairs* several months before the 1994 elections, the charting of a new foreign policy for South Africa was a "key element in the

---

[5]DeKlerk, the last president of the apartheid era, and his Afrikaner-based National Party won only 21 percent of the popular vote.

creation of a peaceful and prosperous country." Toward this end, South African policymakers during the Mandela and Mbeki administrations pursued several strategies to adapt South African foreign policy not only to the realities of the post-apartheid era, but also to the demands of the post–Cold War era. This latter point cannot be overstated given the geopolitical vacuum created by the Soviet Union's collapse in December 1991. Whereas the ideological concerns of the Cold War penetrated domestic politics throughout Africa after World War II, the demise of the world's strongest communist power transformed the landscape of African politics in the 1990s and propelled dramatic shifts in many countries toward democratic and economic reforms. In this context, the strategies pursued by South African leaders, described in the following sections, were emulated by other countries in Africa and elsewhere that were undergoing historic democratic transitions.

THE RESTORATION OF CIVILIAN CONTROL

One of the most delicate tasks facing post-apartheid leaders was the restoration of civilian control over a security apparatus that had become all-powerful in the formulation of South African domestic and foreign policies. An agreement reached between the military leaders of the apartheid-era SADF and the military wing of the ANC prior to the general elections of 1994 outlined the creation of a civilian-managed Ministry of Defense, civilian control over the military budget, and civilian-based approval of senior promotions (Kriger and Bond 1995). Military officers during the apartheid era had been responsible for actions deemed illegal under domestic and international law. In response, the constitution stipulated that all security forces "must teach and require their members to act in accordance with the constitution and the law, including customary international law and international agreements binding on the Republic."[6]

The process of demilitarization also included profound changes in military doctrine (see Cilliers and Heinecken 2000). As opposed to the apartheid-era practice of launching counterinsurgency wars and retaliatory strikes against neighboring countries, current military doctrine emphasizes the overriding importance of national self-defense. In this respect, the South African military will be deployed beyond the country's borders only under restrictive circumstances. These include multilateral peacekeeping operations, humanitarian relief missions, and, as witnessed by the South Africa–Botswana intervention in Lesotho in 1998, the restoration of democracy.

---

[6]The 1996 constitution replaced the "transitional" constitution of 1993, which in turn replaced the apartheid-era constitution of 1983.

An important challenge confronting Mandela was the necessity of integrating previously opposed military forces into the newly created South African National Defense Force (SANDF). These included 85,000 largely white SADF soldiers, 30,000 predominately black ANC forces from *Umkhonto we Sizwe*, 6,000 guerrilla fighters from the Azanian People's Liberation Army, and 7,000 soldiers from four black homelands (Transkei, Bophuthatswana, Venda, and Ciskei) that were granted independence by the former apartheid regime but were never recognized by other countries (Crawford 1995). An important reason for the success of this effort was the decision by Defense Minister Joe Modise to maintain an oversized defense force of at least 70,000 soldiers with the intention of gradually reducing this force over time through attrition. As noted by Mbeki (quoted in Crawford 1995, 101), "We could hardly take 30,000 combatants from the ANC and throw them on the streets." Similar to their counterparts from other portions of the armed forces, continued Mbeki, these guerrilla fighters were "proud of their role" in the struggle to create a multiracial and democratic South Africa and understandably "wanted to keep their jobs in an economy where unemployment is high."

RESTRUCTURING THE FOREIGN-POLICY ESTABLISHMENT

A second strategy to adapt South African foreign policy to the new era was the restructuring of the foreign-policy establishment. As detailed later, the 1996 constitution clearly established the roles to be played by a wide variety of institutional actors. The creation and consolidation of democratic practices encouraged input from a wide variety of nonstate actors as well. In short, as South Africa became more democratic, so did its foreign policy.

One of the most profound examples of institutional change revolved around the restructuring of the former Ministry of Foreign Affairs to ensure that it assumed a leading role in the formulation and conduct of foreign policy (Landsberg, le Pere, and van Nieuwkerk 1995). An important step in this process was the creation of a new diplomatic agency—the Department of Foreign Affairs—that would integrate diplomats from the foreign service of the former apartheid regime, the ANC's Department of International Affairs, and the foreign ministries of the four homelands (Mills 1997, 21). This restructuring process prompted heated interagency debates because the Department of Foreign Affairs was the only bureaucracy allowed by the Public Service Commission to expand substantially, which it did by nearly 10 percent in 1995 alone. However, as demonstrated by simply one indicator—the growth of South African diplomatic representation abroad from twenty-five foreign embassies in 1985 to forty-three in 1995—South Africa's emergence from the shadows of its "diplomacy of isolation" demanded an enlarged diplomatic corps capable of responding to new foreign-policy challenges and opportunities.[7]

A LEADING ROLE IN THE "AFRICAN RENAISSANCE"

An emphasis on South Africa's unique position as the leader of the "African renaissance" constitutes a third important component of the country's foreign-policy adaptation to the new era. This renaissance refers to the strengthening of democratic practices and economic liberalization that has occurred across Africa since the fall of the Berlin Wall in 1989. South Africa's leading role was designed to emphasize the centrality of Africa in its foreign policy. Further, it underscored the importance of South Africa as the embodiment of Africa's future political and economic potential. Finally, it highlighted the critical role of South Africa as an intermediary between the African continent and leading foreign powers in other regions of the world (Crouzel 2000). Interestingly enough, the African renaissance, arguably one of the most cited and debated themes in African politics at the beginning of the new millennium, was initially popularized due to repeated usage by then Vice President Mbeki (Vale and Maseko 1998). It has since emerged as the defining foreign-policy concept of his presidential administration.

Mbeki's strong attachment to the concept of the African renaissance reflects several classic African foreign-policy concerns that have become integral to South African foreign policy.[8] Among the most important of these is the promotion of regional integration and development, as witnessed by South Africa's membership and leadership role in the Southern African Development Community (SADC; formerly SADCC).[9] Also viewed as crucial is the government's unequivocal support for nuclear nonproliferation. This position was vividly demonstrated by South Africa's dismantling of a nuclear weapons program that successfully tested a nuclear device during the apartheid era. Mandela punctuated this point by playing a crucial role in convincing other developing countries to accept an indefinite extension of the Nuclear Non-Proliferation Treaty.

Another component of Pretoria's role in the African renaissance relates to its heightened sensitivity to the concepts of territorial integrity and state sovereignty. This was most poignantly symbolized by Mandela's

---

[7]Statistics are drawn from a larger data-based research project directed by the author that seeks to explore trends in African diplomatic representation from the 1960s through 2000.

[8]For an introduction to this rich literature and its foreign-policy themes, see Wright (1999).

[9]The other SADC member countries are Angola, Botswana, Lesotho, Malawi, Mozambique, Swaziland, Tanzania, Zambia, and Zimbabwe.

impassioned rejection of U.S. demands that South Africa avoid diplomatic contact with Libya and Cuba, both of which were designated as "rogue states" (later as "states of concern") by the Clinton administration. South Africa also emerged as an ardent supporter of the peaceful resolution of conflicts, a position made clear by Mandela's willingness to serve as a third-party mediator in an attempt to resolve ethnic conflict in Burundi.

South Africa's interpretation of the African renaissance is consistent with several new themes in African foreign policy that are accepted to varying degrees throughout the continent. A commitment to the promotion of democracy and human rights has gathered strength throughout Africa since the Cold War's end. Such a commitment reflects the emergence of democratic governments in Latin America and other regions that were formerly ruled by military dictators. Although many democratic transitions have been disrupted in recent years amid domestic turmoil, the global trend toward democratic governance is inescapable.

Nonetheless, South Africa's support for democratization makes even some elected African leaders uneasy due to its inevitable clash with the cherished principle of sovereignty (see Landsberg 2000). In the case of South Africa, the Mandela administration's joint undertaking with Botswana of a 1998 military intervention in Lesotho to restore democratic rule suggests an expansive interpretation of what means can be employed to promote democratic values and human rights. This interpretation, of course, assumed global proportions in the 1990s as the UN approved dozens of missions to preserve democratic transitions throughout the world. These missions often included the deployment of peacekeeping forces to separate warring factions and to allow elected governments the time necessary to implement political reforms.

A willingness to adopt the liberal economic model of free trade and investment has also gathered strength in post–Cold War Africa and has been especially invoked by the technocratically minded Mbeki administration (see Evans 1999). Although recognizing that domestic reconstruction and development constitutes the singular priority of South Africa's population, the Mbeki administration, like its predecessor, has underscored the critical role of foreign trade and investment, not to mention foreign aid, in this process. Toward this end, the government's close cooperation with South African businesses has yielded enormous success in developing regional markets and penetrating overseas markets. Once again, South Africa has taken advantage of a global trend in this regard as a record number of countries in the world have discarded statist economic strategies and have instead embraced export-led models of development. This has been a remarkable achievement in South Africa given the potentially contentious relationship between the post-apartheid regime and major corporations in South Africa, many of which are owned by whites and based in foreign countries.

ADHERENCE TO THE "UNIVERSALITY" PRINCIPLE

A fourth adaptation strategy, adherence to the foreign-policy principle of "universality," is designed to bridge the foreign-policy gap between the apartheid and democratic eras. This principle underscores the willingness of South Africa to establish diplomatic relations with all countries of the world regardless of their domestic and foreign policies. In the Middle East, for example, Mandela and Mbeki sought to strengthen diplomatic links with Israel, historically an ally of the apartheid regime, while at the same time establishing and strengthening diplomatic ties with Libya and Iran, which were strong supporters of the ANC's guerrilla struggle. In some cases, such as the ongoing diplomatic battle between the People's Republic of China (PRC) and Taiwan as to which capital, Beijing or Taipei, is recognized as the official seat of the Chinese government, South Africa's desire to maintain a two-China policy proved untenable. This led South Africa to choose Beijing, largely for economic reasons (Geldenhuys 1995).

The willingness of the Mandela and Mbeki administrations to choose economic self-interest over regime type in the case of China—Taiwan is a democracy and the PRC remains a dictatorship—has led to sharp critiques of South African foreign policy. This is most notable when one realizes that the ANC, during the period of guerrilla struggle, strongly denounced any government (including the United States) that emphasized economic self-interests in their refusals to impose sanctions against the apartheid regime. In this regard, there has been a tendency for South Africa to err on the side of maintaining diplomatic ties even with authoritarian regimes such as Fidel Castro's Cuba, which strongly supported the ANC during its insurgency.

South Africa's diplomatic ties with countries considered by U.S. leaders to be terrorist states (most notably Libya, Iran, and the Sudan) caused repeated diplomatic tensions with the Clinton administration. The tensions continued after Clinton's departure in January 2001 and the coming to power of the much more strategically minded administration of President George W. Bush. South Africa's policy, however, has been widely praised in other capitals as reflecting a more independent stance that is able to overcome pressure, and occasional intimidation, from the great powers. In this respect, South Africa has emerged as a role model for other emerging powers that wish to assert themselves in regional and global politics.

GROWING ACTIVISM IN INTERNATIONAL ORGANIZATIONS

A final strategy for adapting South African foreign policy to the new era is a commitment to upholding and strengthening the norms and practices associated with the UN and its member agencies. This commitment also applies to a wide range of other intergovernmental organizations at the regional and global levels, whose numbers and responsibilities have increased substantially in recent years and have played a major role in fostering democratic transitions.

One of the most important objectives of the immediate post-apartheid era was to ensure that South African diplomats quickly reasserted South Africa's "rightful place" as both a member and a leader within the international community. Less than two months after Mandela took power in 1994, South Africa was admitted to the OAU, joined the Non-Aligned Movement, and was readmitted to the British Commonwealth of Nations. South Africa has especially embraced its reclaimed UN membership, joining the governing councils of several specialized agencies and organs such as the International Telecommunications Union.

South African diplomats consistently argue that their country's historic role in the UN, of which South Africa was a founding member, and its current status as the embodiment of the African renaissance, make South Africa the ideal African candidate for a permanent seat on an enlarged UN Security Council. This campaign is not unlike those launched by other emerging powers covered in this volume, including Brazil, India, and Indonesia. South Africa's potential African rivals for a permanent UN Security Council seat are dismissed as either undemocratic (Egypt), beset by internal conflict (the Democratic Republic of the Congo), or lacking sufficient economic resources (Nigeria).[10]

A More "Democratic" Foreign Policy

The study of the sources of African foreign policy traditionally has been dominated by three bodies of scholarship (Schraeder 2000). The first body of research, often referred to as the "big-man" theory of African foreign policy, emphasizes the overriding importance of the personal whims of authoritarian leaders to explain the formulation and conduct of African foreign policies (e.g., Chan 1992). A second body of scholarship focuses on the impact of the larger geopolitical setting of great-power competition, most notably the Cold War struggle between the United States and the Soviet Union (e.g., Weiss and Blight 1992). Finally, a third body of scholarship emphasizes the constraints imposed on African foreign policies by the continuation of "dependency" relationships between African states and their former colonial powers (e.g., Shaw and Okolo 1994). In essence, all three bodies of scholarship simplistically imply that one has only to grasp the preferences either of African leaders or foreign powers in order to understand the key sources of African foreign policy.

---

[10]Confidential interview with an official in the South African embassy in Washington, D.C., September 16, 2000.

The primary argument of this chapter is that these explanations constitute at best exaggerations of more dynamic foreign-policy processes, especially in those cases, such as South Africa, that have made transitions to democratic forms of governance. Specifically, students of African foreign policy have neglected the simple but logical hypothesis that the process of democratization, typically examined in terms of its impact on domestic politics, should also foster the democratization of African foreign-policy institutions. The implication of this trend is that the process of democratization has favored the emergence and strengthening of a wide variety of state and nonstate actors, all of which are capable of shaping foreign policies. African democracies, including those newly established and in the process of consolidation, embody open political systems that, by their nature, permit wider involvement in the foreign-policy-making process.

In this respect, it is crucial to note the important role played by many actors in the formulation and conduct of South African foreign policy today. The constitution of 1996 clearly stipulated the overriding importance of the president in the formulation of South African foreign policy. This constitutional prerogative was further strengthened by what is often referred to as the "Mandela effect," which relates to Mandela's emergence from captivity into one of the most celebrated, admired, and charismatic figures of the twentieth century.[11] Rather than seeking to punish his former jailers once he and the ANC won the 1994 elections, Mandela extended the olive branch to all ethnic and racial factions in South Africa. This surrounded the former guerrilla leader with an aura of near sainthood within the international community. It is precisely for this reason, lament critics of the Mandela administration (see Mills 1997, 24), that South African foreign policy often followed Mandela's public statements rather than the sometimes opposing contours of consensus opinion within the foreign-policy establishment.

It will be up to future historians to sort out the long-term impact of the "Mandela effect" within the foreign-policy realm. In any event, the election of the more technocratic and less charismatic Mbeki as president in 1999 heralded a greater "depersonalization" of South African foreign policy that is more in line with the 1996 constitution (Evans 1999). Having served as the foreign minister of the ANC during its years in exile, Mbeki is clearly familiar with the multitude of foreign-policy issues confronting post-apartheid South Africa. Unlike his predecessor, Mbeki is more open to compromise and more willing to rely on the expertise of specialists within the executive branch, most notably the Coordination and Cooperation Unit, a sort of "kitchen cabinet" directly answerable to Mbeki that is comprised of young and energetic, but initially inexperienced foreign-policy staffers.

---

[11]For a personal account of the Mandela story, see his autobiography (Mandela 1994).

THE DIFFUSION OF BUREAUCRATIC CONTROL

The foreign affairs bureaucracies of the executive branch also serve as an important source of South African foreign policy in the democratic era. A fascinating aspect of the emerging bureaucratic blueprint of South African foreign policy is that the existing foreign affairs bureaucracies, most notably the Department of Foreign Affairs and the Ministry of Defense, were transformed. This involved a synthesis of the personnel of the former apartheid regime, the guerrilla armies, and the black homelands. In this sense, the foreign affairs bureaucracies remained works in progress by the beginning of the Mbeki administration. Bureaucratic actors have attempted to further rationalize their administrative structures and organizational routines. They have set out clear organizational goals and priorities, recruited and trained new personnel, and learned through trial and error the best means of ensuring a preferred foreign-policy outcome via negotiations and bureaucratic competition with other members of the foreign-policy establishment.

Several revealing trends can be noted in the relative positions of power and influence of individual bureaucracies within the foreign-policy hierarchy. The Department of Foreign Affairs has regained a substantial portion of the influence that it lost during the apartheid years. It does, however, struggle to train enough capable diplomats to staff South Africa's quickly expanding diplomatic network. The department has also been stung by criticism that its first head, Foreign Minister Alfred Nzo, an ANC stalwart, was not proactive enough and did not have the proper administrative credentials to be an effective leader. This perception has softened in large part due to the more assertive policies of his successor, Nkosazana Dlamini-Zuma. Joe Modise, the first head of the Ministry of Defense, won praise from many quarters for his handling of the reorganization and integration of the South African armed forces. This bureaucracy, however, has played a more restrictive foreign-policy role due to the lingering suspicions associated with its role during the apartheid era.

South Africa's trade-oriented, foreign-economic policy, not surprisingly, has made the Department of Trade and Industry one of the most prominent bureaucracies within the foreign-policy-making establishment. This bureaucracy, however, has found itself in competition with the Department of Foreign Affairs. Critics (e.g., Bischoff and Southall 1999, 159) have suggested that the two departments be merged in order to avoid unnecessary bureaucratic competition and to ensure a more integrated foreign-policy approach. This dispute, similar to that which has long been waged within Japanese foreign-policy circles (see Chapter 5), is no doubt inevitable given South Africa's heightened international stature and foreign-policy ambitions in the post-apartheid era.

Finally, the South African parliament has emerged as an important foreign-policy actor in the democratic era. This constitutionally independent branch of government plays an important oversight role that, although not as powerful as originally envisioned by ANC leaders and advocates of civil society, clearly goes beyond the foreign-policy prerogatives enjoyed by legislatures during the apartheid and pre-apartheid eras. The leading legislative actor within the foreign-policy realm is the Portfolio Committee on Foreign Affairs. This committee holds well-attended hearings in which established tradition requires the appearance of executive branch officials to answer questions related to South African foreign policy. The Portfolio Committee has not hesitated to criticize executive branch policies. Most notable have been the policies fashioned by the Department of Foreign Affairs, despite the fact that both the presidency and the parliament are controlled by the ANC.

Within parliament, the Select Committee on Defense, modeled after a similar arm of the German *Bundestag*, is charged with making recommendations concerning the military's budget, organization, and policies. "Under the National Party and the previous Westminster parliamentary system, the Select Committee on Defense had proved little more than a rubber stamp for the executive," noted Jakkie Cilliers and Lindy Heinecken (2000, 252), two specialists of civil–military relations in South Africa. "Now, with its powers enshrined in the Constitution, Parliament has taken an active and vigorously independent role in monitoring defense relations and the military as a whole." The committee perceives itself as an "active participant" in all major decisions undertaken by the Ministry of Defense and has played a critical role in restoring civilian control over the South African military. It is precisely for this reason that the "relative power and influence" of civilian managers within the Ministry of Defense in the near future "will be comparable to that in most Western armed forces."

GREATER INPUT FROM NONSTATE ACTORS

A wide variety of nonstate actors also plays a significant role in the formulation of South African foreign policy. This pattern has emerged in other newly democratic countries, particularly those in Eastern Europe, and demonstrates how a more pluralistic government structure produces greater public involvement in foreign affairs. Importantly, nonstate actors are widely viewed as an essential pillar of civil societies. As such, Western aid donors have broadened their efforts in recent years and have provided vast sums to political parties, labor unions, news organizations, and other nonstate actors whose influence is seen as vital to the consolidation of democratic rule.[12]

---

[12]The U.S. government's recent focus on supporting private groups associated with civil society in newly democratic countries, including South Africa, reflects a "learning curve" in its foreign aid programs. See Carothers (1999) for a detailed examination of the lessons learned by the U.S. government and other major aid donors since the Cold War.

Among these groups in South Africa, the ANC is particularly influential due to its status as the ruling party in both the executive branch and the parliament during the democratic era. The ANC's victory in two sets of legislative elections and the transition of power from the Mandela to the Mbeki administrations have even led some scholars (e.g., Giliomee 1998) to refer to South Africa as a "dominant-party system" in which the ANC will likely continue to rule for the foreseeable future. Yet the ANC's ideological stance on foreign-policy issues, and therefore its impact, has significantly changed since the party's inception in 1912 (Thomas 1996). At least three phases can be discerned (Evans 1999). The first phase (1912–1960) involved liberal support for international law and international organizations. The second phase (1960–1993) embraced the socialist ideals of international revolution and redistribution. Finally, the third and current phase (1993–present) calls for a more pragmatic, self-interested approach that emphasizes the importance of "geoeconomics." This latter position is widely shared within the South African government and among business leaders. It is also endorsed by most northern industrialized countries and international organizations.

Mbeki's election reflected the strengthened position of adherents to the current pragmatic phase. Many ANC members in parliament, however, maintain strong attachments to the ideals of socialism, while many groups in the executive and legislative branches share the ideological leanings of liberal internationalism. The ideological differences between the ANC's adherents in the executive and the parliament partly explain the ongoing foreign-policy tensions between these two branches of government. Some have even argued that the contradictory nature of South African foreign policy (i.e., the primacy of geoeconomics in some cases and the primacy of human rights concerns in others) is "in no small part attributable to the push/pull effects of this competing triad of theoretical perspectives and the lack of consensus the tensions between them have generated within the ranks of the ruling party" (Evans 1999, 623).

Not only do political parties play a key role in democratic governments; labor unions have also exerted strong influence in domestic and foreign policy. The South African labor movement, under the leadership of a nationwide umbrella group, the Congress of South African Trade Unions (COSATU), is particularly important in this regard. Its influence derives in large part from the Congress's central role in the transition to the democratic era and its contribution to the electoral success of the ANC in national elections. Although principally focused on domestic priorities, such as the creation of a National Economic Forum and the passage of the Reconstruction and Development Program, COSATU's leadership has actively pursued a wide variety of foreign-policy initiatives, especially when supported by "fraternal" unions in neighboring countries.

It has been argued, for example, that pressures from COSATU played an important role in Mandela's decision to seek a restoration of the democratically elected government of Ntsu Mokhehle in Lesotho (Bischoff and Southall 1999, 175). The group's lobbying efforts were also critical in prompting Mandela to place pressure on King Mswati to oversee a return to democracy in Swaziland (Bischoff and Southall 1999, 176). In both cases, COSATU's actions were driven by a desire to lend support to trade unions that took the lead in calling for democratization in neighboring countries.

Finally, a wide variety of international actors has also served as an important source of South African foreign policy. South African leaders especially have been influenced by "role expectations" within the African continent and the wider international community. As aptly stated by Aziz Pahad, former deputy minister of foreign affairs, there exists a "tremendous expectation" from other capitals that South Africa will play a major role in shaping the world politics of the new millennium. In this regard, many African leaders expect South Africa to take the lead in promoting the most cherished aims of African foreign policy. The northern industrialized democracies, meanwhile, expect South Africa to continue to serve as a role model for economic and political reforms throughout the African continent. It therefore should come as no surprise that Mbeki has made the African renaissance and South Africa's unique place at the intersection of the African continent and the northern industrialized democracies the cornerstones of South African foreign policy.

The impact of economic factors in shaping foreign policy in post-apartheid South Africa cannot be overstated. Struggling to overcome the disparities of the apartheid era that included a 45-percent unemployment rate, largely within the nonwhite majority population, South Africa has aggressively sought foreign aid, trade, and investment. In 1995, the first full year of democratic transition after Mandela's election, South Africa received $386 million in Official Development Assistance from a wide variety of foreign governments (Organization for Economic Cooperation and Development 1996, 178). Industrialized countries, meanwhile, exported $27 billion in goods and services to South Africa (U.S. and Foreign Commercial Service 1997, 81). South Africa's leading economic partners, including the member-states of the European Union (most notably Germany and the United Kingdom) and the United States, thus have a material as well as normative interest in the consolidation of democratic rule in South Africa.

The link between political reform and economic development is clearly demonstrated by the explosion of foreign direct investment (FDI) that has been directed toward Africa's most dynamic emerging market. In just the first two years after apartheid was abolished, FDI inflows to South Africa increased dramatically from $29 billion to $43 billion (U.S. and Foreign Commercial Service 1997, 85). This surge in private investment was also due to the simple fact that wide-ranging sanctions were dropped after South Africa emerged as a "legitimate" actor in the international community. The recognition among South African leaders that foreign capital is crucial to internal reconstruction and development has made South Africa a firm proponent of the neoliberal model of development. This consensus, which rejects the once-heralded models of import substitution, trade protectionism, and government control of key industries, is only one of many surprising developments in South African foreign policy since the apartheid era.

TOWARD THE FUTURE

Several issues will continue to set the tone of debates over South African foreign policy in the future. The first is the degree to which the South African policy-making establishment should be focusing on foreign affairs as opposed to the serious domestic challenges confronting South Africa's nascent democracy (e.g., see Thompson 1999). The extraordinary domestic challenges inherited from the apartheid era include a 35-percent unemployment rate among the majority black population, which constitutes 75 percent of a total population of approximately 43 million people. Also of concern is the impoverished condition of the historically neglected black townships, in which 7.5 million citizens still lack access to running water and 3 million citizens lack adequate housing.

To these apartheid-era remnants one can add the more recent but related challenges of an AIDS pandemic that currently afflicts more than 4.2 million people and a dramatic rise in crime. The murder rate in South Africa, for example, is an astounding 58.5 killings per 100,000 South Africans, a rate nearly ten times higher than the U.S. rate of 6.3 murders per 100,000 Americans. In short, many South Africans who have yet to receive the material benefits of the democratic transition are increasingly prone to question the usefulness of spending limited national resources on costly foreign-policy initiatives when so much needs to be done at home to resolve the inequities of the apartheid era.

Even if a consensus is reached as to the proper balance between foreign and domestic policy priorities, the South African foreign-policy-making establishment remains in a process of flux that limits its effectiveness in foreign policy. Although the *restructuring* of the foreign-policy apparatus has been largely completed, the *interaction* both within and between the various branches of government remains unclear and often chaotic. For example, the balance of power between the executive branch and the parliament has yet to be clearly defined, especially as legislators increasingly balance their traditional focus on reconstruction and development with a greater interest in foreign affairs. Even within the executive branch, interaction among the various foreign-affairs bureaucracies remains fluid as each seeks to master its area of expertise. In short, the process of making South African foreign policy remains a work in progress.

Not surprisingly, the lack of consistency within the foreign-policy-making process has fostered seemingly contradictory foreign-policy behavior. Critics particularly underscore the tension between South African rhetoric over the need to promote human rights and democracy and the more apolitical demands associated with the principle of universality, state sovereignty, and the pursuit of economic self-interests. Needless to say, all countries must contend with competing foreign-policy objectives. Few, if any, are successful in creating a hierarchy of goals in which the most important is rigidly and consistently pursued.

As noted earlier, Mandela's decision to recognize Beijing over Taiwan served as one example of a wider and intensifying foreign-policy debate. Its primary concern is whether "universality" and economic self-interests should serve as the guiding principles of South African foreign policy. Indeed, the unwillingness of both the Mandela and Mbeki administrations to be outspoken over the human rights violations of Castro's Cuba and other supporters of the anti-apartheid struggle has prompted critics to charge that post-apartheid South Africa is guilty of doing exactly what it condemned others for doing during the apartheid era: turning a blind eye toward human rights violations in the name of promoting economic self-interests.

Regional relations will be of particular importance to South Africa's emerging foreign-policy role. The ongoing civil war in neighboring Angola and heightened racial tensions in neighboring Zimbabwe serve as important daily reminders of the fragile nature of democratic reform in southern Africa and across the continent. Such conflicts not only hinder the prospects for further regional integration, one of the cornerstones of the regional initiatives undertaken by Mandela and Mbeki, but they also invariably affect South Africa itself as refugees and armed groups cross its international boundaries.

Like it or not, South African policymakers must respond to these problems. The role expectations associated with South Africa's self-proclaimed status as a leader of the African renaissance have ensured such complications in its regional relations. In the case of the large-scale war that has engulfed the Democratic Republic of the Congo (formerly Zaire), dubbed Africa's "First World War" by many observers, South Africa's appeals for a nonviolent resolution stand in sharp contrast to its direct military involvement in Angola, Namibia, and Zimbabwe. Denunciations of South Africa's approach to the Congo war reflect a high degree of regional hostility toward Pretoria that was once thought to be a by-product of South Africa's hated apartheid system. In short, South Africa's newfound status as a legitimate, post-apartheid foreign-policy actor has in many respects harmed its regional relationships as smaller, less-powerful neighbors seek to limit the influence of what in essence constitutes a regional superpower.

These cross-pressures in the regional security context raise fundamental questions as to what sort of balance should be struck in South Africa's links with Africa and the wider international community. From the day of his inauguration, Mandela sought to set the tone of his and future administrations by stating that South Africa was, first and foremost, an African country with primary responsibilities to the African continent. The vast majority of South Africa's economic and financial links, however, are with the major northern industrialized democracies. In this regard, South African leaders are quick to note the overriding importance of maintaining economic access to the industrialized world as the best means of promoting successful internal reconstruction and development.

The crucial and as yet unresolved questions are as follows: Should South Africa primarily focus on strengthening its links with the northern industrialized democracies? Or does cultural solidarity demand a greater focus on the African continent and other countries within the Southern Hemisphere? Although some would argue the necessity of simultaneously expanding and strengthening links in all directions, others rightfully claim that the rational use of limited resources requires some kind of geopolitical hierarchy. Only time will tell if South Africa emerges as the preeminent representative of African foreign-policy interests, a rising middle power that serves the interests of the northern industrialized democracies, or some combination of the two. In any event, a democratic South Africa will inevitably play a crucial role in shaping the destinies not only of its own people, but of those far beyond its borders.

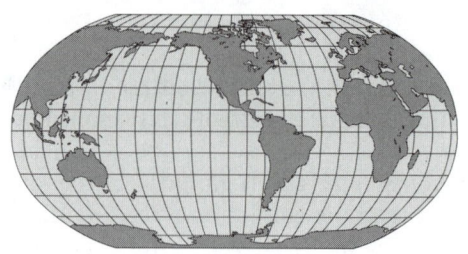

BIBLIOGRAPHY

Agung, Ide A. *Twenty Years of Indonesian Foreign Policy, 1945–1965*. The Hague: Mouton, 1973.

Aidit, D. N. *Set Afire the Banteng Spirit*. Beijing: Foreign Languages Press, 1964.

Akbar, M. J. *Kashmir, Behind the Vale*. New York: Viking, 1991.

Alexander, Yonah, and Allan Nanes, eds. *The United States and Iran: A Documentary History*. Frederick, MD: Aletheia Books, 1980.

Allison, Graham T. *Essence of Decision: Explaining the Cuban Missile Crisis*. Boston: Little, Brown, 1971.

Ambrose, Stephen E., and Douglas G. Brinkley. *Rise to Globalism: American Foreign Policy since 1938*, 8th rev. ed. New York: Penguin, 1997.

Anwar, Dewi Fortuna. *Indonesia in ASEAN: Foreign Policy and Regionalism*. New York: St. Martin's, 1995.

Arbatov, Alexei G. "Military Reform in Russia: Dilemmas, Obstacles, and Prospects." *International Security* 22 (spring 1998): 83–134.

Aron, Leon. "The Emergent Priorities of Russian Foreign Policy." In *The Emergence of Russian Foreign Policy*, ed. Leon Aron and Kenneth M. Jensen, 17–34. Washington, D.C.: United States Institute of Peace Press, 1994.

Baker, Richard W., and Charles E. Morrison, eds. *Asia Pacific Security Outlook 2000*. Tokyo: Japan Center for International Exchange, 2000.

Baldwin, David A. *Economic Statecraft*. Princeton, NJ: Princeton University Press, 1985.

Baldwin, Richard E. "The Eastern Enlargement of the European Union." *European Economic Review* 39 (April 1995): 474–481.

Barber, James, and John Barratt. *South Africa's Foreign Policy: The Search for Status and Security, 1945–1988*. New York: Cambridge University Press, 1990.

Barbosa, Rubens. "The United States and Brazil: Strategic Partners or Regional Competitors?" Statement by Ambassador Rubens Barbosa to Subcommittee on Western Hemisphere Affairs, Committee on International Relations, U.S.

House of Representatives, Washington, D.C., 26 July 2000. <www.house.gov/international_relations/wh/usbrazil/RBarbosa.htm>

Beasley, William G. *The Rise of Modern Japan: Political, Economic, and Social Change since 1850*. New York: St. Martin's, 1995.

Bill, James A. *The Eagle and the Lion: The Tragedy of American–Iranian Relations*. New Haven, CT: Yale University Press, 1988.

Bischoff, Paul-Henri, and Roger Southall. "Early Foreign Policy of the Democratic South Africa" In *African Foreign Policies*, ed. Stephen Wright, 154–181. Boulder, CO: Westview Press, 1999.

Bose, Sumantra. *The Challenge in Kashmir: Democracy, Self-Determination, and a Just Peace*. Thousand Oaks, CA: Sage, 1997.

Breslauer, George W. "What Have We Learned about Learning?" In *Learning in U.S. and Soviet Foreign Policy*, ed. George W. Breslauer and Philip E. Tetlock, 825–856. Boulder, CO: Westview Press, 1991.

Breslauer, George W., and Philip E. Tetlock, eds. *Learning in U.S. and Soviet Foreign Policy*. Boulder, CO: Westview Press, 1991.

Bresnan, John. "Indonesia." In *The Pivotal States: A New Framework for U.S. Policy in the Developing World*, ed. Robert Chase, Emily Hill, and Paul Kennedy, 15–39. New York: W. W. Norton, 1999.

Broadbent, Jeffrey. *Environmental Politics in Japan: Networks of Power and Protest*. New York: Cambridge University Press, 1998.

Bulletin of the Atomic Scientists. "Nuclear Notebook: Russian Strategic Nuclear Forces, End of 1997." *Bulletin of the Atomic Scientists* (March–April 1998): 70–71.

Butts, Kent H., and Paul R. Thomas. *The Geopolitics of Southern Africa: South Africa as a Regional Superpower*. Boulder, CO: Westview Press, 1986.

Calleo, David P., and Benjamin M. Rowland. *America and the World Political Economy: Atlantic Dreams and National Realities*. Bloomington, IN: Indiana University Press, 1973.

Cameron, Fraser. *The Foreign and Security Policy of the European Union: Past, Present, and Future*. Sheffield: Sheffield Academic Press, 1999.

Carothers, Thomas. *Aiding Democracy Abroad: The Learning Curve*. Washington, D.C.: Carnegie Endowment for International Peace, 1999.

Carré, Herve, and Karen H. Johnson. "Progress toward European Monetary Union." *The Federal Reserve Bulletin* 77 (September–December 1991): 769–783.

de Carvalho, José Murilo. "Dreams Come Untrue in Brazil: Burden of the Past, Promise of the Future." *Daedalus* 129 (spring 2000): 57–82.

Chan, Stephen. *Kaunda and Southern Africa: Image and Reality in Foreign Policy*. London: British Academic Press, 1992.

Chase, Robert, Emily Hill, and Paul Kennedy, eds. *The Pivotal States: A New Framework for U.S. Policy in the Developing World*. New York: W. W. Norton, 1999.

Chauvel, Richard. "Ambon: Not a Revolution but a Counter-Revolution." In *Regional Dynamics of the Indonesian Revolution: Unity from Diversity*, ed. Audrey R. Kahin, 236–264. Honolulu, HI: University of Hawaii Press, 1985.

Chicago Council on Foreign Relations. *American Public Opinion and U.S. Foreign Policy*. Chicago, IL: Chicago Council on Foreign Relations, 1995, 1999.

Chilcote, Ronald H. *Theories of Development and Underdevelopment*. Boulder, CO: Westview Press, 1984.

Cilliers, Jakkie, and Lindy Heinecken. "South Africa: Emerging from a Time Warp." In *The Postmodern Military: Armed Forces after the Cold War*, ed. Charles C. Moskos, John Allen Williams, and David R. Segal, 242–264. New York: Oxford University Press, 2000.

Clad, James. "Fin de Siecle, Fin de l'ASEAN?" *PacNet Newsletter* 9 (3 March 2000).

Cock, Jacklyn, and Laurie Nathan, eds. *Society at War: The Militarization of South Africa*. Johannesburg, South Africa: Thorold's Africana Books, 1989.

Coker, Christopher. "Britain and the New World Order: The Special Relationship in the 1990s." *International Affairs* 68 (July 1992): 407–421.

Colbert, Evelyn S. *Southeast Asia in International Politics, 1941–1956*. Ithaca, NY: Cornell University Press, 1977.

Commission of the European Communities. "One Market, One Money: An Evaluation of the Potential Benefits and Costs of Forming an Economic and Monetary Union." Study of the Directorate-General for Economic and Financial Affairs. *European Economy* (October 1990).

Corrales, Javier, and Richard E. Feinberg. "Regimes of Cooperation in the Western Hemisphere: Power, Interests, and Intellectual Traditions." *International Studies Quarterly* 43 (March 1999): 1–36.

Cossa, Ralph A., ed. *Restructuring the U.S.–Japan Alliance: Toward a More Equal Partnership*. Washington, D.C.: Center for Strategic and International Studies Press, 1997.

Cottam, Richard W. *Nationalism in Iran*. Pittsburgh: University of Pittsburgh Press, 1979.

Crabb, Cecil V., Jr., and Pat M. Holt. *Invitation to Struggle: Congress, the President, and Foreign Policy*, 4th ed. Washington, D.C.: CQ Press, 1992.

Crawford, Neta C. "South Africa's New Foreign and Military Policy: Opportunities and Constraints." *Africa Today* 42, no. 1–2 (1995): 88–121.

Croft, Stuart, ed. *British Security Policy: The Thatcher Years and the End of the Cold War*. London: HarperCollins, 1991.

Croft, Stuart, John Redmond, G. Wynn Rees, and Mark Webber. *The Enlargement of Europe*. Manchester, UK: Manchester University Press, 1999.

Crouzel, Ivan. "La 'renaissance Africaine': Un discours Sud-Africain?" *Politique Africaine* 77 (March 2000): 71–182.

Daviddi, Renzo, and Fabienne Ilzkovitz. "The Eastern Enlargement of the European Union: Major Challenges for Macro-Economic Policies and Institutions of Central and East European Countries." *European Economic Review* 41 (April 1997): 671–680.

Deutsche Bundesbank. "Exchange Rate Movements within the European Monetary System: Experience after Ten Years." *Monthly Report* 41 (November 1989): 28–37.

Diamond, Larry. "Promoting Democracy." *Foreign Policy* 87 (summer 1992): 25–46.

Dijk, Cornelis van. *Rebellion under the Banner of Islam: The Darul Islam in Indonesia*. The Hague: Nijhoff, 1981.

Dmytryshyn, Basil. *USSR: A Concise History*, 3rd ed. New York: Scribner, 1978.

Dobriansky, Paula J. "Russian Foreign Policy: Promise or Peril?" *Washington Quarterly* 23, no. 1 (2000): 135–144.

Ehteshami, Anoushiravan. *After Khomeini: The Iranian Second Republic*. New York: Routledge, 1995.

European Central Bank. "The International Role of the Euro." *Monthly Bulletin* (August 1999): 31–45.

Evans, Graham. "South Africa's Foreign Policy after Mandela." *Round Table* 352 (October 1999): 621–628.

Evans, Peter B., Harold K. Jacobson, and Robert D. Putnam, eds. *Double-Edged Diplomacy: International Bargaining and Domestic Politics*. Berkeley, CA: University of California Press, 1993.

Fairclough, Gordon. "Standing Firm: Asia Sticks to Its View of Human Rights." *Far Eastern Economic Review* 156 (April 1993): 22.

Forrester, Geoff. "Introduction." In *The Fall of Soeharto*, ed. Geoff Forrester and R. J. May, 1–23. Singapore: Select Books, 1999.

Forster, Anthony, and William Wallace. "Common Foreign and Security Policy." In *Policy-Making in the European Union*, ed. Helen Wallace and William Wallace, 411–435. New York: Oxford University Press, 1996.

Freedom House. *Freedom in the World, 1998–1999*. New York: Freedom House, 2000.

Friedman, Thomas L. *The Lexus and the Olive Tree*. New York: Anchor Books, 2000.

Frieman, Wendy. "International Science and Technology and Chinese Foreign Policy." In *Chinese Foreign Policy: Theory and Practice*, ed. Thomas Robinson and David Shambaugh, 158–193. Oxford: Oxford University Press, 1994.

Funabashi, Yoichi. "Bridging Asia's Economics-Security Gap." *Survival* 38 (winter 1996–1997): 101–116.

———, ed. *Japan's International Agenda*. New York: New York University Press, 1994.

Gardner, Paul F. *Shared Hopes, Separate Fears: Fifty Years of U.S.–Indonesian Relations*. Boulder, CO: Westview Press, 1997.

Garnett, Sherman W. "A Nation in Search of Its Place." *Current History* 98 (October 1999): 328–333.

Garten, Jeffrey E. *The Big Ten: The Big Emerging Markets and How They Will Change Our Lives*. New York: Basic Books, 1997.

Gasiorowski, Mark J. *U.S. Foreign Policy and the Shah: Building a Client State in Iran*. Ithaca, NY: Cornell University Press, 1991.

Geldenhuys, Deon. *The Diplomacy of Isolation: South African Foreign Policy Making*. New York: St. Martin's, 1984.

———. *Isolated States: A Comparative Analysis*. New York: Cambridge University Press, 1990.

———. *South Africa and the China Question: A Case for Dual Recognition*. Working Paper Series No. 6. Johannesburg: University of the Witwatersrand, 1995.

Gerges, Fawaz A. *America and Political Islam: Clash of Cultures or Clash of Interests?* New York: Cambridge University Press, 1999.

Ghirshman, Roman. *Iran: From the Earliest Times to the Islamic Conquest*. New York: Penguin, 1979.

Giliomee, Hermann. "South Africa's Emerging Dominant-Party Regime." *Journal of Democracy* 9 (October 1998): 128–142.

Gilpin, Robert. *War and Change in World Politics*. New York: Cambridge University Press, 1981.

Goldmann, Kjell. *Change and Stability in Foreign Policy: The Problems and Possibilities of Détente*. Princeton, NJ: Princeton University Press, 1988.

Gordon, Philip H. "Europe's Uncommon Foreign Policy." *International Security* 22 (summer 1998): 74–100.

Green, Michael J., and Patrick M. Cronin, eds. *The U.S.–Japan Alliance: Past, Present and Future*. New York: Council on Foreign Relations Press, 1999.

Greenhouse, Steven, and Richard Stevenson. "Unions March in Washington, Urging Congress to Defeat Trade Agreement with China." *New York Times*, 13 April 2000, A8.

Gretschmann, Klaus. "EMU: Thoughtful Wish or Wishful Thinking." In *Economic and Monetary Union: Implications for National Policy-Makers*, ed. Klaus Gretschmann, 3–26. Boston, MA: Nijhoff, 1993.

Gros, Daniel. "Paradigms for the Monetary Union of Europe." *Journal of Common Market Studies* 27 (March 1989): 219–230.

Gros, Daniel, and Niels Thygesen. *European Monetary Integration*. New York: St. Martin's, 1992.

Haas, Ernst. B. *Beyond the Nation-State: Functionalism and International Organization*. Stanford, CA: Stanford University Press, 1964.

———. "Collective Learning: Some Theoretical Speculations." In *Learning in U.S. and Soviet Foreign Policy*, ed. George W. Breslauer and Philip E. Tetlock, 62–99. Boulder, CO: Westview Press, 1991.

Haas, Peter M. "Do Regimes Matter? Epistemic Communities and Mediterranean Pollution Control." *International Organization* 43 (summer 1989): 377–403.

Hanrieder, Wilfram F. *Germany, America, Europe: Forty Years of German Foreign Policy*. New Haven: Yale University Press, 1989.

Hardgrave, Robert L., Jr., and Stanley A. Kochanek. *India: Government and Politics in a Developing Nation*, 6th ed. Fort Worth, TX: Harcourt Brace College Publishers, 2000.

Hermann, Charles F. "Changing Course: When Governments Choose to Redirect Foreign Policy." *International Studies Quarterly* 34 (March 1990): 3–21.

Hiebert, Murray, and Nayan Chanda. "Dangerous Liaisons." *Far Eastern Economic Review* (20 July 2000): 16–17.

Hill, Christopher. "The Foreign Policy of the European Community: Dream or Reality?" In *Foreign Policy in World Politics*, 8th ed., ed. Roy C. Macridis, 108–142. Englewood Cliffs, NJ: Prentice Hall, 1992.

———. "The Capability-Expectations Gap, or Conceptualizing Europe's International Role." *Journal of Common Market Studies* 31 (September 1993): 305–328.

Hiorth, Finngeir. *Timor, Past and Present*. Townsville, Australia: James Cook University of North Queensland, 1985.

Holsti, K. J. *Why Nations Realign: Foreign Policy Restructuring in the Postwar World*. Boston, MA: Allen and Unwin, 1982.

Holsti, Ole. "Public Opinion and Foreign Policy: Challenges to the Almond-Lippmann Consensus." In *American Foreign Policy: Theoretical Essays*, 3rd ed., ed. G. John Ikenberry, 361–393. New York: Longman, 1999.

Hook, Steven W. *National Interest and Foreign Aid*. Boulder, CO: Lynne Rienner Publishers, 1995.

Hook, Steven W., and Jeremy Lesh. "Privatizing Foreign Policy: Interest Groups and Sino–American Trade Relations after the Cold War." Forthcoming in *Contemporary Cases in U.S. Foreign Policy: From Terrorism to Trade*, ed. Ralph G. Carter. Washington, D.C.: CQ Press, 2002.

Hook, Steven W., and John Spanier. *American Foreign Policy since World War II*, 15th ed. Washington, D.C.: CQ Press, 2000.

Hook, Steven W., and Guang Zhang. "Japan's Aid Policy Since the Cold War: Rhetoric and Reality." *Asian Survey* 38 (November 1998): 1051–1066.

Huelshoff, Michael. "Domestic Politics and Dynamic Issue Linkage: A Reformulation of Integration Theory." *International Studies Quarterly* 38 (June 1994): 255–279.

Hunter, Shireen. *The Transcaucasus in Transition: Nation-Building and Conflict.* Washington, D.C.: Center for Strategic and International Studies, 1994.

Hurrell, Andrew. "Brazil and the International Politics of Amazonian Deforestation." In *The International Politics of the Environment: Actors, Interests, and Institutions*, ed. Andrew Hurrell and Benedict Kingsbury, 398–429. New York: Oxford University Press, 1992.

Hutton, Will. "Britain in a Cold Climate: The Economic Aims of Foreign Policy in the 1990s." *International Affairs* 68 (October 1992): 619–632.

Hyland, William G. *Clinton's World: Remaking American Foreign Policy.* Westport, CT: Praeger, 1999.

Iriye, Akira. *Power and Culture: The Japanese–American War, 1941–1945.* Cambridge, MA: Harvard University Press, 1981.

Johnson, Chalmers A. *MITI and the Japanese Miracle: The Growth of Industrial Policy, 1925–1975.* Stanford, CA: Stanford University Press, 1982.

———. "Korea and Our Asia Policy." *The National Interest* 41 (fall 1995): 66–77.

Jolliffe, Jill. *East Timor: Nationalism and Colonialism.* St. Lucia, Australia: University of Queensland Press, 1978.

Jones, Howard P. *Indonesia: The Possible Dream.* New York: Harcourt Brace Jovanavich, 1971.

Jopp, Mathias. "The Strategic Implications of European Integration: An Analysis of Trends in the Integration Policies and Their Consequences for the Transatlantic Partnership and a New European Security Order." Adelphi Paper, no. 290. London: Brassey's, 1994.

Kadian, Rajesh. *The Kashmir Tangle: Issues and Options.* Boulder, CO: Westview Press, 1993.

Kahin, Audrey R., and George M. Kahin. *Subversion as Foreign Policy: The Secret Eisenhower and Dulles Debacle in Indonesia.* New York: New Press, 1995.

Kahn, Joseph. "Why West's Billions Failed to Give Russia a Robust Economy." *New York Times*, 2 November 2000, A7.

Kaiser, Karl. "Reforming NATO." *Foreign Policy* 103 (summer 1996): 128–143.

Kaltenthaler, Karl C. *Germany and the Politics of Europe's Money.* Durham, NC: Duke University Press, 1998.

Kapstein, Ethan B., and Michael Mastanduno, eds. *Unipolar Politics: Realism and State Strategies after the Cold War.* New York: Columbia University Press, 1999.

Katouzian, Homa. *Mussadiq and the Struggle for Power in Iran.* New York: St. Martin's, 1999.

Kattenburg, Paul M. *The Vietnam Trauma in American Foreign Policy, 1945–75.* New Brunswick, NJ: Transaction Books, 1980.

Keck, Margaret E., and Kathryn Sikkink. *Activists Beyond Borders.* Ithaca, NY: Cornell University Press, 1998.

Keddie, Nikki R., and Mark Gasiorowski, eds. *Neither East nor West: Iran, the Soviet Union, and the United States*. New Haven, CT: Yale University Press, 1990.

Kegley, Charles W. Jr., and Eugene R. Wittkopf. *American Foreign Policy: Pattern and Process*, 5th ed. New York: St. Martin's, 1996.

Keohane, Robert O. *After Hegemony: Cooperation and Discord in the World Political Economy*. Princeton, NJ: Princeton University Press, 1984.

Keohane, Robert O., and Stanley Hoffmann, eds. *The New European Community: Decisionmaking and Institutional Change*. Boulder, CO: Westview Press, 1991.

Keohane, Robert O., and Joseph S. Nye, Jr. *Power and Interdependence*, 3rd ed. New York: Longman, 2001.

Keohane, Robert O., Joseph S. Nye, Jr., and Stanley Hoffmann, eds. *After the Cold War: International Institutions and State Strategies in Europe, 1989–1991*. Cambridge, MA: Harvard University Press, 1993.

Khadiagala, Gilbert M. *Allies in Adversity: The Frontline States in Southern African Security, 1975–1993*. Athens, OH: Ohio University Press, 1994.

King, Dwight. "Indonesia's Foreign Policy." In *The Political Economy of Foreign Policy in Southeast Asia*, ed. David Wurfel and Bruce Burton, 74–100. New York: St. Martin's, 1990.

Kirchner, Emil J. *Decision Making in the European Community: The Council Presidency and European Integration*. Manchester, UK: Manchester University Press, 1992.

———. "Second Pillar and Eastern Enlargement: The Prospects for a European Security and Defence Identity," in James Sperling, ed., *Two Tiers or Two Speeds? The European Security Order and the Enlargement of the EU and NATO*. Manchester, UK: Manchester University Press, 1999.

Kissinger, Henry. *Diplomacy*. New York: Simon & Schuster, 1994.

Klare, Michael. *Rogue States and Nuclear Outlaws: America's Search for a New Foreign Policy*. New York: Hill and Wang, 1995.

Krasno, Jean. "Brazil." In *The Pivotal States: A New Framework for U.S. Policy in the Developing World*, ed. Robert Chase, Emily Hill, and Paul Kennedy, 165–194. New York: W. W. Norton, 1999.

Krauthammer, Charles. "The Unipolar Moment." *Foreign Affairs* 70 (January–February 1990–1991): 23–33.

Kriger, Norma, and Patrick Bond. "Negotiations and the Military in South Africa." *Africa Today* 42, no. 1–2 (1995).

Kubicek, Paul. "Russian Foreign Policy and the West." *Political Science Quarterly* 114 (winter 1999): 547–568.

Lafer, Celso. "Brazilian International Identity and Foreign Policy: Past, Present and Future." *Daedalus* 129 (spring 2000): 207–238.

Lake, Anthony. *Caution and Concern: The Making of American Policy toward South Africa, 1946–1971*. Doctoral dissertation, Princeton University, Princeton, NJ, 1974.

Lamb, Alastair. *Kashmir: A Disputed Legacy, 1846–1990*. Hertingfordbury, UK: Roxford Books, 1991.

Landsberg, Chris. "Promoting Democracy: The Mandela-Mbeki Doctrine." *Journal of Democracy* 11 (July 2000): 107–121.

Landsberg, Chris, Garth le Pere, and Anthoni van Nieuwkerk, eds. *Mission Imperfect: Redirecting South Africa's Foreign Policy*. Johannesburg, South Africa: Foundation for Global Dialogue and Center for Policy Studies, 1995.

Laurence, John C. *Race, Propaganda, and South Africa*. London: Gollancz, 1979.

Layne, Christopher. "The Unipolar Illusion: Why New Great Powers Will Rise." *International Security* 17 (spring 1993): 5–51.

Leifer, Michael. *Indonesia's Foreign Policy*. London: Allen & Unwin, 1983.

Lieven, Anatol. "Restraining NATO: Ukraine, Russia, and the West." *Washington Quarterly* 20 (autumn 1997): 55–77.

Lindberg, Leon N. *The Political Dynamics of European Economic Integration*. Stanford, CA: Stanford University Press, 1963.

Lindberg, Leon N., and Stuart A. Scheingold. *Europe's Would-Be Polity: Patterns of Change in the European Community*. Englewood Cliffs, NJ: Prentice Hall, 1970.

Lockwood, William W. *The Economic Development of Japan: Growth and Structural Change*. Princeton, NJ: Princeton University Press, 1968.

Lodge, Tom, et al. *All Here, and Now: Black Politics in South Africa in the 1980s*. New York: Ford Foundation and the Foreign Policy Association, 1991.

Mackie, J. A. C. *Konfrontasi: The Indonesia–Malaysia Dispute, 1963–1966*. New York: Oxford University Press, 1974.

Macridis, Roy C., ed. *Foreign Policy in World Politics*, 8th ed. Englewood Cliffs, NJ: Prentice Hall, 1992.

Mahncke, Dieter. "European Interest and Southeast Asian Security." *Journal of European Studies* 5 (July–December 1997): 1–25.

Mandela, Nelson. "South Africa's Future Foreign Policy." *Foreign Affairs* 72 (November–December 1993): 86–97.

———. *Long Walk to Freedom: The Autobiography of Nelson Mandela*. Boston, MA: Little, Brown, 1994.

Marks, Gary, Liesbet Hooghe, and Kermit Blank. "European Integration from the 1980s: State-Centric v. Multi-level Governance." *Journal of Common Market Studies* 34 (September 1996): 341–368.

Masson, Paul R., and Mark P. Taylor. "Fiscal Policy within Common Currency Areas." *Journal of Common Market Studies* 31 (March 1993): 29–44.

Mastanduno, Michael. "Preserving the Unipolar Moment: Realist Theories and U.S. Grand Strategy after the Cold War." In *Unipolar Politics: Realism and State Strategies after the Cold War*, ed. Ethan Kapstein and Michael Mastanduno, 138–181. New York: Columbia University Press, 1999.

Masumi, Junnosuke. *Contemporary Politics in Japan*. Berkeley, CA: University of California Press, 1995.

Mattox, Gale A., and Daniel Whiteneck. "The ESDI, NATO and the New European Security Environment." In *Two Tiers or Two Speeds? The European Security Order and the Enlargement of the European Union and NATO*, ed. James Sperling, 121–138. Manchester, UK: Manchester University Press, 1999.

Maull, Hanns W. "Germany and Japan: The New Civilian Powers." *Foreign Affairs* 69 (winter 1990–1991): 91–106.

Mayhew, David R. *Congress: The Electoral Connection*. New Haven, CT: Yale University Press, 1974.

McFaul, Michael. "A Precarious Peace: Domestic Politics in the Making of Russian Foreign Policy." *International Security* 22 (winter 1997–1998): 5–35.

Mearsheimer, John. "The False Promise of International Institutions." *International Security* 19 (winter 1994–1995): 5–49

Meyer, Mahlon. "Class Politics: Taiwanese, Chinese Students Don't Mix, Even on U.S. Campuses." *Far Eastern Economic Review* (1 December 1994): 56–58.

Meyer, Stephen M. "The Devolution of Russian Military Power." Defense and Arms Control Studies Program Working Paper, Center for International Studies. Cambridge, MA: Massachusetts Institute of Technology, 1995.

Michener, James A. *The Voices of Asia*. New York: Random House, 1951.

Milani, Mohsen M. *The Making of Iran's Islamic Revolution: From Monarchy to Islamic Republic*. Boulder, CO: Westview Press, 1994a.

––––––. "Iran's Post–Cold War Policy in the Persian Gulf." *International Journal* 49 (spring 1994b): 328–354.

Mills, Greg. "Leaning All Over the Place? The Not-So-New South African Foreign Policy." In *Fairy Godmother, Hegemony, or Partner? In Search of a South African Foreign Policy*, ed. Hussein Soloman, 19–34. Johannesburg, South Africa: Institute for Security Studies, 1997.

Milward, Alan S. *The European Rescue of the Nation-State*. Berkeley, CA: University of California Press, 1992.

Missiroli, Antonio. "CFSP, Defence and Flexibility." *Chaillot Paper* 38. Paris: Institute for Security Studies, Western European Union, 2000.

Modelski, George. *Indonesia and Her Neighbors: Policy Alternatives for the West*. Princeton, NJ: Center of International Studies, Princeton University, 1964.

Moïsi, Dominique, and Michael Mertes. "Europe's Map, Compass, and Horizon." *Foreign Affairs* 74 (January–February 1995): 122–134.

Moravcsik, Andrew. "Preferences and Power in the European Community: A Liberal Intergovernmentalist Approach." *Journal of Common Market Studies* 31 (December 1993): 473–524.

Morgenthau, Hans J. *Politics Among Nations: The Struggle for Power and Peace*. New York: Knopf, 1948.

Munger, Edwin S. *Notes on the Formation of South African Foreign Policy*. Pasadena, CA: Castle Press, 1965.

Muñoz, Heraldo, and Joseph S. Tulchin, eds. *Latin American Nations in World Politics*, 2nd ed. Boulder, CO: Westview Press, 1996.

Muravchik, Joshua. *Exporting Democracy: Fulfilling America's Destiny*. Washington, D.C.: AEI Press, 1991.

Naughton, Barry. "The Foreign Policy Implications of China's Economic Development Strategy." In *Chinese Foreign Policy: Theory and Practice*, ed. Thomas Robinson and David Shambaugh, 47–69. New York: Oxford University Press, 1994.

Nazaruddin, Sjamsuddin. *The Republican Revolt: A Study of the Acehnese Rebellion*. Singapore: Institute of Southeast Asian Studies, 1985.

Nehru, Jawaharlal. *India's Foreign Policy: Selected Speeches, September 1946–April 1961*. New Delhi: Government of India, Ministry of Information and Broadcasting, 1961.

Noer, Thomas J. *Cold War and Black Liberation: The United States and White Africa, 1948–1968*. Columbia, MO: University of Missouri Press, 1985.

Norman, E. Herbert. *Japan's Emergence as a Modern State: Political and Economic Problems of the Meiji Period*. New York: International Secretariat, Institute of Pacific Relations, 1940.

Nuttal, Simon. *European Political Cooperation*. Oxford, UK: Clarendon Press, 1992.

Odom, William E. *The Collapse of the Soviet Military*. New Haven, CT: Yale University Press, 1998.

Organization for Economic Cooperation and Development. *Geographical Distribution of Financial Flows, 1995*. Paris: OECD, 1996.

Orr, Robert M., Jr. *The Emergence of Japan's Foreign Aid Power*. New York: Columbia University Press, 1990.

Osborne, Robin. *Indonesia's Secret War: The Guerilla Struggle in Irian Jaya*. Boston, MA: Allen & Unwin, 1985.

Pérez, Louis A. *Cuba and the United States: Ties of Singular Intimacy*, 2nd ed. Athens, GA: The University of Georgia Press, 1997.

Peterson, John. "Decision-Making in the European Union: Towards a Framework for Analysis." *Journal of European Public Policy* 2 (March 1995): 69–93.

Peterson, John, and Elizabeth Bomberg. *Decision-Making in the European Union*. New York: St. Martin's, 1999.

Peterson, John, and Erik Jones. "Decision Making in an Enlarging European Union," in James Sperling, ed., *Two Tiers or Two Speeds? The European Security Order and the Enlargement of the EU and NATO*. Manchester, UK: Manchester University Press, 1999.

Posen, Barry R., and Andrew L. Ross. "Competing Visions for U.S. Grand Strategy." *International Security* 21 (winter 1996–1997): 5–53.

Putnam, Robert D. "Diplomacy and Domestic Politics: The Logic of Two-Level Games." *International Organization* 42 (summer 1988): 427–460.

Radelat, Ana. "Congress Renews Efforts to Lift Sanctions." *CubaInfo* 11 (27 October 1999): 1–2.

Ramazani, Rouhollah K. *Iran's Foreign Policy, 1941–1973: A Study of Foreign Policy in Modernizing Nations*. Charlottesville, VA: University Press of Virginia, 1975.

Reardon-Anderson, James. *Yenan and the Great Powers: The Origins of Chinese Communist Foreign Policy, 1944–1946*. New York: Columbia University Press, 1980.

Reddaway, Peter, and Dmitri Glinski. *The Tragedy of Russia's Reforms: Market Bolshevism against Democracy*. Washington, D.C.: United States Institute of Peace Press, 2001.

Ripley, Randall B., and James M. Lindsay, eds. *U.S. Foreign Policy after the Cold War*. Pittsburgh, PA: University of Pittsburgh Press, 1997.

Risse-Kappen, Thomas, ed. *Bringing Transnational Relations Back In: Non-State Actors, Domestic Structures, and International Institutions*. New York: Cambridge University Press, 1995.

Rix, Alan. "Japan's Emergence as a Foreign Aid Superpower." In *Foreign Aid toward the Millennium*, ed. Steven W. Hook, 75–89. Boulder, CO: Lynne Rienner Publishers, 1996.

Roett, Riordan. *Mercosur: Regional Integration, World Markets*. Boulder, CO: Westview Press, 1999.

Rojansky, Matt. "At Russia's Door: NATO Expansion and the Baltic States." *Harvard International Review* 21, 3 (summer 1999): 22–25.

Rosati, Jerel A., Joe D. Hagan, and Martin W. Sampson III, eds. *Foreign Policy Restructuring: How Governments Respond to Global Change*. Columbia, SC: University of South Carolina Press, 1994.

Rose, Gideon. "Neoclassical Realism and Theories of Foreign Policy." *World Politics* 51 (October 1998): 556–565.

Rosenau, James N. "Foreign Policy as Adaptive Behavior: Some Preliminary Notes for a Theoretical Model." *Comparative Politics* 2 (April 1970): 365–387.

Rubinstein, Alvin Z. *Soviet Foreign Policy since World War II: Imperial and Global*, 2nd ed. Boston, MA: Little, Brown, 1985.

Ruggie, John G. "Consolidating the European Pillar: The Key to NATO's Future." *Washington Quarterly* 20 (winter 1997): 109–124.

Rushdie, Salman. *The Satanic Verses*. New York: Viking, 1988.

Sakwa, Richard. *Gorbachev and His Reforms, 1985–90*. New York: Philip Allan, 1990.

Samuels, Richard J. *The Business of the Japanese State: Energy Markets in Comparative and Historical Perspective*. Ithaca, NY: Cornell University Press, 1987.

SarDesai, Damodar R., and Raju G. C. Thomas, eds. *Nuclear India in the 21st Century*. New Delhi: Oxford University Press, 2001.

Scalapino, Robert A. *Democracy and the Party Movement in Prewar Japan: The Failure of the First Attempt*. Berkeley, CA: University of California Press, 1962.

———. *The Politics of Development: Perspectives on Twentieth Century Asia*. Cambridge, MA: Harvard University Press, 1989.

Schmitt, Eric. "Business-Minded Democrats Create a Party Split on China." *New York Times*, 13 April 2000, A8.

Scholte, Jan Aart. *Globalization: A Critical Introduction*. New York: St. Martin's, 2000.

Schraeder, Peter J. *United States Foreign Policy toward Africa: Incrementalism, Crisis, and Change*. New York: Cambridge University Press, 1994.

———. *African Politics and Society: A Mosaic in Transformation*. Boston, MA: Bedford/St. Martin's, 2000.

Scott, James M., ed. *After the End: Making U.S. Foreign Policy in the Post–Cold War World*. Durham, NC: Duke University Press, 1998.

Sedelmeier, Ulrich, and Helen Wallace. "Policies toward Central and Eastern Europe." In *Policy-Making in the European Union*, ed. Helen Wallace and William Wallace, 353–388. New York: Oxford University Press, 1996.

Sestanovich, Stephen, ed. *Rethinking Russia's National Interests*. Washington, D.C.: Center for Strategic and International Studies, 1994.

Shanker, Thom. "Who Needs Treaties?" *New York Times*, 10 June 2001, 1, 4.

Shaw, Timothy M., and Julius E. Okolo, eds. *The Political Economy of Foreign Policy in ECOWAS*. New York: St. Martin's, 1994.

Shin, Dong-Ik, and Gerald Segal. "Getting Serious about Asia–Europe Security Cooperation." *Survival* 39 (spring 1997): 138–155.

Sick, Gary. *All Fall Down: America's Tragic Encounter with Iran*. New York: Random House, 1985.

Simes, Dimitri K. "The New Soviet Challenge and America's New Edge." In *Soviet Foreign Policy in a Changing World*, ed. Robbin F. Laird and Erik P. Hoffmann, 422–439. Hawthorne, NY: Aldine, 1986.

Simmons, Beth A. *Who Adjusts? Domestic Sources of Foreign Economic Policy during the Interwar Years*. Princeton, NJ: Princeton University Press, 1994.

Sisson, Richard, and Leo E. Rose. *War and Secession: Pakistan, India, and the Creation of Bangladesh*. Berkeley, CA: University of California Press, 1990.

Smith, Jonathan. "Foreign Policy for Sale." *Presidential Studies Quarterly* 28 (winter 1998): 207–220.

Smith, Michael. "The EU as an International Actor." In *European Union: Power and Policy-Making*, ed. Jeremy J. Richardson, 247–262. London: Routledge, 1996.

Sokov, Nikolai. "Russia's New Concept of National Security." *East European Constitutional Review* 9, no. 1–2 (2000): 83–87.

Sperling, James, and Emil Kirchner. "The Security Architectures and Institutional Futures of Post-1989 Europe." *Journal of European Public Policy* 4 (June 1997a): 155–170.

———. *Recasting the European Order: Security Architectures and Economic Cooperation*. Manchester, UK: Manchester University Press, 1997b.

Stankevich, Sergei. "Toward a New 'National Idea.'" In *Rethinking Russia's National Interests*, ed. Stephen Sestanovich, 21–32. Washington, D.C.: Center for Strategic and International Studies, 1994.

Stares, Paul, and Nicolas Regaud. "Europe's Role in Asia-Pacific Security." *Survival* 39 (winter 1997–1998): 117–139.

Starobin, Paul. "Is NATO About to Make a Bad Move in the Baltics?" *Business Week* (13 November 2000): 74.

Stavrianos, Leften S. *The Global Rift: The Third World Comes of Age*. New York: Morrow, 1981.

Stepan, Alfred. *Democratizing Brazil: Problems of Transition and Consolidation*. New York: Oxford University Press, 1989.

Strobel, Warren P. *Late-Breaking Foreign Policy: The News Media's Influence on Peace Operations*. Washington, D.C.: United States Institute of Peace Press, 1997.

Stubb, Alexander. "The Amsterdam Treaty and Flexible Integration." *ECSA Review* 11 (spring 1998): 1–5.

Subrahmanyam, K., ed. *India and the Nuclear Challenge*. New Delhi: Lancer International, 1987.

Sukma, Rizal. *Indonesia and China: The Politics of a Troubled Relationship*. London: Routledge, 1999.

Suryadinata, Leo. *Indonesia's Foreign Policy under Suharto: Aspiring to International Leadership*. Singapore: Times Academic Press, 1996.

Taylor, John. G. *Indonesia's Forgotten War: The Hidden History of East Timor*. Atlantic Highlands, NJ: Zed Books, 1991.

Teague, Elizabeth. "Russians Outside Russia and Russian Security Policy." In *The Emergence of Russian Foreign Policy*, ed. Leon Aron and Kenneth M. Jensen, 81–106. Washington, D.C.: United States Institute of Peace Press, 1994.

Teitelbaum, Michael. "Immigration, Refugees, and Foreign Policy." In *On the Agenda: Current Issues and Conflicts in U.S. Foreign Policy*, ed. Howard Wiarda, 319–333. Glenview, IL: Scott, Foresman/Little, Brown Higher Education, 1990.

Thomas, Raju G. C. *The Defence of India: A Budgetary Perspective of Strategy and Politics*. Columbia, MO: South Asia Books, 1978.

———. *Indian Security Policy*. Princeton, NJ: Princeton University Press, 1986.

———. *Democracy, Security, and Development in India*. New York: St. Martin's, 1996.

———. *India Files*. Jane's Sentinel Country Assessment/Jane's Information Systems, Andover, Hampshire, UK: International Thompson Publishing Company, 2000.

Thomas, Raju G. C., ed. *Perspectives on Kashmir: The Roots of Conflict in South Asia.* Boulder, CO: Westview Press, 1994.

———, ed. *The Nuclear Non-Proliferation Regime: Prospects for the 21st Century.* New York: St. Martin's, 1998.

Thomas, Raju G. C., and Amit Gupta, eds. *India's Nuclear Security.* Boulder, CO: Lynne Rienner Publishers, 2000.

Thomas, Scott. *The Diplomacy of Liberation: The Foreign Relations of the African National Congress since 1960.* New York: Tauris Academic Studies, 1996.

Thompson, Leonard. "Mbeki's Uphill Challenge." *Foreign Affairs* 78 (November–December 1999): 83–94.

Travkin, Nikolai. "Russia, Ukraine, and Eastern Europe." In *Rethinking Russia's National Interests*, ed. Stephen Sestanovich, 33–41. Washington, D.C.: Center for Strategic and International Studies, 1994.

Trumbore, Peter F. "Public Opinion as a Domestic Constraint in International Negotiations: Two-Level Games in the Anglo-Irish Peace Process." *International Studies Quarterly* 42 (September 1998): 545–565.

Truth and Reconciliation Commission, Government of South Africa. *Truth and Reconciliation Commission of South Africa Report.* London: Macmillan, 1999.

Ulam, Adam B. *Expansion and Coexistence: Soviet Foreign Policy 1917–73.* New York: Praeger, 1974.

Ungerer, Horst, et al. "The European Monetary System: Developments and Perspectives." Occasional Paper 73. Washington, D.C.: International Monetary Fund, 1990.

U.S. Central Intelligence Agency. *The World Factbook.* Washington, D.C.: Central Intelligence Agency, 1998–2001.

U.S. and Foreign Commercial Service. *Country Commercial Guide: South Africa, Fiscal Year 1998.* Washington, D.C.: U.S. and Foreign Commercial Service, 1997.

Vale, Peter, and Sipho Maseko. "South Africa and the African Renaissance." *International Affairs* 74 (April 1998): 271–287.

Valencia, Mark. J. "The Spratly Imbroglio in the Post–Cold War Era." In *Southeast Asia in the New World Order: The Political Economy of a Dynamic Region*, ed. David Wurfel and Bruce Burton, 244–272. New York: St. Martin's, 1996.

Varg, Paul A. *Foreign Policies of the Founding Fathers.* Baltimore, MD: Penguin, 1963.

Vatikiotis, Michael R. J. "Indonesia's Foreign Policy in the 1990s." *Contemporary Southeast Asia* 14 (March 1993): 362–377.

Vig, Norman J., and Michael E. Kraft, eds. *Environmental Policy in the 1990s*, 3rd ed. Washington, D.C.: CQ Press, 1997.

Wallace, William. "Europe as a Confederation: The Community and the Nation-State." *Journal of Common Market Studies* 21 (March 1982): 57–68.

Waltz, Kenneth. *Man, the State, and War: A Theoretical Analysis.* New York: Columbia University Press, 1959.

———. *Theory of International Politics.* New York: McGraw-Hill, 1979.

———. "Structural Realism after the Cold War." *International Security* 25 (summer 2000): 5–41.

Weatherbee, Donald E. *Ideology in Indonesia: Sukarno's Indonesian Revolution.* New Haven, CT: Yale University, Southeast Asia Studies, 1966.

————. "The Indonesianization of East Timor." *Contemporary Southeast Asia* 3 (April 1981): 1–23.

————. "The Diplomacy of Stalemate." In *Southeast Asia Divided: The ASEAN–Indochina Crisis*, ed. Donald E. Weatherbee, 1–30. Boulder, CO: Westview Press, 1985.

————. "ASEAN: Indonesia's 'Dual Track' Diplomacy." *Indochina Issues* 64 (February–March 1986): 7–10.

Weinstein, Franklin B. *Indonesian Foreign Policy and the Dilemma of Dependence.* Ithaca, NY: Cornell University Press, 1976.

Weiss, Thomas G., and James G. Blight, eds. *The Suffering Grass: Superpowers and Regional Conflict in Southern Africa and the Caribbean.* Boulder, CO: Lynne Rienner Publishers, 1992.

Whiting, Allen S. *The Chinese Calculus of Deterrence: India and Indochina.* Ann Arbor, MI: University of Michigan Press, 1975.

Wiarda, Howard J. *American Foreign Policy: Actors and Processes.* New York: Harper Collins College Publishers, 1996.

Williams, William A. *The Tragedy of American Diplomacy.* Cleveland, OH: World Publishing Co., 1959.

Woodhall, Brian. *Japan under Construction: Corruption, Politics, and Public Works.* Berkeley, CA: University of California Press, 1996.

Wright, Stephen, ed. *African Foreign Policies.* Boulder, CO: Westview Press, 1999.

Zegart, Amy B. *Flawed by Design: The Evolution of the CIA, JCS, and NSC.* Stanford, CA: Stanford University Press, 1999.

Zwick, Peter. *Soviet Foreign Relations: Process and Policy.* Englewood Cliffs, NJ: Prentice Hall, 1990.

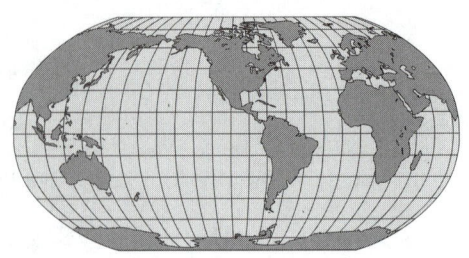

INDEX